BARBARIANS, MARAUDERS,
and INFIDELS

BARBARIANS, MARAUDERS, *and* INFIDELS

The Ways of Medieval Warfare

Antonio Santosuosso

Westview PRESS

A Member of the Perseus Books Group

Copyright © 2004 by Westview Press, a Member of the Perseus Books Group

Published in the United States of America by Westview Press, a Member of the Perseus Books
Group, 5500 Central Avenue, Boulder, Colorado 80301-2877, and in the United Kingdom by
Westview Press, 12 Hid's Copse Road, Cumnor Hill, Oxford OX2 9JJ.

Find us on the world wide web at www.westviewpress.com.

Westview Press books are available at special discounts for bulk purchases in the United States
by corporations, institutions, and other organizations. For more information, please contact
the Special Markets Department at the Perseus Books Group, 11 Cambridge Center,
Cambridge, MA 02142, or call (617) 252-5298 or (800) 255-1514, or e-mail
special.markets@perseusbooks.com.

Library of Congress Cataloguing-in-Publication Data

Santosuosso, Antonio.
  Barbarians, marauders, and infidels : the ways of medieval warfare / Antonio Santosuosso.
    p. cm.
  Includes bibliographical references and index.
  ISBN 0-8133-9153-9 (hardcover)
    1. Military art and science—History—Medieval, 500–1500. 2. Military history, Medieval.
  I. Title.

U37.S25 2004
940.1—dc22

2004005198

The paper used in this publication meets the requirements of the American National
Standard for Permanence of Paper for Printed Library Materials Z39.48–1984.

Set in 11-point AGaramond by the Perseus Books Group

10   9   8   7   6   5   4   3   2   1

for Alma with Love

Contents ~

Illustrations

Acknowledgments

THE MEDIEVAL PAST WAS AN ever-present entity in my native hill town. A medieval castle, vastly altered through the ages, stood on what seemed to be Roman ruins flanked by Longobardic towers at one side and, just behind the castle's main gate, by a square Norman tower. The old section of the town was guarded by two gates that at one time must have barred the entry of any intruder. Medieval stories were often my companions at night or the object of stories endlessly narrated to other children: Venetians scaling fortifications in the Near East; blond-haired, blue-eyed strangers in our midst and now present in the physique of many among us; the lone old chapel at the edge of town; the long, thin, dark small-town streets articulating from a long, tight road, incongruously called *piazza*, that moved like the dorsal spine of the most ancient district.

It was then logical that I would continue my journey of the vicissitudes of warfare through the Middle Ages after my view of Classical Greece and Republican Rome (*Soldiers, Citizens, and the Symbols of War*, 1997) and of Imperial Rome (*Storming the Heavens*, 2001) through the Middle Ages. Like the previous two books, this sequel explores the roots and motivations of organized violence.

I am grateful to the support of fellow scholars and to the insights of my university students through my years of teaching. The smiles and sounds of my wonderful, very young granddaughters, Dakota and Georgia, were a constant source of company and inspiration when my day was gray as a somber sky. My beloved sons, Derek and Kevin, and Derek's dear wife, Kris, have been at my side in moments of spiritual need. Finally, special thanks go to Trish Goodrich, associate publicist at Westview, to Lisa J. Teman, senior project editor, who directed the final stage of the project with grace and skill, to Jon Howard for his accurate and speedy role in the later stages of production, and especially to

Steve Catalano, senior editor at Westview Press, for his encouragement, advice, and insightful, tireless comments and suggestions in the preparation of my work.

The greatest debt goes to my wife, Alma Santosuosso, at Wilfrid Laurier University in Waterloo. She has been a constant source of encouragement and appreciation and critique of my work, as well as my travel companion through European archives and battlefields—her researching medieval music history, while I tried to make sense of the sources of medieval history. I dedicate my book to her with love.

A grant from the University of Western Ontario's former dean of the faculty of social science, Peter Neary, supported a research trip to Europe.

Antonio Santosuosso
March 2004

Introduction ~

BARBARIANS, MARAUDERS, AND INFIDELS: *The Ways of Medieval Warfare* is a sequel to my two previous works, *Soldiers, Citizens, and the Symbols of War* and *Storming the Heavens*. It covers the period from the end of the Roman Empire in the fifth century to the last stages of the Middle Ages in the fifteenth century, placing the main changes in warfare and its motivations within the political, cultural, and social contexts of that period.

The book is divided into four parts. Part One (476–814) is devoted to the "barbarian" kingdoms from their emergence to the successful establishment of the Carolingian hegemony in western Europe. Part Two, which is roughly a chronological parallel to Part One, deals with the Prophet Muhammad and the origins of Muslim warfare, followed by an account of the immense success of its soldiers in conquering, in a brief period of time, Syria, Iraq, Persia Egypt, and North Africa before crossing into Spain. Part Three (800–1300) discusses a new, aggressive, empire-building West. After containing new threats to its security from the Vikings in the north and the Magyars in the east, the forces of the western states engaged in a process of counterattack. Their armies spread east against Slavs, west to regain the Iberian Peninsula from the Muslims, and across the Mediterranean to wrest the Holy Land away from their religious enemies. It is a story mixing success and failure, great acts and miserably atrocious behavior, the memory of which the erosive power of centuries has not fully cancelled. It was also during this period that the system of military, political, and cultural values—feudalism, with its attendant features of chivalry and knighthood—was established. The great confrontations of the time take the reader to the battlefields of Hastings, Courtrai, Bouvines, and Antioch as a viewer of brilliant or incompetent leadership and the terrors and savagery of war. Finally, Part Four (1300–1453) treats the Middle Ages from its peak around 1300 to the waning years in the fifteenth century. War remained endemic in both East and West; England and France continued to be at each other's throats for more than a century; and the last remnants of the Roman Empire—Constantinople—fell at the hands of the Ottoman Turks.

One of the main themes of the book is the idea that medieval war was carried out for God, personal profit, and honor. Waging war was a condition defining the ruling groups of all societies and, as such, a necessary and pursued status of the human condition. The upper classes fought or organized other people to fight because war advanced one's position socially; it fulfilled the will of their God who expressed His blessing by making them victorious; and it increased their material wealth and political prestige. Finally, if you were from a lower-class background, war helped one to make a living in a period of chronic underemployment and little prosperity.

PART ONE

The Barbarian Kingdoms

Chapter One

Attila Is Dead:
The Early Barbarian Kingdoms

THE NEWS SPREAD LIKE WILDFIRE among the men who had grouped to celebrate his wedding.[1] Their great man, their king, had died a few hours after marrying another of his many wives, the beautiful Ildico, probably a German. When he had not come out of the place where he had taken his new wife, his servants had forced the entry: they found Ildico in tears, her face covered by a veil, and their king sprawled on the bed, his face smeared with his own blood. No wounds were found on his body. His nose had bled again (not an unusual occurrence) during the night, suffocating him.[2] What neither the Romans of the East nor the Romans of the West, what the many Germanic and Iranian tribes could not do, destiny had achieved in a few seconds. It was a base end for Attila, the king of the Huns, dying in such a manner, not in the turmoil of battle with enemy blood on his hands. Soon other stories of his end circulated, suggesting that the Hunnish king had died in other ways: murdered by Ildico.[3]

As was the custom of their ancestors, Attila's men placed his body in state in the middle of a plain, probably a reminder of the windy, desolate, flat places they had come from. A silk tent was the abode of the dead man. Soon hundreds of his followers, their hair cut and their faces slashed with their blades as a sign of despair, rode their horses, circling the tent in the manner of circus games to honor the spirit of their leader. And they sang his deeds. He was the son of the sire Marduch, lord of the bravest tribes; Attila was the lord over the lands of the Germans and of all people of Scythia; he had terrified both Empires, East and West, and stopped his conquest only after receiving annual tributes from them.

The Huns continued their display of grief and lamentation over Attila's body in their traditional manner, where outbursts of tears and joy were mixed.

Then in the secrecy of night they carried his body enclosed in three coffins, the first gold, the second silver—both symbols of the man who had been feared and honored by both Roman Empires—and the third iron, to embody the strength of the leader who had united the previously disunited Huns and killed his brother in the process and who had conquered so many nations. And then they placed in his tomb weapons of the foemen he had conquered, luxurious trappings, gems and ornaments of all sorts. And when his body had been hidden under the soil, the earth ran with the blood of the men who had interred him so that no one would desecrate the resting place of their great king.

Shortly after, the many tribes that, from the Black Sea to the Hungarian plains, had been subjects of the Huns rebelled against their overlords[4] and overwhelmed separately those men who "used to inspire terror when their strength was united." From then on the Huns, who had come from the Mongolian plains and spread in pockets from the East to the West, would slowly vanish from history as a major multiethnic group; yet no citizen of the Roman Empire would forget the damage they had caused to the dominion. They— the Huns—would reappear in small groups over and over again in the armies of the emperor at Constantinople. They were, as a Goth would write about one hundred years after their first foray into Europe, the offspring of witches that had repaired to the Maeotic swamp in the farthest reaches of Europe. Witches had begotten there a savage race that "dwelt first in the swamps," a "stunted, foul and puny tribe, scarcely human and having no language save one which bore but slight resemblance to human speech." Their features alone inspired terror, their heads were nothing but "a sort of shapeless lump, not a head, with pin holes rather than eyes," terrifying not only because of their natural ugliness but also because their sparse beard barely covered the scars received in battle or self-inflicted at the death of a great chief. Nor was their stature impressive. They were "short" with firm necks always "erect in pride," and though they lived in the form of men, they had "the cruelty of beasts."[5]

Attila died in 453, but the damage that his men had created to the Empire, both East and West, had been incalculable. Actually, the Hunnic chief's demise coincided with the third wave of barbarian movements into the Empire of the West, which would not survive the unrelenting attack of the barbarians.

For the citizens of the Roman Empire, all the Germanic or non-Germanic people pressing on their borders were akin to savage beasts, half-dressed, dirty, smelly in words akin to Jordanes's description of the Huns. Their language was barbarous and unintelligible. No Roman could trust them: they were fickle, unreliable, eternally prone to petty theft. True, the Romans would admit, the barbarians may be formidable opponents in battle, but they fought without organization and tended to give up at the first reversal in the tide of battle. They were so wild that some fed on raw flesh and drank the blood of slain enemies.[6] Any man, including slaves, wearing leather clothes and sporting long hair, which was the attire of the barbarians, ordered the Code of the Emperor Theodosius and was forbidden to enter the city of Rome and any location nearby.[7]

The Romans had the attitude shared by all advanced civilizations toward people who were not like them and used stereotypes that have never disappeared when judging humans whom we fear or who do not follow the customs to which we are accustomed. On one level, however, the Romans were correct. In customs and behavior, the invaders were different from them, and they came from places where fear and hunger were supreme. For these were the main factors of the great movement of people who spread into the territories of the Empire between the fourth and sixth centuries. Their migration became irresistible, like the sudden flush of a river, by the end of the fourth century. It began in the 370s when about 200,000 Goths, moved by hunger and fear, crossed the Danube River that separated them from the Empire. The invaders were a crowd of half-starved individuals whose lands had been taken over by the fearsome Huns. In their minds, the Empire was the land of plenty, luxuries, and wealth of which they could only dream.

What is remarkable is that the Romans, at least in the beginning, seemed unaware that the invaders of the fourth century were quite different from the small tribes they had come in contact with in earlier centuries. Yes, most of them still spoke a variety of German dialect, they still looked wild and undisciplined like the enemies of the past, their most common attire still evoked feral images in the Roman mind, but their numbers—the core still numerically small—had become much larger as other tribes had fused their identity with that of the primary tribe. Moreover, their training in matters of war was at a much higher level.

There are great problems in assessing the preinvasion German civilization. The best written source is the treatise of the great Roman writer Tacitus, composed toward the end of the first century. For the rest we must rely on nonwritten sources often difficult to interpret. For the culture of the invaders was oral. The view of descendants of the invaders, like the Longobard Paul the Deacon, the Goth Jordanes, or the Frank Fredegar, was often filtered through Roman eyes and written years later. The exceptions are few and do not appear before the seventh century—*Beowulf* for instance. Even the saga of the Nibelungens is a creation of the twelfth to fourteenth centuries, although based on oral memories of a previous period. Yet a few elements about the invaders emerge clearly.

Not all the invaders were Germans, and not only because of the presence of people like the Huns, the Avars, the Sarmatians, or the Alans. Large congregations of invaders that go by the name of a single tribe were aggregations of different ethnic groups, not always Germanic and certainly, if Germanic, not always from the same tribe. Usually the members of the confederation going by a single name—Frank or Longobard, for example—had come together over a period of many years of migrations, often contaminating the culture of the primary nucleus and always liable to a continuous process of integration and disintegration or exchanges with other people.[8] The idea that all barbarians shared a common cultural, physical, political, and linguistic origin, identified as German, was a much later creation of the eighteenth and nineteenth centuries, although an earlier formulation had appeared in the Carolingian eighth and ninth centuries, almost 300 years after the invasions.[9]

Originally, people speaking German dialects are found along the areas east of the Rhine and north of the Danube. The tribes were numerous but numerically small (at most probably 10,000 individuals) and often characterized by different burial practices. What tied the people of each tribe together was generally the belief in a common origin, a similar view of the world, a common form of worship in which goddesses symbolizing fertility were uppermost, a common language, and certain aspects of the law. On the Rhine the most important tribes were the Franks on the north side of the Main River and the Alamans on the south. East of them we find various groups like the Saxons, Thuringians, Burgundians, Bavarians, and farther from the Rhine the Vandals. The Franks emerged in the long run as the dominant tribe and to them eventually would go the greatest prize of all: Roman Gaul. North of the Danube the dominant tribes were the Goths, who eventually spread from the Black Sea to the Balkans, divided into two main groups, the Visigoths (Goths of the West) and Ostrogoths (Goths of the East). In that region, however, there were also people who originally had come from the Iranian highlands or from the eastern side of the Black Sea like Sarmatians and Alans.

In 166 Quadi and Marcomans, both German tribes, had broken through the imperial defense perimeter and marched deep into the West, reaching Aquileia, an important town in northeastern Italy. Emperor Marcus Aurelius beat them back, and although serious danger kept the Empire in turmoil for a good part of the third century, it seemed that the main threat had disappeared by the beginning of the fourth. In reality it was an ominous quiet broken in the second half of the fourth century by a wide-ranging migration process of various peoples, German and non-German, who eventually would destroy the structure of the Empire, whose center was Rome.

These new invaders were different from the past. By the fourth century, the small tribes of previous years had undergone crucial changes. They had become large confederations of people, gathered around one of the dominant tribes and led by charismatic kings who boasted wealth and power, often by serving at least temporarily in the imperial armies. Actually the tendency of the Empire to prefer dealing with strong chiefs instead of a variety of less important leaders may have helped the process of strengthening the various confederations. On the surface the situation favored the Romans, who now could deal with a few individuals in controlling the populations across the Rhine and the Danube, yet this also strengthened the authority of these kings, who defined their supremacy by being the "managers" of war—those who brought victories and material benefits to the confederation. Moreover, the contact with people used to fighting on horseback, like Alans and Sarmatians and later Huns, provided some tribes with a form of attack—cavalry—that they had rarely used in the past. It was symptomatic of another change toward a more aggressive posture: the primacy of gods like Wotan or Woden replacing the fertility female gods like Nerthus in the barbarian pantheon of religious worship.[10]

The main reason for the new migration was the arrival of a Mongolic tribe from Central Asia—the Huns. Fear of these new invaders, who spread from the Black Sea to the Hungarian plains, became the major motivation for the Goths, deprived of their lands, to cross the Danube in 366 to escape the famine ravaging their kind and fear of death at the hands of the invaders from the East. Their aim was to settle in the lands of the emperor of the eastern Roman Empire; at that time the empire was divided in two parts—the West, with its capital in Rome, and the East, eventually with its capital in Constantinople. The Goths, supported also by groups of Alans and even some Huns, were received by the eastern emperor with a policy mixing optimism (they could serve as cheap recruits for the imperial army) with exploitation, that is, a mob from which dignity and hope could be taken away (Roman profiteers traded the flesh of a dog for each person—adult or child—who gave up his liberty or his son to slavery).[11] The only alternative for the Goths was to perish or face the imperial troops in battle. Unexpectedly they won, killing even the emperor of Constantinople, who had come to lead his troops. It was August 378, the place Adrianople, just south of the Danube River.

The Goths were the first wave of a continuing population movement,[12] but a major one, since it is likely that before the battle about 200,000 individuals of every age had crossed the river, settling, after their victory, in the imperial territories from the Black Sea to the Balkans. Adrianople was crucial also because for the next few decades the ruler of the western part of the empire was left practically alone to contest the invaders coming from the east south of the Danube and from those pressing on the Rhine's frontier.

On 31 December 406 a new major movement began. Waves of Vandals, Sueves, and Alans moved relentlessly from the east across the Rhine River near Mainz. Eventually Suebians and Alans would settle in Spain, the former establishing a kingdom that would last for about 200 years. But the Vandals were hunting a greater prey. After twenty years on the Iberian Peninsula they crossed the Strait of Gibraltar and took from Rome the granary of the empire, North Africa. Meanwhile, four years after Vandals, Alans, and Suebians had crossed the Rhine, the Visigoths (the Goths of the West) marched into Italy in search of food. But Italy was not the place where food could be found, for the peninsula survived on the grain that came from Africa. Unable to build a navy to cross the Mediterranean, the Visigoths proceeded along the edges of the Mediterranean, some settling in southern France and the rest in Spain. Meanwhile, by 407 the last of the imperial troops had left Britain, which would be fought over by Picts, Scots, and the Germanic tribes of Saxons, Angles, and Jutes. Around the same time, Visigoths, Alamans, and Burgundians were destroying what was left of imperial power in Gaul (roughly modern France).

The plight of the western empire did not end there, for in the middle years of the fifth century the third wave of migrations began. Most of the tribes this time were part of the Ostrogoth confederation. Again, hunger was the principal motivator. Italy suffered the most. Rome, already ravaged by the Visigoths in 410, suffered another sack in 455, this time at the hands of the Vandals, coming from Africa. In 476 a barbarian leader named Odovacar took control of the Italian peninsula, sending the symbols of the empire to Constantinople. He would not last long. In 488 the emperor in Constantinople gave Theodoric, the leader of the Amals, an Ostrogothic tribe, permission to enter Italy and remove Odovacar from the throne. Five years later the Amal chieftain defeated Odovacar and later killed him with his own hands.

So by 500 the Roman Empire of the West had disappeared (Figure 1.1), and even though the invaders were numerically inferior to the local population—at most only 5 percent or even lower[13]—several barbarian kingdoms had been

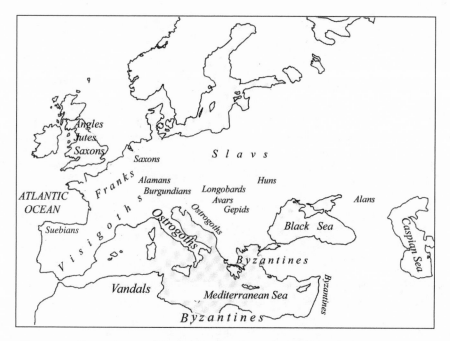

Figure 1.1 Byzantines and Barbarian Peoples in the Early Sixth Century

established with Angles, Jutes, and Saxons in England; Alans and Suebians in northern Spain; Visigoths in the rest of Spain and in about half of Gallia with a kingdom that extended from the Atlantic to the Mediterranean; Franks, Burgundians, and Alamans in the rest of Gaul; Ostrogoths in most of Italy; and Vandals in North Africa. The Byzantines were the only past presence remaining, clinging to a few regions in Italy and on the other side of the Adriatic Sea. But peace did not return. War was to become an endemic feature of the new barbarian kingdoms. Moreover, more destructive than any of the wars brought by the invaders would be the foolish attempt by the emperor of the East, Justinian, to recover the lands of Italy. It was a decision fraught with dangers for the "Romans" now at peace under the Ostrogoths.

Chapter Two

A Double Pestilence: Ostrogoths and Byzantines in Italy

L ED BY THEIR CHARISMATIC KING, Theodoric, the Ostrogoths and other ethnic groups that had joined the original tribe moved toward Italy, young and old, males and females, wagons heavy with the few things they owned.[1] They arrived in 489. Four years later their ruler wrested the power from Odovacar, the man who had brought down the last remnants of the Empire of the West, killing him with his own hands at a banquet that supposedly should have cemented joint rule over the peninsula.[2] For a few years an uneasy peace reigned in the land. It would not last long for the Byzantines, the Roman heirs of the Empire of the East; the same people who had urged the Goths to move against Odovacar arrived now to displace them from the kingdom.

The Last Romans

While the Roman Empire of the East would endure for another millennium, the Empire of the West would disappear by the end of the fifth century. Several barbarian kingdoms would be formed in its place. Some kingdoms would last a short time (the Burgundians in southeast Gallia and the Vandals in Africa), others (the Franks in Gallia and the Saxons, Jutes, and Angles in Britain) would establish states that became the foundation of modern society.[3] The invaders were defined as a society at war, an attitude that many of them would display even after their initial success. This was the case of the Longobards in Italy; others (the Ostrogoths, in Italy also) would have to switch their posture from offensive to defensive. Those were societies where freeman equated to soldier and where the king's most important role was that of manager of war. Unlike Roman society, based on the concept of peace at home and defense or aggression at the frontier, the barbarian kingdoms—the Franks, for instance—lived in an endemic state of war both internally and externally. Normally the original inhabitants of the barbarian kingdoms were, more likely than not, to be excluded from war participation. This was the case in Ostrogothic Italy, where the Goths were the warriors. Yet in that case the "Romans"—that is, the former citizens of the vanished empire—still kept important positions in the administration of the kingdom and monopolized the Catholic hierarchy because the Goths subscribed to the Arian heresy. In some cases, the Longobards, initially in Italy, and the Vandals in Africa excluded local populations from the military as well as from the civil apparatus and sometimes even from the religious hierarchy. The most successful of all barbarian kingdoms would instead be the Franks in Gaul, who easily absorbed the social hierarchy of the Gallo-Roman population, forming the basis of their strong kingdom in partnership.

The events in Italy are a strong example of how an initially acceptable compromise between invaders and local populations led in the end to catastrophe and death to both. But then the fault lay with the emperor of the East, who misguidedly tried to reestablish an empire on lands he was powerless to hold.

The Italian population did not consider Odovacar's rule as oppressive when he deposed the last Roman emperor of the West in 476. True, they were despoiled of one-third of their lands, or of the shares of tax assessment of those lands, which were distributed among Odovacar's followers.[4] But Odovacar revealed himself to be a strong defender of the old Roman Senate and a guardian of the basis on which the empire had rested. In reality, Odovacar suited the interests of the ruling groups in Italy, for he respected their prerogatives, whether that meant the army—that is, the barbarians—or the Roman Church, which was assuming an increasingly important role in society, or the senatorial group representing the civilian elite of the Italian peninsula.[5]

The eleven years of peace that Odovacar brought to the peninsula were broken when the eastern emperor, Zeno, tried to solve an internal problem in the lands near Constantinople by encouraging the source of the turmoil, Theodoric's Ostrogoths, to remove Italy from Odovacar's control. While the western branch of the Goths, the Visigoths, had moved away from the territories they had migrated to in the fourth century and tried first to settle in Italy at the beginning of the fifth century and later in southwest Gallia and Spain, the eastern branch, the Ostrogoths, had remained in the east. With the passing of time famine, which had forced them to abandon their lands in the first place, periodically afflicted them, and they became the agents of disorder and unrest with other ethnic groups of the Balkans. As the Gothic historian Jordanes writes, "The Goths began to lack food and clothing." Moreover, peace became distasteful to men for whom war had long furnished the "necessities of life."[6] Zeno, the eastern emperor, tried to avoid the perils that the situation created in the Balkans and in territories too close to Constantinople by dispatching Theodoric's Ostrogoths to Italy to force Odovacar out of power.

The new ruler brought no meaningful changes to the Italian peninsula. As the contemporary Greek historian Procopius writes, Theodoric enforced just laws, kept Italy safe from invasions, and did not change the old customs or abuse his power over the subjects. Even the lands that he distributed among his population were only those that already had been taken over by Odovacar's men. "Theodoric was a tyrant [i.e., an illegitimate ruler] by name, but in fact he was a true and real emperor."[7] The Ostrogothic king did not intend to fuse his own people with the "Romans," at least for the moment, or consider the conquered people as a defeated population. What he tried to do was to keep the two people divided, each under their own laws. The "Romans" kept the civilian posts of the kingdom's administration, while the Goths formed its army. What existed was the creation of a state in which Goths and Italians were "distinct" but "codependent."[8] Generally the ruling groups in Italy accepted their new ruler because he defended their interests, even those of the Church, in spite of the fact that the Ostrogoths were not Catholics but Arians.

It was an idyllic situation that could not last. The Ostrogoths thought in terms of independence, although theoretically they still realized that the ruler of the peninsula was the eastern emperor. During the last years of Theodoric's rule the strain became evident even in the action of the fair-minded monarch when he executed two of the greatest minds of the period, Boethius and Symmachus, members of the powerful senatorial group. Theodoric never came to terms with the realization that the Italian population tolerated his rule yet considered the emperor at Constantinople their legitimate ruler. For its part, Constantinople felt that it could never give up the control of Italy to a Gothic king. When Theodoric died of dysentery in 526, instability fell on Gothic Italy. His throne went to his grandson Athalic, who was only ten years old, but the reign's control fell to the boy's mother, Amalasuintha. When Athalic died in 534, wasted by a life of debauchery, the Goths elected Vitigis, whose connection to Theodoric's dynasty was his marriage to Amalasuintha's daughter. A year later in 535 Roman armies landed in Sicily and eighteen years of bloody wars began. The initiator of the war was the new, powerful Roman emperor of Constantinople, Justinian. His aim was to restore the lost portion of the Roman Empire of the West to his throne.

Justinian's first act was to wrest control over North Africa from the Vandals. Under the great general Belisarius, the reconquest was a simple operation. Italy was a different case. The wars of Italy lasted eighteen years, from 535 to 553. In the end Justinian was an ephemeral conqueror, for the destruction of the peninsula was enormous, and the way was open to a new barbarian migration: the Longobards.

The conflict between Byzantines and Ostrogoths is an excellent field from which to analyze the way of war between an important Germanic people and the last Romans, although instead of the term *Roman*, as they called themselves, I shall use the anachronistic term *Byzantine*, as they were later called.

The Opposing Armies

The Goths we find in Italy in the sixth century were quite different from those of the past. They had been in close contact with the Roman population since the 370s, and most of them had likely served in Roman armies. Also, unlike the later invaders, the Longobards, who had had minimal contact with the Romans before their invasion of Italy, the Goths had assimilated many of the values that we associate with either Rome or Constantinople. Yet they still differed on matters of religion; they were Arian Christians and, as such, a threat to the Christianism of the empire. This would be an element of conflict for two reasons: the empire looked at Christianity as a state religion, and thus all dissenters were considered potential internal enemies.

Probably the fighting men of the Gothic army were as few as 20,000 when they crossed the Alps in 489.[9] But once in Italy their number must have grown tremendously in the typical manner of armies of successful leaders. The original group included not only individuals who claimed a direct ancestry from the Gothic tribe but also people who by a process of ethnogenesis had assimilated with them since they had crossed the Danube. Men from the Pannonian provinces (Germanic Rugians, Herulians, Scirians, Thuringians, Suebians, Turcilians, and Caucasian Alans and Sarmatians, and probably even Huns) became part of Theodoric's army besides the ethnically variegated remnants of Odovacar's host.[10]

Theoretically, all free Gothic men were obligated to serve in the army. Initially, the Italians were specifically excluded, the main reason being that the Goths did not want to deplete the ranks of those who tilled the land. The same rule did not apply to the upper classes of Italian society. Actually, in the last stages of the Gothic kingdom even peasants and lower classes were encouraged to join the Goths against their masters, who had kept their allegiance to Constantinople. In reality, however, Theodoric's army or those of his successors were a polyethnic entity.[11] As Patrick Amory writes, "The [Gothic] army was an extremely variegated body in constant flux, knit into the tight fabric of Italian civil society."[12]

Although the account of the Gothic war by Belisarius's secretary, Procopius, the great Byzantine historian of the Gothic wars, seems to contradict this, the Ostrogoths were primarily horsemen. Probably, the mistaken impression that the reader receives is based on the fact that the more sophisticated Byzantine cavalry overshadows the less successful Ostrogothic horsemen. In normal circumstances, even when the infantry played an important role in battle, the killing blow was left to the cavalry charge. The Goths on horseback were, Herwig Wolfram says, like the lance-riders of other nomadic peoples, with an extra-long thrusting lance held with two hands, using a sword and small shield as secondary weapons,[13] a role that they must have learned probably because of their contact with horse-riding people like the Alans more than with the Huns. The bowmen of the Ostrogothic army, unlike the Huns and the Byzantines, were footmen. Sophisticated body armor seems to have been a luxury in the Gothic army, probably the privilege of the leaders and units fighting on the front lines. Infantrymen carried long spears, swords, and large oblong shields. They were protected either by leather pants or leather or quilted tunics that may have reached the knees.[14] Few must have worn helmets. At least this is the impression one receives from reading Procopius. Clearly their mode of protection and their defensive armor were inferior to the Byzantines. Before the Battle of Taginae, for instance, the Roman commander Narses reminded his soldiers that they were superior in valor, numbers, and "in every sort of equipment."[15] That is not surprising, because the notion of "people under arms" meant that different social levels were part of the Gothic army. What they lacked in armor, they made up in physique, as we can deduce from the reaction of the Gothic women when they saw the Roman soldiers enter Ravenna at the end of a siege. These very beautiful women, says Procopius elsewhere,[16] spat in their husbands' faces. They were cowards, they said; unlike what the husbands had told them, the Romans were neither big nor too numerous.[17]

The Gothic army was a sophisticated entity, as the struggle for Italy would show. Like the Byzantines, they built fortified camps in which to take refuge or to fight from. They also were able to construct besieging towers and rams, and when they realized that pulling rams with oxen made the animals an easy target for defenders, they pushed their towers by teams of men under some form of protection. Their deployment on the battlefield, preceded often by scouting, also conformed to the classical form of combat: footmen in the center and cavalry at the wings. Sometimes they liked to open the encounter with a duel, as at Taginae, and preferred pitched battles, but they also recurred often to more devious or complex ways of engagement. They used various tactical devices to gain the initiative on the battlefield—surprising the enemy with sudden attacks by both horse and foot, preceded by war cries and intense beating of shields and weapons as they moved to contact; outflanking the enemy; charging and regrouping in case of failure behind the protection of spear-armed infantry; and ambushing.[18] They also had a valid grasp of strategic warfare, as they showed when they cut the water supply of Rome under siege. In the later stages of the war, under the leadership of a great king like Totila, they destroyed bridges, built dikes, and cut ditches to flood the likely routes of the enemy.[19] Yet Theodoric's well-trained and well-supplied army broke down during the last stages of the Italian war.[20]

The Byzantines began their recovery of the western half of the Roman Empire by a strike in Africa against the Vandals under the command of their great general, Belisarius, who also directed the initial stages of the Italian campaign. In Africa Belisarius's men may have numbered about 15,000. Eventually at its peak in Italy the Byzantines would have about 18,000 soldiers, but when Belisarius landed in Sicily in 535 the general had only about 5,000 men under his direct control.[21] The Byzantine army was organized in a manner similar to the hosts of the last stages of the empire before the division between Rome and Constantinople. Recruitment was based partly on volunteers, partly on landownership.[22] Moreover, mercenaries like the Huns and many others were used extensively. The pay was poor, but one has to take into account that even a modest wage was preferable to unemployment in a preindustrial society. Also, besides the normal pay, soldiers could increase their income by looting in wartime and receive cash grants at various times and during the accession of a new emperor.

Contact with Central Asiatic Avars on the Danubian frontier and with Persians on the east seems to have influenced greatly the armies of Constantinople both in terms of armor and tactical priorities.[23] Unlike in traditional Roman armies, the bow became an essential part of the cavalry. By the late sixth century, although not yet used at the time of the war in Italy, the stirrup, an innovation borrowed from the Avars, had been introduced. The quality of the armor depended on the soldier's battle-line position. Both cavalrymen and infantrymen fighting on the front lines were much better protected than the rest. For horsemen this meant a padded cloth over which there was a long mail coat down to the knees, a helmet, a small round shield strapped on the left shoulder, a lance, a sword hung on the left side, and a bow and quiver placed on the right side. The first and second infantry ranks also wore sophisticated armor: breastplate, helmet, and iron, leather, or felt greaves. Infantry shields, either oval or round and with spikes where the boss stood, were about 1.5 meters at their longest side. Their weapons included spear and sword. The other ranks of both cavalry and infantry seem to have been protected much less. In all cases, however, soldiers fighting behind the front ranks still were well protected with quilted or padded coats and extra leather protection for the chest. The primary units were the cavalrymen, and although the Romans did not shy away from face-to-face combat, their primary weapon seems to have been the bow, which they shot from horseback.[24] They also used different types of heavy-firepower machines. At the first siege of Rome they used stone throwers like the onager, the ballista (a type of large bow), and planks with inserted spikes that they would drop on the besiegers.[25] Finally, the Byzantines were able to use a sophisticated logistical support for their armies since they had no challenge in the Mediterranean almost until the conflict's end.

But Belisarius had a decided advantage against the Goths: the discipline and the steadiness of both infantry and cavalry under his command. Although there is no evidence that Byzantine commanders had less confidence in their footmen's efficacy, the war in Italy would show a tendency to increase the number of cavalrymen in comparison to infantry, especially of heavy armored cavalry, armed with firepower, the bow, and both shock weapons, the lance and the sword. The main change from the past was that whereas the Romans of the West had relied on mercenary arrow-shooting light cavalry, the Byzantines tended now to include also heavily armed bow cavalrymen, probably based on the examples of the Alans and of the Persians.[26] Moreover, in the case of the army sent to Italy with Belisarius it is likely that the proportion of foot to horse (normally 3:1[27]), had been altered in favor of the cavalry. In spite of the presence of many mercenary units, command was firmly in Byzantine hands. Of the twenty-two commanders in Belisarius's army, three were Huns, one of Germanic origin, and the rest, eighteen, Roman natives from Thrace.[28]

The Byzantine armies of the sixth century were in general much smaller than the Roman armies of the ancient past, one reason probably being that the events of the Empire of the West taught that large armies could be the worst enemy of state stability. For the emperor's relationship with the soldiers was based on the assumption that "war was an unfortunate necessity."[29] Byzantine hosts, then, were small, but normally they involved a fine balance between the various units with the cavalry assuming a preponderant role. Horsemen armed with bows, spears, and swords could hit from a distance and then charge with lances. Moreover, some of their auxiliary units—Huns and Moors, for instance—would also perform a harassing role without coming to face-to-face combat. In general, Byzantine armies were best used to fight as long as possible from a distance, delivering a shattering charge only when the enemy was disordered and had suffered heavy losses. Although cavalry was still primary among their ranks, the Goths relied on face-to-face combat. They too had bowmen but apparently none of them on horseback. Belisarius would exploit this situation with great cleverness. As he explained to his secretary, Procopius, he had noticed in his first clashes with the enemy that the Goths, if not superior in number, could inflict no injury to his men. The difference was that the Byzantines and their allies, like the Huns fighting for Justinian, were able horsemen accustomed to fighting with bows from a distance. The Goths, besides being poor horsemen (but here Belisarius was wrong, as Totila would show in the prologue to the Battle of Casilinum), instead attacked with spears and swords. Their bowmen were only on foot.[30]

Goths and Byzantines at Rome's Walls

Belisarius's approach to the conquest of Italy was masterful (Figure 2.1). He began by assuring the supply line with Constantinople and a careful, but also at times daring, strategic control of Italy. The first thing he did after reconquering North Africa was to monopolize the sea-lanes of the Adriatic Sea that linked a possible supply line with Constantinople. The next stage was to bring Sicily within the sphere of the empire. Once this was achieved, Belisarius moved against the most important city of southern Italy, Naples, before moving on to Rome. While in Rome, most of the strongholds of southern and central Italy, still in Ostrogothic hands, fell, often without resistance, into Byzantine hands.[31] Moreover, the advance was coordinated on Belisarius's flank with supply ships carrying wheat from Sicily.[32]

Belisarius's march to Rome, with forays into Tuscany and Umbria, was favored by the decisions that the new Gothic king, Vitigis, was forced to make. Vitigis posted 4,000 soldiers in Rome[33] and left for Ravenna to marry Theodoric's granddaughter, Matasuntha, necessary, he felt, to legitimize his rule and to make sure that peace be made with the Franks so that he could use

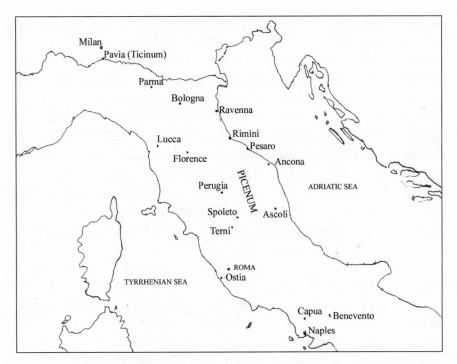

Figure 2.1   The Main Theater of the Ostrogothic War

the Gothic troops stationed against them. He also reequipped the army with offensive weapons and armor.[34] Vitigis's decision to withdraw "reveals the well-planned moves of the seasoned commander,"[35] but this is debatable, especially considering the strange behavior of the men left in Rome. When Belisarius, after the conquest of Naples, approached Rome's walls, the 4,000 Goths left the city to join their king in Ravenna. They streamed through Rome's gates the same day that Belisarius's troops entered.[36] If they had remained it would have been difficult for Belisarius to move into the city.

On the surface, Belisarius's decision to take Rome does not make sense. The civilian population, dreading the anguish of a siege, was lukewarm at best about his arrival. Moreover, he entered a city that in appearance would have been impossible to defend with 5,000 men. The wall circuit alone was about 20 kilometers,[37] and in many locations the walls built under the emperors Aurelian and Honorius were in disrepair. Supplies could not be received easily if the forthcoming siege were to last a long time since the enemies could block traffic on the Tiber River by conquering Portus, Rome's harbor, on the Tyrrhenian Sea. But in reality, unless he received reinforcements quickly,

Belisarius had no other choice. A pitched battle against an army much more numerous than his own would have been foolish. He needed to be in a city that the enemy could not disregard. If he had remained in Naples or moved on to Perugia or Spoleto, both cities with impressive fortifications, the Goths could have left him there forever, trusting time and desertion to defeat the Byzantine effort. But Rome was different. The important symbolical meaning of the city dictated that it had to remain in Gothic hands. Belisarius needed his enemies to attack *him*. At least in Rome, his strength could be magnified by the walls that still encircled the city. In other words, Belisarius's decision to remain in Rome must be seen not as a defensive maneuver but as a sophisticated offensive challenge to the Goths. No doubt, however, the position of the Byzantine army was problematical. Five thousand soldiers in a city with a wall circuit of 20 kilometers were too few.

Belisarius did not get discouraged (Figure 2.2). Immediately he decided to strengthen the fortifications as much as possible before the inevitable return of the Goths. First, to ensure the safety of his men fighting from the city walls, he built in some places a cross-wall on the defenders' left side to avoid making them vulnerable to arrows and javelins coming from that direction. He also surrounded the fortifications, where necessary, with a ditch. Second, he collected the food supplies from ships that had moved along his left flank since he had left Sicily, as well as anything edible from Rome's vicinity.[38] And then he waited for the enemy to arrive. At this stage he seemed confident about his chances, for there is no evidence that he requested reinforcements from Constantinople. He would do that later.

Vitigis began with a strange move. He sent a large army not against Rome but to take Dalmatia on the eastern side of the Adriatic Sea.[39] The Goths accomplished nothing. But even if successful, possession of Dalmatia could have created only minimal damage to Belisarius's supply line because control of the Mediterranean was in Byzantine hands. A better move was instead making peace with the Franks, because that allowed Vitigis to recall his troops from southern Gaul. It was a heavy blow to the Byzantines, for they had reached an agreement with the Franks before Belisarius moved into Italy assuring Constantinople that the Franks would continue hostilities against the Ostrogoths in exchange for a financial reward. When the Franks reneged on the promise, the danger on Vitigis's northwest vanished, and more men became available for his war effort against Belisarius.

The Gothic king reached the outskirts of Rome on 21 February 537.[40] According to Procopius, he had 150,000 people under his command.[41] The

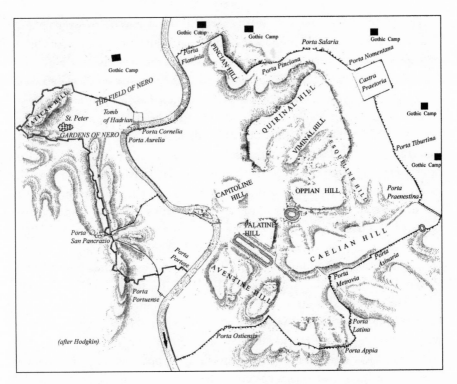

Figure 2.2　*Rome*

Greek historian is, however, not to be trusted with such figures. No doubt, Vitigis's army was large, for the Goths, like all barbarians, were a people under arms and, as such, could rely on all freemen of a certain age for military service.

The first clash between Goths and Byzantines took place at Narni, north of Rome. The Byzantines were successful, but the event meant nothing to the confrontation at Rome because Narni is quite distant from Rome and apparently not many men were involved. Meanwhile, Belisarius tried to slow the enemy's approach to the city by building a fortified tower on the Milvian Bridge, about two miles north of Rome.[42] Belisarius thought that the bridge would have been the most likely place for crossing the Tiber from the western to the eastern bank, where the main gates of Rome stood. As soon as they saw the large Gothic army approaching, about twenty-two tower guards deserted immediately to the enemy; the rest ran away toward Naples, worried about finding any safety in Rome.[43] Thus the enemy crossed the river in perfect safety and without Belisarius's knowledge.

This event almost cost the great general his life. Unaware that the enemy had crossed the river and was now stationed near Rome, Belisarius, at the head of 1,000 horsemen, moved out of the city to scout the area the next morning. Unexpectedly they met the Goths, who had already moved on the Tiber's left bank. They too were horsemen. Belisarius should have run away to safety. Instead, rather foolishly, he engaged the enemy. The deserters in the Gothic army recognized the general because of his dark-roan steed, a wonderful animal, and were urged to direct the attack with words and gestures where Belisarius stood. The general, now in serious danger, fought back ferociously, assisted by his grooms and guard. Many on both sides fell where the general stood. In the end, the Goths ran to their camp while Belisarius and his men retreated to a nearby hill.

As the Goths entered camp, news that they had engaged the enemy general convinced another group of cavalrymen to leave the camp and move against Belisarius. This time the struggle did not go well for the Byzantines. Finally, while one man tried to delay the Goths' pursuit, the rest of Belisarius's men ran madly toward Rome's Salarian Gate, but when they arrived at Rome's walls they were refused entry. The news had spread that Belisarius had died, and the soldiers inside the city were unwilling to open the gate to the men pressing outside. Their own sight encumbered by the waning light of dusk, and fearful that the Goths would enter too, the defenders could hardly recognize their comrades covered with blood and dust. Belisarius had no choice but to counterattack. By voice and gesture he rallied the men around him and suddenly assailed the enemies who were trying to cross the ditch around the walls. Helped by the coming of darkness, Belisarius caught the enemy by surprise. The Goths withdrew, afraid that probably reinforcements had come from the city. Finally, the Romans recognized Belisarius and opened the gate to safety. The engagement had lasted the whole day. Begun in the morning, it ended in the evening. Afterward, Belisarius must have been afraid of a night attack, and before returning to his wife, he disposed trusted men to guard the gates and ordered all his soldiers to be on the alert and to illuminate the fortifications' perimeter with continuous fires.[44]

As the light of the following day spread over the walls, both sides prepared for a major clash. The Goths decided to concentrate their attacks against five of the fourteen major gates of Rome's walls. The disposition of the Gothic camps suggests that they planned to spend their major effort north and east of the city against about half of the walls' perimeter. The five gates involved were the Porta Flaminia, the Pincia, the Salaria, the Nomentana, and the

Praenestina. Corresponding to these gates, on the right side of the Tiber the Goths had established six of their seven camps, all under Vitigis's direct command. The seventh camp, across the Tiber in Nero's Plain, right of St. Peter's Church as it stands today, was intended to prevent Belisarius's soldiers from escaping toward the Mediterranean. Moreover, the men in the seventh camp could also harass the defenders at the Porta Aurelia. Its commander was a man named Marcia. All the camps were set in the pattern of the old Roman camps, probably based on their experience of living for more than a century on the territories of the eastern emperor. They dug a deep ditch around each camp, massing the earth on the lodgings' side and placing sharp stakes on the earth's top. The Goths also broke all the aqueducts, stopping fresh water from reaching the city, although of course the besieged could always use the Tiber's waters, to which they had access as the river crossed most of the city on their side of the walls.[45]

Belisarius established his headquarters on the hill between the Porta Pinciana and the Porta Salaria overlooking the area where he expected the greatest Gothic effort.[46] The area was a wonderful location because it allowed him also a fairly clear view of the eastern side of the city against which six of the enemy camps were located. Each gate was locked, and entry into the city was barred by placing large rocks against the gates.

After a fruitless attempt by Vitigis to convince Belisarius to surrender (he sent ambassadors to the Roman general), the Gothic king had prepared for a full-scale attack by building wooden towers, four rams, and several ladders. On the other side Belisarius had prepared several ballistae (large machines launching large arrows with great violence), onagri (a type of catapult throwing stones), and machines, nicknamed wolves, that dropped wooden planks into which sharp pikes had been inserted over the attackers trying to scale the walls.[47]

The attack against Rome's walls started on 21 March 537, the eighteenth day since the siege had begun. It started with crowds of Goths rushing into the northern section of the fortifications toward Porta Salaria, throwing fascines to fill the ditch in order to facilitate the advance of the towers and rams. At the same time, oxen and men (about 50 soldiers per tower) pulled and pushed the towers and rams toward the walls to the defenders' great distress. But Belisarius seemed unworried, and he actually laughed as the towers approached. When the machines reached the killing range of his archers, he ordered his men to target only the oxen. Soon the machines, the animals wounded or dead, stopped moving and remained stationary. Vitigis's aggression, however, did not end there. He kept the northern walls under attack by lining his men deep and keeping a steady flow of arrows against the Porta Salaria. At the same time, the main assault switched to the Porta Prenestina on the east and the Porta Aurelia on the northwest.[48]

The Tomb of Hadrian (the modern Castle St. Angelo) provided an obvious place of defense for the Byzantines. However, the Goths avoided a direct approach (it would have been suicidal to do so) and advanced concealed by the portico of the nearby St. Peter's Church, which at that time was much smaller than the church built during the Renaissance. Finally, covered by their large oblong shields, they emerged to surround the Tomb of Hadrian, targeting the defenders with volley after volley of arrows. They also carried ladders. The Byzantine contingent was in great danger. They could not use their ballistae, for once the Goths had reached the walls of the Tomb of Adrian the ballistae were useless because they shot only in a straight line. Nor were their bows enough to contain the enemies coming over the ladders. Then in desperation they found a solution to their plight in the many marble statues erected around the perimeter of the building. They broke them into large pieces and threw them against the Goths as they massed on the ladders near the building's wall. The enemies withdrew in disarray to avoid the marble falling on their heads, some probably dropping their shields to move faster. They then became an easy target for the archers and, as they ran away farther, for the ballistae.[49]

The push against the Prenestina compelled the defenders to call Belisarius for help. In the end, however, the Gothic attack failed miserably. Unable to make headway against the fortifications, Vitigis's men tried to penetrate into the city by breaking part of a wall that had been the Vivarium, the location where the ancients kept the wild beasts for the circus. The Vivarium was near the Prenestina Gate and in appearance was a much easier target. By breaking it the Goths had hoped that they would enter the city. They were stunned when they were faced by another wall (the city's normal wall) and more soldiers. Meanwhile Belisarius, upon reaching the Prenestina, gave orders to open its doors, falling upon the rear of the Goths pressing nearby. At the same time, up in the northern part of the fortifications, the Romans opened the Salarian Gate and routed the enemies assembled there. By the end of the day, Procopius claims, obviously with exaggeration, 30,000 Goths had lost their lives, while Belisarius's men had suffered only light casualties.[50] But the Byzantine general also had serious problems. He must have realized that he could not resist forever with only 5,000 men—and many of them ready to desert: he sent a letter to Justinian asking for reinforcements. Those would eventually arrive, but not for a while and then only in small numbers. An even greater problem was the lack of food supplies in the city. The situation became very serious when the Goths, three days after the battle, took the harbor, Portus, on the right side of the Tiber's estuary, cutting the normal flow of supplies to Rome. Now supplies had to land at Anzio, a day's distance from Ostia; then, with the harbor and the road to Rome on the river's right side in Gothic hands, supplies had to be carried on foot along the track on the left of the Tiber, a difficult track often encumbered by woods.[51]

To relieve some of the food pressure by people unable to serve in the defense of the city, Belisarius sent his soldiers' wives and children as well as slaves to Naples. But it was not enough. Rome's lower classes, deprived of the possibility of working because of the siege and having no money to buy food even if it were available, were starving. Belisarius pressed them to share guard duty along the city walls with the soldiers. It was a skillful solution heightening the degree of safety by having more men on the walls, and giving civilians some relief in the form of provisions. Besides burning the machines abandoned by the Goths, Belisarius also refined safety measures within the city. For fear of treason he changed the locks of each gate twice a month and moved the guards from gate to gate, far away from the original post. And to make sure that the enemy would not engage in a sneak attack, he sent his nimble Moors and dogs to patrol the moat surrounding the walls at night.[52]

Finally, in early April 547, twenty days after the fall of Portus, the harbor on the Mediterranean now in Gothic hands, a few reinforcements arrived for the Byzantines: 1,600 Slavonians, Antae (Slavs), and "Huns," that is, soldiers ethnically similar to Huns. Now with more horsemen at his disposal Belisarius switched to an offensive posture: he brought war to the Goths. He ordered one of his bodyguards, Trajan, to lead 200 guard horsemen toward the enemy camp, to take control of a hill nearby, and to remain there. If the enemy advanced toward them, he was to engage them with bows from a distance. When no arrows remained in their quivers, or if the enemy was dangerously close, they were to gallop back toward Rome. It happened just as Belisarius predicted. The enemy attacked in a dense mass, making an easy target for the Byzantine bowmen. No arrow was wasted, and when the Goths moved too close, Belisarius's men scurried toward Rome with enemies in pursuit. However, a nasty surprise awaited the Goths: as they rushed toward the walls, the giant bows, the ballistae, brought death and disorder among their ranks.[53] Not less than 1,000 Goths perished that day. Belisarius used the same trick two more times, the bait being 300 men, with similar results. In all about 4,000 Goths died in these three engagements.[54]

The countermeasure that Vitigis undertook demonstrated how different the two armies were, as well as the Gothic king's unsophisticated understanding of war. He ordered 500 horsemen to a hill near Rome but at a certain distance from their camps; they were to remain out of range of the machines on the battlements. Belisarius countered by sending 1,000 men forward. They surrounded the hill and shot at the Goths until they were forced to descend to the plain, where most of them were massacred.[55] Three days later Vitigis sent 500 more horsemen, chosen among the bravest of each camp, and launched them toward the walls of Rome. This time Belisarius countered with 1,500 horsemen. The Goths, outnumbered 3:1, were routed, and most of them perished.[56]

The continuous success experienced during the skirmishes raised so much the spirits of both soldiers and populace that they kept pressing Belisarius for an all-out effort. After much hesitation the general, probably also pressed by the limited flow of supplies entering Rome, agreed to try to capitalize on the high spirit of his men and the obviously low morale of the enemy. It was a mistake for which he would pay dearly. He began his attack against the northern posts, three of the seven enemy camps, and, worried about the fourth camp on the northwest in Nero's Plain, he tried to make sure that the Goths there would not take part in the forthcoming encounter. But the soldiers located on the Tomb of Hadrian, and thus in the same area of the Gothic camp, were too few to hold the enemy, and he increased their number by allowing members of the Roman populace to join them. Many civilians had constantly begged him to let them fight alongside the soldiers. Belisarius's order was clear and precise: Do not engage the enemy; remain still and visible so that the Goths there, in fear of you, will not bring aid to their comrades in the area between the Porta Flaminia and the Porta Salaria, where the main Roman attack was to take place.

The ploy worked magnificently at the opening as the light of the day spread over the Roman walls, even better than Belisarius had anticipated. While the rest stood ready to battle, the North African horsemen located near the Tomb of Hadrian kept harassing the enemy with their bows. Soldiers and civilians posted there—carried on the wings of enthusiasm—rushed the enemy, which was not what Belisarius had ordered. The Goths were routed in fear, taking refuge atop the nearby hills. And there Belisarius's men made their second mistake: they stopped to loot the enemy camp instead of delivering the killing blow to the enemy. Moreover, with their minds clouded by greed, they disregarded either cutting the bridge over the Tiber (and thus relegating Vitigis' army to only one side of the river), or crossing the bridge themselves and attacking the rear of the main Gothic army engaged between the Flaminia and the Salaria Gates. They would pay dearly for their greed and lack of lucidity. The Goths, who had taken refuge on a nearby hill, realized that many of the enemies were civilians, not soldiers, and counterattacked with rage. Those who did not fall victims to the Goths left the enemy camp with empty hands; for those who perished, the only consolation was to die with the loot still in their grasp.

The main encounter between the Flaminia and the Salaria Gates also started well for Belisarius's men. Vitigis deployed his men in the classical manner, foot in the middle, cavalry at the wings, as close as possible to Rome's walls. Confident that he would rout the opponents, he wanted his own soldiers to stay near the obvious line of retreat—Rome's gates, so that they could easily slay them during the pursuit. Belisarius's problem at this location of the front line was twofold: what to do with the many civilians who had insisted on joining his army, and what to do with the many footmen who, by getting horses from the enemy during past encounters, now wanted to fight like professional horsemen. He solved the civilian problem by marshaling them either on the battlements or behind the moat, away from the first line, so that if panic ensued among them it would not spread to the rest. Moreover, stationed at the ditch they could screen the regrouping cavalry. To strengthen their will to fight, he also had, after much soul-searching and under the insistence of the people involved, allowed two commanders very dear to him to deploy with the civilians. The would-be horsemen were marshaled with the rest, the reason probably being that Belisarius felt that a larger number might dishearten the enemy.

Passing through the smaller Porta Pinciana, located between the Porta Flaminia and the Porta Salaria, Belisarius's men deployed, walls to their backs. Facing them were the soldiers of the three nearby enemy camps, hopeful that a frontal encounter, in which they thought they were superior to the Byzantines, would give them victory. The Byzantines attacked in the manner familiar to their style of waging war, their arrows causing many opponents to bite the dust as blood spurted from their bodies. But there were so many enemies that their front line, as it was thinned by the Byzantine bows, was also immediately replenished. Yet by midday the Goths had been forced to withdraw almost to where their camps stood. At this stage many among the Byzantines thought that they should have been happy with the result and that they should have withdrawn from the battlefield and taken repair behind Rome's walls. That solution would have been appropriate because attrition was working in favor of the Goths who, with the camps now behind them, fought vigorously under the protection of their large shields. Moreover, by then Vitigis's men must have realized that their adversaries were much fewer. Either Belisarius did not give the order of withdrawal or, more likely hoping for a definitive victory, had to pursue his attack until the enemy's annihilation.

The tide of battle changed at this stage. The Gothic cavalry on the right wing charged the Byzantines who, faced by the spears of their enemy (clearly their archers must have been unable to stop the Goths), were broken. The whole of Belisarius's line ran to safety. Many would have perished if not for the bravery of the two commanders of the mainly civilian infantry lined up at the moat surrounding the walls. One of them, Principius, fell quickly, his body hacked to pieces; the other, Tarmutus of the Isaurians of Asia Minor, kept resisting until his brother Enne came to help him. Although his body was covered by wounds, Tarmutus ran to safety behind the walls, two javelins still in his hands. He died two days later.

Meanwhile the brave stand of the footmen allowed the routed Byzantine cavalry to reach Rome's walls, but safety was still far away, for the people atop the walls refused to open the gate in fear that the Goths would penetrate into the city together with the fugitives. Their backs pressed against the walls, the Byzantines were in danger of death, but they could not fight back because, unable to use their bows (the enemy was too close), they could hardly maneuver their spears, most of them having broken during the previous fight. What saved them was the presence of the crowd on the battlements. Afraid that their own lives could be in danger if Belisarius's men descended from the walls and counterattacked, the pursuers stopped at the moat, allowing the Byzantines to seek refuge behind the city walls as finally the people inside the gates decided to open the gate when they saw the enemy in retreat. The battle, begun early in the morning, ended as the day waned.

Both sides licked their wounds in the aftermath. Belisarius realized that for the moment it would be suicidal to engage in pitched battles. So far the Ostrogoths had been humiliated and beaten several times in their siege attacks and in skirmishes, but there was nothing that would suggest that they would throw away their weapons and shields and run away in the next major confrontation. From then on the Byzantines engaged the enemy in the manner that was most efficient: cavalry engagements and sallies. Moreover, as winter came, the main brunt of hostilities ceased.

The new sun of spring was sullied by the arrival of famine and pestilence among Belisarius's men. But not all was gray and deadly just for them. Both besiegers and besieged shared the same plight: plague and hunger. The Goths soon stripped the resources of their surroundings. At the same time, there was some relief for Belisarius, for Constantinople controlled the supply line. Also, Belisarius finally received considerable reinforcements and eventually supplies: 500 men recruited by Procopius, historian of the expedition, in Naples; 3,000 Isaurians, 800 Thracian cavalrymen, and 1,000 other horsemen of nonspecified origin from Naples.[57] Eventually another contingent of 5,000 men under the command of Narses landed at Picenum, an area northeast of Rome on the Adriatic Sea.[58]

Vitigis was the first to approach for an armistice. Belisarius agreed, and the proposal was sent to Justinian for approval. The truce that the armistice should have brought was continuously broken, probably more by Belisarius than by Vitigis. Now with more men at his disposal the Byzantine general slowly but methodically enlarged his sphere of military control. First he assured that food supplies and men could reach him safely, then he started to move northeast of Rome into Umbria and the Marches. Belisarius's men were given specific orders: occupy the most important strategic spots; respect the Romans but despoil all Ostrogoths of their possessions and take their women and children (whose male relatives were fighting near Rome) as slaves.[59] The initiative of a daring commander named John actually brought the Byzantines close to strike even the capital of the Ostrogothic state, Ravenna. It was at this stage that Vitigis decided to abandon the siege.[60] It was 12 March 548.[61] A full year and nine days had passed since the Goths had arrived near Rome. As Procopius tersely states, sixty-nine major encounters had been fought between Goths and Byzantines during the siege.[62] But the bloodshed did not end then; as the Goths left, the Byzantines attacked them viciously during the crossing of the Milvian Bridge north of Rome. Belisarius came out from the Porta Pinciana and caught the Goths unprepared, divided into two sections, one safe already across the river, the other still near the Pinciana. In the beginning the Goths fought with bravery and withstood the Byzantines well but then in panic ran to cross the bridge and reach the opposite bank and safety. In their mad rush they bumped into each other, fighting not just the Byzantines pressing on their backs but their own kind as well. Many died on the bridge; many others fell into the Tiber and drowned, sucked to the bottom by their armor's weight.[63]

The existence of an armistice that was not an armistice, and the switch to battlefields north of Rome, changed the tenor of warfare. Belisarius by all appearances seemed on the edge of a final triumph, but the arrival of Byzantine reinforcements under the command of the Armenian Narses, a eunuch with considerable military experience, was a hindrance more than an asset. Jealousy and antagonism between the two generals, and especially among their subordinate officers, weakened the Byzantine army since the two men pursued different aims. It was at this stage that the most horrendous event of the war took place. The Goths, who had conquered the city of Milan that had remained in the emperor's camp, slaughtered all Italian males of any age there, their women given as slaves to the Burgundians, who had come to help the Goths during the siege. In all, 300,000 men were massacred. The body of the civilian commander was cut to pieces and fed to the dogs. The only ones left unscathed were the Byzantine soldiers, for this had been agreed before the city's surrender.[64]

At this stage the Goths initiated a fine strategic move. They realized that Constantinople's war effort depended on peace on their eastern frontier with the Persians. Vitigis sent ambassadors to Persia to entice it to attack the Byzantines again. When Emperor Justinian realized the danger, he ordered Belisarius to bring the war in Italy to a close as quickly as possible.[65] It took some time for the general to obey the emperor, but in the end he took Ravenna, and Vitigis agreed to abandon the throne and leave for Constantinople, where he died about two years later. In 540 Belisarius departed for Asia Minor.[66] By then the Goths had been reduced to a corner of Italy in possession only of a major city, Ticinum (Pavia).[67]

The End of the Goths

Finally the Goths seemed beaten and in disarray. Two men whom they elected to the throne were both murdered while they pleaded with Constantinople to leave their people in control of northern Italy. But then the incompetence of the Byzantine leaders in Italy and the election of a new Gothic leader, Totila, the greatest of them since Theodoric, started a Gothic revival throughout the peninsula.

After beating the Romans in two major battles, Totila bypassed Rome and struck into southern Italy. The new king not only was a great tactician but also had a clear sense of strategy. Before besieging and eventually taking Naples, he destroyed the walls of Benevento to deprive Constantinople of using the city as a military base. The conflict was then renewed on a large scale.[68] By the summer of 544, when Belisarius was again sent to Italy to redress the fortunes of war for Constantinople, the Gothic king had recovered most of Italy. He would be more than a match for the great general. Yet his dream of reestablishing Gothic rule in the peninsula was impossible for several reasons. The resources available to Constantinople were much greater than those left in the ravaged peninsula for Totila. Moreover, the Italians and a good section of the Gothic aristocracy were more than willing to find an accommodation with the emperor. Actually Belisarius's main task was not so much to defeat the Goths on the battlefield but to restore order to a place where his own men acted as thugs, looting the local population. In any case, Belisarius's second tenure as a commander was a failure. Things turned around when the emperor decided to replace him with a brilliant general, Narses, a eunuch who had already been in Italy toward the end of Belisarius's first tenure in office. At that time jealousy and misunderstandings among the officers' core of both generals had made Narses's presence a hindrance more than a benefit to the emperor's cause.

Narses's march toward Italy was fraught with dangers, and while crossing the Balkans he barely escaped the Avars, an Asiatic people settled in the Danubian area. When Narses reached the peninsula's borders two more formidable enemies stopped his way: Franks in the Venetian territory, and Goths at Verona in locations that Narses apparently had to cross to move into central Italy. Daringly the Byzantine general moved very close to the edge of the sea with the Byzantine fleet on his flank.

Narses remained nine days at Ravenna and then struck toward central Italy, his aim to reach the outskirts of Rome, which Totila had again besieged (Figure 2.3). But there were major obstacles along the way, first at Ariminum, and then, as he moved on the Flaminian Way across the Apennines, the fortress of Pertusa. Again, Narses, in a series of splendid moves, outflanked the enemy. First he crossed an Ariminum river, the Marecchia, on a pontoon after the leader of the Goths, who had contested his passage, met his end in a skirmish; then the Byzantine general struck south along the Flaminian Way. He abandoned the old Roman road north of Seni Gallica, for he did not want to pass near Pertusa. Probably near the mouth of the River Sena he struck right and began his crossing of the peninsula in very difficult terrain. Even when he reached Ad Calem, the march's extreme westward point, the terrain must still have been very difficult. From there he moved southward and finally stopped on the plain near Taginae (Gualdo Tadino), almost a niche between the hills of the Apennines.[69]

Totila, who was nearby Rome, could still have stopped Narses's army by adopting a defensive posture in the Apennines, for Narses was still in the

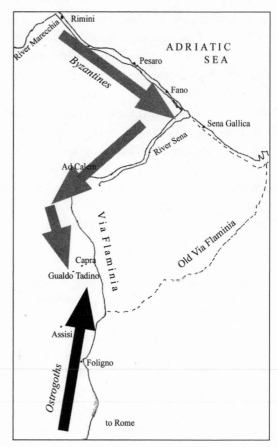

Figure 2.3
The Gualdo Tadino (Taginae)
Campaign of 551–552

midst of the mountain chain. Strangely he moved forward to answer the Byzantine's challenge in spite of the fact that the 2,000-man reinforcement he was expecting from Verona had not yet arrived. He camped about 15 miles from the Byzantine army.[70] When Narses proposed a pitched battle, Totila answered that he would be ready to do so in about eight days, but actually the next day he marched on, stopping at a distance of two bowshots (ca. 300–400 meters) from Narses's camp. He was disappointed, for his move did not surprise Narses (the Byzantine had expected it, and he too was ready for battle).

We are not sure about the numerical strength of the two armies, but according to Procopius the Byzantines were vastly superior. Narses's soldiers were a combination of several ethnic groups coming from all parts of the empire; they included many "Roman" soldiers, that is, citizens of the empire from Italy and elsewhere, and large number of mercenaries, 400 Gepids, a large band of Heruli, under two commands (one of the bands included 3,000 men on horseback), Longobards, Huns, and even Persians who had deserted to the Byzantines during their war in the East.

Procopius mentions the speeches of the opposing leaders, and although their words must be seen as the creation of the writer's imagination, they do make sense in pointing out the obvious ideas in the minds of the two generals. The Ostrogoths, said Narses, were nothing but thieves and robbers; their leader had come from the gutter; they were vastly inferior numerically; and they could not win because the Byzantines represented law and good government, not theft and disorder like their enemies. Totila stressed the victories of the past: we have defeated them before, and we shall defeat them again. True, they were superior in number, but they were mercenaries coming from all parts of the world whose only interest resided in their wages. They had already received their pay, which meant that they would run away at the first chance.

The terrain on which the two armies stood was a plain surrounded by many hills. One of the hills was strategically important, for whoever controlled it could outflank the Byzantines (Figure 2.4). The night before the encounter Narses sent 50 footmen to occupy it. At daybreak Totila vainly tried to displace Narses's men, but in spite of repeated cavalry charges he had to give up. Helped by the difficult terrain of the hill, their spears, and the noise of their shouts and the shields clashing together, they frightened enemy horses and men. Narses's 50 men kept control of the hill.

Unlike the Byzantines, the Goths deployed cavalry in front and infantry on a second line. They were also told to use neither bow nor sword but only spears, to Procopius's great surprise.[71] That strange deployment was ominous for Totila and his men. It became worse when, outflanked on both sides, the Goths were funneled into the center of the Byzantines. For the Byzantines had divided their army into the traditional center and wings. The center lined up barbarians like Heruli, Longobards, and Gepids, who usually fought on horseback but this time were ordered to fight dismounted. Narses wanted to make sure that they would fight, not flee on their horses at the first reverse. The soldiers on the wings, all cavalrymen, were among the best in the Byzantine army. Narses was stationed on the left. Just ahead of the two wings and flanking the center he deployed 8,000 dismounted archers, 4,000 each side. And Narses's preparations did not end there, for he placed 1,500 horsemen at an angle near his left wing, 500 in support of any unit retreating from the battlefield, 1,000 to assault the enemy's infantry if they moved to attack.[72]

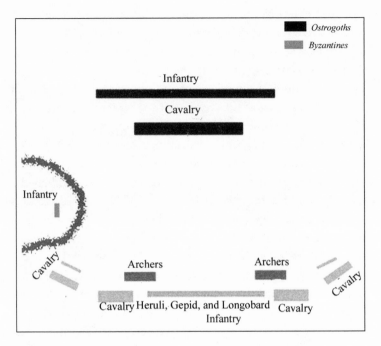

Figure 2.4 **Taginae 552**

Totila rode from one side of the line to the other, encouraging his men; Narses enticed his soldiers by displaying on poles what the brave could expect—bracelets, necklaces, and bridles, all in gold, the symbols of the brave.[73] But the preliminaries had not ended yet. A Byzantine deserter named Coccas, a man with a great reputation as a fighter, rode forward, challenging any of his former comrades to single combat. One of Narses's guards, an Armenian named Anzalas, moved forward. Coccas rushed toward him, his spear pointed to the Armenian's belly, but as he drew near Anzalas the Armenian moved sideways and stuck his own spear into the enemy's side. Coccas fell dead while loud shouts of victory ran through the Byzantine line—another blow to the confidence of the Gothic host.

Totila had another problem. He nervously must have been waiting for the arrival of the 2,000 horsemen from Verona and, probably to give them more time to arrive, he engaged in a stunning war dance. But it was a dance of death more than victory. He advanced in the space between the two lines in shining armor plated in gold with purple favors (purple the color of kings) flowing from his spear and helmet. And there in the midst of the two lines he reverted to some ancestral rite. He performed the *djerid*, the lance-ride typical of the steppe nomads.[74] He rode his horse in circles clockwise and counterclockwise, and while riding he threw the javelin in the air, grabbing it before it fell to the ground and passing it again and again from hand to hand.[75] And then after he stopped his dance, he sent an emissary to Narses. He wanted to talk, but the eunuch sent the messenger away, asking Totila to stop his silly display and engage in battle instead.

Meanwhile, the 2,000 Goths had arrived, but since the sun was now high in the sky Totila withdrew his army for the morning meal. They did not remain in their camp long, for they soon were back on the battlefield in a rush, again hoping to surprise Narses; but the old general had never left the battlefield and distributed food to his soldiers while they remained in line.[76] Totila, probably desperate by now, played his last card. He quickly tried to break the center of the wider enemy line; he deployed all the cavalry in the first line and all the footmen in the second. He ordered his horsemen forward in a suicidal move, leaving the infantry behind. As the Ostrogoths galloped forward, the two groups of Byzantine bowmen advanced, creating a crescent with their footmen as the center. The Goths' targets were the footmen, but few of Totila's cavalrymen reached them, for they had to advance among the deadly showers of arrows. And when they reached Narses's center, the footmen stood valiantly to meet their enemies. Clearly Totila had tried to win by breaking the enemy center, unleashing only his horsemen to the attack. He failed, but the fight still must have lasted long, for only as light faded did the Gothic cavalry withdraw toward their own panicked infantry, which instead of supporting them ran away, often fighting with each other.

Normally, any death in Procopius is rendered in heroic terms. The champions of both sides disappear after heroically killing scores of enemies. The end of Totila is instead a strange combination in which heroism, savagery, and humdrum are mixed together with behavior that it is hard to explain logically. After his magnificent dance, Totila entered the fray with the armor of a common soldier. He who had been a great and brave soldier would end his life in a manner not worthy of past achievements, according to Procopius. Actually his end was mysterious. He was buried at Caprae, a place miles from the battlefield. One story claims that he was speared in the back while trying to escape, succumbing miles away; another story says that he was struck by an arrow and, unable to endure the pain, left the fray to succumb a few miles away. At the end of the day 6,000 Goths lay on the battlefield. The rest, taken prisoner, were slain soon afterward. Byzantine casualties were probably minor.

Totila was followed by two more kings, neither a real danger to the Byzantines. The last major battle was at Mons Lactarius in 553 nearby Vesuvius, with the Goths making their last stand around their king, Teias, who died in the heroic manner. Teias fought with desperation to the end, his shield encumbered over and over again by the weight of enemy spears and often dropped in exchange for a clean one. He never retreated but kept charging again and again toward anyone trying to displace him, causing death and despair among the enemy. But the end was near: when again he urged for a new shield and turned his body to grasp it, an enemy javelin struck him. He, Teias, the last Gothic king of Italy, a man who had savagely slaughtered 300 Roman children not long before, fell to the ground and died instantly.[77]

The Many Faces of Death

As Procopius moves on in his narrative of the war in Italy, the light tone of the initial pages disappears. His prose becomes harsh and dry; optimism disappears and pessimism and gloom enter his account.[78] Even his hero, Belisarius, practically unblemished in his first five years, becomes flawed. And for the first time Belisarius's secretary starts to show admiration for the Goths, making a real effort to understand their viewpoint.[79] Simply stated, the Goths felt that they had conquered Italy on Constantinople's behalf and that they had ruled the land given to them with fairness and justice. Until the last stage of the conflict, their ruling class—that is, the aristocracy—really wanted some kind of accommodation with the emperor.[80] Procopius was correct in looking with sadness at the whole enterprise. The men that the Byzantines had gone to free were often unwilling to reject the Goths and translate their allegiance to the rule of a man—the emperor in the East—so distant and insensitive to their needs.

By the end of the war, the senatorial class (the ruling class of Italy) together with the upper clergy had been practically destroyed. Those who escaped left Italy for the safety of Constantinople. Once there they never returned.[81] And the ones who remained in the peninsula would soon know a harsher life at the hands of the Longobards.

If the senatorial group suffered, the anguish of the rest of the Italian population was to be much greater. Although the figures given by Procopius on any fact are suspect (yet we have no other reliable source), they give a general impression of the plight of the population. Often the writer's account is nothing more than a death list mostly of the Italian population but also of the Goths, rarely of the Byzantines.

Death came in many forms: famine, illness, torture, on the battlefield; behind the walls of a city; in one's own house, among one's friends, in the midst of enemies, while escaping toward safety; suddenly, slowly, while holding treasures in one's own hands, on green grass, on sand, in the water of sea and rivers; with the body lacerated by hunger and rotted by disease, with muscles and strength intact and still in the prime of youth; the smile of a child still on one's face, or the body decayed and devoured by the passing years; with gold in the purse or in the midst of misery and poverty. Death respected no one in the fields of Italy, as Rome's greatness was no more and its heir from the East was the herald of destruction and chaos in one's own lands.

Civilians were the target of the contestants more than the enemy soldiers. Goths often offered Byzantine soldiers the option of either joining their forces or leaving in safety without weapons and armor, after taking an oath not to fight anymore against them. Harsh treatment was usually reserved only for the enemy leader. In one case they cut off both his hands, penis, and testicles before killing him.[82] The Goths considered civilians traitors, for they had called in Justinian's army in spite of the just and fair rule of the Ostrogoths. The senators, the highest social group, were often their target, but sometimes their rage knew no limits. Before Taginae, Totila had taken 300 children from notable Roman families. After the battle Teias, the new Gothic king, would kill them all.[83]

According to Procopius, 30,000 Goths died during the first siege of Rome and 6,000 in the battle of Taginae; what was left of the Gothic host were slain by the Byzantines afterward. But the battlefield was just one place where people met their end. At the siege of Milan, 300,000 men died at the hands of the Goths, and the civilian commander was cut to pieces and fed to dogs.[84] And later at Tibur, a city not far away from Rome, all the civilians were massacred with tortures that Procopius finds too awful to describe. Meeting one's own end by the sword was not necessarily the worst thing to happen to civilians during a siege; starvation and inhumane behavior became often the norm, as when the Goths under Totila besieged Rome for the second time during the war. The siege lasted almost two years from 544 to 546. The city became isolated, and Belisarius, the hero of the first siege, was incapable and ineffective in resolving the situation. Soon, as hunger joined the other nightmares of civilian life, food was distributed to the soldiers alone. What was left was sold at prices that only the wealthy could afford. Anything left in the city that could be swallowed became food: mice, dogs dead or alive, dead horses, even corpses of human beings. Looking like ghosts, people moved throughout the city, picking up even the dung of other human beings. Some sought relief in suicide. One case was particularly pitiful. When a father's five starving children kept gathering around him, crying and begging for food, he took them to a bridge over the Tiber, covered his face with his cloak, and jumped into the waters of the river, meeting his end in front of his screaming family.[85]

Famine or the threat of famine were a constant. At one point under the fear of war and the diminishing resources in their own lands, the civilian population of Umbria, north of Latium, and of Aemilia, the area north of modern Bologna with Piacenza as its center, migrated to Picenum, northeast of Rome. Their hope was that food supplies would not be scarce there, because, being on the Adriatic Sea, they may have received supplies from Constantinople. But the famine was also there. It is said, Procopius writes, that not less than 50,000 died.[86] Procopius saw the desperate condition of these people with his own eyes. They were lean and pale, their skin barely hanging on their bones. As time went on, their skin was marked by a thousand wrinkles until their body changed from purplish to blackish: they ended looking like torches, death in their eyes. And when they died, even wild animals and birds refused to ravage their corpses, for they were mostly bones with no flesh. Some in desperation collapsed and died while trying to feed on a grassy patch; others were always found ready to cannibalize the bodies. Two women in the countryside around Ariminum (Rimini) killed, while asleep, seventeen vagrants passing through their lands. But the eighteenth intended victim woke up just when they were ready to slaughter him and ended up killing them instead. Even when food became available life ended for many, for they stuffed their stomachs with as much food as possible until they collapsed and died.[87]

Constantinople had won, but the damage inflicted on Italy in eighteen years of war was enormous. It destroyed its resources, decimated the ruling class, and inflicted horrible punishment on the civilian population. For Italy the future would have looked brighter if the Ostrogoths had continued their supremacy. In the long run it was more than likely that the two peoples, Goths and Italians, would have blended. Instead, the catastrophic conditions on the peninsula at the end of the Gothic wars made easy the invasion of the next barbarian population, the Longobards, who would impose a much harsher rule than either the Goths or the men from Constantinople.

Chapter Three

The Arrival of the Longobards

THE SCRIBE CAREFULLY CLEANED his quill and then, helped by a makeshift ruler, copied the next few lines on the pricked parchment. Outside a soft wind whistled through gentle branches of majestic trees. He read again the lines to copy, dipped the quill into the black ink, and bent his hand to the parchment, but suddenly the quiet was broken by the tone of agitated voices. First one, then two, three, then a throng. They came from the cloister, normally a place of silence and peace.

The scribe's hand left the parchment while a sense of foreboding chilled his heart. The voices came closer and closer. Then the library's doors opened violently, smashing against the walls. The Longobards were arriving, screamed the group of monks as they crowded the exit. They could be here any moment. The scribe's first reaction was to throw his quill on the ground and run away, but then he stopped, picked up the quill, and wrote: *Longobardorum invidia non explicit musica.* (This treatise on music was not finished because of the evil deeds of the Longobards.) The work he was copying was *De Institutione Musica*, the great work of Boethius, the Roman senator whom Theodoric had executed in his last mad days during a reign that had known only peace and prosperity in its early years. Boethius's original was lost in the next decades. The only copy left to the future was the unfinished copy that the scribe was writing.[1]

The Longobards had crossed the Alps a short time earlier. A tall blond man with grey-blue eyes[2] moved slowly but energetically uphill toward the summit of the Mountain of the King, as it was named afterward.[3] A motley group of other warriors followed, many physically like the man in the lead. They had long, pear-shaped white faces covered with beards, burned here and there by the sun, the top of their long hair parted in the middle and then flowing down to mouths level but oddly shaved all around, starting from one temple to the other, the long sword bouncing along their side, spear held in one hand, legs enveloped in whitish dirty leggings underneath wide tunics flowing down to the knees, their feet in sandals laced up to the calves. Many must have been tall (an average height of 171.7 centimeters among the males and 161.1 among the females on the basis of 870 skeletons examined by István Kiszely).[4] But not all were of the same ethnic group. The most common speech sounded Germanic, but there were also others whose voices reflected strange, unusual accents and whose features denoted a much more exotic origin.

The leader stopped at the summit and excitedly indicated the lands in the valley below. Soon others joined him. Some, after a quick look, ran back toward the lower reaches of the mountain from which they had come and where women, children, and other warriors stood. They shouted that they finally had reached the territory of the "Romans," that is, the Italians. Fear of the Asiatic Avars who controlled Pannonia, or the Hungarian plains (roughly the area between the Danube and the Sava River),[5] the desire of new land, and the incessant need for more and more plunder had forced them to leave their homelands.[6] Their long trek from the flat lands of Pannonia seemed to have come to an end. The date was 2 April 568.[7]

They were Longobards, their leader and king Alboin. The Longobards had remained in Pannonia for forty-two years,[8] but their movement southward from their ancestral home had begun centuries earlier. Originally from Scandinavia, as their historian Paul the Deacon claims,[9] or from near the estuary of the Elbe River, as most historians today believe,[10] they had moved incessantly toward the south during eight centuries of wanderings (Figure 3.1). In the process they had mixed with many other Germanic tribes that they met. An examination of their skeletons shows that the original Longobardic blood became diluted as they moved south.[11] Yet this was not necessarily true of their nobility. All the found skeletons of the upper classes show retention of northern European bodily features.[12] It is likely then that while the aristocracy insisted on keeping the racial purity of the origins, this was not the case with the social groups of their free people (*arimanni*), whose characteristics remained northern European only in a general sense. Their lowest classes (*aldiones*) show instead features of the other populations (non-Germanic) that the Longobards had met in their quest southward.[13]

The immediate place of departure of Alboin's followers was that cauldron of violence, disorder, and everlasting change that the southern banks of the Danube River had become during the last stages of the fall of the Roman

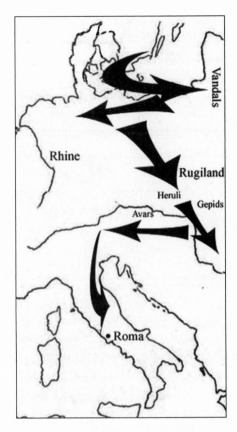

Figure 3.1
Longobards from c. 100 to 570

Empire of the West. It was a place in which roamed remnants of the old Roman army, constantly fighting each other, elements of many German tribes, and people who had come from Asia and from the Russian steppes. Alboin's soldiers then included not only Longobards but also other barbarians and former Roman soldiers or their descendants—Goths, Saxons, Bulgarians, Gepids, Thuringians—and probably even some of those Asiatic Avars from whom the Longobards were running away.[14] Some of them had already fought on Italian lands, from which they had been forced to depart when the leader of the Byzantine forces in Italy, Narses, a man not unknown for his ruthlessness, had been appalled by the wanton destruction and savagery of his 5,500 Longobard mercenaries against the Ostrogoths and the Italic populations: they set fire to any building found during their march and violated women who had taken refuge in sanctuaries.[15]

The army led by Alboin was not that large, especially if we exclude the other ethnic groups. At most it reached 100,000 in all, including women and children, and not counting the 20,000 Saxons who after a stay in Italy moved back to their German lands to meet a most bitter end. There, another Germanic tribe, the Suebians, who had taken over their lands, destroyed them to the last man.[16] Yet the Longobards themselves must have been more than the 15,000 warriors attributed by some historians (Kiszely gives a 50,000 total including women and children).[17] If we accept the 20,000-plus figure that Longobard historian Paul the Deacon gives to the Saxons,[18] we must assume that the promoters of the invasion, Alboin's Longobards, were likely more numerous than the Saxons. But how many of them we do not know, and in any case they numbered at most 100,000, not counting the Saxons.[19] Certainly the invaders were a minority compared to the roughly 4 million people in Italy.[20] If these figures are correct, they constituted, after crossing the Alps, about 4.5 persons for every 1,000 members of the local population.[21]

Longobard society was characterized by a small minority of aristocrats as the ruling class: 4 percent, it seems, in a population where about 60 percent were freemen and about 20 semifree. They lived on war, and in Pannonia, it seems, the only activity besides that was the breeding and training of horses. They were divided for social and military reasons into the *fare*; that is, social groups tied mostly by blood that became the nuclei during campaigns. Theoretically they followed the precepts of the Arian religion.[22] But in reality, as their cemeteries show, mostly they seem to have remained heathens. They tended to restate solidarity with savage rites dating to a very distant history. For instance, 100 years after their conquest of the Duchy of Benevento they still gathered outside the walls of the city, hung a viper on a tree, took turns hitting it, then meticulously divided it into small pieces and ate it. Also they decapitated a goat to honor their ancient god Thor. Their definition as a people was based on the idea of personal freedom, victory on the battlefield, and superiority over any other people, whether Germanic, Slavic, Asiatic, or Latin. However, although the indigenous people of the Italian peninsula were religiously excluded from positions of power, this did not apply necessarily to those ethnic groups that had come with them to the peninsula. There were, for instance, dukes (the regional lords of the kingdom) who were not Longobards.[23]

That such a relatively small number of warriors should be able to establish rule over Italy is not surprising, although they never controlled the entire country: the Byzantines would hold not only Ravenna but also Rome, Naples, Sicily, and the heel and toe of southern Italy. Alboin's men arrived in a time of great social and economic distress.[24] Decades of bloody, destructive wars had been waged between the Romans of the East—that is, the Byzantines of Constantinople—and the Ostrogoths who had come to Italy, on the emperor's beckoning, to displace the barbarian Odovacar. And there were also other ills. The plague had surfaced in most of northern Italy, from the mountains on the east to the beaches of Liguria. Another calamity followed: famine brought more misery and caused many deaths.[25] The civilian population had no weapons or training to oppose the invaders. The only soldiers were the Byzantines left in the peninsula by an emperor whose priority was the border with Persia and, later, the irrepressible Muslim advance toward the Mediterranean coast. In Italy they were to protect mainly easily defended areas, like Sicily, or places considered essential for Constantinople's political and economic interests, like Ravenna, the seat of Byzantine dominance in northern Italy, Rome in the center, and Naples in the south. That the Longobards may have been invited to come to Italy, as is sometimes said and was recently suggested by Neil Christie,[26] seems unlikely. Although several bishops met the invaders on friendly terms, this was not the case of the holders of the major ecclesiastical sees of Milan and Aquileia. They would not have remained hostile if they had, at least initially, invited the Longobards to settle in Italy either on their own or because the Byzantine emperor or his representatives in the peninsula had done so.

The Longobards spread forcefully but not always quickly throughout Italian lands, conquering all the territories that the Byzantines were unable to defend. Eventually they settled in three main areas: in the north, in the Duchy of Spoleto in central Italy, and in the Duchy of Benevento in the southern peninsula (Figure 3.2). But initially they behaved in the manner of nomads, for whom permanence was not the main goal. Instead of concentrating on the peninsula, they crossed the western Alps, coming into the lands of the Franks. But the Franks were not an easy target. They pushed the Longobards to the other side of the Alps, often with high casualties, and kept their own foothold on the Italian side of the mountains, which they had established during the waning years of Gothic domination.[27]

To contemporaries the Longobards looked like Huns with blond hair and western eyes: their advance was a catalogue of sack and spoliation. What they could not carry they seemed to have destroyed for the sake of destruction. The violence struck every level of society, Italians and barbarians alike, for they battered not only the conquered but at times their own kind. The first king, Alboin, was assassinated by a conspiracy woven by his wife in his third year of reign; the second ruler, Clefi, was slaughtered by a servant midway during his

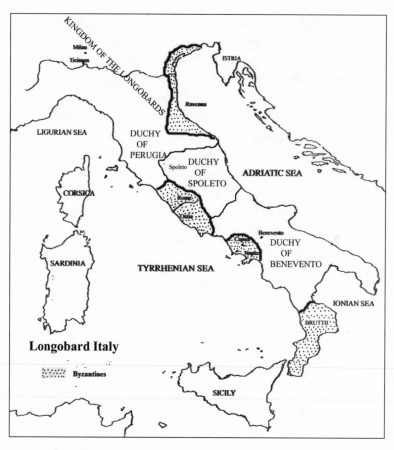

Figure 3.2 Longobard Italy

second year; the third, Autari, was poisoned in his sixth year of reign.[28] And then the kingdom split into more than thirty separate duchies,[29] with almost eleven years of internal disorder and civil war; no king was elected even though the drive toward expansion remained constant. It was during the interregnum that the Longobards actually extended their dominion in parts of southern Italy.[30]

There is no better example of their wild, violent lifestyle than the end of the king who led them to Italy. Alboin loved drinking wine from a goblet made from the skull of a king he had killed in the lands of Pannonia. (The king was Cunimund, leader of the Gepids.) One day during a drunken feast he forced his own wife, Rosamund, to drink from that skull. She drank, but with hatred in her heart, for she was the daughter of the slain man. From then on, revenge stormed her heart. First to come to her side was a man, probably the instigator of the plot, named Helmichis. He sought Alboin's throne and had been nourished by the same woman from whose breast Alboin had sucked his milk; then a valiant warrior, Peredeo, probably a Gepid like the queen, joined the plot. Peredeo had refused at the beginning to be part of the conspiracy, but he had fallen under Rosamund's control after making love to her during a night in which unknown to him, she had taken the place of Peredeo's lover in his bed. The queen had revealed her identity after intercourse. "My husband will destroy you when he knows of the adultery. You have no choice but to kill him first." Soon after, while Alboin took his usual nap, Rosamund had taken all the weapons away from the bedroom. She left only a sword, which she tied to the bed, making it impossible to use. It was then that Peredeo came in. Alboin woke up in time. Desperately he defended himself with a chair, but in the end he succumbed to the blows of the assassin. He had reigned three and a half years in Italy.[31] It was a pattern of violence that continued throughout the two centuries of rule in northern Italy and for two centuries more in the Longobard Duchy of Benevento. Murder was commonplace. Often adversaries had their eyes removed or their lifeless bodies defiled. Nothing similar had been witnessed in past centuries on Italian lands; probably not even the Huns had been that cruel.

When they first arrived in Italy, the Longobards kept behaving like people who only momentarily would remain there. *Razzia*—taking from the local population of anything they could lay their hands on—was their method of warfare. The second stage was harsher, including rape, spoliation, and wanton destruction of any element, human or physical, that could help the local population recover. It was only in the third stage that they adopted a more rational form of conquest. They became settled landowners, excluding the Italian population from political and social power, forcing small landowners to provide a third of their harvests to the ruling class, and forcing peasants to remain tied to the land as another form of chattel.[32] The third phase of occupation must also have implied a strong sense of individual property and probably in the long run the weakening of the collective ties of the *fara*, the original nucleus that typified the army.[33] Yet the Longobards never completely abandoned their policies of spoliation and destruction. In 873 the Longobard duke of Salerno raided the territories on Italy's tip. When he withdrew, the lands had no human beings left. It seemed like the aftermath of a deluge.[34] The words come from a Benevento chronicle of the ninth century. In 843–844 the duke of Salerno forced the Montecassino abbey to "loan" their treasures (gold, silver) to finance his confrontation with the duke of Benevento.[35] As late as 888, the duke of Benevento filled the water wells of a neighboring valley with stones to slow down the recovery of the territories that his men had pillaged.[36]

Now that the original Italian upper classes had been either destroyed or rendered powerless like the Catholic clergy, the invaders organized a state in which the local populations were "servants" of a warrior class, their "masters" being Longobards or those who had come with them from Pannonia. Probably for the Italian lower classes this did not mean a radical change from the past. The only different thing was that the masters looked physically different.[37] When the upper clergy began to regain social primacy, they too were different from the past. Mostly of Longobardic origin, eventually accepting Catholic orthodoxy, they were tied in kinship and ideology with a worldview based on war.[38]

The Longobards, like all Germanic peoples during the early medieval period, were a nation in a constant state of war. The kings were ultimate warriors, elected initially by all the warriors in a general assembly; later only the dukes (the military commanders of well-defined territories, mostly Longobards, or part of the original group of invaders[39]) participated in the ceremony. The dukes eventually agreed to give the king half of their income,[40] likely for the organization of warfare either in attack or defense. As in most barbarian kingdoms the king's main duty was as war manager: his prestige and power were based not only on his ancestry but also on his ability to lead men to victory on the battlefield.[41] Armed conflict was the only occupation worthy of a man. The term *exercitus* (army) was synonymous with *people*; adulthood was reached at age twelve, when the adolescent was able to handle his sword.[42] The exclusive right of the Longobards to bear arms implied political supremacy and internal surveillance over the Italian population, reduced to servile status, and even over freemen and small landowners.[43]

In the territories that remained under the Byzantines (mainly Ravenna and Rome), military service was based on landownership; that is, military service was a personal duty of the man of a certain substance, a duty that the landowner could not devolve to another individual, as was the case during the later stages of the Roman Empire.[44] In appearance this was the same arrangement that the Longobards adopted: land ownership equaled military service. In reality, it was different at first. The Byzantines recruited Italian-born for the army, whereas the Longobards did not.[45] The first changes came under Liutprand (713–744), who gave political and legal rights even to people who were neither potentially nor in fact warriors.[46] And a few years later during the reign of King Astulf (749–756) there were changes suggesting the inclusion of Italians into the Longobard host. In his edict of 750, Astulf divided the Longobard population into four groups of declining territorial property. When called to arms the highest three groups had to come with weapons, armor, and horses of declining sophistication. The fourth had to be armed with bow and arrows.[47] This arrangement, based on landed property, must have eliminated most Italians after the spoliation of their possessions during the initial decades of invasion. Yet Astulf, aware of the social changes among his subjects, integrated militarily city people whose personal wealth was not necessarily based on land. This must have implied the inclusion of Italians, although, one suspects, not in the upper ranks of the army. The new Italian recruits were organized into three groups in a way parallel to the Longobards. The lowest group in this case also had light armament: bows and arrows.[48] The equipment required from the higher groups included horses, a long spear with the inevitable long sword (*spatha*) typical of all Germans, a shorter saber (*scramasax*), a round shield, eventually helmets, and, by the end of the seventh century, lamellar armor.[49]

The Italian historians of the nineteenth century wasted time and talent claiming that the Longobards were too few to make any difference in the social, political, and racial makeup of the Italian population; in other words, the Italian bloodlines had remained pure.[50] Besides the fact that such claims for most of Europe, with the possible exception of certain parts of Scandinavia, are generally nonsensical, it seems reasonable to assume that the inclusion of 100,000 newcomers must have diluted the original ethnic mix only minimally. But the reality from the political viewpoint is different. It is true that culturally the impact of Rome triumphed. The invaders lost their language and in the end adopted Latin as their own. Yet in political and social terms this was not the case.[51] The Longobard invasion represented a crucial break in the history of the peninsula.[52] The newcomers were ferocious defenders of their ethnic primacy and constituted the basis of the aristocracy for future generations, at least for a few centuries.[53] Even during the Renaissance, nearly 800 years later, it was not unusual for some of the leading Italian families to claim distant origins to Germanic ancestors.

Unlike what happened in the French territory, where the Gallo-Roman upper levels were integrated in the upper strata of the Visigoths, Burgundians, and later Franks,[54] the old Roman-Italian ruling class in most of Italy was disenfranchised in a process that combined extermination with an ideology that emphasized the superiority and separateness of these foreign warriors, who were bound together by a network of family ties, the memory of old myths, and a nebulous history of common origin.

By the time the Longobards started to include the Italian population in their army, the world around them was changing radically. The Byzantine foothold on the Italian peninsula was becoming increasingly more tenuous, and the Longobards' own domination in most of central and northern Italy had encountered an old enemy: the heirs of the Franks who had invaded Gaul and, after almost three centuries, finally moved in large forces to Italy to displace the Longobards. In 774 the Longobard domination of most of Italy came to an end before the army of Charlemagne. Only the Duchy of Benevento continued to remain autonomous until the turn of the first millennium. The fall of the Longobard kingdom was not a surprise because probably their reign was the weakest of those produced by other Germanic peoples like Visigoths, Franks, and Burgundians.[55]

Chapter Four

The Franks and the Emergence of France

OVER ABOUT TWO CENTURIES, the Franks had already become accustomed to the landscape when they finally moved to what is modern France in larger and permanent numbers during the fifth century. They would establish the most successful of all barbarian kingdoms, France, that in succeeding centuries would become one of the playmakers in Western civilization. The key was that the Franks, unlike the Ostrogoths and the Longobards in Italy or the Visigoths in Spain, assimilated easily into the existing Gallo-Roman aristocracy and became champions of the religion that would become the trademark of the Middle Ages: Christianity as interpreted by Rome.

Tacitus, the great Roman historian who wrote a successful tract on the German tribes, does not mention the Franks. They appear for the first time in the middle of the third century as predators of the Roman Empire in Gaul (roughly modern France), but eventually at least some of them became soldiers in Rome's pay. Where the Franks came from and what their name means has been a matter of scholarly debate. In Late Antiquity the name was synonymous with "brave" or "fierce," not with "free," as interpreted later by the French aristocracy. Gregory of Tours, a Gallo-Roman aristocrat who wrote a history in the sixth century, saw the Franks as originating in Pannonia (roughly modern Hungary), but there is no other evidence confirming it. It is likely that their place of origin, except for some groups among them, was the lower right bank of the Rhine River from midway in its course to the sea and westward as far as the Elbe and the Main.[1] Actually their varied and sometimes contrasting attacks against the Roman Empire during the earlier stages indicate that they were not a cohesive unit originally and that instead of a single ethnic group they were a confederacy of different Germanic and sometimes non-Germanic tribes that eventually found a common identity.[2] These are the origins of the Franks.

By the middle of the fifth century, Gaul and the territories immediately east of the Rhine were parceled among a mix of ethnic groups, with Germanic people being the dominant population (Figure 4.1). One region, roughly corresponding to the modern northern French region of Brittany, remained out of the contest for supremacy. Brittany included several ethnic groups, among which Gallo-Romans, Alans, and Celts prevailed. Next to them was the Kingdom of Syagrius, symbolizing the last stronghold of the vanishing Roman Empire and host to an ethnic mix of former imperial soldiers, and groups of Alans, and likely also Franks. Syagrius's reign, which extended from the Loire to the Somme, would be absorbed by the Franks by the beginning of the sixth century. The Franks, sometimes on friendly terms but more often hostile to the ancient amalgam of Gallic and Roman populations, occupied around the mid–fifth century the northern land, roughly north of the Loire River, and eastward well across the Rhine. On the south there were two other Germanic peoples, the Visigoths and the Burgundians. The former controlled the area with the Atlantic on the left, the Pyrenees on the southwest, and the Mediterranean on the south. Burgundian neighbors to their east touched the border of the Franks on the north, their dominion stretching across the Rhine in the east. The Burgundians were neighbors of the last of the four major Germanic people, the Alamanni, settled around the right bank of the Rhine, and inhabited the area up to the Frankish border. In the northern lands, now part of Holland, Belgium, and northern Germany, were the Saxons. However, all the Germanic groups were never larger demographically than the Gallo-Roman population.

Contact with people who were ruled by a strong tradition of kingship like the Huns probably stimulated the emergence of a strong centralized power among the Franks. Kingship may have acted as a rallying focus not only for the Franks but also for the smaller German units displaced by the violent invasions. The final product was the subjugation of all the other ethnic groups—Gallo-Romans, Germanic, and others—a feat in which the Frankish King Clovis (481–511), a strong, powerful, and clever man, played the central role. By 561 the longhaired kings, as contemporaries called the Merovingian Dynasty (Clovis and his descendants), had extended their rule from the Pyrenees to the Rhine.[3] In 534 they conquered the Kingdom of Burgundy; in 536 they reached the Mediterranean, displacing the Visigoths from southern France.

Figure 4.1   The Kingdoms of the Merovingian Franks in 561

Fusion with the Gallo-Romans

Clovis was the son of Childeric I, a shady man who at one time had been forced from his throne for his intimacy with the daughters of the kingdom's magnates (so says Gregory of Tours). He became a symbol of all the ethnic groups living in Gallia. For the Christians he was the new Constantine, as his conversion to orthodox Christianity had vanquished the threat of the heretic Arians; for the Gallic population he was the logical heir of their Gallo-Roman masters; for the Franks he was the embodiment of the strength, fierceness, and primacy of their traditions[4]; and for the various Germanic ethnic groups who had assimilated into the Frankish identity, one would assume, he became a symbol of unity. Accommodation with the Gallo-Roman population was a pattern already found among the Visigoths who had conquered the lands of southern France. Although the Visigoths tried to keep a separate identity in the long run, they also accepted Roman culture and actually encouraged its preservation.[5] The Franks moved farther along in the process of assimilation.

It was easier to do so because they accepted orthodox Christianity like the Gallo-Romans (the Visigoths remained Arians), and because of intermarriages among higher-level Franks and local aristocracies.[6] This was a process that had appeared in Gaul at the beginning of the barbarian waves settling lands once controlled by Rome. Faced by the appearance of new masters, the old ruling class had a few options. Some could leave, but to where? Those who left soon faced the same problems they had escaped, and those who remained to oppose the barbarians' way of life faced continuous danger and probably daily humil-iation. The best option was to come to terms. This did not imply the aban-doning of social leadership but rather the switching of primacy from the mili-tary sphere to a monopoly over the highest ecclesiastical position—the office of bishop.[7] The Roman Church became the special reserve of the Gallo-Roman senators even when they had to share it with the other ethnic groups by the sixth century. Those positions were few, but the Gallo-Roman aristocracy found another method to preserve its leadership. It became the high priest of classical culture, the heir to Rome both culturally and ideologically. The policy worked well, and by the eighth century ethnic distinctions between the new and the old elites had disappeared.[8] It was a solution benefiting both sides, and in the long run it would make the Frankish dominion the strongest and most enduring of all barbarian states. It preserved the image of the past while blend-ing with it the heritage of those who had forcefully occupied these lands.

As Frankish Gaul came to terms with the remnants of the Roman heritage both socially and ideologically, it was also mandatory to ideologically refash-ion its past. Their myths claimed that the Franks were not barbarians, after all, but shared common roots with Romans. Their ancestor, as for the Romans, was a Trojan named Frigas, a brother of Aeneas. Frigas had left Troy for the Danube, and from there a group of Franks under the leadership of Francio had moved on to the Rhine. This legend combined brotherhood with the Romans (after all, their founder Frigas was Aeneas's brother), religious ele-ments (the Trojans were descended from Noah), and memory of the later con-tact with people like the Huns (who may have influenced the rise and strengthening of the Frankish concept of kingship).[9] It was thus despite the fact that the legend had no historical foundation, except for evoking the migration of some ethnic groups among the Franks and as testimonial of their accommodation with the Gallo-Romans dominating the region in the past. Certainly by the fifth century this agglomeration of Germanic peoples embodied not only Germanic roots but also an acquaintance with Roman civ-ilization. Childeric I's tomb, discovered in 1653 and the richest burial site of the early Middle Ages, is not entirely barbarian nor entirely Roman.[10] Rome and the Germanic populations had met and given each other new strength.

The Franks at War

Kingship was certainly one of the factors that made the kingdom of the Franks powerful. The ruler's control of the wealth of the land was central to his supremacy.[11] He received not only the income of his large personal estate but also the fruits of plunder and taxation of defeated enemies. This income became even larger through confiscation of subjects' property if, for one reason or another, they challenged the king's supremacy. Tribute from defeated neighbors could be another source of income. The Saxons, for instance, were forced to pay an annual tribute of 500 cows after their defeat in 556.[12] A similar request was placed upon the Goths, who first decided to pay with a gold dish weighing 500 pounds, then redeemed it for a substantial amount of money.[13] Even diplomacy could reap considerable benefits, as when they exacted compensation from the Byzantine emperor who tried to use the Franks to displace the Longobards from Italy.[14] But in a manner suggesting the feudal arrangement of the future, the Merovingian rulers could not hoard all the wealth coming into their coffers. Generosity—that is, distributing gold or land—was essential to maintain the loyalty of followers, from the great magnates to the so-called *leudes*, military supporters lower socially than the aristocracy.[15]

As among the Longobards, being a Frank meant being a warrior. War, bravery in battle, and success on the battlefield were essential elements of kingship. There was no Merovingian ruler who could avoid the baptism of fire. Reading the most important chroniclers of the time, Fredegar and the pious Gregory of Tours, one cannot escape the sensation that the supremacy of the ruler was based upon how many opponents he had slain in face-to-face combat.

The national weapon of the Franks was, at least until the end of the sixth century, the *francisca,* a battle axe that could be used either as a hand weapon or as a projectile. A recent study on the weapons found in Frankish and Alaman graves in southern Germany shows that in the period 440–530 the axe is found in 53 percent of the Frankish burials and only 20 percent of Alaman burials. The second most popular weapon among the Franks was the spear, found in 31 percent of the locations.[16] "You keep neither your spear nor sword nor axe in serviceable order," Clovis reproached a man during a convening of the Frankish army at the Field of Mars. Then he grabbed the man's axe, throwing it in disgust to the ground. When the man bent to pick it up, the king drew his own axe and struck the man dead. It was repayment for a previous insult.

At a loot distribution in the city of Soissons, Clovis had wished to retain a sacred vase that he desired to return to the bishop of a church that the Franks had looted. But one of the king's chieftains, the man he later killed, had angrily struck the vase with his own axe, screaming, "You shall get nothing here except what the lot fairly bestows you."[17] When a man killed his father out of greed and then went to pay homage to Clovis, showing the treasure chest he had taken from the victim, he ended up dead, hit by an axe when he kneeled to uncover his loot of gold coins to the king.[18] And Clovis himself again used the battle axe to dispose of a person whose cowardly behavior had caused humiliation to the king's family.[19] Of course the *francisca* was used in a battle array. According to a Greek writer (whose accuracy on this account has been impugned), Franks threw the *francisca* during their first charge with such strength that they killed their adversaries or shattered their shields.[20]

Although the *francisca* was the weapon that differentiated the Franks from other Germanic groups, the most-used weapon on the battlefield must have been the spear. The Franks seemed to have used an array of spearheads, but generally at least three categories can be distinguished. A short iron head of various shape but usually flat and very sharp characterized their most common weapon. The next two types were javelins more than spears. Both had barbed heads and both must have been used mainly for throwing. One had a wooden shaft with a normal-size head; the other, the *angon*, had a very long iron head (80–125 centimeters), with a shaft smaller than normal. The *angon* measured about 2.15 meters on average.[21] The shaft was similar to the Roman *pilum*. According to Agathias (ca. 532–580), a native of Asia Minor, the *angons* were used for both thrusting and throwing. If it hit an enemy body, it would cause terrible damage when withdrawn; if it was embedded in his shield, the barbs would prevent it from being drawn out and discarded. The Franks moved to step their foot on the dragging *angon*, pulling the enemy to the ground, where his head and chest would be exposed for the final blow.[22]

The soldiers of the Merovingian Dynasty used at least three sword types: one, rather rare, was long, about 75–90 centimeters, with a thin blade and its gravity center located toward the point. It was heavy and probably the weapon of horsemen. Its rarity suggests that it was the weapon of the upper levels of society. Another sword type was much shorter, about 40 centimeters, and a third type, usually called a *scramasax* or *sax*, could be as long as 85 centimeters with, like the scimitar, only one cutting edge and a blade 6–8 centimeters wide and 1–1.2 centimeters thick. There were also smaller versions of this sword about 20 centimeters long. But not all warriors were armed in this manner. The more modest burials of sixth- and seventh-century Franks usually contain only a bow and arrows, the arrow points between 6 and 8 centimeters.[23]

The Franks' defensive armor always included a shield and may have included some kind of body armor and a helmet. The shield had a particular symbolical meaning for the Frankish warrior. It defined entry into adulthood, when he was given one, and to lose or discard it afterward would have been a dishonorable action. The warriors would strike their shields to express approval in assemblies or trial verdicts. Shields were also used during the proclamation of a new king. The Frankish shield was either circular or elliptical, between 0.8 and 1.2 centimeters thick. Covered with leather, it displayed a boss in the center, concave around 500, convex later. Finally, body armor was rare and normally made of link chain. There were large variations in the warriors' armor and weapons. For instance, a burial place at Mezières in the Ardennes had three tombs of warriors with a complete panoply, and fourteen more had only a few swords, *franciscae*, *scramasaxes*, and spears but no shields.[24]

The Merovingian army was probably the most sophisticated of all Germanic peoples. To a certain extent this was the result of the Franks' long connection to the Roman Empire. This was evident especially in siege warfare, which they patterned on technology inherited from the Romans.[25] The fortifications of Dijon as described in Gregory of Tours and the siege of Covenae are good examples, where besiegers and besieged used methods normally beyond the expertise of most other barbarian groups.[26] The efficacy of the Frankish army was also tied to their quick integration into the ruling class and local populations they had invaded. Finally, the powerful influence of Catholicism over the heretical Arianism strengthened them psychologically and materially; the bishop could play an important role in military affairs.

The Merovingian army was composed mainly of foot, although their leaders and some groups, probably the guard units of the different chieftains, must also have been on horseback. It could easily engage in a military campaign, as it was something of a permanent army. The king and the magnates, of Frankish and Roman backgrounds, had armed followers, called *trustis*, *antrustiones*, *pueri* in the sources, probably some kind of guard units, together with the *leudes*, military followers at a lower level than the guard units.[27] What happened in the long run would spell disaster for the Merovingian kings, for the magnates, able to master personal armies, became increasingly powerful.[28] Finally, the Merovingian kings could theoretically call to arms any free citizen if needed and sometimes even slaves, the latter likely in humble roles.[29]

War remained an endemic part of Frankish life but at a much more sophisticated level than with the Longobards. Loot was distributed among the chieftains, who in turn, one suspects, would have shared it with followers. Moreover, they kept close vigilance on the status of soldiers' preparedness, for the military forces of the kingdom were periodically called together for inspections of weapons and readiness. Finally, even logistics were well-organized, as the siege of Covenae shows, where both attackers and defenders seem not to have suffered from any supply problems.[30]

A superficial observer may feel that after Clovis's disappearance in 511 the Merovingian Dynasty began a spiral of decline marked by degeneracy and astonishing cruelty. In reality there were many conquests after Clovis, and the Merovingians achieved almost complete control of Gaul and surrounding territories about fifty years after their king's disappearance. Moreover, the violence of Clovis's successors must be placed in the context of an age where cruel and ruthless acts were the rule.

The Merovingians Against the Byzantines

We can see how the Merovingian Franks fought by looking at their 554 invasion of Italy at the end of the Gothic wars. Desperate after their defeat at Mons Lactarius, the Goths sent an emissary to the Franks. "Help us," they begged, "for once the Romans have destroyed us, they will march against you." But the new Merovingian king, Theudobald, still a boy, dismissed their plea. Yet two brothers named Leutharis and Butilinus, Alamans by birth, were given permission to bring relief to the Goths. They invaded Italy with a large army of Franks and Alamans, but certainly not the 75,000 reported by Agathias.[31]

Franks had appeared previously in Italy, causing problems for both Goths and Byzantines. Now they had come to pillage what was left after eighteen years of war. The invaders had no fear of the "puny little man" left in charge of the Roman troops in Italy. He was an individual of "diminutive stature and abnormal thinness" and a eunuch "without the testicles and penis of a real man, especially a soldier." He was used to the softness of the bedchamber. He had "nothing masculine about him."[32] A few months later the Franks and Alamanni paid in blood, for Narses was also a shrewd individual and leader of men, capable of facing any eventuality, a rhetorical master, a wolf on the battlefield.[33] Even Procopius, no friend of his, had to recognize Narses's charismatic personality. When Justinian appointed him to lead the last stages of the Gothic wars in Italy, commanders and soldiers flocked to his army, for Narses was a man famous as well for generosity.[34]

Narses was aware of the new threat, but for the moment he was busy crushing the Ostrogothic resistance, so he entrusted the conduct of the operations against the invaders to other men. His plan at this stage was to deploy men in a continuous line around Parma to bar the Franks' march to Tuscany, where Narses stood. His generals, afraid of the enemy's large number, instead withdrew to Faenza. Scolded by Narses, they finally moved again to Parma's neighborhood, but by then it was too late for the general's plan to be effective.

The Byzantine problem in Tuscany was finally solved after three months of siege. By then it was late autumn, and winter was near. It would be foolish to fight then, Narses decided, for the Franks were accustomed to battle in cold weather. Better to wait for spring. The Byzantine general ordered his troops to winter quarters and instructed his generals to assemble in Rome at the beginning of spring.[35]

As spring came, Narses's men began converging on Rome. Meanwhile the armies of Butilinus and Leutharis bypassed Rome and struck south. Butilinus took to the right along the Tyrrhenian Sea until he reached the tip of the boot; Leutharis marched along the Adriatic Sea until he reached Otranto, the tip of the heel. Their march carved a path of destruction. The Franks (who were Catholics) spared the churches, but the Alamans (who were Arians) spared nothing. They pillaged churches and monasteries, destroying even the roofs of the holy places and leaving bodies to rot in the chapels or in fields. But when the heat of summer arrived and the plague started decimating their rosters, Leutharis's army decided to withdraw northward. He promised his brother Butilinus that he would place prisoners and spoils in a safe location in the north and then return south to make the inevitable confrontation with the imperial troops of the East in central Italy.

Leutharis's progress toward northern Italy had many problems. Ravaged by the plague, his army started to vanish. He also lost 3,000 men north of Fanum, near the Adriatic coast, many falling from a cliff into the sea, many others drowning as they crossed the Po River. The rest, with most of their loot gone (the Byzantines had sacked their camp during the encounter near Fanum), were cut down by the plague in the flatlands of northern Italy. Ravaged by high fever, some died of violent seizures, others fell into coma, some succumbed to delirium. But the worst death was that of their leader. Leutharis fell to malarial fever marked by chills and pain. He must have lost his mind, for he began biting his own arms and eating the flesh stripped from his body. He gradually wasted away and died.[36] Meanwhile Butilinus, unaware of his brother's end, prepared for the inevitable attack of Narses's forces. He camped at Casilinum, in the area near Capua, and waited for the arrival of his enemies while the plague visited his camp. Narses had not been inactive but rigorously trained his troops for combat, marching them on the double, refamiliarizing them with trumpet signals, and urging the cavalry to perform elaborate maneuvers of all types. Finally, when Butilinus camped near Capua, he left Rome to destroy his enemy.[37]

After an initial encounter that favored the Byzantines, the day of battle finally arrived. Butilinus, angry at the outcome of the earlier confrontation, deployed his host for battle.[38] Narses had problems from the start: an important component of his battle line, the normally faithful and ferocious Heruli, were missing. They had refused to fight because one of their leading men had been executed for having killed a slave in violation of Narses's express prohibition. At the last moment, however, the Heruli changed their minds. Yes, they would join, but not right away. Meanwhile Narses had deployed his men. As at Taginae, the weakest component was at the center, where the footmen stood. Probably afraid that his central line (without the Heruli for the moment) could have been pierced, he placed light troops, archers, and slingers in reserve behind the center. The cavalry on the right wing was led by Narses himself, supported by the men of his household. On the left was the rest of the cavalry, half-concealed and half-protected by woods.

Agathias describes how the Byzantine line was protected with armor, especially in the front ranks of the 18,000-strong army. In contrast, the 30,000 enemy soldiers were poorly protected, their chests bare, leather or linen pants enclosing their legs, some without helmets. They used no bows, only spears, especially the barbed *angones*, and throwing axes.[39]

When deserters from the Herulian contingent informed Butilinus that their compatriots had refused to join Narses (that was only partly true, for the Heruli would come to the battlefield eventually), the leader of the Franks and Alamans moved quickly to the attack. To the deafening sound of shouts and the beating of shields and weapons they marched on, brave but undisciplined: their advance was, says Agathias, not a deliberate and ordered progress but a wild and impetuous rush. Apparently devoid of cavalry, they had formed into a wedge shape that was full up front but empty in the center as the line extended toward the back.

Their clash against the infantry fractured the Byzantine line, weakened by the absence of the Heruli, but as Butilinus's men moved through the ranks their piercing action must have slowed down because of opposition from the rest of the Byzantines. The solution to the enemy's shattering blow came from the cavalry at the wings: the horsemen turned until their front was parallel to the wedge, then targeted the enemy with a deadly fire that was especially effective if the arrows hit the enemies' backs, where they had little or no protection. The Byzantine arrows were not aimed at the men closest to them but at the interior of the wedge, probably to weaken the force against the center line. Meanwhile the edge of the enemy line that had forced through Narses's infantry met the Heruli, who finally had decided to join the fray, and the slingers and bowmen that Narses had deployed as support of the first line. Butilinus's men were an easy target, especially when they thought that they had fallen into an ambush. Mostly fell on the battlefield. Only five, says Agathias (obviously an exaggeration) escaped. Narses's casualties were very light, only eighty.[40]

Events at Casilinum should be approached with great caution in assessing how the Merovingians fought. In many ways the invading army was unusual. The lack of cavalry at Casilinum suggests that this army was unusual or, more likely, that attrition took its toll during the long expedition. A better example was the encounter near the walls of Rimini, which took place before the two Frankish armies struck into southern Italy.[41] The fight involved some 2,000 Frankish forces of horse and foot against 300 horsemen of the great general Narses.

Narses had taken refuge behind the walls of Rimini to avoid the main Frankish army. However, a small enemy contingent had been left behind to forage and plunder the countryside. This was done in full view of Narses, who could observe them from atop Rimini's walls. Upset by the Franks' gall, Narses decided to punish them. Riding at the head of his personal guard, about 300 horsemen, he ordered the gate opened. The Franks were easy targets, split into small groups. Those who escaped withdrew to a location near a forest where their rear and flanks were protected. Once there they deployed, the footmen in a compact formation in the center—"a solid mass of shields," says Agathias[42]—with the cavalry at the wings.

Three hundred horsemen were not enough to charge the enemy, and in any case a charge would have been untypical of the way a Byzantine army operated. Narses used bowmen to thin the enemy ranks. But when Byzantine bows and Frankish javelins brought no resolution to the battle, Narses resolved to a stratagem of feigned withdrawal. After a frenetic exchange of blows he ordered his men to simulate a panic retreat. Believing that the enemy had been routed, the Franks abandoned their secure position and pursued, splitting into smaller groups. It was then that Narses ordered his troops, obviously by a trumpet signal, to turn around and to concentrate methodically on eliminating the small groups. The only Franks who survived were the horsemen, who were able to withdraw in safety. The Frankish footmen (more than 900) were "slaughtered like a herd of swine or cattle."[43]

Although in this encounter the Franks met a deadly end, it seems more in tune with the way they must have deployed for battle. Their formation was a mixed force of foot and horse; their deployment—close rank infantry in the center and cavalry on the wings—was the classical choice of most armies; their weapons were spears or javelins but not bows. The awkward armies of the Merovingians were radically changed once the Carolingians took power in Gaul.

The Warrior with the Long Hair

The Merovingian Dynasty, which had ruled France from 481 to 747, faded. Childeric III, the last Merovingian king, was shut inside a monastery, his flowing hair, the symbol of royalty, shorn. But his power had ended long before. Without the wealth of his ancestors he had become king only in name. His estate was hardly large enough to support him and his servants. When the time came for the yearly meetings, where assembled Franks decided on past and future affairs of the kingdom, he arrived like a peasant in a cart yoked to oxen. The only symbols of his royalty were his long hair and flowing beard. Well before his accession to the throne, power had passed into the hands of the Mayors of the Palace.[44] At the time of Childerich's deposition in 751, Peppin the Short was mayor, an office that his grandfather and father had held. And to him, on the authority of the Bishop of Rome, was granted the title of king. It was the beginning of the Carolingian Dynasty (747–888), which eventually disintegrated in discord and disunion as well. But for a time its greatest representative, Charlemagne, would rule most of the western Roman Empire and would be crowned emperor in the year 800.

Charlemagne (742–814) was a man with a strong body and impressive features. His unusually large eyes, piercing and investigative, and large nose were the most impressive elements of his round face. His neck was too short for such a massive body, and as the years passed his stomach became heavier than normal. He was tall and muscular and loved hunting, riding horseback, and swimming so much that during his last years he remained in his palace at Aachen, where he could swim in a warm-water pool. He was sober and sparing in both food and drink. He hated drunkenness in any man. An aura surrounded his person, and authority seemed second nature to him. The only element out of tune was his voice, too thin for a man so large and physically strong. In general he liked to speak so much that he was too close to being garrulous. Although awed by the Latin intellectual achievements of the past and intensely religious, he never learned to write Latin, although he seemed to have mastered it orally. He remained very proud of his Frankish ancestry, and except in two cases, while in Rome at the request of popes, he dressed in the humble national attire of the Franks. When ready to sleep, he dropped every item of clothing from his person and slept naked. He was a strong man, attached too much to his daughters (he kept them close, not allowing them to marry before his death), and was unusually prone to tears.[45]

He died at Aachen, where he fell victim to high fever in January. As usual, he tried to weaken the onset of the illness by fasting, taking only liquid at rare intervals. But then pleurisy attacked his system. On the seventh day after taking to bed he received communion, and not much later he died at seventy-two. He had been on the throne for forty-seven years, all of them marked by war.[46] His journey upon earth had been an uninterrupted series of military campaigns building on the achievements of Charles Martel and those of his great father, Peppin the Short. Each year one or more campaigns were marshaled against the enemies at the border of his ever-expanding dominion; they were repeated if they had not achieved their initial goals. Pitched battles were rare and sieges commonplace. Although he masterminded the campaigns' timing and goals, Charlemagne led his army only in 4 pitched battles: at Lubeck in 775, nearby Bocholt, Westphalia, in 779, and at Detmold and at the River Hase in 783.[47]

One year after his ascension in 768 (he would have to share the throne initially until 771 with his brother Carloman) Charlemagne strengthened the basis of Frankish control over Aquitaine in the southwest, a business begun skillfully by his father. In 773–774 he engaged in one of the easiest campaigns, displacing the Longobards from most of Italy and reducing their remaining centers of power in the Duchy of Spoleto and in the Duchy of Benevento. He also established the pope as the ruler of a new state that extended from Rome northward. The Byzantines were left in possession of a few coastal cities (Ravenna and Venice). In 777 he moved into Muslim Spain, the first of the campaigns across the Pyrenees. This time it ended in tragedy when the rearguard of the Frankish army was ambushed at Roncesvalles in 778 and destroyed to the last man by the Basques, led by the sons of a Muslim governor. The "lightness of their arms" and the "nature of the terrain" (mountainous and uneven) won over "the heavy equipment and armor of the Franks."

Among the casualties was Roland, Lord of the Breton March and the subject of *Song of Roland*, a masterpiece of French literature.[48] His death left an indelible imprint on the collective memory of the French people.[49] The Franks again marched south of the Pyrenees: in 785 they conquered Gerona, in 803 Barcelona, and in 808 Tarragona, besides major expeditions in 806 and 813. But their hold on Spain remained tenuous at best.

In 786 and again in 799 and 811 Charlemagne's soldiers marched into the northwest—Brittany—to control a region never happy with Frankish rule. Between 763 and 787 the time arrived to bring the Bavarians under the supremacy of the Franks. Between 791 and 803 another problem demanded Charlemagne's attention: the eastern frontier, where the Avars, a tribe originally from Asia, were dominant. In the end the Avars were destroyed, and their wealth—the fruits of endless past campaigns—fell into Carolingian hands. The Franks went from a poor people to one in possession of gold, silver, and other riches.[50] But the greatest struggle during Charlemagne's reign was against the Saxons, who occupied the area bordering the northern sea between the River Ems on the west and the Elbe and Saal on the east.[51] No war waged by Charlemagne lasted longer, and none was "more full of atrocities or more demanding of effort." Both sides, Franks and Saxons, engaged in murder, robbery, and arson.[52] It ended only when Charlemagne, as an extreme remedy, deported 10,000 Saxons and resettled them into small groups in Gallic and Germanic lands, thereby compelling them to abandon their pagan gods in favor of Christianity.[53]

By the end of Charlemagne's life the new empire included the whole of ancient Gallia, most of what is now modern Germany up to the Elbe River in the east, to the North Sea in the north, and then across the Danube into the northern section of the Balkans; all of northern and most of central Italy; with the rest of the peninsula granted either to the popes or subservient to the Franks (e.g., the Longobard Duchy of Benevento in southern Italy). Surrounding the empire's border they established safeguards, territorial units called marches, in Spain, Pannonia, eastern Italy, and modern Austria (Figure 4.2).

The continuous successes under Charlemagne were the result of the policy that his great-grandfather, Peppin de Herstal, and his grandfather, Charles Martel, first formulated and that his father, Peppin the Short, had applied with consistency and daring. By the time Charlemagne ascended to the throne, the Franks possessed the largest and most sophisticated army in western Europe. It could be raised in any season, good weather or bad, could march hundreds, even thousands of kilometers in any direction without sup-

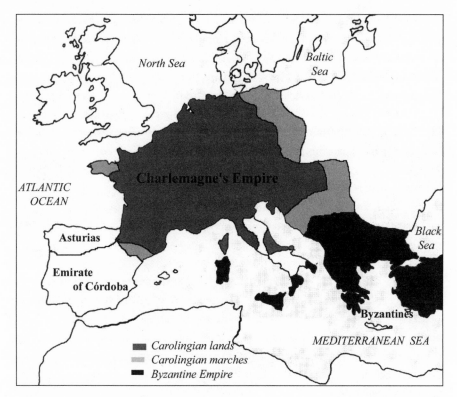

Figure 4.2   Carolingian Empire in 814

ply problems, and was available year after year.[54] The truth is that the Carolingian Dynasty could recruit more men than anybody else in Europe, and
it could deploy soldiers to several tasks, whether sieges or battles. Its soldiers
became veterans quickly, for Franks at this time were reared amid ongoing
conflict. In only five years between 714 and 768 (740, two more before 751,
759, and 764) did peace prevail during the reigns of Charlemagne's grandfather and father. The long reign of Charlemagne (768–814) saw peace only
twice, 790 and 807, when Franks did not march across their borders to subject an enemy.[55]

The Carolingian rulers could use many recruiting sources. In a moment of
great necessity they could call the general levy of all freemen to protect the
kingdom under menace; the select levy that provided the rank and file for
aggressive campaigns; the household troops of magnates and ruler (the professional element of the host); and auxiliaries from outside the kingdom.[56]
Unlike in Longobard Italy, technically all able-bodied freemen age twelve and

above, of any ethnic background, had the duty to serve in the army when the Frankish kingdom was under threat. Persons refusing to serve were fined heavily (sixty *sous*, the *sou* being one-twentieth of a pound of silver), the equivalent of twenty mares or thirty cows, a fortune for a man of limited means. If unable to pay, the culprit became a slave of the sovereign. Deserters were punished with death and confiscation of their property.[57] In other words, the Franks, like most barbarian societies, were a people under arms, and military obligations were paramount. What differentiated them from other barbarians was the obligation of all to serve, whether or not they were ethnically Frankish. In reality, however, the general levy contained many restrictions and was rarely called, and then only in areas where the threat was greatest. More normal was the recruitment based on property ownership, with duties commensurate to one's wealth. The process had begun long before Charlemagne, but it was under him that the system reached its peak.

Thus Charlemagne's army was based on public and private obligations. Some were public in the sense that all individuals of authority—counts, bishops, abbots, abbesses—had a duty to support the sovereign's military campaign in person and with a suitable retinue (in case of laymen) or with a set number of well-equipped soldiers (in the case of ecclesiastics). The obligations were private in the sense that they included vassals—individuals to whom land had been granted by the ruler or by any of the magnates in exchange for military service. This was the system upon which feudalism would later be built. The devolution of land to potential soldiers went back to the Romans, but it was with Pepin II and Charles Martel that the system expanded greatly. The lands parceled out came from the patrimony of the Carolingians, from the royal fisc, or, more often, from the Church.[58] The obligation of how many warriors each vassal or magnate should contribute probably varied according to power and land, respectively. Normally laymen could exempt four men, two to protect their dominion, two for the administration of their property. Ecclesiastics could reserve two to supervise the harvest, maintain public order, and control the serfs.[59] For instance, Archbishop Hincmar of Rheims, a strong defender of the rights of the Church, saw nothing objectionable when two-fifths of his see's income was used for military defense.[60]

The obligation to serve extended to the rest of the population. All freemen were required to serve depending on the extent of their property and were responsible for their own equipment and supplies. Normally the owner of four manses (sixty-four hectares, each manse being sixteen hectares) had to join the army when called. Lesser owners had to combine resources with others of similar means so that one man could be chosen to serve.[61] This must have created large armies, because at the peak of his rule Charlemagne could count on the support of about 2,000 magnates (200 abbots, about 100 bishops, 500 counts, and about 1,000 vassals).[62] It is also clear that the contribution of the Church was an essential element of Charlemagne's power: many vassals were created with Church land, and high prelates were required to provide soldiers.

There is a lively controversy over the numerical strength of the Carolingian armies. Ferdinand Lot, writing in 1946, argued that at most the Carolingian rulers could assemble an army of slightly less than 5,000 heavy cavalry, a figure often repeated but misunderstood because Lot did not mean the whole army but just the heavy cavalry.[63] Timothy Reuter recently argued, without specifying the proportion between foot and horse, that Carolingian armies were normally not more than 2,000 strong; logistical problems would have prevented any higher number.[64] But Reuter is in the minority. Most of recent scholarship sustains a much higher number. Bernard S. Bachrach, although he maintains that the heavy cavalry was "usually a small part of any large army,"[65] is of the opinion that "several [Carolingian] armies in any given year . . . when taken in aggregate could reach a total in the neighborhood of 100,000 effectives."[66] K. F. Werner has argued that Charlemagne could rely on 15,000–20,000 horsemen. J. F. Verbruggen estimates that the largest army numbered 2,500–3,000 horsemen and 6,000–10,000 footmen, a figure that Philippe Contamine seems inclined to accept.[67] But the strength of the Carolingian state rested not only on the size of their host (in any case, normally larger than any enemy) but also on the ability of raising new armies easily in every corner of the dominion. The ruler's authority extended over about 1 million square kilometers, not the 200,000 previously accepted as the norm.[68] For instance, in the campaign of 778 against Saragossa, the Carolingian host included horsemen from Aquitania, Burgundy, Austrasia (the northeastern region of the kingdom), Bavaria, Septimania (southern France), and Italy. During the campaign against the Avars in 791 there were Saxons, Thuringians, Frisons, and Longobards in addition to the Franks. In 806 the Frankish host included Bavarians, Alamans, and Burgundians.[69]

Charlemagne's call to arms was apparently very detailed, perhaps being one of the secrets to the efficiency of his armies. For instance, this was the order he sent abbot Fulrad in 806,

> Be aware that we have convoked a general assembly this year in east Saxony on the River Bode at a place called Strasfurt. We order you to be there,

the 15th day before the calends of July, with all the men well armed and equipped, with weapons, baggage, and all the items necessary for waging war in terms of food and vestments. Each horsemen should have a shield, a lance, two swords, one long, one short, and a bow and quiver full of arrows. Make sure that your wagons carry utensils of all types and food necessary for three months from the place of departure, and clothing for six months.[70]

As these instructions sent to the abbot show, the campaigns were organized well in advance and all logistics were anticipated. Also, troops from the time of the early Carolingians were trained for the battlefield as well as siege warfare. Actually, says Bachrach, their mastery of how to conquer a well-defended city was extraordinary because they could rely on a large number of men: a defending city needed one man for every meter or so of wall, whereas the besieging force must have a numerical advantage of at least 4:1.[71]

The heavy cavalry, the heart of the Carolingian armies even if numerically smaller than other units, was armed for offense and defense. Heavy cavalrymen carried a long spear, a round or oval shield of medium girth that could be hung from the neck, a long sword about 90–100 centimeters long, and a short sword. But what distinguished the Carolingian heavy cavalryman was his armor. He wore a conical helmet, probably with an ornament on top, protective defense on the arms, hands, and legs, and a tunic of leather or other heavy material covered with metal scales or rings down to the knees. It was expensive equipment worth about 600 *sous* of silver.[72] The mail coat alone cost more than a warhorse.[73] The requirements of the light cavalry were much less expensive. It involved a long spear, javelins, bow and quiver, helmet, and shield. The infantry carried spears, shields, and, against Slavs and Avars, bow and quiver.[74]

A comparison with the Merovingians shows how different the Frankish armies had become by Charlemagne's time. Footmen were no longer the core of the host, their weapons had changed (there is no mention of the *francisca*), and cavalrymen now played the key role. Yet, according to P. Contamine, the Carolingians represented only a period of transition between the Early Middle Ages and the successive period. They did not witness a tactical revolution, as Lynn White Jr. claimed in the early 1960s. White argued that the introduction of the stirrup stabilized the horseman on top of his horse and made him able, with lance couched under his arm, to deliver strong and deadly blows against opposing horsemen.[75] An invention of Asiatic nomadic people, the stirrup was known to the Byzantines in the sixth century, and it reached the Carolingians in the seventh, but its adoption was not universal and not in a logically progressive manner. Of 135 horsemen found in Frankish graves, only 13 had stirrups.[76] Also, we have no evidence that the lance was couched under the arm in the manner of the knight of later centuries. The first clear evidence of this manner of attack comes from the Bayeux Tapestry toward the end of the eleventh century, and even then it was not used by all the horsemen of William the Conqueror. The lance of the Carolingian period was employed in the traditional manner: thrown like a javelin, held high abreast, struck in a downward motion, or pushed straight forward with the arm resting at the side of the body.

Cleverness in strategy strengthened the Franks' tactical advantages. In a combination of diplomacy and force of arms, Charlemagne at times rendered his enemies powerless even before any blow was struck. It was, says Verbruggen, a *stratégie des armées convergentes*; that is, attacking the target with armies approaching from different directions, making the enemy uncertain where and when to concentrate forces.[77] In reality Charlemagne's approach was even more sophisticated than Verbruggen suggests. It seems like an early version of the blitzkrieg—break through the center of the enemy line of defense, disregard secondary posts, avoid when possible the attrition of a pitched battle, and concentrate on the heart of the enemy's government and power. Although most of his campaigns were short (perhaps two or three months), Charlemagne was ready, when necessary, to leave his soldiers on campaign even during winter.[78] Depending on the nature of the goal, he was also ready to keep coming like a bulldog against particularly difficult enemies. He attacked the Saxons year after year—782, 783, 784, and 785.[79] And when the campaigns did not bring the results he expected, he was not squeamish about using the most brutal means, as when he massacred 4,000 Saxons at Verden in 782.[80] But his favorite mode was to point different armies against his goal, advancing concentrically and ravaging the land as they moved forward. In the spring of 773, during his war against the Longobards in Italy, he sent an army through the Moncenisio and another through the St. Bernard Pass, which means that the Longobards defending the Moncenisio were outflanked and had to retreat. Both Frankish armies then advanced, besieging the heart of Longobard rule, the city of Pavia. Against Bavaria, Charlemagne sent three armies in 787, one from Augsburg on the west, one from the north along the Danube, and the third from Bolzano on the south. Three armies were also deployed against the Avars in modern Hungary: one from the south (Italy), another along the left bank of the Danube, and the third along the right bank of the same river (Figure 4.3). In 796 he moved against the Avars, whose

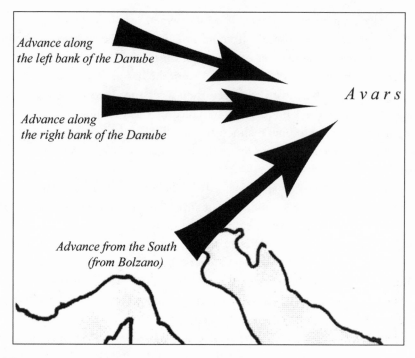

Figure 4.3   Charlemagne's Avar Campaign of 791

dominion was finally destroyed with armies from Bavaria and Italy. In 794 the Saxons were rendered powerless when caught between two armies, one led by Charlemagne, the other by his son Charles. In the siege of Barcelona in 800, led by the sovereign's son Louis, the Carolingians used three armies with different tasks—one to besiege the city, one to prevent any attempt at relief, and one in reserve.[81]

Yet Charlemagne's uncanny strategic sense and tactical primacy on the battlefield do not explain everything about the Franks' military superiority. Charlemagne also used diplomacy with great skill and exploited the internal weaknesses of enemies. This was the case in Italy, where the Longobards never stopped quarreling with each other and never came to some mutual agreement with the popes. This was also the case in Spain, where Muslim chiefs were reluctant to accept the authority of the Emir of Córdoba. This may have been also the case with the Saxons, split between the aristocracy willing to come to terms with Frankish rule and the lower classes reluctant to give up their freedom and ancient pagan beliefs.[82]

The New Emperor

Alcuin, the English intellectual in Charlemagne's entourage, probably was the first to hear of the scandal in Rome. On 25 April 799 a crowd led by two high members of the papal administration and relatives of the preceding pontiff attacked Pope Leo III in public.[83] The assailants' intention was to blind the prelate and to cut his tongue. After the assault they dragged the victim to the monastery of Saints Stephen and Sylvester, where they subjected him to more beatings, leaving the pontiff half-dead and, in their understanding, mute and blind. Finally, they moved their prisoner to another institution, the monastery of Saint Erasmus, where they thought that their control over the pope was more secure. But Leo kept his voice and sight and with the support of Wittigis, Duke of Spoleto, took refuge in the duchy's capital.

We do not know the nature of the accusations against the pope except in general: fornication and perjury. The person who knew more, Alcuin, destroyed the letter from Rome itemizing the pope's conduct so as not to create more scandal in the future. Urged to intervene, Charlemagne hesitated at first but in the end arrived in Rome toward the end of 800. The problem was serious: Did anybody have the authority to depose a pope, even one who had committed crimes? Alcuin, often the heart and soul of the sovereign in theological matters, thought that no one, not even a council of bishops, had such authority.

Charlemagne entered Rome on 24 November 800. By then he had decided to defend the pontiff. The coming events were carefully staged in pursuit of that goal. A week later in the crowded Church of Saint Peter, Leo III, the New Testament in his hand, ascended the pulpit and swore that the accusations of his enemies were false. Probably that same day or a day before, the Patriarch of Jerusalem arrived, bringing the keys of his city and of the Holy Sepulcher, thereby making the pope the highest figurehead in Christendom. The stage was set for the final drama.

On 25 December 800 in front of a crowded congregation of Franks and Romans, before mass began, Charlemagne, accompanied by his son, knelt in prayer in front of St. Peter's Tomb. When Charlemagne rose, the pope placed a crown on his head. The crowd, obviously primed beforehand, followed with an exclamation repeated three times, "Long life and victory to Charles Augustus, crowned by God, great and peaceful emperor of the Romans!" This was followed by the pope's prayer and, according to the *Annals of the Franks*, by proskynesis, in which the pope knelt in adoration in front of the emperor.[84]

Einhard comments that Charlemagne was unaware of what had been planned. If he had known, he would have refused to enter church that day.[85] Whether we believe Einhard or not, what is important is the role usurped by the pope in investing Charlemagne with the imperial crown. At Constantinople, where similar ceremonies took place, the city's patriarch intervened only after the new emperor had been approved by the army, the Senate, and the people. In other words, the patriarch confirmed what the traditional elective agents had done. In Rome the pontiff had initiated the crowning, and the people's approval came only after the crown had been placed on Charlemagne. Even if proskynesis had been performed, the actual authority of the coronation rested in the pope's hands: the pope had become the "creator" of the emperor, and until the end of the Middle Ages emperors were crowned at St. Peter's.[86] It was one important aspect of the role of the Church in medieval Europe. The strength of Charlemagne rested on the support of his high ecclesiastics; now his elevation to emperor was the work of the highest head of the Church.[87] Yet the situation was not agreeable to the new emperor. When at the end of his life it came time to crown a new emperor in the person of his son Louis, Charlemagne himself placed the crown atop his head.[88]

At his death in 814 Charlemagne left a great empire. It would not last. Internal conflicts among his descendants weakened the empire as new enemies came to the fore and old enemies revived hostilities: Vikings from the North, Magyars from the East, and Muslim pirates in the Mediterranean.

PART TWO

The Muslim Empire

Chapter Five

God, His Prophet, and War: The Origins

THE DAY STARTED WITH A BAD omen for the Quraysh tribe when a man sent to scout Muhammad and the Medinans came back with these words: "Yes, they are quite fewer than us. But death rides astride their camels. Their only refuge is the sword; dumb as the grave, their tongues they put forth with the serpent's deadly aim." Muhammad had drawn his army into wings and center, probably like the formation of his enemy, which slowly advanced toward them. His instructions were a clear summary of the way he understood a battlefield encounter: "Do not move to break your lines but stay on; do not commence fighting until I order; do not waste your arrows while the enemy is still beyond reach; when the enemy approaches, begin throwing stones with your hands; on his nearer approach use lances and spears, the sword being drawn only finally for hand-to-hand fighting."[1] But before weapons were crossed, three men—two brothers and the son of one of them—moved forward, challenging the Medinans to individual combat. It ended with the death of all three challengers. Death came to two of them quickly, but the third lasted longer. When his opponent's blade cut his tendons and he fell to the ground, the two other Muslim champions who had dispatched their adversaries quickly ran over and took the life out of him. That was the beginning of the Battle of Badr, the first great victory of Islam.

The upheaval that led to the downfall of most of the Byzantine Empire and of the Persian Empire emerged from a most unlikely location: the barren, dry, avaricious territory east of Syria and south to the Strait of Aden—the vast Syro-Arabian Desert. The southern part of the land had never been conquered by the major powers of the Near East. In the past they had struggled to control it with alliances, gifts, and subsidies. Arabia was a tribal society, where the population had remained ethnically pure since its establishment in the ninth century B.C.,[2] but at the beginning of the seventh century A.D. they were unstoppable and spread over lands of civilizations on the east, north, and west. They conquered, as Patricia Crone so eloquently puts, "in the name of . . . a God that dwelt among the tribes and spoke in their language," and regardless of where the new conquerors went, "morally they did remain in Mecca."[3] Their conquest bred a new civilization, unlike the various western barbarian kingdoms that had conquered the Roman Empire of the West, but that in the end they too had succumbed to the lure of Roman civilization.

The Arabian Peninsula

The Arabian peninsula is a large landmass of about 3 million square kilometers (Figure 5.1). The desert that occupies most of the territory continues north on the eastern edge of Syria. The Red Sea on the west, the Persian Gulf on the east, and the Indian Ocean on the south surround the rest of the peninsula. The western edge is characterized by a thin strip of land with a mountain range eastbound. The northern part of the range is the Hejaz. The southern coastland, where modern Yemen is located, and the northeastern coast near the Arabian Gulf, are the only locations that receive enough rain to make them fertile. The rest, the central and northern part, is dominated by sand, dotted in some place by oases. The most important town in pre-Islamic times was Mecca, mainly because it was an obvious resting place for caravan routes and because it housed the black stone, called Kaaba, an object of particular veneration.[4]

Kingdoms with a differentiated and socially stratified society had emerged only in the southern part of the land, such as the Kingdom of Saba.[5] For the rest, power remained in the hands of tribes who, despite their feuds and conflict, were strikingly uniform culturally. The tribe, as defined by Fred McGraw Donner, was "a body of blood relations . . . [including] all those people descended in the male line" from some real or legendary ancestor.[6] The tribe was the place of defense and refuge and the agent of solidarity among its members.

Not all tribes were equal, but all cherished martial values. It was a society in northern and eastern Arabia, where the bedouin, the individual who extracted a meager living out of the desert by hard work or violence, was the favorite type. The dominating tribes were members either of a warrior aristocracy, that is, groups that in the distant or more recent past had established supremacy through their fighting ability; or of a religious aristocracy, that is,

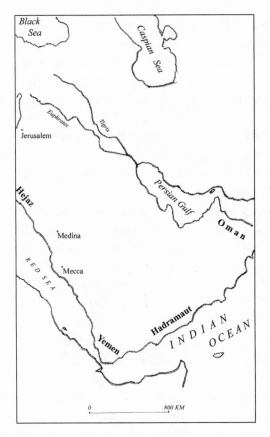

Figure 5.1
The Arabian Peninsula

groups claiming their hegemony because they had become guardians of the cult of one of the gods and goddesses who were worshiped before the advent of Islam.

Although tribal ties cut across all types of inhabitants, the people of the peninsula and of the Syrian Desert, excluding the population in Yemen, the area south, could be divided into sedentary, nomad, and seminomad.[7] The sedentary lived in oases and mountain valleys, making a living from their contacts with the other two groups of people; their livelihoods were interdependent. The sedentary groups were more numerous than the others, although spatially they inhabited a more limited area. Nomads were of two types. One covered most of the territory of the Arabian peninsula, herding flocks of camels in small groups of five to twenty people and surviving from camel's milk, dates, and other staples they received by bartering hides, leather, cloth woven from camel hair, and livestock with sedentary populations. Another type of nomad herded sheep and goats. Because their animals needed water much more often compared to camels, they tended to live near water sources at the edge of the desert. Like the camel-herders, they based their worldview on martial values. These seminomads were numerically larger than the nomads. The migratory patterns of their sheep, goats, or camels were changed according to weather conditions and were shorter, as herders lived part of the year in villages in Mesopotamia or on the fringe of the Syrian Desert. Sometimes they even tilled the land, an occupation despised by other bedouins, although like nomads they saw themselves essentially as fighters and retained great pride in the memory of past military exploits.[8]

Pre-Islamic society seemed unchanged and unchangeable, with a few tribes being the leading social units. It was warlike, but not so much an internal feud as outright war against the inhabitants of the two empires on its borders, Byzantium and Sassanian Persia. Although the rulers of those empires had no intention of conquering them, they were constantly worried about raids on their territory. This led both empires to come to terms with the tribes, either by establishing alliances or by paying subsidies. The Byzantines relied on the confederacy of tribes called the Ghassanids operating south of Palestine, and the Sassanians on the Lakhmid kings living around al-Hira on the fringes of Mesopotamia.

The system worked until the early seventh century, when a new element emerged among the Arabs: belief in the words of the Prophet Muhammad and in a God who would not compromise with those who did not believe in Him. Either you believed in Him or you were to be conquered.[9] And then, neither the might of the Byzantines nor of the Sassanians could stop the servants of God. Piece by piece, the Sassanian Empire was dismantled, the Byzantines were expelled from the Near East and the southern coast of the Mediterranean, and even Egypt fell. And the new believers would not stop at Gibraltar: they crossed the strait and crushed the Visigoths in Spain. They even attempted to bring down the Frankish kingdom and never stopped threatening the southern coast of France and the Italian peninsula, even wresting Sicily from the Byzantines. They had become an irresistible machine of conquest once their natural martial tendencies combined with the words of the Prophet, the emissary of God.

The Prophet of God

Muhammad (ca. 569–632) was born in a family of the Hashim tribe, one of the lesser clans of the powerful Quraysh tribe that controlled the city of

Mecca. A man with a bright future, known for self-control and diplomatic skill, he made a living in the caravan trade. Although a merchant by profession, Muhammad was also sensitive to the problems of his environs, plagued by injustice and suffering and marked by extreme wealth and poverty. Around his fortieth year he had a vision from God that made him question the society dominated by the Quraysh tribe in Mecca.[10]

While the leading tribe looked at him with scorn, Muhammad's life in Mecca remained secure because of the powerful influence of an uncle and of Muhammad's own wife, Khadija. When the two died, he felt forced to escape from Mecca and to seek refuge at Yathrib, later called Medina, a rural town of about 3,000. With him came followers, whose number had continually increased after the first difficult years, when only the poor and members of socially undistinguished families responded to his call. The date was 24 September 632, the year of the Hegira (migration from Mecca to Medina) and the beginning of a new era. Muhammad would soon become the political chief of the city and begin his mission of conquering the rest of Arabia with his creed or his sword.

Muhammad's message was based on the notion that the Islamic community—the believers of the God preached by the Prophet—was a unique community where authority was centralized and whose believers had to follow God's dictates as revealed to His Prophet.[11] The duties of a Muslim were codified in the holy book, the Quran, which contained God's revelations to Muhammad transmitted to the Prophet by the archangel Gabriel between 609 and 622 (the Quran was compiled after Muhammad's death by the Caliph Othman between 644 and 646). They included belief in one God, the angels, the emissaries of God (i.e., the prophets), the truth as revealed in the holy books, the last judgment, and the resurrection. The believer had to accept the notion that there is only one God and that Muhammad was His Prophet; had to pray five times a day (morning, noon, midday, evening, and night); give alms to the poor and disadvantaged; had to observe a fast for 29–30 days during Ramadan (the ninth month of the Muslim calendar); and make a pilgrimage to Mecca during his lifetime.

Muhammad's teachings were revolutionary and changed the nature of Arabian society in an irreversible way. The early stage involved Muhammad firmly establishing control over competing agencies in Medina, especially the Jewish contingent; it continued with a bitter struggle for the control of Mecca against the Quraysh tribe; it ended with Muhammad consolidating power first in the neighborhood of Medina and then in the rest of Arabia. This was particularly important because it meant the subordination of the various tribes to a simple goal as expressed in Muhammad's teachings. In the end a completely new arrangement emerged on the peninsula. Tribal particularism was submitted to a centralizing agency, the new creed, and the creed's hierarchy, a new ruling elite that included the early converts to Islam, the followers of Muhammad from Mecca to Medina (the muhâjirûn), the Medinese Helpers (the *ansar*), and the members of the Quraysh tribe after their defeat. It was essentially a Hejâz ruling elite and meant a revolutionary transfer of power from the nomadic tribes to sedentary groups.[12] In this sense it was a radical event on the Arabian peninsula because for the first time in history a state was created out of both faith and force of arms.

Muhammad's death in 632 was followed by a period of internal turmoil, the *ridda* wars (632–633), between the various contenders to power within the Islamic community. The struggle ended with the triumph of a gifted, moderate, natural leader named Abû Bakr, the father of Muhammad's favorite wife, Aisha. Bakr extended the power of Islam over all the people of Arabia. Soon afterward, armies of Muslims, that is, the followers of Islam, moved into Byzantine and Sassanian territories, beginning a period of exciting conquest. Little is known about the military history of the preconquest Muslim army in spite of the importance of later events. Ella Landau-Tasseron argues that the military actions that took place during Muhammad's lifetime laid the basis for future conquests. She distinguishes five types of hostile actions during that time: caravan looting, raids against bedouin tribes, attacks on settled communities, frontal encounters, and defensive warfare. All of them, with a slight exception for pitched battles, involved small numbers of participants and limited bloodshed.[13]

Landau-Tasseron argues that Muhammad initially took part personally in caravan looting, as that was one way of gaining a livelihood for people who had left Mecca for Medina without riches. Also, it required little military skill and involved small parties of men, as few as eight; the reward could be great; and the experience gained by the participants could be put to effective use in more difficult encounters. The bedouins were a particular target during a *razzia* (predatory raid) not only because it was the traditional manner of attack among Arabs but also for strategic reasons: to discourage supporters of the Qurayshi at Mecca or of Jewish opponents or to gain control over particular routes. Usually the participants were small numerically (from 100 to 800, even as low as two dozen in one case). The highest number of participants were in attacks against settled communities and may have reached 10,000 men against Mecca (likely a much inflated number, however). Mecca was the biggest prize because of its importance and because it was the seat of the powerful Qurayshi. It was finally conquered in 630 after five years of war. Another target was the Jewish settlements, the conquest of which was easy and fruitful in terms of material gain.[14]

Settled communities were not difficult to conquer even when they had a system of defensive fortifications; inhabitants were forced to surrender out of fear that the besiegers would cut supplies into the city or destroy the trees outside the city walls on which their livelihoods depended. The booty gained in the suppression of the Jewish tribe of Banú l-Nadír resulted in the acquisition of mail coats, helmets, and hundreds of swords.[15] Defensive warfare was unusual during this period, for the besieged eventually left the city walls to resolve the issue through a pitched battle.

Only four encounters can be considered to be real pitched battles: Badr in January 624, Uhud in January 625, Mu'ta in 629, and Hunayn in February 630. At Badr the Muslim armies included 300 soldiers, at Uhud 700, at Mu'ta 3,000, and at Hunayn 12,000. The casualties were limited: 14 at Badr, 70 at Uhud, 8 at Mu'ta, and 4 at Hunayn.[16] Among the non-Muslim forces there were 70 casualties at Badr and 22 at Uhud.[17]

Under the leadership of the Prophet there was a crucial change in terms of military leadership during the preconquest period. In the past, leaders were either self-appointed or chosen after consultation with the leading men of the army. With Muhammad the process of election was abolished. The leader was the spiritual head of the Muslim forces, and it was he who appointed the subordinate chieftain.[18] It was also Mohammed who set the army's strategic and tactical goals.

It seems that preconquest soldiers were personally responsible for providing their own weapons and food. In later centuries the leader had to make sure that enough provisions were available for both men and animals.[19] Although a central armory was established, soldiers had to come with their own weapons.[20] But the most striking aspect of a preconquest army was the logistical, strategic, and tactical sense of its leader. Unless we doubt the evidence as the creation of a later period describing the life of the Prophet, there are various events connected to the campaigns and battles that show Muhammad had a sophisticated understanding of warfare.

Peace did not mean abandoning the prospect of war, for leisure could be used to sharpen one's military skills. During periods of peace Muhammad encouraged his men to practice archery. Moreover, he organized competitive footraces and horseraces in a place near a mosque, personally distributing prizes to the winners. The scholar Muhammad Hamidullah sees a substratum of military exercises even in the religious obligations of the faithful, like the need to wake early for the morning prayer; the ordered manner and almost military formation of praying shoulder to shoulder; the fasting during Ramadan, when no food or drink is consumed between dawn and sunset, making people accustomed to deprivations; and the pilgrimage to Mecca, where life is conducted in the open under heavy sun or sudden storms.[21] But much more important was the belief that war was waged in the name of God to enlarge the dominion of the Muslim community and, later, not so much to destroy the infidels as to convince them of the error of their ways.

Maneuver was conducted to mislead the enemy and to achieve surprise. The army often marched away from the target and then, by using unusual routes, suddenly appeared where the enemy had camped. Sometimes the real intent of the expedition was kept even from subordinate leaders. The advance was carried out stealthily, during the night, after cutting the bells on the camels and horses. Sometimes Muhammad used devices to convince the enemy that his forces were much greater than they really were. For instance, he would order extra fires to be lit during the nighttime rest so that the enemy might imagine there was a much larger army.[22]

Tactically he was always ready to adopt what he had found impressive among the enemy. For instance, in a confrontation with a Jewish tribe in 629, his soldiers came face-to-face with an instrument of war, the catapult, that was unknown to them. One year later they had not only catapults but also covered wagons for carrying siege weapons.[23] He was also cognizant about how to restrain an enemy on horseback. In 627 he used ditches, a practice apparently unknown in northeastern Arabia. Muhammad also seemed aware of how to exploit weather and terrain to his advantage. When possible, Muhammad deployed in such a manner that the sun would shine in his enemy's faces. He also realized that the army holding higher terrain would have a great advantage.[24] Finally, he made sure that the loot was divided evenly among his followers after a fifth was left to the Prophet, who then would use it to strengthen the state socially and militarily.[25] Although practice did not always follow actual behavior, Muhammad provided detailed rules on how to deal with defeated enemies. It was forbidden to treat the enemy brutally. During battle most actions were permissible, but they should not burn or mutilate their corpses. Children and women should be respected, and prisoners, once captured, had to be treated humanely.

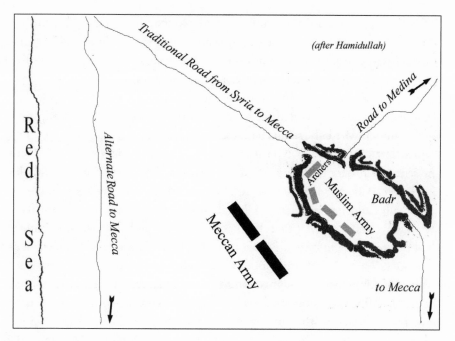

Figure 5.2   Battle of Badr

The Battle of Badr

The Battle of Badr, fought in 624, demonstrates how Muhammad understood war, although one should be cautious because old traditions and myths are mixed with the evidence (Figure 5.2). It was not Muhammad's plan to engage in a pitched battle with the Qurayshi when he left Medina with a little more than 300 men in early January 624.[26] He only intended to ambush a Meccan caravan upon its return from Syria with more than 1,000 camels and a value of some 50,000 gold pieces.[27]

Muhammad had prepared the raid carefully, establishing friendly relations with the tribes along the caravan's route. Also in early January he sent two scouts west of Medina to Badr, the normal stopover of a caravan coming from Syria. Once they ascertained the caravan's intended arrival, they were to return to Medina with the news. When his scouts did not return, Muhammad became impatient and on 12 January, a Sunday, he marched his army out of Medina. It was a host of footmen, with only two horses and seventy camels, which they took turns riding.[28] Muhammad set out for Badr.

Before appearing in the vicinity of Badr, Muhammad tried again to find out when the caravan would arrive by sending two scouts ahead. At Badr the scouts heard that the caravan was expected either the next day or the day after that. But the caravan's leader had done his homework and seemed to have arrived at Badr soon after the departure of the Muslim scouts. There he heard that two strangers had visited the village a short while before. An investigation of the ground where the scouts had rested showed that their camels' dung contained small pits of dates typical of the crop grown at Medina. Immediately he sent an emissary to Mecca asking for help and then, instead of crossing the land from Badr to Mecca, chose an alternate route along the Red Sea before eventually moving westward to his destination. As the caravan left Badr behind, its leader realized that they had escaped the ambush that Muhammad had prepared. He informed Mecca then that they did not need military help anymore. The new information did not change the decision to counter Muhammad's move, although some Meccans remained in their city, worried about shedding the blood of relatives and friends who had converted to Islam. The rest, a little more than 900 men with 700 camels and 100 horses, decided after heated discussion to push forward to Badr and to intercept Muhammad's army.[29] Meanwhile Muhammad was moving toward Badr, for he did not know that the caravan had escaped the trap. It was Thursday when he found out that an enemy army, not a caravan ripe for pillage, was waiting for him at Badr. By then he was on his last march. It would have been foolish to return to Medina, for the enemy was much more mobile with their camels and horses and could have intercepted him before they reached safety. Muhammad quickly convened his council of war. It was agreed that they could not escape and that God would be on their side against the idolaters from Mecca.

Before reaching Badr, Muhammad sent a small party to reconnoiter. They surprised three women at a well. One escaped to the camp of the Meccans; the other two were captured. While his men were beating the women to learn more about the enemy, Muhammad bid them to stop. He had discovered the enemy camp. It stood behind the sand hills on the western side of the valley. The valley had hills on the north and east, low, broken terrain on the south, and a number of small hills on the west. Muhammad deployed his forces on the east. His position forced the enemy to advance with the sun in their eyes. But as the evening drew on, Muhammad made another preparation. He diverted the water of the wells near the enemy, except for a particular good spring, which would be in the center of his line. If the battle lasted long, he intended to deprive the enemy of water.

The night was broken by a storm. The downpour over the camp of the Qurayshi seems to have been stronger than that over Muhammad's camp. As first light arrived, the smaller Medina contingent had some advantages. Their line rested on the high ground, where the sand had become firm during the night's storm. The Meccans had to start their advance from a quagmire created by the downpour. Moreover, the terrain, a chain of hillocks, made their advance fatiguing. But Muhammad was also aware of his weaknesses—too few men and little mobility. He deployed archers on one flank as protection against a cavalry envelopment, although in the end the Qurayshi used neither horses nor camels. Also, Muhammad ordered his men to stay still and let the enemy advance, compelling the Meccans to undertake a difficult advance from soft terrain toward the firm hillock where the Muslims were deployed.

The battle opened with a duel, three from each side, all favorable to the Muslims. The losses of the challengers must have disheartened the Qurayshi army, whereas the Muslims found a new source of inspiration and courage in the promise that casualties would be rewarded in Paradise. It is said that a young, strong, handsome man threw to the ground the dates he had in his hand, crying, "Are these dates that hold me back from Paradise? I shall taste none of them until I meet my Lord." He ran to the battlefield and met his end there.

The weather also seemed to conspire against the Meccans. The sound of thunder twice broke the din of metal and despairing cries. Muhammad cried out that the angels, Michael and Seraphim, had come to fight with his comrades. As the wind rushed sand in the enemies' faces, Muhammad grabbed a handful and threw it in the direction of the adversaries. "Let confusion disorder their ranks," he cried. When the Meccans started to retreat, the Muslims followed them, cutting down any they met. By the end of the day the bodies of 70 Meccans and 14 Muslims covered the battlefield. Roughly 70 Meccans also fell prisoner to the men from Medina. The Prophet ordered that no harm be done to the captives, except for two men who were executed, probably because they had killed Muslims in Mecca. The rest were treated well. Sometimes their captors fed the prisoners better than themselves. Eventually they were set free after paying a ransom. If poor, they were let go without any ransom. The literate among the prisoners were let go on condition that each of them would teach young Muslim children to read and write.[30] Muhammad also ordered that no mutilation of the enemy corpses should be carried out, but he had them buried in a place separate from his own fallen soldiers.[31]

The Battle of Badr is a crucial event in the history of Islam because Muhammad defeated the powerful Quraysh tribe and started to gain the upper hand in his conquest of Arabia. It also shows some of the key elements of Islamic warfare during the preconquest period: the promise of Paradise for people fighting for the faith, deference to the battlefield casualties, whether friend or foe, respect of prisoners and of nonparticipants like women and slaves, and the laws to be followed in dividing the loot.

Chapter Six

The Conquest of
the Fertile Crescent:
Muslims in Syria and Iraq

ONCE THEY LEFT THEIR LANDS, Muslims surged to conquer other places with the violence and unpredictability of a flash flood. Syria fell quickly, followed by Iraq and Persia. Then they took over North Africa before crossing the Mediterranean Sea to the Iberian Peninsula.

Why the Arabs Left Their Homeland

Historians have been at a loss to explain why a people who for 2,500 years had left the desert only for predatory raids would abandon ancestral homelands and bring two great empires to their knees. With no consensus to speak of, explanations usually center on three points. Leone Caetani, writing in the early twentieth century and developing an idea first raised by Hugo Winkler, argued that the exodus of the Arabs was caused by ecological factors, including climate changes and increases in population. Increasing poverty and the competition for fewer resources among a growing population convinced them to move. It was a movement that the early caliphs—that is, Muhammad's successors—could not control, at least initially. One strong point in favor of this thesis is that the initial drive aimed at conquest, not at the conversion of the people conquered. It is a thesis that either denies or minimizes the impact of religious motivation.[1]

A more modern view emphasizes accidental factors. The movement was not coherent and did not obey principles stemming from a central authority. The advance of the Muslims was a series of raids in the fashion of past behavior. The idea of a mass movement bent on conquest of the two empires is a "historiographical myth" fashioned by Muslims of the later generations.[2]

F.M. Donner rejects both views. He argues instead that the conquest was organized ideologically and strategically by the center, that is, the caliphs.[3] As he maintained in the 1980s, there are much more logical explanations of the conquests. It is not to be overlooked that the leaders of the movement—the first converts to Muhammad's preaching—felt that it was their religious duty to increase the domain of Islam. It was a belief that the continuous string of victories must have easily spread among the lower ranks of the movement. It may have also been the case that the leading Arabian tribes—the Qurayshi, for instance, one of the leading groups of the Muslim elite—saw conquest as a means of expanding into new markets. Conquest also meant new properties, new taxes to impose on the conquered, slaves, and booty that would benefit those on the battlefield as well as the elites in Medina. Finally, it may also be possible that the elites used conquest as a means to retain primacy in the state.[4] As Machiavelli would write almost a millennium later, a state is kept strong if it is continually engaged in absorbing other states.

The Conquest of Syria

The move against Syria (the region that today includes Lebanon, Israel, Palestine, Jordan, and Syria) should not have been a surprise for commercial, political, religious, or strategic reasons (Figure 6.1). The Arabian desert extends beyond the borders of modern Saudi Arabia and divides Syria into two opposite regions. On the east are desert and steppe; on the west winds coming from the Mediterranean bring enough rain to make the coast and the mountain valleys fertile. It was a region split into two cultural identities, Arabic in the interior, Byzantine in the west (Syria had been under Roman and then Byzantine domination for more than 500 years). Cities were divided: Arab for Aleppo, Hims, and Damascus; Byzantine for Beirut and Jerusalem.

Muhammad himself showed great interest in the area, and when he was alive a Muslim contingent penetrated into the region, only to be defeated at Mu'ta by an array of Byzantine soldiers and local troops. He was probably trying to bring under Muslim control the rest of the nomadic tribes operating outside Arabia in the Syrian Desert. That was essential to stabilizing Muslim hegemony over Arabia proper. But there were important practical and religious reasons as well. The Qurayshi, who had become members of the Muslim elite after accepting Muhammad's creed, had important commercial ties with Syrian tribes. Moreover, Jerusalem, a most holy city for Muslims, was also there.[5]

Syria had been for centuries a place of contrast between the Roman Empire of the West (and later of the East) and whoever held power in Persia. The rul-

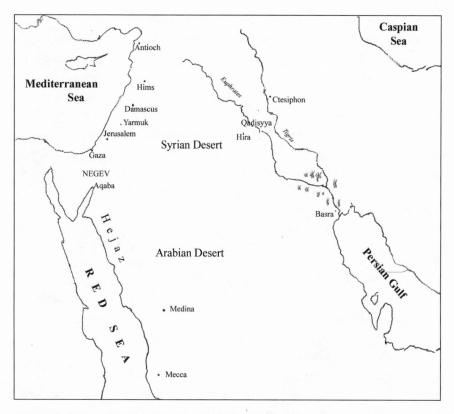

Figure 6.1   Syria and Iraq During the Muslim Conquest

ing Persian dynasty, the Sassanians, had conquered the area, relinquishing it to the Byzantines around 629–630. Then, on the eve of the Muslim assault, the Byzantines reentered a region where their previous system of government and system of alliances had been disturbed or destroyed. Delicate diplomacy was required, but the Byzantines, haunted by financial distress and probably cocky about their recent success against the Sassanians, were reluctant to reestablish old ties or perhaps were blind as to how to rebuild political and social supremacy.

Whether the Byzantine army was strong enough to defeat the Muslim onslaught has been a matter of controversy. Certainly the empire's population was much larger than the Muslim population. Originally around 28–34 million, it had declined by 630 probably to around 17–27 million. By the time of the invasion there were at least 1.9 million people in Syria and Palestine and 3 million in Egypt.[6] Michael Whitby is of the opinion that if the wars after

Justinian's reign had often begun in defeat for the Byzantine armies, in the end victory had been theirs on the Danube against the Avars and in the east and south against the Sassanians. What weakened them was war against the Persians, which never seemed to end, together with civil war within the empire's borders and the recurrent bouts of plague. They lost the Middle East, says Whitby, not because they were weak but because their adversaries, the Muslims, were more energetic and determined. W. E. Kaegi paints a different picture. The Byzantine Empire, he says, although strong on paper, was "fiscally, psychologically, and militarily unstable and potentially volatile."[7] But even if we share the opinion that the Byzantine army was not in decline tactically, there were important strategic reasons why it could not contain a decisive thrust into the empire's territories.

In the 620s, only about ten years before the Muslims penetrated Syria, the Byzantine emperor, Heraclius, had led a campaign against the Sassanian control of the Persian Empire. At that time Syria was in Persian hands, but strangely enough Heraclius led his soldiers far away from there, striking into the heart of enemy territory. His primary objective was not to regain the lands he had lost to the Sassanians but to humiliate the enemy. In the manner of a medieval *chevauchée* (a destructive medieval war ride) he mixed military and civilian targets, like the fire temples of the Sassanians. What interested Heraclius was honor (after all, the Sassanians had carried a similar campaign into Byzantine territories) and the majesty of the imperial throne. In his seeking such goals, the defense of the frontier seemed to have been relegated to second priority. To paraphrase, it was more important to humiliate the enemy than to disarm him. The truth was that "the Byzantine army in the province was never capable, or meant to be capable against full scale invasion." Cities were organized to withstand a siege, but the countryside was open to the invaders. For instance, the Negev, the region in southern Syria near the Gulf of Aqaba, likely had few Byzantine soldiers. Their troops numbered only 300 in their first pitched battle against the Muslims.[8] Moreover, we have to add to this the empire's disregard of the barrier traditionally created by bedouin allies against the southern Arabian tribes, losses and attrition due to the chronic conflict with the Sassanians, financial distress, and plague. Thus although the Byzantine army was strong on paper, it was not ready to defeat a determined adversary that had little to lose and much to gain (religiously and materially) and that combined battlefield bravery with strategic sophistication.

The plan that Abû Bakr, Muhammad's successor and the first caliph of the Muslim state (632–634), devised was strategically perfect. The first stage of conquest involved the achievement of supremacy over the nomadic tribes operating south and east of Syria. The process began in 633 and lasted almost a year. For the moment generally no attack was unleashed against the walled cities of the Byzantine Empire. Also, the Muslim armies remained away from the key agricultural regions of central Palestine. They reached a maximum of 24,000 men, mainly settled people from the Hijâz and the Yemen.[9]

The Byzantines seem not to have reacted at the first onset of the invasion. One of the reasons must have been the way they understood warfare: avoid pitched encounters; rely instead on "endless patience, dissimulation and false negotiations, timing, cleverness, and seemingly endless maneuvering." More than trusting everything to a single battle, it was much wiser withdrawing to the safety of the walled cities.[10] Their reluctance to engage the Muslims on the field may have reflected the belief that they were facing only a series of predatory raids that would eventually vanish when limited goals had been reached. Another problem might have been the smaller size of their military force in Syria. But its defeat there had consequences out of proportion to the number of men lost in the encounter: it left southern Palestine in the hands of the Muslims.[11]

One of the deadly mistakes the Byzantines made, even before the Muslims started their trek for Byzantine territory, was their treatment of tribes that buffered Syria and the Hejâz. The tribes usually received payments for being the first obstacle against any northern advance of Arabian forces. When the tribesmen living in the buffer zone had come to the Byzantine commander, a eunuch, to receive the customary payment, they had been greeted with an insult. The emperor, he said, "scarcely pays the soldiers, how much less these dogs."[12] The bedouins' answer came soon thereafter: the Muslims found the door wide open when they moved north, divided into four armies (Figure 6.2). One was directed from the south against Palestine, moving from Aqaba across the Negev until reaching the neighborhood of Gaza and Dathin. The other three attacked from east of the Jordan River. Marching from the eastern part of Arabia, one was sent against Jordan in the region south of Balqâ and east of the Wâdi 'Araba; another struck in the direction of Balqâ, east and northeast of the Dead Sea; the fourth column moved into the Golan Heights.[13]

The decisive event that closed the first phase and initiated the second phase (634–637) of the conquest of Syria was the arrival from Iraq of a Muslim contingent that initially had operated in Mesopotamia against the Sassanian Empire. There is controversy on the route that the contingent took, but regardless of its route into Syria and its relatively small number

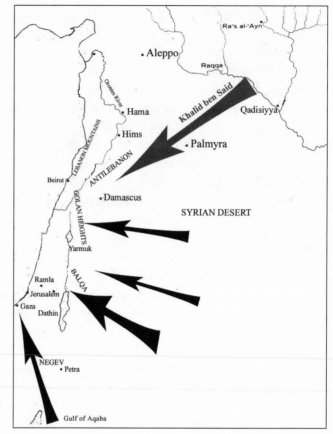

Figure 6.2
The Muslim Attack
on Syria 632–637

(500–800 men, says Donner), its advance, carried through the desert, an environment forbidden to the Byzantines, must have disconcerted the Byzantines. It is likely that the commander, a gifted war leader named Khâlid ben Sa'îd, must have appeared from the north, pointing toward Damascus.[14] The arrival of Khâlid opened another front, this time in the rear of the Byzantine forces. Moreover, it shows the Muslims' mastery of the desert and the quickness of their movements. It also points to the existence of a central authority directing operations on the field, likely the seat of the Caliphate in Medina.[15]

The Byzantines' decision to rely on fortified walls to stop the Muslims did not work. The nomads' supremacy in the surrounding territories strangled the cities, and in the end the Muslims, after gaining support from local tribes, decided to move against the cities. The Byzantines were left with no choice but to engage in pitched battle. As the main cities started to fall to the Muslim onslaught, the Byzantines decided to face the enemy in a series of encounters culminating in the Battle of the Yarmûk in August 636.

The Battle of the Yarmûk

Heraclius, the Byzantine emperor, realized the seriousness of the Muslim threat when they challenged his supremacy in the cities. Whether he intended to create a defensive line or face the invaders in a pitched battle is uncertain. Taking the traditional response of the Byzantines into consideration, probably the idea of a defensive line, made up of troops in the field, garrisons, and fortified cities, must have made more sense to an emperor who had decided early on that a pitched battle was too dangerous. Yet he must have changed his mind and instructed his generals to meet the threat head-on, although later Byzantine writers tried to exonerate him, claiming that the initiative came from the generals in the field against the express order of the emperor.

Heraclius's decision is logical if we examine the nature of the terrain where the battle was fought. The area was traditionally the granary of southern Syria and thus of considerable value to the empire. Militarily, Adhri'at on the southeast of the Yarmûk was the gateway to the south, and whoever held it could be a threat to the Muslim motherland. At the same time, the Muslims, who had assembled there, could easily strike toward the northern part of Palestine where Damascus and Hims were located, knowing that any attack on their rear would have been impossible because of the difficult nature of the terrain from the Mediterranean onward.[16]

As the Byzantines assembled their forces, the Muslims, worried about overexposing their lines, abandoned their posts in central and northern Syria, at Hims and Damascus, regrouping east of the Golan Heights in the proximity of the Yarmûk River, where they remained for several weeks facing the Byzantine army. No major clash took place for about two months. The Muslims asked for reinforcements. When they arrived, they must have been small. At most the host reached 24,000 men against a much larger army, probably around 40,000.[17] The commander in chief of the Muslim army was Abû 'Ubayda b. al-Jarrâh. Among his subordinates was the brilliant Khâlid b. al-Walîd, head of the cavalry. Initially the Muslims had chosen to line up near the town of Jabiya. Worried by the advance of the larger Byzantine host and by the presence of women and children in their midst,[18] they withdrew south, deploying in the stronger defensive line between Dayr Ayûb and Adhri'at. It is likely that at this stage the Byzantines established their camp near Jabiya or

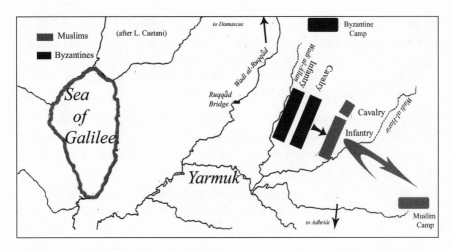

Figure 6.3   Yarmûk 636: The Initial Stage

across the right side of the upper course of the Wâdi Ruqqâd between the wâdi and the old Roman road.[19]

The terrain the Muslims had chosen to make a stand was a plain protected by mountains and the Sea of Galilee on the left and was without major obstacles (Figure 6.3). The area was intersected by three wâdi flowing south from the northeast, while the Yarmûk River flowed southeast, creating a triangular terrain in the junction with the major wâdi, the Ruqqâd. The peaceful nature of the flow of the wâdi (an irregular course of water) hid a trap, however. At one point during the southward course their waters were marked by sharp falls (about 160 meters in the case of the Wâdi al-Ruqqâd, 80 for the Wâdi al-Harir, which ran on the extreme right). It was less precipitous in the case of the central Wâdi al-Állan in the center. The sudden falls created deep holes in the terrain with water incongruously the color of snow in the scorched landscape.[20]

When the Muslims withdrew in the direction of Dayr Ayûb, the Byzantines must have followed and probably deployed parallel to the enemy. That was a mistake. Assuming that the terrain south was within the Muslim sphere of influence, any Byzantine retreat had but two alternatives: north (but what would happen if the Muslims closed that road?) or west. Any retreat west would have been difficult. The Ruqqâd was almost impossible to cross, because at the battle's location it ran into a gorge. The only solution could have been an old Roman bridge existing across the wâdi, and the Byzantines did post a guard there. But how could a single bridge accommodate thousands of men in retreat with enemies at their backs?

The Byzantines were, as usual, a composite army that included Armenians and Christian Arabs, besides the regular units (Greeks and auxiliaries from various parts of the empire). Having soldiers from various ethnic groups, using different languages and cultural traditions, might not have meant lack of cohesion under normal circumstances. But this situation was not normal. They operated in a region where soldiers had stirred up great animosity among the Jewish and Christian civilians living there. The support of the Christian Arab tribes was not firm. Not even the highest Byzantine officer at Hims in northern Syria had responded to the Byzantine army's requests; when asked for logistic support, he had denied it. Moreover, mistrust and conflict poisoned the army's leaders from the two top commanders, Vahân and Theodore Trithurios, to the lower chiefs.[21]

No major clash took place for about two months while the Byzantines uselessly tried to sow discord within the enemy camp and to make their men familiar with the way the Arabs looked. But why go to such lengths unless some had never met the Arabs in battle? So in about three days, beginning around 20 August 636, the destiny of Syria was decided. The Muslims might have started the battle with some kind of ruse, for they retired from the battlefield quickly and sought refuge in their camp. But in the meantime they left scores of warriors hidden among the bushes and rocks, likely on the Byzantines' left flank; this may have been the commanders' initial plan, or they may have become separated from the rest during the clash. They stayed hidden until the next day, when the Byzantines sought to land the killing blow.

John W. Jandora assumes that the Muslims deployed in a linear formation with two wings, center, and an advance or rearguard, with the right flank anchored on the river as a protection against envelopment.[22] A linear formation makes sense for infantry, although it is unlikely that they would also have had soldiers for either the advance or rearguard. The cavalry under Khâlid ben al-Walâd took its place on the right flank. The line must have been a colorful display of banners of red, yellow, and green.[23]

The Byzantines placed all the cavalry in the first line, supported by the infantry in the second line. The footmen, at least at certain times during the encounter, stood with their shields so close that some would say the soldiers had been chained together. The deployment of the Byzantine cavalry makes sense if we assume that they had been ordered to perform what Kaegi calls a mixed formation, that is, the cavalry would move to the attack and then quickly withdraw through the ranks of the infantry. The footmen had to abandon their close formation to let the horses filter through their ranks before closing up ranks again. When the cavalry regrouped, it would then again gallop through the infantry ranks to strike the enemy, repeating the maneuver over and over.[24] The mixed formation would have been difficult even in training; it must have been challenging during the confusion of battle. In any case, the first clash again favored the Byzantines on the right and the left. Apparently the Muslims, defeated all along the line, ran in panic toward the safety of their camp.

Was the Arabs' flight a feigned withdrawal? Or was it a way to draw the Byzantines toward the Muslim camp, where other soldiers, likely archers, were poised to unleash arrows from the safety of a defensive shield formed by animals (camels?) or by the palisade that must have surrounded the camp? Or were the Muslims really running in panic and shamed into action by their women, who greeted them with insults and stones? Regardless, it is logical to assume that the Byzantines must have arrived in the proximity of the enemy camp in disorder and that a gap could have opened between the cavalry and the infantry, either because of the pursuit or because of problems maintaining the mixed formation. At this stage, Khâlid brilliantly took advantage of the situation (Figure 6.4). While the Muslim infantry turned to face the Byzantines, he dashed his horsemen between the enemy cavalry and infantry and struck the infantry's left (now without the support of their horsemen and already in disorder because of their attempt to rout the enemy). Surprise came, and pursuit turned to flight. Many must have been slain by Muslim cavalry and infantry, or by those hidden on the battlefield the day before. A dust storm must have increased the plight of the Byzantines, who likely were less accustomed to such an event. Some gave little resistance and sat on the ground, hoping that the Muslims would take them prisoner and thus spare their life. They were slaughtered on the spot, for Muslims took no prisoners.

The Muslims followed up their tactical superiority with strategic brilliance (Figure 6.5). The cavalry moved to displace the Byzantine guard from the bridge that crossed the Ruqqâd while other soldiers moved to occupy the Byzantine camp located to the north, near Jabiya. With the enemy pressing from the west, the south also under enemy control, the bridge guarded by Muslim troops, and the north crowded by those who had stormed their camp, the Byzantines' only exit must have been across the Ruqqâd Gorge.

As night descended the fighting stopped. But darkness brought neither silence nor rest. The Muslims launched a new attack, and the Christian Arabs who had fought alongside the Byzantines left the battlefield. Soon the terrain echoed with the terrifying din of Muslim shouts and battle cries. Shadows suddenly changed into blades that penetrated flesh. The wind brought the cries of comrades as the enemy stealthily penetrated the ranks among the

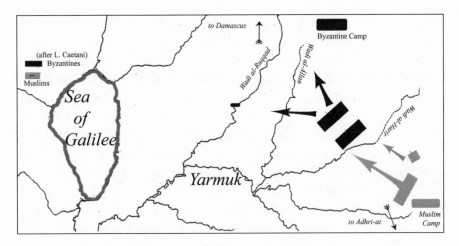

Figure 6.4   Yarmûk 636: The Muslim Counterattack

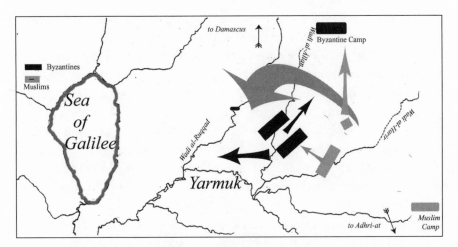

Figure 6.5   Yarmûk 636: The End of the Battle

infernal noise of cymbals, drums, and battle cries.[25] It must have been even more terrifying because they had not expected the Muslims to attack by dark. Dying on the spot meant a less fearsome end compared to those who tried to escape across the Ruqqâd Gorge. There they had to contend with the enemy as well as the pitch-black water, lightened by the silvery streaks. Many escaped the battlefield only to be swallowed up by the waters of the wâdi.

Even with the battlefield in their possession and after three days of fighting, the Muslims were not satisfied. Smarting from the heavy losses they had suffered, the Muslims realized that total destruction of the enemy may have meant mastery over Syria. They spared no one on the battlefield and pursued the Byzantines many kilometers north,[26] until those who escaped, men and leaders, had few choices. Some, like the Christian Arab tribes, joined the Muslim war machine, although not necessarily embracing Islam; others reached the safety of northern cities under Byzantine control like Antioch and Edessa; others, especially the leaders, may have entered monasteries to escape the hunt as well as the wrath of the emperor, quick to find scapegoats; others sought refuge in the garrison cities where they could survive until those places fell. There was no meaningful reaction from the emperor. As Kaegi writes, Byzantium "became completely numb or inert" as its supremacy in Syria crumbled. "It was a thorough and catastrophic defeat."[27] But Whitby doubts that the battle showed that the Byzantines were inferior militarily to the Muslims. They lost, he says, because of friction among the army's commanders, the rebellious behavior of some contingents, inferior tactics, logistical problems, and adverse weather conditions.[28] So if the Byzantines lacked proper logistics and tactics, they must have been inferior to the Muslims.

After Yarmûk, the third phase of the conquest of Syria took place. It lasted about eleven years (from 637 to 647–648), during which the main cities fell into Muslim hands: Damascus, Aleppo, Jerusalem, Caesarea, Tyre, Sidon, Beirut, Antioch. After Yarmûk the Byzantines did not dare face Muslim armies on the battlefield, and so the process of Islamic conquest was carried out by smaller forces according to the objective of the moment. Byzantine resistance, fractured during the second phase, was virtually eliminated during the Muslim consolidation despite the fact that Byzantium still commanded good support at the local level. Actually by the end of the period Muslim armies had moved into Egypt and now were attacking the Byzantines even in their lands in Anatolia. In 642 Alexandria, the seat of Hellenism, fell to the Muslims, and the Byzantine fleet, with the army aboard, set sail for Byzantium, leaving behind a land that for centuries had been an integral part of the Roman Empire. Arab armies then penetrated deep into Asia Minor. The region that suffered most was Cappadocia, which was sacked repeatedly. It was only in the eighth century that the Muslim advance was stemmed.[29]

The Conquest of Iraq

Unlike Syria, the core of Iraq is flat, its fertility assured by two great rivers, the Tigris and the Euphrates, as well as their tributaries. Mountains appear on the border with Persia and in the north. It was a land of contrasts, the people divided by geography, class, religion, and ethnic backgrounds. Arab nomadic tribes were prevalent in the desert and steppe along the western fringes of the flatlands. The Sassanians had kept the populations living there under control through a variety of means: building garrisons where the desert ended, absorbing certain tribes into the Persian army, and using the Lakhmid kings of al-Hira to keep the nomadic tribes in check. But by the time the Muslims appeared on the edge of the desert, the rule of the Sassanians (226–651) had been considerably weakened by years of war with the Byzantines who, in one of their forays into Sassanian lands, had sacked the Great King's estates and threatened even Ctesiphon, the capital. Moreover, the Sassanians, during their most recent conflict with the Byzantines, had lost Egypt, Syria, and northern Mesopotamia and had been compelled to pay an annual indemnity to Byzantium, an onerous task since floods had decimated the land. If this were not enough, succession conflicts had marred the empire when the king was murdered by his own son and the state fell prey to various claimants to the throne.[30] Finally, the buffer zone provided by the Lakhmids disappeared once the Sassanians, upset over the king's lack of support in a trying moment, had thrown him to his death under the feet of an elephant and established an ephemeral ruler (he did not last long) in al-Hira.[31] Taking these conditions into consideration, the surprise is, says Donner, that the Sassanians "could still put up very stiff resistance to the invading Muslims."[32]

One reason for the strong resistance must have resided in the faulty Muslim conquest policy (Figure 6.6). While the attack on Syria was unrelenting, the invasion of Iraq went hot and cold, always secondary to what happened on the eastern shores of the Mediterranean. Yet if Medina could be criticized for uncertain policy on Iraq, strategy was, as always, masterful. For a long time they kept their troops on the edge of the alluvial lands within or close to the desert. The idea was to first conquer the nomadic tribes before moving against the urban centers in the center and the eastern side of the Tigris and Euphrates—but always in a careful manner. Even at the eve of the Battle of al-Qâdisiyya, Caliph Umar (634–644), the successor of Abû Bakr, specified what should be the policy of the army: "Let your people be on the border between the desert and the cultivated land, on the sandy tracks in between; then stay in your place, and do not move from it," he warned the army's commander. The commander had to remain in that location, for "if you lose your battle, the desert will be behind you. You will retreat from the edge of the cultivated land to the edge of your desert; there you will have more courage and will know the terrain better. Your enemies, on the other hand, will be fearful and

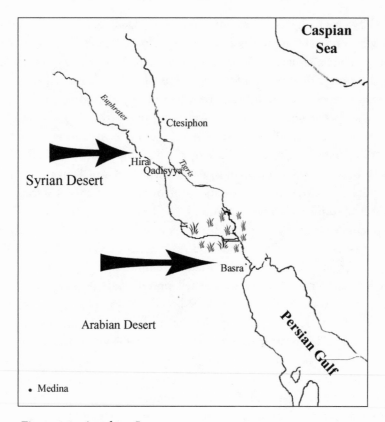

Figure 6.6   Attack on Iraq

ignorant of the terrain. Eventually, God will grant you victory over them and provide you with another opportunity to attack."[33]

Another problem was the fact that the Muslim armies were separated due to the terrain, as a large swamp separated the south from the center. This meant that action in the south, where the population was smaller, was directed against small Sassanian garrisons and the various villages. Supremacy north of the swamp involved large urban centers, which meant large confrontations on the battlefield. Actually, the first major encounter ended in defeat for the Muslim forces at the Battle of the Bridge. The conflict had taken place on the banks of the Euphrates in a location where a bridge connected the opposite banks. The Muslim commander had inexplicably crossed the bridge and engaged the Sassanian troops on the opposite side. It was foolhardy, for he cut off his own troops and placed his soldiers in dire danger. Something terrifying awaited the Muslims on the opposite side, where they came face to face with elephants whose noise and ferocity surprised them. One of the elephants trampled a leader to death. In desperation an Arab from the Thaqif tribe cut the bridge to destroy all hopes of salvation and to compel his comrades to fight. But nothing could be done to save the day. Most ran away from the battlefield; the others met their end under the blows of the Sassanians.[34]

After the Battle of the Yarmûk the caliph decided that the time had arrived for a final confrontation in Iraq. The army that assembled under the command of Saʿd Abî Waqqâs, a veteran of Badr and one of the first companions of the Prophet, was quite different from those sent to Iraq from 633 to around 636. Previous armies had been composed only of Medina volunteers or from the city's neighborhood, tribal units gathered on the way to Iraq, and Iraqi tribesmen who had converted to Islam. Those who had fought earlier against Islam, and any late converters, had been excluded. The final push for supremacy was carried instead by a heterogenous host, including those who had finally seen the light.[35]

As Saʿd marched toward Iraq, new recruits from the Njid tribes and from Caliph Umar, who kept sending new troops from Medina, swelled his host. Saʿd wintered on the edge of the desert. With the arrival of spring he moved closer to central Iraq, stopping at Sharaf while new tribal units joined him. By the time he arrived near al-Qâdisiyya, Saʿd commanded a host somewhere between 6,000 and 38,000.[36] (Donner thinks that it was between 6,000 and 12,000.[37]) By this time the Sassanians had become aware that the Muslims were a threat to their empire. They assembled a rather large army, probably between 20,000 and 30,000, although the estimates of Muslim writers range from 60,000 to more than 100,000.[38] What we can say with certainty is that the numbers of both armies have been inflated. Donner maintains that in spite of its importance "the battle of al-Qâdisiyya appears to have been a clash between two rather small armies."[39] Yet the behavior of the Sassanian king (unable to assemble another large army after al-Qâdisiyya), and the importance of the encounter to the Muslims, suggest the likelihood of larger hosts, less than 20,000 for Saʿd, less than 30,000 for the Sassanians.

Al-Qâdisiyya was a small town on the edge of the desert, not far from al-Hira. It had a fort, cultivated fields, and a palm grove (Figure 6.7). The desert was four to six miles on the west. Saʿd set his camp at ʾUdhaib, where the desert ended.[40] The Sassanian king, Yadzdgard, had recalled his general, Rustam Farrukhzâd, the head of the Sassanian host, from his command of the armies in Azerbaijan. But when Rustam's army approached al-Qâdisiyya, he remained largely inactive for about four months trying to find some kind of

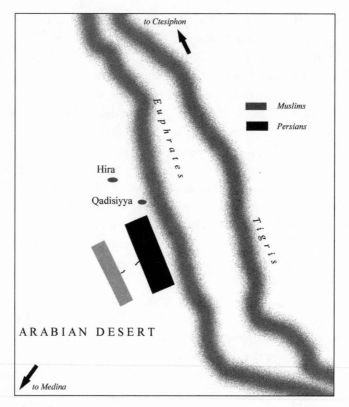

Figure 6.7   Qâdisiyya, July 637

diplomatic solution. The Muslims were deaf and blind to his proposals, and the battle was joined around the middle of June 637.[41]

The clash involved three to four days of intensive fighting. The Muslim army commander, Sa'd, was unable to lead his men into battle. Afflicted by either boils or sciatica and unable to ride a horse, he lay face-down on cushions while observing the action from a distance.[42] But apparently he was able to convey instructions to his troops, combining religious fervor and practical advice: "Handle your enemies like lions of the forest; be stern like tigers, and let dust be your armor. Trust in God and lower your eyes. If your swords become blunt . . . throw stones at your enemies, because it is permitted to do with stones what is not permitted to do with iron."[43]

As seems to have been the common initial stand in all Muslim pitched encounters, they waited for the enemy to move against their line. "Stay in your position," ordered Sa'd, and do not move anything before you perform the noon prayer. When you complete the noon prayer, I shall proclaim "God is most great." Proclaim the same and prepare yourselves. Know that none before you was given [the right to proclaim] "God is most great," and know that it was given to you as a sign of support for you. Then when you hear me proclaiming "God is most great" for the second time, proclaim the same and let your equipment be ready. When I proclaim "God is most great" for the third time, proclaim the same, and let your horsemen [the commanders] encourage the people to step forward and charge their adversaries. When I proclaim "God is most great" for the fourth time, all of you must move forward, mingle with the enemy, and say: "There is no power or strength except in God."[44]

Rustam, the Sassanian commander, placed himself away from the first line but in easy communication distance to his subordinate commanders. He sat on a throne covered with a sunshade. He arranged his elephants along the whole line, eight on the right, eighteen in the center, and seven on the left.[45] The battle opened with individual combats every day of the encounter, as the Muslims seem to have done since Muhammad's time.[46] When the duels ended, the elephants rushed against the Muslim line, causing great distress to Sa'd's troops, who initially were unable to deal with the pachyderms. Finally, they realized that if they stepped at the side and cut the girth of the howdahs, it would cause the riders to fall to the ground, rendering the animals leaderless. The ploy worked well, and as the sun fell to the west and darkness started to envelop the battlefield, the Muslims were able to push the enemy attack back.[47] At this stage the advantage must still have remained with Rustam's troops.

The battle turned decisively in the Muslims' favor on the second day. After the opening duels between the champions, the Muslims used a stratagem to cause disarray among the Sassanian ranks, who were unable to use their elephants since their howdahs had not been repaired during the night. The Muslims placed veils and some kind of platform atop their camels so that they would appear to be elephants. Surrounded by protective screens of cavalrymen, the camels moved toward the Sassanian lines, causing chaos among their horses. As Al-Tabarî dryly puts it, "These camels were not able to withstand anything, yet the Persian horses took fright and fled."[48] The Muslim cavalrymen remained on the battlefield from sunrise to midday. From midday on the infantry took its turn.[49] They stayed on the battlefield until midnight. But the most important event of the day between sunrise and midnight was the arrival of a Syrian contingent from the east. Recalled from there on the caliph's order, they had marched across the Syrian Desert to join their comrades. They seem to have arrived in small groups; as they reached the battlefield they were fed into the fray, bringing new and unexpected forces to the battle.[50]

When the new day opened the Sassanians again sent the elephants to the attack. This time the pachyderms advanced while surrounded by a screen of infantry protected by cavalry.[51] The Sassanians, beaten physically and morally the previous day, made no headway against the Muslims, whose morale must have been high indeed. The fight continued until night; probably it never stopped. In any case, the next day the Sassanians began their retreat. By noon, Muslim pressure, and probably a dust storm, were instrumental in breaking the stability of the Sassanian line. A gap opened, placing the whole army in danger. And then General Rustam lost his life. When the sandstorm blew away the sunshade from his throne, Rustam had taken refuge behind mules standing nearby, their loads still on their backs. It was not a safe place. A Muslim cut the ropes of one mule's load: it fell on Rustam. The weight displaced a vertebra in his spine. Still, the general tried to save himself by escaping to a nearby river. But the Muslim warrior pursued him, entered the waters, grabbed the general by a leg, dragged him to the bank, and killed him. As the sandstorm began to settle, the Sassanians fled, seeking safety eastward.[52]

The Battle of al-Qâdisiyya found a special place in Muslim history. The victory gave Muslims control over the rich alluvial lands between the Tigris and the Euphrates. Yet the Muslim victory at al-Qâdisiyya did not mean the end of Sassanian rule in Iraq and Persia. It did deprive the Sassanians of the ability to assemble another large army. After al-Qâdisiyya, action shifted to the walled cities.

It took some time for the Muslims to realize the magnitude of their success, and they seem to have hesitated in launching an attack against Ctesiphon (al-Madâin). The capital, located along both banks of the Tigris, was actually a group of cities, the most important being Ctesiphon and Selleucia, besides six others. Surrounded by strong walls, Ctesiphon withstood the Muslim siege for about two years (the sources say that the Muslims were able to consume fresh dates twice). In the long run, famine and unrelenting Muslim pressure were more than the defenders could withstand. When King Yadzgard, with a retinue of thousands, escaped east, the defenders opened the gates to the Muslims, who found unbelievable treasures in dresses, jewels, and weapons.[53]

The last encounter was at Jalula, where the Sassanian troops surrounded their camp with a palisade of wooden and iron stakes. Afterward the conquest of the remainder of the Persian Empire continued with smaller encounters and sieges in Media, Kurisân, Sistân, and Transoxiana, but the Muslims never forgot that their main prey was Yadzdgard, the king. After escaping again and again, he fell at the hands of a nameless assassin in 651.[54]

Why the Muslims Won

It is nearly impossible to gain a clear view of the armies of the Muslim conquest. Muslim sources are often unreliable, especially in regard to numbers and the way the fighting was carried out. The main obstacle seems to have been the fact that the accounts followed *topoi* (themes) that were often identical for all descriptions of warfare.[55] Despite the inaccuracy and exaggeration, it is possible to describe some distinctive features of early Islamic warfare.

The defeat of the Byzantine and Sassanian empires appears impossible on paper, for the early Muslim armies were not as sophisticated or as strong as their adversaries. Yet they did have strategic primacy, organization, and leadership. Caliphs played a central role during the early stages. Armies were recruited from the most eligible or the most willing warriors of each tribe. Then, after assembling near an urban center, mainly Medina, the caliph dispatched the men to the front lines, in Syria or Iraq, depending on the needs of the moment. Caliphs seemed to have kept a close eye on what the campaigns needed as well as how units should be used even after the troops reached the operational zone. All this implies centralization of authority, a subject of intense debate among Islamists. Donner thinks that Medina exercised control over most of the decisions on how, when, and where to unleash the Muslim soldiers.

If the caliph was a careful overseer of the military situation, early Muslim armies seem to have been blessed by skillful military leaders, most of them early supporters of Muhammad during his lifetime and thus early converters to Islam. Even more crucial was their strategic mobility. Coming from unexpected places and covering enormous distances must have struck fear into the hearts of opponents. For a long time their armies were footmen, horsemen assuming a primary role in the ninth century. But the reality was that the footmen may have come to the battlefield on horses and camels, which they dismounted before joining battle as archers or spear-holding infantry. Hugh Kennedy, like most historians, finds the lightning success of the early Muslim armies puzzling and agrees that mobility must have been one of the Muslims' advantages.[56] D. R. Hill argues that "the superior mobility of the Arabs was . . . one of the most important factors in ensuring their success in the early conquests."[57] The key was the capacity of the camels and dromedaries to cover distances in a desert environment that would have killed horses. This held true in Syria, Iraq, and Egypt, but not in Persia, Armenia, or Asia Minor, where horses performed better.[58] Thanks to their mounts, Muslims were able to switch armies quickly from one front to another and appear in places seemingly out of nowhere. Moreover, they were able to keep their lines of communication open and use them efficiently even on the battlefield. For instance, before the great Battle of al-Qâdisiyya, the Muslims, conscious of their inferiority vis-à-vis the Sassanians, operated only from bases at the fringes of the desert, where they could strike quickly into enemy territory before returning to the desert, where neither Sassanian horse nor footmen dared to enter.[59] If victorious, they pursued the enemy ruthlessly, aiming at total destruction. Such was the case at Yarmûk.

The mobility of the Muslims was heightened by the small number of noncombatant followers. But women did accompany them. At Yarmûk the women seemed to have been instrumental in convincing their men to stop their retreat and make a stand against the Byzantines. At al-Qâdisiyya there were 1,000 unmarried and 700 married women with the army, but never enough for all the soldiers. After al-Qâdisiyya the warriors were compelled to take Christian and Jewish women as wives.[60]

Finally, an essential element of the Muslim success was without doubt their religion. This is not to deny the importance of religion among the Byzantines. Emperors consciously used icons, the cult of the virgin, and the image and relics of the cross to gain their soldiers' loyalty and to heighten their fervor in battle.[61] Yet the Christian God had not yet become the God of the Crusades, whereas the Muslim God promised His faithful not only great earthly rewards but a prize in the afterlife, which made sacrifice on the battlefield much more easy to face.

As for the tactical characteristics of the Muslim armies, the evidence offers diverging conclusions. The soldiers of each tribe may have fought as a single, monolithic unit. More likely such was not the case. The tribal leaders did play an important role on the battlefield but as part of an elite group, not necessarily at the head of their tribal units, which were dispersed along the battle line.[62]

It seems that Muslims divided their battle line in several main blocks. Always present was the "heart" (center) together with two wings (flanks). More often the deployment also included an advance and rearguard. The core of the Muslim army remained the infantry (archers and spearmen). The cavalry, if present, was made up of spearmen.[63] Muhammad himself considered archers to be essential. He encouraged archery training, and at Badr he deployed them to defend a flank menaced by enemy cavalry. Archers must have been important against the Sassanian and Byzantine armies, in which cavalry was the most prized unit.

Battles opened with individual duels. This was the case at al-Qâdisiyya and at Badr, the first great victory of the Prophet. After the duels the encounter may have continued with a discharge of arrows before the spearmen, red, yellow, and green banners flowing in the wind, moved to the hand-to-hand clash, where first spears and then swords tried to finish the adversary. The advance was marked by intense noise and shouts, which could be religious statements of praise to a great warrior from the distant past to which each group claimed association.[64]

As Hugh Kennedy discusses in his excellent book on the armies of the caliphs, our knowledge of the armor and equipment of the armies of the conquest is limited.[65] What can be said with certainty is that the Muslims' primary weapons were the sword, spear, and bow. The most cherished weapon of both horsemen and footmen was the straight sword, probably about 100 centimeters in length. It was used in both a cutting and a thrusting motion. The lore about the qualities of the sword is an obligatory topic in Arabic literature. Iron maces and bars were also common. Muslims used different types of spears. One was quite long (6–7 meters), although that spear, mentioned at times, must have been unusual and probably used only for standards. After arrow volleys, spears must have been the primary weapons in the initial clash of infantry both in thrusting or, held in both hands, in a slashing motion from side to side. The spear was also extremely effective against cavalry charges. Cavalrymen used swords in face-to-face combat after first using lances. The other type of spear was shorter, less common, and more like a javelin. Another unusual weapon was the *naft*, an incendiary material, likely manufactured from the oil surfacing in some regions of the Middle East, but not similar to the so-called Greek fire that the Byzantines used against the Muslims during the siege of Constantinople in the seventh century. We do not know what machine was used to throw the *naft*. Finally, bowmen may have used two types of bow: the typical light one of the Arabs, and the heavier one of Persian armies. It was the weapon of footmen, although with the passing of time and the integration of men from the former Sassanian Empire, its use expanded to the cavalry. It seems that the range of a bowshot was between 180 and 240 meters.[66] Of course, its killing range depended on the type of target, whether one wore armor, and the body part that was hit.

At least initially, armor must have been the privilege only of leaders and elite units. Their most important item was the mail coat, probably a leather or quilted cloth garment onto which small plates of mail had been sewn. It seems that at times two coats were worn: a smaller one of armor over a longer one, probably made of leather or quilted cloth. Sometimes a coif to protect the neck was worn beneath the helmet; sometimes an aventail (a protective piece of iron) hung on the back of the helmet for the same function. Also, some protection was devoted to legs and arms. Both infantry and cavalry carried small shields, although at times individuals entered the fray without them, even without armor, for they must have sought martyrdom in falling for the cause of the faith. Shields were circular and rather small, normally less than 1 meter in diameter.[67] Stirrups were introduced slowly.[68] In the West the introduction of the stirrup was an important element in the development of heavy cavalry, but such was not the case in the East, where Muslim armies preferred lightness and mobility over power.[69]

The Muslims' lightning conquest was not due to numerical superiority. At the battle that spelled the beginning of the end for the Sassanian Empire in Persia, the Muslim force was 6,000–12,000 and no more than 20,000; at Yarmûk, the battle in which the Byzantines lost the Middle East, the Muslim host had no more than 40,000 and probably as few as 20,000–24,000; the conquest of southern Iraq was carried out by a host of 2,000–4,000.[70] Nor were the Muslim armies the result of a vast movement of peoples, as with the barbarians in Europe. Rather it was an elite force of nomadic tribes, with sedentary people usually joining from Mecca and Medina. But what they lacked in numbers and technology was counterbalanced by the belief that God was on their side here on earth and in the afterlife. Nor was the lure of riches secondary in their minds. In a region where deprivation was the rule, the lands of Byzantium and Persia must have seemed like an Eldorado. And even if conquest did not translate into riches, the expectation of a steady salary must have been powerful.

As the Muslims advanced into territories during the first wave of conquests, they did not seek proselytes to their creed. They created new garrison cities or set up garrisons within the cities they had conquered. There the invading forces were stationed and rewarded in a manner that took into consideration their allegiance to Islam and to its military expansion. All the warriors were registered in *diwân* and paid a certain amount of money yearly and rations in kind monthly. The pay was scaled according to the date of the individual's acceptance of Islam. This meant that early converts received a much higher compensation than later ones—2,000 dirhams (silver coins) for the highest, 300 for the lowest. Moreover, at least initially, the warriors received shares of the revenues derived from the lands they had conquered. Wives and children of the warriors also received a stipend—100 dirhams for wives and 700 each for both male and female children. The registered men paid no taxes but were obliged to give alms to the poor *and* to perform military service. The penalty for refusing military service could involve the cancellation of the stipend permanently.[71]

The assumption behind this arrangement was that leaders did not want soldiers to settle down but to remain an army of occupation to keep order and to be ready for future military campaigns. This system worked well at the beginning and must have been a great inducement; once one was registered in the *diwân*, the pay applied to descendants. However, problems developed on two main issues: who among the newcomers to Islam should be registered in the *diwân*; and how much of the income from the provinces should be forwarded to the head of the Muslim community, the caliph. Also, if the campaign was unpopular it was difficult to gather an army.[72] And the army, once gathered, could not be efficient, for the people registered in the *diwân* may have lost the desire to fight like the ancestor who had first entered the ranks.

The early army was essentially a Muslim army, but with victory important enemy soldiers started to pass into the ranks. For instance, on the eve of the Battle of al-Qâdisiyya it is reported that 4,000 soldiers of the Sassanian host passed into the Muslim army in exchange for a salary and the authorization to settle anywhere they wanted. The same happened for 4,000 more soldiers from northern Iran, also in the war against the Sassanians, again for a paid salary. At the civil war Battle of Siffîn there were about 8,000 non-Arabs out of 70,000 soldiers.[73] Yet for quite a long time it was not the policy of the Muslim armies to recruit soldiers from other ethnic groups. In the long run, as the idea of conversion started to apply also to non-Arabs, the initial genetic pool (at most 500,000 Arabs) became diluted as some kind of assimilation or acceptance of non-Arabs into the military became commonplace. It could not have been otherwise when we realize that 500,000 Arabs would eventually rule over 20–30 million non-Arabs from Persia to North Africa.[74]

Muslim success benefited from the attitudes of the subject civilian populations. Syria, Palestine, and Egypt had become accustomed to a continuous changeover of governors. The new conquerors may have seemed even better than those of the past. The government changed, but their lifestyles did not.

As long as they paid taxes, they could keep their religion and even occupy important civilian posts, for the Muslims realized from the beginning that they had to rely on the experience of the former Byzantine and Persian administrators.[75]

The conquest of Syria, Egypt, Iraq, and Persia changed that world forever. But the conquest did not stop in Persia. Central Asia, or at least a portion of it, was open to the Muslims. Eventually, the Indian subcontinent would be another prize, but for the moment the coast of northern Africa was more tempting. It was the road to Spain and to Sicily.

Chapter Seven

The Muslim Strike into North Africa and the Iberian Peninsula

THE MUSLIMS SAW THE BERBERS from a distance. They were lined up on the rocky terrain not far from a group of houses vividly painted in powerful earth color, mostly red on white but at times also blue and yellow. Their standing seemed incongruous with the vitality of the habitations, for they sat motionless on the ground, closely jammed to each other, a forest of long spears in their hands in the first line, shorter spears in the rear ranks. They were covered from head to toe in indigo clothing that seemed black in the distance. The only uncovered parts of their bodies were the eyes, hands, and feet. There were also a few men on horses, a colored cloth functioning as a saddle-cloth. The sky was a clear, cobalt blue. Far away one could discern the beginning of a sandy landscape golden in color.

The Muslim commander kept a careful eye on the Berber flag's position, which for the moment was held at the diagonal. He knew that when the flag was raised, the Berbers would rush to the attack. He had been told that Berbers were magnificent fighters, willing to die more than surrender. In combat they knew only one motion: to move forward, never retreat, never run away. Their long spears in the front ranks were used mainly to defeat an attack, while the short spears were formidable instruments of death, for they rarely missed. They also launched attacks from the backs of horses and camels. They could have been much more formidable opponents if only the various tribes had formed larger confederations, leaving behind the old hatreds and vengeance.[1]

The Conquest of North Africa

There is controversy on the origins of the Berbers. One reasonable theory is that the Berbers were the result of the union between prehistoric inhabitants and an eastern population, the Libou (ancient Libyans). Clearly those living in the areas close to the Mediterranean must have intermarried with Semitic people like the Carthaginians and, later, with Romans, Byzantines, and Vandals. It was from the Romans that they received their name: Berbers, from the Latin word *barbari* (barbarians), that is, people speaking neither Latin nor Greek. On their south, where the Sahara dominated, Berbers must have intermingled with blacks. This meant that the Berbers had experienced cultural and genetic contacts with ancient Libyans, Egyptians, Phoenicians (Carthaginians), Romans, Byzantines, Vandals, and black Africans.[2]

Their original region was called Maghrib (Land of the Sunset) by the Arabs (Figure 7.1). The term meant all the area west of Egypt, including the modern nations of Libya, Tunisia, Algeria, and Morocco. The Arabs also used "Ifrîqiya" only to refer to the eastern section, roughly from Tunisia to the coast up to Egypt. The Maghrib consists of a coastal strip of about 4,200 kilometers from the border of Egypt to the Atlantic Ocean. Most of the area, from Tunisia to Morocco, is highland. The average altitude in Tunisia is 300 meters, 900 in Algeria, and 800 in Morocco. The area bordering the sea has a Mediterranean climate with fertile regions. Where the Mediterranean climate ends, there is, except in Egypt, an intermediate region in which arid conditions become increasingly prevalent as one moves south, where the Great Sahara begins. Algeria and Morocco are characterized by mountain ranges; the highest peak, the Tubkal, reaches 4,150 meters.[3]

The conquest of Egypt was easy for the Muslims. The Byzantine troops stationed there gave little resistance when 'Amr b. al-'As invaded in 642. The successive conquest of the African coast west of Barqa seems not to have been intended initially as a strategic necessity. For the next twenty-five years, all forays westward were for looting.[4] Several reasons dictated the Muslims' reluctance to move west of Alexandria and then Barqa. The central authorities, first at Medina and later at Damascus, were far from the area in question and did not have a good grasp of the geography beyond Egypt. Moreover, they saw that area as an ideal target for lucrative raids more than for occupation; and when the results of the raids were made public, they increased conflicts within the Muslim community between those who insisted that all revenues should go to the original Muslims, and those who

Figure 7.1 North Africa

felt that populations in North Africa who had shared in the military campaigns should also share in the benefits.[5]

The raids along the African coast began the same year of the conquest of Egypt when a contingent of about 4,000 men under 'Amr pushed west, conquering Barqa. They continued afterward with several small expeditions. The next major campaign took place in 647. It was an enterprise engineered from Medina. The Caliph 'Uthmân b. 'Affân (644–655) was instrumental in assembling volunteers, providing them with equipment, camels, and words of encouragement before they departed for Egypt. The army of about 9,000–10,000 men (with a few Copts as guides) struck past Tripoli, still in Byzantine hands, to move into southern Tunisia. There it met a strong Byzantine host, which they defeated, killing its leader and taking prisoner his daughter. But the Muslims did not settle in the area (a sign that looting, precious metals, and slaves, women, and children were their main concerns) and came back to Egypt with unbelievable riches after fourteen to eighteen months of conquest. Horsemen received a bonus of 3,000 dinars (gold coins worth 12 to 20 dirhams), infantrymen 1,000.[6]

The civil war that broke out among Muslims as a result of the murder of the Caliph 'Umar ibn al-Khattâb (634–644) by a slave in 644, and then also of the next caliph, 'Uthmân b. 'Affân (644–655), slowed the Muslim drive into the new lands. However, the rise of the dynasty of the Mu'âwyids to the caliphate, begun in 661, brought new energy. In 665 a large army of about 10,000 was assembled in Egypt and launched against the west. It penetrated deep into North Africa, defeating a Byzantine army before returning to Egypt carrying heavy spoils, of which the infantry share was 200 dinars. But again their return without bothering to occupy any territory shows that the main goal had been looting.[7]

More than twenty years after their first campaign, the Muslims decided that the time was ripe to despoil the Byzantines of their last remaining strongholds in North Africa, thereby extending the Muslim world up to the Atlantic Ocean. The new policy is symbolized by 'Uqba b. Nâfi' al-Fihrî. 'Uqba was harsh, arrogant, a strong believer in the supremacy of the Arab people, but also gifted with military skill and clear policy goals for the North African territories. Starting probably around 666, at the head of a large army of 10,000 horsemen, he advanced along an unusual route and conquered the southern Tunisian cities of Gudâmis, Qafsa, and Qastîlya, slaughtering all the Christians living there. From there he moved toward the north, founding al-Qayrawân in 670. The city, which was completed about five years later, became the Muslim capital in North Africa. It was far enough from the sea to avoid a surprise attack from the Byzantine fleet and located on the North African steppe, for "we," said the founders, "are camel herders and without them we cannot launch any war." 'Uqba felt that the Byzantine strength in North Africa rested on the support of the Berbers. It was then necessary to establish a permanent basis in North Africa, thus the foundation of Qayrawân, both to ensure the safety of his troops against any rebellion of the local population, and as a base for further conquests in the interior where the Berber tribes dominated.[8]

The sudden and unexpected dismissal of 'Uqba in 675 may have been dictated by the realization that a new approach was needed to bring the Berber tribes to the Muslims' side. The Muslims switched to a policy of accommodation with indigenous populations, respecting their structures and local concerns.[9] But seven years later 'Uqba again was appointed head of the North African territory under Muslim control. Leading an army of 5,000 infantry (some sources say 10,000 horsemen) he joined the troops stationed at Qayrawân. As he moved westward from there, 'Uqba increased his host to 15,000.[10] That figure suggests that he must have recruited among the local populations. After failing to subdue Baghâya, to the north of the Aurès Mountains, he arrived at Zâb in Numidia, where he engaged a Berber and Byzantine army. From there, after another engagement, he reached Tangiers before striking south as far as al-Sûs. Later writings said that when he reached the Atlantic, he forcefully moved his horse into the ocean's waters, swearing total dedication to the cause of Islam.[11] It was a gesture—if it really happened—typical of the behavior of a knight whom nothing could stop except the sea.[12]

'Uqba turned east from there. He carried considerable loot, including wonderful horses and women so beautiful that, once in the region controlled by the Muslims, they would fetch 1,000 dinars each. But when he reached Tahûda, south of the mountains, near Biskra, Berber troops attacked and killed him and his party. He had with him 300–5,000 men, having sent ahead most of his forces with the loot. 'Uqba's end points out that the real adversary was not Byzantium, which held nominal control of the Berber coast, but the various Berber forces.[13] They had provided the main opposition in the early stages of 'Uqba's campaign, and they killed him in the end. 'Uqba's death was disastrous for the Muslim forces. They abandoned their posts in North Africa and withdrew to Egypt.

In 688 a new attempt was made with 4,000 Arabs and 2,000 Berbers under the command of Zuhayr b. Qays al-Balawwith. Zuhayr's campaign was successful, but on his return east he was killed when he tried to displace the Byzantines from Barqa, which they had reconquered while Zuhayr was campaigning in western North Africa.[14] So far the whole North African theater had seen failure following success. But finally in 693–694 the Muslims assembled a large army, estimated at 25,000–40,000, under the command of Hassân b. al Nu'mn al-Ghassânî. The caliph's intentions in Damascus had been very clear when he appointed Hassân: "I give a free hand so that you can use the Egyptian revenues to assemble the army. Pay all soldiers that accompany you." In other words, treat Arabs and recruited Berbers equally.

In 695, after a long delay caused by internal turmoil in Iraq, Hassân moved toward Qayrawân. Several Berber tribes joined him as he methodically reestablished Muslim rule in places that either had rebelled or had never been conquered in the past. Reaching Qayrawân with probably 12,000 soldiers and conquering Carthage was fairly easy. But in the interior, near the mountains of western Algeria, he met a formidable opponent in the Kâhina, the charismatic Berber queen of the Jârawa tribe. The Kâhina was a woman who combined an irreducible fighting spirit with the reputation as a prophet and magician. She commanded a great following among the Berber tribes, at least initially. When Hâssan moved against her, she defeated him, slaughtering a great part of his men and pursuing the rest up to Qadis on the Mediterranean coast. Hâssan himself withdrew to Barqa, where he remained for about five years awaiting reinforcements. Once again the Muslim troops had failed and were compelled to withdraw.[15]

Hâssan remained at Barqa for at least three years. In the meantime, the Kâhina gained control of eastern North Africa, except for the city of Qarawân, which she did not conquer, probably fearing a harsh Arab reprisal if the town's civilians were slaughtered. However, she tried to find some means for discouraging them to come again. "The Arabs," she thought, "search for towns, for gold and for silver, but we only seek for pasturage."[16] But she destroyed towns in the region and, as far possible, any trees. Among her Muslim prisoners was a man, Khâlid b.Yazîd al-Qaysî, of whom the Kâhina became so fond that she adopted him as a son. "You are," said the queen one day, "the handsomest and bravest man whom I have ever seen. I wish to give you my milk so that you will become a brother of my two sons." She mixed barley flour with oil, applied the paste to her breast, and then invited Khâlid to eat it together with her two biological sons.[17]

Defeating the Kâhina became a major goal of Hâssan when he finally received reinforcements. This time there was nothing that the Berber queen could do to stop the Muslims because some Berber tribes had deserted her, angry over the destruction she had brought to the land. She went into battle certain of death. Her army was defeated, and she was pursued until Hâssan himself cut off her head with his sword. But just before the battle the Kâhina, worried about her two children and certain of her end, asked the man that she had adopted, Khâlid, to take her two sons to Hâssan, where they converted to Islam and later assumed high positions in the Muslim army and in the administration of the lands the Muslims conquered.[18] The Kâhina's defeat was the last major act of resistance of the Berber tribes. Afterward, the chiefs of several tribes joined the Muslim cause, and 12,000 Berbers were recruited to be part of the Muslim armies under the command of the Kâhina's two sons.[19] Now the coast demanded Hâssan's attention, for the Byzantines had reconquered Carthage. He again expelled them from the city and founded a new town nearby, Tunis, which would become the base of the Arab fleet in the western Mediterranean. Tunis was built on a very strong location, next to a small lake with an isthmus that Hâssan cut, connecting the lake to the sea.[20]

The last stage of the conquest of North Africa was the work of Hâssan's successor, Mûsâ b. Nusair. Mûsâ put an end to the ties between the remaining Byzantines on the coast and their fleet by moving the residents away from the coastal cities and resettling them in the interior. He continued Hâssan's policy of pacification and assimilation of the Berber tribes and brought the western parts of North Africa under Muslim control. Although he was not always completely successful, on the whole his tenure coincided with the suppression of most of the Berber opposition to Islam. He was cruel and ruthless against any tribe that opposed the tenets of the Muslim faith, but generous and lenient to those who converted. He made a point of confirming the old chiefs so that conversion took place with minimum social displacement. Unlike the lightning campaigns of Syria, Iraq, and Persia, the conquest of North Africa had taken about seventy years. After his successful campaigns, Mûsâ moved to Qarawân, leaving in 708 a Berber named Târiq b. Ziyâd as governor of Tangiers and in command of a large array of Berber troops.[21]

The Conquest of Spain

The next target of Muslim expansion was Spain, where another barbarian kingdom had been established in the waning years of the Roman Empire. While the great Roman general Stilicho was engaged in stemming the Visigoths in the early fifth century, new tribes had crossed the Rhine: the Indo-European Alans and the Germanic Suebians and Vandals, the latter divided into two branches, the Silings originating from the river Main, and the Asdings from the River Tiza in Hungary. After ravaging Gallia in 409, those tribes escaped the Roman forces that had moved forward to stop them and crossed the Pyrenees into Spain. The 30,000–40,000 Alans settled in the center, the 80,000 Asdings and the 20,000–25,000 Suebians in the northwest, and the 50,000 Silings in the south.[22] In the manner of all barbarian kingdoms, the peaceful arrangement did not last long. Between 416 and 418, urged by the Romans, the Visigoths who had settled in Gallia moved into central and southern Spain, inflicting terrible losses on the Alans and the Siling Vandals before withdrawing to Gallia. Worried about the Gothic threat always present on their flank and taking advantage of internal disarray in North Africa, the Vandals moved across the Strait of Gibraltar in 428, challenging Constantinople's supremacy in North Africa. They would remain masters of the region until the Byzantine general Belisarius defeated them in 533.

The final barbarian act on the Iberian Peninsula came when the Visigoths moved into most of Spain between 468 and 477. About a century later, the Visigoths assailed the kingdom established in the north by the Suebians in 411, but they never completely subdued the northern part of the peninsula. Pride in independence among the local populations (the Basques most of all) and of the remaining Suebians meant that northern Spain, including the northern part of Portugal, remained conquered only on paper. In the meantime, the troops of Constantinople reappeared in 554, gaining control of southern Spain until 629.

When the Visigoths arrived in Spain in 416, they had shown no respect for the Catholic Church. Either because they belonged to the Arian Church or because they behaved in the manner typical of armies bent on looting, they had sacked churches, defiling and breaking altars, kidnapping nuns, and despoiling the clergy of their vestments.[23] When they returned in 468 to settle indefinitely on the peninsula, they behaved instead with moderation and concern for all. Yet the fact that they were Arian created conflict. The first step was to remove the prohibition of intermarriage during the reign of the Visigothic King Leovigild (567–586). His successor, Recared, went farther. He converted to Catholicism in 587. It was a master stroke that strengthened royal authority and the military power of the kingdom, for now the king could easily use the sources of the religious magnates to his advantage. The administrative mechanism involved summoning all bishops and other primary ecclesiastics together with the powerful lay representatives at regular assemblies that considered religious as well as lay matters. It was a clever way to harness the resources of the kingdom and another example of manipulating religion to rule and to conquer. By the beginning of the sixth century there were some "Romans," that is, former citizens of the Roman Empire, among the soldiers of the Gothic king. It was a tendency that increased over time. King Wamba (672–680) tried to extend the obligation of military service to all regardless of ethnic background and to draft slaves for military duties.

The Iberian Peninsula was a fairly easy conquest for the Muslim armies. Usually three interpretations have been advanced to explain it. The Middle Ages saw it as the punishment of God for a society that had lost its ways. St. Boniface in 746 pointed a finger at the spread of homosexual practices as the cause of the loss of Spain to the Muslims.[24] Modern historiography has moved away from the medieval interpretation and seen the collapse of Spain due to the internal decay of the Visigothic kingdom or as the logical development of the Muslim policy of conquest. Recently the Spanish scholar Pedro Chalmeta has combined the two interpretations. Spain fell because it was a state in "a deep crisis that affected the efficacy and stability of its political, military, juridical, ecclesiastical, economical, and social structures"; the people, once they conquered the Maghrib, were ready to continue their policy of aggression and conquest.[25]

Chalmeta depicts a Spain barren of social peace and justice. The Kingdom of Toledo had experienced in the forty years before the invasion a series of rebellions and upheavals that resulted in the disintegration of central authority and misgovernment at every level. From 672 to 711, four kings were deprived of their throne, and no less than five serious rebellions took place. Nor were the various sovereigns able to rely on the aristocracy, for each ruler tended to reward those who had supported him and to punish those who had not. Rodrigo, the ruler at the time of the Muslim invasion, was considered illegitimate, for he had wrested the throne from King Witiza. Considering the frequent changes of rulers, this meant that the aristocratic bloc, upon which rested the military strength of the state, was never a monolithic entity but fragmented into factions. As the *Crónica del 754* says, "Most soldiers of the Visigothic army were intent only on dethroning Rodrigo [king at the time of the invasion] and on replacing his faction."[26]

Recurrent famine afflicted the country in the 680s and in 707 and 709; and in 708–709 it was the bubonic plague. The problems were heightened because of low productivity, the flight of slaves from their masters, low demographic increases, and lack of technical innovations. The government complicated matters with increasingly harsh taxation and the devaluation of gold coins. It is not surprising that the economic difficulties were reflected in the deterioration of quality of life. Abortions became common; babies were left to die or were sold into slavery. In spite of increasingly harsh punishments, the number of fugitive slaves increased so much that in 702 there was "no city, castle, village, farm where fugitive slaves are not found." One can imagine the attitude of slaves forced to fight for their masters.[27]

While the poverty level increased among the middle and lower classes, the rich tended to become richer as they extended their lands and gained legal control over the poor, who often lost free status to become serfs. At the same time, poverty pushed many to become bandits, others to seek safety as hermits in locations far away from inhabited centers, others to seek spiritual refuge in ancient cults from the pagan past, and others to choose the ultimate act of despair, suicide. As the Toledo Council of 693 pointed out, an atmosphere poisoned by the "contagion of desperation" had fallen over the country.[28] The disadvantaged saw no hope around them. Lack of loyalty and misbehavior were present at all levels of life, even among the privileged people. The aristocrats were ready to betray the loyalty that they had sworn to the crown; the kings were unable to check the rapacious policies of their tax collectors and of the nobility; the most powerful clergymen made a mockery of their vows of chastity and obedience to the precepts of Christ.[29] It was a condition that called either for disintegration of central power or for the reception of any benevolent invader who promised a better world.

The invasion of Spain in 711 is tied to three men: a mysterious individual named Julian of uncertain ethnic background who from sovereignty over Tangiers had been forced to move to Ceuta; the governor of Tangiers, a Berber named Târiq; and the governor of North Africa, Mûsâ. We are not certain who Julian really was, probably a Byzantine or a Visigoth or even a

Berber, but initially he seemed to have been entrusted with safeguarding Visigothic interests across the strait. For instance, when the Arab general 'Uqba arrived at Tangiers in the early 680s, he discouraged him from attempting an invasion of Spain. It was much easier, he said, to move south against the many Berber tribes. But by 709 or so he had changed his attitude. Probably he realized that now that the Muslims had conquered most of North Africa, he had to be their friend to keep what was left of his dominion. Sending the Muslims across the strait may have helped his survival. Probably it was resentment against the Kingdom of Toledo, whose new king, Rodrigo, may have stopped paying the subsidy that Julian had received in the past. The story that Rodrigo had raped the daughter whom Julian had sent to the royal court to refine her manners is likely a fable invented later. The version that either the caliph or Mûsâ had accepted Târiq's proposal to move across the waters also seems to be a later creation. Târiq, probably encouraged by Julian, reached the decision on his own.[30]

The invasion of al-Andalus, the land of the Vandals, as the Muslims would call the Iberian Peninsula, was slow at first, almost a series of predatory raids, but then it became relentless, powerful, and unstoppable. Before Târiq crossed the strait that eventually received his name (Gibraltar, from Gabal Târiq), there had been other attacks against the Spanish coast. They had begun with Julian at the head of 250 men and continued with 500 soldiers led by Tarîf, and then with 1,000 under the command of Abû Zur'a. The army that accompanied Târiq in 711 numbered about 12,000 men, although there were probably only 1,700 at the first landing. At their disposal were four ships owned by Julian. The invaders intended to land at Algeciras, which is the shortest distance between the North African coast and Spain, but when Julian's ships approached the coast, they realized that soldiers were waiting for them, rendering any landing difficult. They followed the coast eastward, landing at the foot of the Rock of Gibraltar. It was toward the end of April 711 (Figure 7.2).

Transporting the troops from Africa to Spain must have taken thirty to forty days considering the limited carrying capacity of only four ships. When all reached the Spanish coast, Târiq had 12,000 Berbers at his disposal. There might have been several dozen black Africans in their midst. The Arabs were few, perhaps less than two dozen.[31] For a while the Muslim troops kept a defensive posture, making sure that all the available soldiers had been transported to the Spanish coast. Also, there were likely few or no Visigoths nearby, or they would have disrupted the landings. King Rodrigo was campaigning in northern Spain, more than 1,000 kilometers distant.

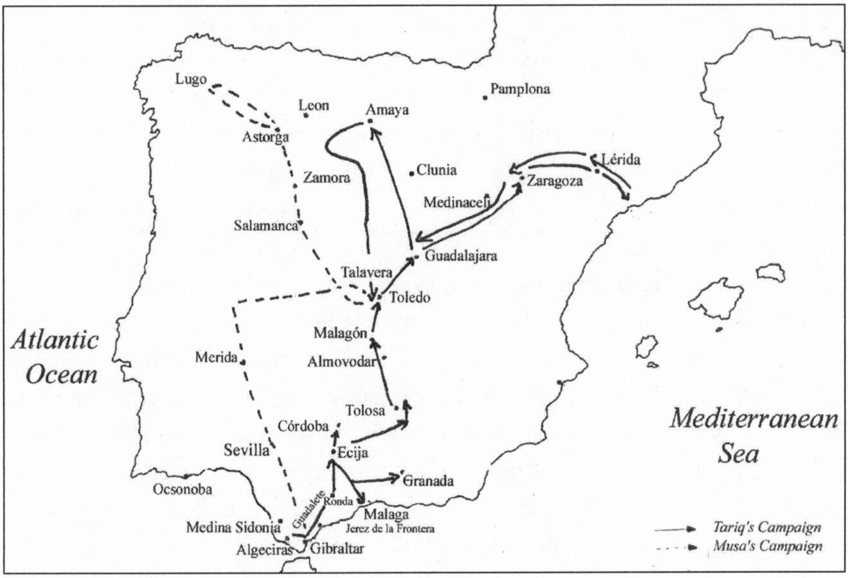

Figure 7.2   Conquest of Spain

Târiq waited patiently for the inevitable reaction of King Rodrigo, who had been informed that "people either fallen from the sky or erupted from the earth's bowels" had come to Spain.[32] In the meantime, the Muslims scoured the neighborhood, especially the Bay of Algeciras, for loot and to get the lay of the land. The confrontation finally arrived about eighty days after Târiq's first landing. The Muslims first touched Spanish soil toward the end of April; they would meet the Visigothic army of King Rodrigo on Sunday, 26 July 711.[33]

Rodrigo's army must have been tired by the time it arrived in southern Spain after a forced march of more than 1,000 kilometers. It was a large host, although the estimates of 40,000–100,000 should be discounted. It was probably, says Pedro Chalmeta, between 24,000 and 30,000, which meant an advantage of 2.4:1 over the Muslims. But the royal host's numerical superiority hid many traps. Some Visigothic soldiers were slaves (by then slaves were being used for military duties). The problem was not that slaves were poor battlefield material but that their marginalization in society and suffering must not have inspired them to fight an invader seen as relieving their disadvantages. But the greatest share of the battle line was in the hands of the aristocracy, which raised another problem. Rodrigo was seen by the supporters of the previous king, Witiza, as illegitimate, and many aristocrats hoped that the Muslims would sweep aside the usurping king and then quickly return to

North Africa with their loot. It was an empty wish, and a misguided desire. But Rodrigo was blind to the situation and tried to come to terms with his alienated aristocracy, trusting both wings of his army to them. Sisberto and Oppa, brothers, not sons as the Arab chronicles maintain, of the former king Witiza, were their commanders. Rodrigo himself led the center.

Likely the encounter took place near the Guadalete River, 30–70 kilometers from Algeciras. We are not sure how long the battle lasted. Guesses are as little as one day from dawn to sunset, to three days, and even to seven between two Sundays, 19 and 26 July 711.[34] The center led by the king fought well. It was at the wings, where the supporters of the former king stood, that the Visigothic host lost the battle. It was probably not due to outright betrayal, and there is no reason to assume that Witiza's supporters passed to the Muslims during the encounter, although it is reasonable to say that their heart may not have been in the fight. Certainly they were the first to flee. In the end the terrain was covered with the dead and dying. King Rodrigo's body was never found. It was said that he drowned in the river or that he sank in mud, an end that symbolically seems fitting for a man who had taken the life of a legitimate king and who lost Spain to the Muslims. Casualties among the Muslims must have reached 25 percent, for after the battle the loot was divided only among 9,000 men; there had been 12,000 on the eve of battle. The casualties among the defeated must have been higher, with almost total destruction of the center. The Visigoths who fought later at Écija must have come from the wings of the Guadalete battle line. The Muslims engaged in a limited pursuit, probably for the next 10–15 kilometers, then regrouped to take care of the wounded and to wait for reinforcements.[35] When news of the victory and loot arrived in North Africa, many more volunteers crossed the waters to join Târiq. It was a badly needed infusion, for if 3,000 were disabled or died, it is reasonable to assume that a similar number may have succumbed to wounds or illness, which meant that the original army of 12,000 had been reduced to about half that number.[36]

Guadalete changed Muslims' Spanish policy. Initially they had been on the defensive. Now they would strike deep into enemy territory. When enough reinforcements arrived to remake Târiq's war machine, the invaders moved toward the main southern centers of Visigothic rule. Their itinerary is a matter of debate, but the most important confrontation, the one that sealed the end of Visigothic Spain, was at Écija, where the remnants of Rodrigo's army had gathered. They would have remained a formidable host if the casualties of the two wings at Guadalete had not been too high. Probably the army was 20,000 men, the same as the Berbers after the arrival of the North African reinforcements. If the Muslims were defeated here, the Visigoths could save their dominion. But failure was near, and any hope that the invaders would soon leave was lost among the Visigoths. After Écija, the military remnants of the Visigothic kingdom would seek refuge in remote locales or to the north and northeast.

The next move by Târiq is remarkable for its military subtlety, although it is likely that he implemented it on Julian's advice. He detached three or four contingents, mostly light cavalry, to conquer the main cities along the northern route and on his right flank as the main body approached the heart of Visigothic Spain, Toledo. One group under the command of a daring leader, Mugît al-Râmî, struck north toward the city of Córdoba; the others took the road southeast toward Málaga and Granada. For the moment, Seville and the northeast, Estremadura and Lusitania, were ignored, probably because Târiq did not envisage any threat coming from there. In reality there was no serious threat arising from any location. After Écija all serious resistance collapsed. The Berbers would find only a few soldiers defending even important cities, the streets populated with the old and the sick. Moreover, it seems that the lower classes were not willing to resist and in several cases joined them. For instance, Córdoba's conqueror, Mugît, had only 700 light cavalrymen. When he stopped in a woods outside the city, a shepherd, captured by his troops, told them that there was a gap in the fortifications near the gate across the bridge. At night an unusually black sky dropped heavy rain. A few Muslims swam across the waters near the gate and reached the gap after scaling the wall with some difficulty. They penetrated the city and captured the guards, who had left their post to take shelter from the rain. As the Berbers gathering outside the gate rushed inside, the city's leader and his men (400 soldiers inside the walls) escaped, taking refuge in a church outside the walls. They resisted there for three months, but eventually their leader was captured while trying to flee toward Toledo. The rest were executed.[37]

The capture of Córdoba is typical of the type of resistance that the Berbers found along the way—few opponents, ready to run away more than to fight, the local population unwilling to support their defenders, although at this stage Christians were badly treated, unlike Jews, whom the Muslims trusted, for the Visigoths had persecuted them. After Guadalete and Écija there were no more important pitched encounters. The Visigoths had given up. They tried to sign favorable terms with the Muslims or moved north and west, where lands were still under the control of Christians. Even Toledo, the capital of their kingdom, seems to have offered no resistance.

There is no doubt that the first phase of the conquest of Spain and most of Portugal was the work of Târiq, a Berber, and of his soldiers, practically all of them Berbers. But then Mûsa, the governor of Ifrîquyia, probably envious of his subordinate's great success, decided to intervene personally. In June–July 712, a year after Târiq's arrival, Mûsâ landed in Spain. He had between 22,000 and 25,000 soldiers, many of them cavalrymen.[38] The governor of Ifrîquiya made a conscious choice to differentiate himself from his subordinate. Mûsâ ordered Julian's ships to land at Algeciras, not at the Rock of Gibraltar; the majority of his men were Arabs, not Berbers; his conquering drive was well-organized administratively; he did not follow in Târiq's footsteps but went to Seville and the west. And after conquering Niebla, Faro, and Meja, he struck toward Mérida. There a Visigothic army came out of the city, inflicting defeat. But where force did not succeed, stratagem would. He laid an ambush in a nearby quarry, achieving a partial victory; it took him few more months of siege and the use of at least one siege engine to defeat the city. Unlike the Berbers, Mûsâ used peace terms that hewed closer to the ideals of the Quran. No civilian was hurt and only the property of those who had died in the ambush or had fled to the north was taken. The rest of the population was subject to taxation.[39]

Mûsâ and Târiq met west of Toledo. It was a contentious meeting that combined envy, anger (Târiq may have used prerogatives to which he had no right), apprehension, fear that the Muslims might have encountered too many dangers in the Iberian Peninsula, and worry over their shares in the spoils. The Berber chief must have feared the encounter, because it seems that he had gone beyond the spirit, if not the word, of explicit orders. When the two finally met, Târiq begged that his behavior be forgiven, passed to Mûsâ the command of his Berber soldiers, and placed all the loot that he had gained at his superior's feet. "I am nothing else than one of . . . your lieutenants. What I have conquered belongs to you," said Târiq humbly. Mûsâ answered, some sources say, angrily, striking him with a whip.[40] But the two patched up their differences and continued the conquest of Spain (Figure 7.3).

The encounter marked the end of Berber supremacy on the peninsula. From then on the Spanish and Lusitanian campaigns were under the direction of Mûsâ and his Muslim followers. Mûsâ seemed to have used Târiq and his Berber men as the vanguard of the Muslim army, that is, for the most dangerous missions and to open the advance for Arab troops. The next three centuries of Muslim Spain and Portugal were Arab times, not Berber times.

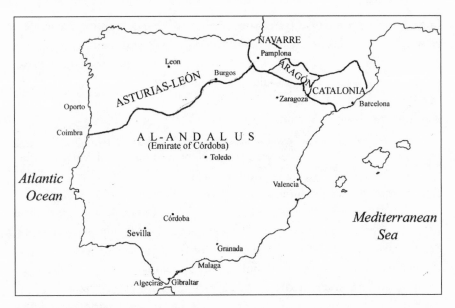

Figure 7.3   Muslim Spain 711–1031

Neither Mûsâ nor Târiq were able to enjoy their success. Both were ordered to leave Spain for Damascus, where Mûsâ was ordered to pay heavy fines and sank into obscurity. He died while traveling to Mecca in 715 or 716. Târiq seems to have encountered a less hostile reception in Damascus, but he disappeared without traces.[41]

War on the West

By 716 the conquest of the Iberian Peninsula was secure. The Christians were not seen or considered to be a threat for the moment. But peace did not return. For decades civil war—Arabs against Berbers, Berbers against Berbers, and Arabs against Arabs—tore apart the social fabric of the Muslim Empire. Despite the conflicts, however, the borders of the dominion remained safe, and an attempt was made to annex French territory. That event marked the limit of Muslim expansion in continental Europe, at least until the Turks brought down the Byzantine Empire.

The Muslim drive across the Pyrenees began soon after the last major pocket of Visigothic resistance fell in 720, but as quickly as they had entered, they had to retrace their steps, for Eudo, Duke of Aquitaine, defeated them near Toulouse. It was a matter that the Muslims could not put to rest. In 725 the governor of al-Andalus, 'Anbasa, penetrated into Aquitaine and conquered the fortified city of Carcassonne before striking deeper into French territory, occupying Nimes, which offered no resistance, and then besieging and sacking Autun in August.[42] He seems to have moved in the direction of Paris, even reaching Sens, about 30 kilometers south. But 'Anbasa died in January 726 during battle. The man that he appointed before his demise brought the Muslim army back to Spain.[43]

The next major expedition took place about eight years later in the aftermath of a strange alliance between the duke of Aquitaine and Munuza, who was in command of a string of Muslim garrison towns on the Pyrenees frontier. Worried about a potential alliance between the Berbers and the Aquitainians, the governor of Spain, 'Abd ar-Rahmân al-Gafîqî, moved against Munuza, hunting him down in the Pyrenees until he finally jumped to his death. Now the turn came for the duke of Aquitaine, who had struck an alliance with Munuza. Gafîqî routed the Aquitainian army near the river Garonne and continued his northward advance, looting as he moved. His goal was the city of Tours, but near Poitiers he met the army of Charles Martel, the Frankish Mayor of the Palace, that is, the actual power in the Frankish lands. The stage was set for a major confrontation.

We know very little about the Battle of Poitiers (or Tours), although mythology has it as one of the greatest battles of all time.[44] But as P. K. Hatti succinctly states, "In reality, it [Poitiers] decided nothing. The Arab-Berber wave already almost a thousand miles from its starting-place in Gibraltar, had reached a natural standstill. It had lost its momentum and spent itself." The main problem was jealousy and discord between the Arabs and Berbers.[45]

What we can say with certainly is that it took place on a Saturday in October 732. The Franks and Muslims faced each other for six days, probably while only skirmishes took place. But the Muslims lost patience and attacked on the seventh day. They played into the hands of the Franks, who were expecting them, deployed in a compact phalanx. They stood like a wall of ice, one source said. The Muslims must have renewed their attack, probably with cavalry, several times. Their casualties were so high that they called the battle's location "the pavement of martyrs." Casualties included their own commander, 'Abd ar-Rahmân al-Gafîqî. The struggle stopped at night's end. In the morning the Franks lined up, ready to renew the fighting; the Muslim forces had left the battlefield during the night.[46]

About two years later the new governor of al-Andalus, 'Uqba b. Al-Hajjâj, again moved into France to avenge the defeat at Poitiers and to spread Islam. It is said that he converted about 2,000 Christians he had captured over his career.[47] After assembling forces at Saragossa he entered French territory in 735, crossed the River Rhône, and conquered and looted Arles. From there he struck into the heart of Provence, ending with the capture of Avignon despite strong resistance. 'Uqba b. Al-Hajjâj's forces remained on French territory for about four years, carrying raids to Lyons, Burgundy, and Piedmont. Again Charles Martel came to the rescue, reconquering most of the lost territories in two campaigns in 737 and 739, except for the city of Narbonne, which finally fell in 759.

The second expedition was probably more dangerous than the first to Poitiers. Yet its failure put an end to any serious Muslim expedition across the Pyrenees, although raids continued. And internal turmoil in the Muslim lands often made enemies out of their own kind.

On to Sicily and Crete

The last major Muslim conquests in Europe were Sicily and Crete in the ninth century. Their conquest was the logical conclusion of a long campaign that challenged the Byzantines on land and at sea. Soon after their conquest of Egypt in the 640s, the Muslims faced a military and logistical problem. As long as they did not have a fleet capable of challenging the Byzantines, they could not long hold any port west of Egypt. However, building such a fleet was not a priority for the caliphs at Medina and later at Damascus. Caliph Umar instructed the conqueror of Egypt: "Let not water intervene between me and thee, and do not camp in any place which I cannot reach with my mount."[48] But a fleet was absolutely necessary to destroy Byzantine control on the southern Mediterranean coast. So eventually two fleets were built, one operating from the Syrian coast, the other from Alexandria. In 649 Cyprus was conquered. In 652 the Muslims defeated a larger Byzantine fleet off Alexandria; the same year they sacked Sicily. Two years later they pillaged the island of Rhodes in the Aegean Sea and in 655 sunk a Byzantine fleet of 500 ships off the southern coast of Asia Minor. About a decade later, in 669, they crossed the Mediterranean to sack Sicily again.[49] In spite of these early successes, it is only toward the very end of the seventh century that the Muslims seem to have gained naval superiority.

In 823 Muslim soldiers, starting in Egypt, began their conquest of Crete. About four years later, in 827, a fleet of seventy vessels with 10,000 warriors and 700 horses, led by a seventy-year-old, left North Africa for Sicily, called there by a rebel. It landed at Mazara on the southeast. Despite the plague, which took the commander, the Muslims advanced to Palermo, which they conquered in 831. It took much longer to subdue the rest of the island. The last Byzantine resistance was centered in Taormina, which fell in 902. But the Muslims had in their sights not only the island but most of Italy. In 837 their fleet threatened Venice and in 846 it landed near Rome. Unable to enter the city, they sacked the Church of St. Peter and the Church of St. Paul outside the walls. The Italian coast remained a favorite hunting ground for Muslim corsair fleets from Spain and North Africa. They also captured Bari, Taranto, and part of Calabria. They were expelled from the mainland by the 880s. Sicily remained in Muslim hands for almost 200 years, until the Normans displaced them.[50]

PART THREE

New Invaders and the Expansion of the West, 800–1300

BY THE EARLY NINTH CENTURY the old Germanic concept that free-man equals soldier weakened. A new concept emerged in the lands controlled by the Carolingians: the soldier was a man of certain means, estimated by how much land he owned and his ties to a greater lord. Over the next five centuries it drastically altered the nature of most Western societies. By 1000 or so, the new soldier that dominates the scene is the *miles*, the armed man, fighting normally but not exclusively on horseback, using lance and sword.

A profoundly different society emerged together with the new soldier. Men would be divided into two kinds: the fighters *(pugnatores)*, and the unarmed people *(inermes)*, whose duty would be to support, with the work of their hands, the new "social managers"—the soldiers. Castles would become omnipresent symbols of the new masters. They were to defend against common enemies and, most of all, stated one's position in society. They would forge and manipulate the destinies of social inferiors. They became symbols of the subjugation of the "unarmed," prisons that were not prisons, places from where taxes and obligatory duties were issued and punishment would come. Eventually, most of the lands were partitioned by royal decree or by force among the lords owing military service to the king, or in turn from the lords to their warriors in exchange for service under arms. The key concept was that land use and land ownership obliged the beneficiaries to provide military assistance at the behest of the lord. This became the system of feudalism.

The period 800–1300 opened with new invaders: Vikings and Magyars. Both were sometimes stopped, sometimes defeated, or redirected toward different goals by the close of the tenth century, although the invasions led to the establishment of new dominions by their descendants, the Normans, in the British Isles and in southern Italy. In tactical terms the impact of heavy cavalry, already crucial under Charlemagne, became even more so in western lands, although in the Muslim territories the primacy of the cavalry, especially light cavalry, seems to have come first. These events took place while major innovations were changing the nature of war. Armor became more sophisticated to meet the challenge of new weapons like the crossbow, or the refinement of old ones like the lance. Soldiers and nobility on horseback were synonymous terms, changing social relationships with the emergence of the knight and the new type of military service. At the same time, the mercenary appeared in increasingly larger numbers. The infantry never disappeared and maintained a crucial role; battle in the open field remained the ultimate choice. Siege warfare would be common, and castles marked the landscape as instruments of defense and even more as statements of power. Finally, internal feuds never ended, especially in places like France and the Italian peninsula. And the West resumed its expansive drive, this time against the Muslims in the Iberian Peninsula and in Sicily, the heathen Slavs in eastern Europe, and the Muslim-controlled Near East.

Chapter Eight ~

Armor, Weapons, and Soldiers

THE IMAGE THAT TYPIFIES AND DISTORTS the period 800–1300 is the armored knight, his lance couched firmly under the arm, riding against the enemy: the rider as master of the battlefield. It is true, however, that this period witnessed a small revolution in the way battles were conducted and how the main combatants fought in attack and in defense. But the knight was not the only effective warrior when it came to face-to-face confrontations.

Riders and Horses

Wearing complex and heavy armor and using the combined power of a couched lance and horse could not have been efficient unless changes were seen in horses, armor, weapons, and the handling of weapons. Mounts had to be sturdy and powerful. By the eleventh century the interpreter of the Battle of Hastings in the Bayeux Tapestry typifies the exalted place given to horses in warfare. He pictures horses in not less than 179 instances and probably in as many as 186. Compare that to five archers in the main account and twenty-three in the lower margin.[1] Horses were part of European warfare from at least the first invasion of Greece by Darius's Persian forces. What became more common in the Middle Ages was the skill for breeding stronger, more ferocious stallions.

It is likely that before the arrival of the Persians, continental horses must have been small, being bred in the wild. The Romans, however, and probably the Macedonians before them must have mastered selective breeding. Yet it seems that this skill had vanished by the early Middle Ages. Breeding seems easy in appearance: one needs a strong stallion and a mare that combine speed, size, strength, and ferocity.[2] Then one selects only those offspring that show more promise and mates them with other promising animals. By continuous and consistent breeding of the best stallions with the best mares, one can develop a much stronger type. It is a four-step process: remove all foals before the age of two, avoiding wasted energy as the dominant stallion chases weaker males from the herd; give them a particular territory to graze; provide feed during the winter when grass is at minimum; and make sure that the stallions do not mate indiscriminately with all the mares available, whether strong or weak. The first two elements and probably the third were practiced in the West at least by the time of Charlemagne.[3] The solution came with better specimens imported from areas where horse breeding had not deteriorated.[4] At that time this meant Muslim lands or those where the influence of the Muslims was paramount—Spain, Sicily, and regions of southern Italy.

The culmination of selective breeding was the destrier, the "great horse" or warhorse which by the late Middle Ages could reach eighteen hands in size and astonishing prices.[5] The warhorse was suited for combat and was the symbol of the aristocracy; its value and rarity meant that not too many soldiers could afford one. Most soldiers seem to have ridden more humble animals, or rounceys. The use of a different horse may have been dictated by other reasons. For instance, the favorite English horse in the *chevauchées* in France during the Hundred Years War was the courser, which combined stamina and mobility.[6] In reality every heavy cavalryman would need several horses: the warhorse, which the knight's squire would lead with his right hand, a more modest horse for the squire himself, and a horse to carry the knight's armor to the battlefield. It was only when confrontation became inevitable that the knight would wear his armor and ride his warhorse into battle.[7]

Breeding a strong horse was not enough to change the nature of combat. The introduction of the stirrup around the eighth century increased the stability of the horseman. Yet it alone was not enough. Other developments were essential: nailed horseshoes, saddles with a high pommel, and the wraparound cantel. Nailed horseshoes allowed the horses to cover longer distances at increased speeds on most terrains; the pommel protected the rider's private parts and stomach; the cantel increased his stability and allowed the soldier to deliver a shattering blow where the lance would be propelled by the power of the horse.[8]

The lance, the main weapon of the mounted rider, underwent a small revolution. Its length and weight varied according to the period. Eventually it would reach the extraordinary length of about 4 meters,[9] although at the time of the Norman Conquest it was probably a little more than 3 meters.[10] Made of strong wood like ash or applewood and with a small cloth pennant showing the lord's insignia attached near the head, it would normally carry a leaf-shaped metal head that provided two lethal functions: the point to penetrate, and the sides to cut. Its penetration was limited by the insertion of a metal cross behind the point to allow its extraction and reuse, although probably most lances would have broken on impact.[11] It is more than likely that the rider would arrive at the battlefield with several lances (and had to gallop back to his line to retrieve a spare). This was feasible because attacks, at least by the fifteenth century, came in waves, allowing riders to gallop back and regroup before delivering the next charge.

On the march the lance was carried vertically, with the butt resting on the stirrup, on the saddle on the right side of the rider, or across the shoulder. During the charge, the lance was held tightly toward the rear beneath the armpit and was placed, at least from the thirteenth century onward, across the horse's neck so that the contenders would attack and be attacked from their left sides. This method created instability; at impact the lance was pushed back into the holder's flank. Starting from the fourteenth century, a rondel, or a thick leather ring called a graper, was placed behind the hand, slowing the backward movement at impact. Also toward the end of that century the rest was developed and affixed to the right side of the breastplate, on which the holder would rest the lance before directing it against the opponent.[12]

The heavy horseman would hold the lance horizontally until the charge began. Then he positioned his body forward while firmly in the saddle, his left hand controlling horse and shield; he grabbed the lance tightly with his right hand almost below his armpit and lined up the weapon on the left of the horse's head. The key was to combine stability with power, which the horse's motion brought to the thrust.[13] Tournament lances were usually longer, with a larger diameter. They also had the wartime head replaced, unless the tournament was *à outrance*.[14]

The introduction of this tactic has been a matter of intensive debate.[15] Lynn White, Jr.'s view, that it was first used under the Carolingians, is usually dismissed today (forcefully by Bernard S. Bachrach).[16] Widely accepted is the view that this manner of combat became prevalent much later, around the end of the tenth century. Certainly the Bayeux Tapestry, from the later eleventh century, shows three cavalrymen holding their lance under the armpit, but even then it must have been unusual. Most horsemen depicted in the tapestry still hold the weapon underarm or overarm. In any case, since the Anglo-Saxons were an army of footmen, it would not have made sense to attack in a manner suitable mainly for combat against an opposing cavalryman.

The Sword

Besides his horse, the main symbol of the horseman's primacy in society and on the battlefield was his sword. Myths about the weapon harken to the barbarian past (Siegfried and Balmus, King Arthur and Excalibur) or from more recent events, where it assumed a powerful role in the psychological heritage of society (the sword of Roland, Charlemagne's paladin, ambushed and killed on his return from Spain, or Charlemagne himself). Trying not to let fall his sword into enemy hands, Roland tried to break it by striking a rock ten times, but his blade "neither broke nor splintered." The pommel of Charlemagne's sword Joyeuse was said to contain the tip of the spear that had pierced Jesus's body.[17]

Burnished and shiny like a mirror, the sword, usually about three pounds, was a double-edged instrument of death.[18] For most of the medieval period, at least north of the Alps, its main use was for slashing and hacking, a method that may have given the best results against chain armor.[19] In the Mediterranean, probably due to Roman influence, the thrust was more common. It required less physical strength and stamina and could be more deadly, for a single hit on a major organ would kill.

The design of the sword did not change much in the period 800–1350. The emphasis was on sharp edges more than a sharp point. But by the fourteenth century, as mounted soldiers switched from chain to plate armor, the old system of slashing was revealed to be insufficient. The tendency was to emphasize the point, which would exploit the joints in plate armor.[20] Its length depended on the holder's stature, but normally it was about 100 centimeters. According to L. Tarassuk and C. Blair, the typical sword of a fourteenth-century knight was long, with the blade itself being almost 1 meter.[21]

The sword remained the privilege of the mounted man-at-arms, but toward the end of the medieval period it became associated with infantry, which in previous times had used simpler swords like the Viking sax and the falchion, essentially long knives with one cutting edge.[22] It is also likely that horsemen and footmen carried daggers, which in the early medieval period were between 45 and 175 millimeters long.[23]

Small war hammers could also be part of the equipment of the mounted man, as well as the mace and short axe—all weapons to be used if the sword was not available or had broken. If fighting on foot, the horseman's favorite weapon might be a small lance or, by early in the fifteenth century, the pole-axe, which combined the shape of an axe with a spearlike spike in front.[24]

Infantry Weapons

The most common infantry weapon remained the spear, which changed name and appearance according to its place of use in Europe, although it was always characterized by a sharp point.[25] The pike, a long spear, which had been so important in the Macedonian armies of the Hellenistic period, returned to dominate the battlefields of Europe under the Swiss by the mid–fifteenth century, but was used rarely before that. When it reappeared, it was associated with other weapons, the glaive, the bill, and the halberd. Both were among the medieval contributions to warfare, developed from the application of the agricultural bill-hook to a pole. Around 1300 or so we find the first variations on this simple instrument. In the case of the glaive, the metal component became longer and included, besides the hook, a long spear in front and a shorter one at the back of the blade. The halberd became something like a great axe with a spearlike top and usually a hook on the back of the axe blade.[26] Both glaive and halberd became deadly instruments against cavalrymen, for they could bring down a horse and finish a horseman who fell to the ground.

Eventually the longbow of the English armies rewrote the history of warfare during the Hundred Years War, but for most of the Middle Ages the weapon that best typifies killing from a distance was the crossbow. This was an instrument of death that the Roman Church vainly tried to outlaw. Constructed initially of wood, it was made of steel by the fifteenth century.[27] It was essentially a bow mounted crosswise that shot metal bolts that could pierce any cuirass at most distances. It could be effective to 370–500 meters.[28] Crossbowmen had two advantages over bowmen: they did not need extensive and continuous training to become adept, and they could prepare the crossbow ahead of time. Yet the complex mechanism to cock the crossbow meant that it was much slower than the longbow (probably six arrows to one bolt) and left the person firing a visible target for enemy bowmen. This meant that crossbowmen often operated in combination with a footman, called a *pavisier*, armed with a spear and a very large shield (*pavise*) behind which the crossbowmen could cock his weapon.

The best crossbowmen were considered to come from Catalonia, Gascony, or Liguria, the Italian region where Genoa is located. They tended to be a large component of most medieval armies, considered an elite corps occupying a central position in the battle line and opening the encounter or attempting to outflank the enemy. Membership in its ranks was so highly valued in Spain that service was considered equivalent to that of a cavalryman.[29]

How to Protect the Troops

Protective items for horsemen and footmen varied according to the times and place, but normally the shield (in the eighth century it was in the form of a kite) among continental soldiers became smaller and more manageable as improvements in body protection took place. Constructed probably of lime wood, at least in northern Europe, they were covered initially with leather reinforced by strips of steel around the rim. Its shape kept changing, first by minimizing the curved top, then by becoming flat more than concave, and finally by assuming a triangular form, the so-called heater, for the cavalryman. Eventually, in the late medieval period, and after a series of refinements in plate armor, horsemen dropped the shield completely. Shields remained an essential protective element for footmen.

Besides the shield, the two most important protective items were the helmet and a mail shirt. The helmet of the ninth century could be segmented, banded, or made of a single piece. The segmented helmet was made of iron or bronze bands linked to a metal plate on top of the head. The framework of the banded helmet, as shown in the Bayeux Tapestry, was based on two semi-circular strips over which four metal plates were laid to form a circular shape. These helmets also included a separate nose bar of varying proportion. They could be worn over mail coifs that were either separate or an extension of the mail shirt.[30] As with the shield, the helmet underwent a series of modifications. By the middle of the twelfth century faceguards were added, often with a short neck guard on the back. Its shape started to become flat-topped instead of conical. It was a development that led to the introduction of the great helmet by the early thirteenth century and remained a favorite protection of most knights until the end of the fourteenth. From 1300 onward another type of helmet, the *basnet*, became popular. It could have various forms, but most included protection for neck and face. A favorite Italian helmet from the fourteenth century onward was the *barbute*, similar to that of the ancient Greek hoplites. By the fifteenth century the *sallet* was also popular. It included modifications to protect the neck and face. At the same time, the *armet* appeared, relatively light and popular.[31] The search for the perfect helmet was an attempt to provide the greatest protection possible with relative comfort. Especially at the height of the sun, even the lightest helmet must have been uncomfortable.

The medieval soldier could also wear protection for legs, hands, and eventually even feet, but the greatest care was initially given to protection of the body. The mail shirt, also called a hauberk or *byrnie*, was worn over some kind of quilted garment, the *aketon*. It covered the body of a medieval horseman to his knees with front and back split so one could sit comfortably on horseback. The sleeves extended to the elbow and sometimes to the wrist. By around 1175 we find that the long sleeves included mail mittens.[32] By the fourteenth century we see shorter shirts, called *haubergeons*, reaching above the knees, usually for footmen. In the fifteenth century it became standard equipment, worn beneath more complex armor. The idea was to provide some protection where gaps in the armor might allow a blade to be inserted.[33] Beginning in the middle of the twelfth century, a long flowing coat, the surcoat, was worn over the mail shirt. It was probably a way to display the insignia of the wearer or, as Ian Peirce suggests, acted as a water repellent after being treated with animal fat.[34]

By 1330 a fully armored cavalryman would wear an *aketon*, the hauberk over the *aketon*, and a coat of plates over the hauberk. The head would be covered with a padded coif over which a heavy, barrel-shaped helmet was placed. Legs and arms would be covered with protective items. Starting in the fourteenth century the coat of plates was increasingly replaced with a complete suit of plate armor, which protected the breast and the back of the horseman. While the armor of the footman always remained second place among the priorities of most armies, the protection of the horseman reached its highest level by 1420. Afterward craftsmen from Lombardy in Italy and from some German cities, especially Augsburg, would bring further refinements. But on the whole the major innovations had taken place by the early fifteenth century.[35]

Chapter Nine ~

Protecting the Borders Against the New Enemies: Vikings and Magyars

A BLACKISH BOAT SPLIT THE DARK waves under a sky barely lit by a cold moon. Its prow was high, the shape of a dragon emerging now and then from the fog. Fear struck the few monks who had left their modest cells to look out to sea. They could barely distinguish the crew except for the sudden flash of weapons, the multicolored shields carefully lined along the gunnels, and the hair, which seemed the color of the sun. Soon they would land and march against the barely defended walls of the monastery. They had been there before, and they were coming back. They were the strangers, the heathens.

The Wild Men from the North

People used different names for the invaders from Scandinavia. For the French they were the Northmen or Danes; the Slav populations referred to them as Rus; the Irish called them gentiles, pagans, and then just foreigners; for the English they were the Danes or the heathens.[1] In the end the name *Viking* came to identify them all. It originated from the word *i viking*, "the man who went plundering."[2] They came from all parts of Scandinavia—Norway and Denmark and Sweden. Swedes operated mainly in the lands of the Slavs; Norwegians in the northern parts of the British Isles, in Ireland, and in the nearby islands; Danes in southern England and on the European continent. Eventually the invaders, Norwegians and Danes, would square off in Ireland as the former moved south and the latter north.

They appeared like a storm on the European continent at the end of the eighth century, writing a story of conquest, violence, and achievement, espe-

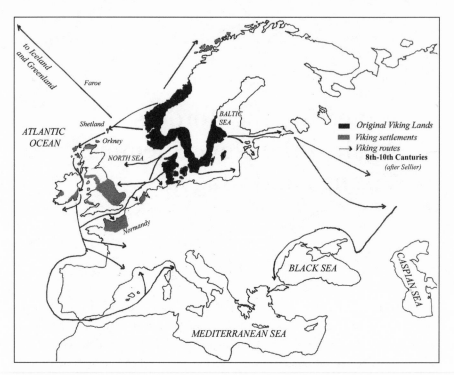

Figure 9.1　Viking Europe

cially in France, where they settled in Normandy, and in England, where they conquered the English throne (Figure 9.1). But they went much farther. They settled in the Orkneys, the Shetlands, the Faeroe Islands, the Hebrides, and in Iceland and Greenland. They even reached North America, certainly the tip of Newfoundland, and probably even farther south, although they had to retreat (possibly because of hostility from native peoples). They entered the Mediterranean, looted North Africa, and besieged Pisa in Italy. In the east they moved to Constantinople and reached the Caspian Sea.

Tales of horrible atrocities preceded them, as they were thought to be unbeatable. They were the new Huns with blue or green eyes and blond hair, the wrath of God on sinful people: "It is a sign that someone has well deserved it," said the English scholar Alcuin. In reality their atrocities were no harsher than those of the past; nor did the new invaders always win. Actually they experienced defeat more often than victory in the few pitched battles that they were forced to fight.

In the past, other invaders may have come from Jutland or Sweden (Cimbri and Teutones in Roman times), then Longobards and Goths, who claimed

that they first moved southward and eastward from Scandinavia, the "
of people" (*oficina gentium*), as the Gothic writer Jordanes wrote in the si
century.[3] But it is not certain why the Vikings left their lands in such an
aggressive manner in late eighth century. The first to suffer was the monastery
of Lindisfarne in 793; it was located on an island off the British coast. Two
years later other monasteries were attacked, always on the British coast, but
also in the Hebrides and on the northeastern coast of Ireland. By the end of
the century, the European continent experienced the violence of Viking raids.
In 799 they pillaged the monastery of St. Philibert, near the estuary of the
Loire in France.[4]

The Vikings' exodus from their lands may have been caused, it has been
argued, by demographic pressures, but that is certain only in western Norway,
not Denmark. In any case, the initial raiders were not interested in settlement;
their goal was loot. Nor did climatic changes render living in Scandinavia
more difficult. Climatic changes did happen, but only after the end of the
Viking period. Nor was it a case of technological innovation such as the use
of ships utilizing both sails and oars. That innovation may have certainly
made the Viking ships cover longer distances, but the problem is that archae-
ologists have not found any ship supporting such a thesis. For that we have to
rely on the evidence of depictions on seventh-century stone carvings.[5] More
convincing are two other explanations. There was a high degree of insecurity
for whoever held a throne in Scandinavian society. For the throne attracted a
host of competing claimants on the basis of ancestry or deed. Losers would
find an alternative in exile, hoping to gain fame and riches outside the Scandinavian area. The situation became exacerbated in the eighth century due to
the centralization of the various kingdoms, a situation that must have displaced several individuals from power positions, convincing them to look
abroad for fortune. It was the right moment for adventure, by raiding or by
trading. The European continent witnessed a process of economic renewal
that brought great quantities of silver, especially from the Muslim lands, to the
region. What Scandinavia offered in exchange were furs and skins—highly
valued items—or else the threat of violence. In other words, the newfound
wealth and increasing contact with Slavic lands and the West may have caused
a domino effect. As some returned home with the riches, others must have
been encouraged to follow.

It was an enticing proposition, for pillaging targets were easy to find. The
favored places for the predatory raids were monasteries and civilian institutions that offered weak resistance or none at all. Although no coastal area

Viking attacks, most of the raids were conducted against
l the northern territories of France. France and Ireland
for most of the first half and middle years of the ninth
n changed in the last third of the century when Britain
of conflict after the landing of a great army in 865. The
...quered two of four English kingdoms, Northumbria and East
Anglia, and established control in parts of Mercia. They failed, however, in
Wessex, where King Alfred the Great made a strong and effective resistance.
The occupation of English soil became permanent between 876 and 880,
when Danes started to settle in the lands that they had conquered—the
Danelaw.[6]

The failure to conquer Wessex may have convinced some of the Vikings
already in England, and the others that eventually left Jutland for gold and silver in western Europe, to focus on France from 879 to 891. They met mixed
success. Their forays deep into France up navigable rivers became increasingly
difficult when the French built a string of fortifications and obstacles over the
river ways, and especially when locals allowed Vikings to settle near the invasion routes of other Vikings. It was thus in 911 that a Viking leader named
Rollo was given the area around Rouen in the lower Seine. It was the foundation of the later Duchy of Normandy.[7]

Misery returned to English lands between 980 and 1016. In spite of creative
defensive strategies, great hardship fell upon the population, for nothing
seemed to work against the invaders—whether it was paying tribute, employ-
ing them as mercenaries, converting them to Christianity, intermarrying, or
praying. Complained one sermon by Archbishop Wulfstan, "Peace has not
gone well for a long time at home and abroad. . . . We pay them [the Vikings]
continually and they humiliate us daily; they ravage and they burn, plunder
and rob."[8] The final event was the Danish conquest of England. In 1015 the
new king of England was a Dane named Cnut who, when he died in 1035, was
succeeded by his two sons. They were followed in 1042 by Edward the Confessor, the son of the former king of England, Ethelred. When Edward died
childless in January 1066, the throne passed to Harold Godwinesson, but not
for long. The duke of Normandy, William, would land in England and defeat
Harold at the Battle of Hastings.

The Vikings at War

In the past the Viking was seen as a wild, undisciplined individual bent on
wanton violence. But the revised picture is that of trader who did not cherish

violence. Régis Boyer says that they were most of all traders.[9] No doubt, the commercial aspect of life was important to the Vikings. Yet in a society where violence was the order of the day, they made little distinction between peaceful trading and the conquest of goods by force and violence. Moreover, widespread fear of their deeds assumed larger-than-life proportions because their targets were defenseless civilian and religious institutions. In the long run, after decades of rampages, they would engage in pitched battles, but those were not their goal. Larger armies started to appear around 830, but it was not until 865 that we see a "great army" in English lands. Viking raiders should be counted in hundreds, not thousands.[10]

Although Vikings did not shy from diplomacy, force was inevitable. Everything conditioned them toward achieving material goals, from religion to fame. Odin, their god of war, combined fierceness and heroism on the battlefield with cunning and treachery, and so it is no surprise that stratagems were a key part of Viking warfare. All hope for future renown was conditioned on what one did while alive; good deeds, unlike in Christian beliefs, were not a prerogative for salvation. The Viking lived in a world where chaos was the reverse side of order and where order could be imposed only by physical confrontation.[11]

The weapon of choice was a double-edged sword about 70–80 centimeters long.[12] Used for slashing, it must have been tiring when used during protracted battle. It is reasonable to assume that the spear, although socially an inferior weapon, must have been as important when one passed from skirmish to a line confrontation or during pursuit. The spear needs less energy and less space. In other words, the spear came into play when the army deployed in a shield-wall or closed ranks, with shields covering not just the holder but half of his neighbor. It is likely that upon landing, or if faced by adversaries with effective long-range weapons, the Vikings must have adopted the *shieldburg* formation, that is, a practically impenetrable hutch using shields.[13] This formation could be abandoned to go on the attack or if the enemy engaged in hand-to-hand combat.

Besides the sword and spear, Vikings used light axes and bows, although probably more for hunting than battle. The two-handed axes found among the mercenaries of King Harold at Hastings seem to have been a later development. The same is true of the oblong shield, also seen at Hastings. The Vikings' shield was round, painted sometimes in contrasting colors, a rather weak defensive instrument (reconstructions based on examples found in burials easily shattered, though the buried shields may have been ceremonial;

battle shields may have been much sturdier). A metal or leather helmet (without horns but with nose protection) was used with a mail or leather coat, although those were luxuries that few warriors could afford.[14]

Once the leader gathered his followers, the next stage was to strike the target. In the west this meant the coasts of Holland, France, and southeastern England for most warriors coming from Denmark, or, if from Norway, Ireland and the northern coast of the British Isles. But when the "great army" was formed we must assume that it included Danes, Norwegians, and even Swedes, although the latter were active mainly in eastern Europe. The Viking's means of transport was a sleek, oared longship that could carry between 35 and 50 men. They would land near estuaries or, if possible, navigate the river directly to the target. Once there they would land and descend as quickly as possible.

Viking raids caused great disarray among European populations until the end of the tenth century. But eventually they stopped, and Vikings who had settled in the British Isles, France, and the Slavic lands were quickly assimilated.

The Magyars

This violent story was repeated in continental Europe by the appearance of the Magyars, who had occupied and settled in the Carpathian Basin, in modern Hungary, an area that had seen several invasions since the Romans. The Romans conquered the region in the later years of Augustus, at the beginning of the common era. They remained there for about four centuries, but around 430 the Huns arrived. The Huns were an Asiatic people identified with the Hiung-nu, originally from the northern frontier of the Chinese Empire under the Han Dynasty. After causing enormous turmoil within the borders of the Roman Empire in both the East and the West, the Huns disappeared after the death of Attila in 453. From then on we find Hunnic contingents spreading from central to eastern Europe, but they never regained the power that they had enjoyed during the fifth century. In any case, it is difficult to identify these others as Huns, for westerners tended to use the term to refer to any ethnic group originating from Asia.

The next invasion came from two Germanic peoples, Longobards and Gepids. They did not last either. The Longobards moved on to Italy; around 568 the Avars, a nomadic horse-riding people from the eastern steppes, moved into the area, defeating the Gepids and forcing the Longobards to seek fortune elsewhere. Eventually the Avars would be defeated in three bloody campaigns carried out under Charlemagne's armies between 791 and 803. At the time of the Magyar conquest, three ethnic groups were predominant in the region: Germans on the west, Slavs in Moravia, and Bulgarians in the remainder. Its inhabitants included groups of Avaric and Hunnish extraction as well as Slavs, Turkic-speaking Bulgars, and Germanic people on the western fringe.[15]

The Magyars were not the ethnic heirs of the Huns, although there is no doubt that the state that was eventually formed in the eleventh century would have included fractions of the Asiatic invaders besides Turkish Bulgars, Slavs, and Avars. The Magyars' place of origin seems to have been the Eurasian steppe along the middle region of the Volga near the Urals and the Caspian Sea. Their language is a branch of Finno-Ugrian, the same group to which today belongs the language of the Finns. Starting in the fifth century they had been subjugated by the Huns, the Avars, the Onogur-Bulgars, and finally the Khazars, an ethnic mix of Asiatic Huns and Indo-Europeans like Alans and Sarmatians.[16] The Magyars' contact with Hunnic, Turkic, and Iranian horsemen must have been crucial to their adoption of the horse and an economy based on animal husbandry. *Magyar* is the name that they used themselves; the name *Hungarian* comes from the Turkic *Onogur*. Actually the Byzantines called them Turks while the West referred to them as Huns or Avars. Their society, divided originally into tribes and clans, was similar to a republic formed of many tribes. Each tribe included a top level of overlords and clan heads; below was a class of warriors, tied to their leaders by myths about a common origin as well as personal obligations. Commoners crowded the lower ranks of society.[17] Leadership remained in the hands of forty or fifty families.[18]

The chronically unstable political situation of eastern Europe forced the Magyars inevitably toward the west. Although the sequence of events is confused, it seems that at first they moved in "the land between two rivers (Etelköz)," the steppe on the lower reaches of the Danube and Don Rivers (Figure 9.2). They did not last long there, for an attack by the Turkic Pechenegs displaced them farther west. By the end of the ninth century, the great plains of Hungary had become their home, a place of high ethnic mix but probably scarcely populated. Their conquest seems to have been quite easy.[19] They may have numbered 400,000 at the time of conquest, moving into an area where the total population was probably half that. The Magyars settled on the plains, for they provided the best grazing area, avoiding the woods, where Slavs were predominant.[20]

The first mention of Magyars in the West is found in a German chronicle for the year 862, in which they are called Ungri. They reappear in 881 as allies of the

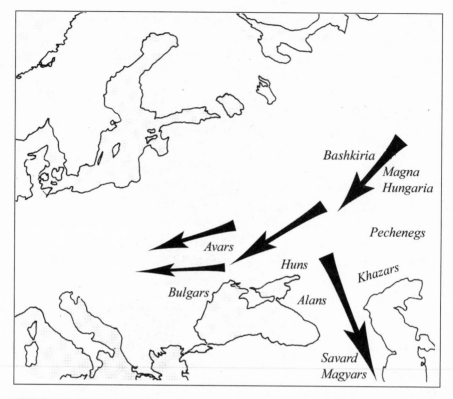

Figure 9.2　Magyars' Road to Hungary

Moravian Slavs against the Franks and again in 892, this time on the Frankish side against the Slavs.[21] Starting in 894, they quickly became a fearsome feature of the European conflicts for more than half a century. They were "lubricious vipers," as a contemporary western source described them.[22] Even many years later a twelfth-century German bishop spoke of them as "monsters of men."[23] In 899 they appeared in Italy. What is remarkable was not only their destructive frenzy but the care with which they prepared their expeditions. Before engaging in successful campaigns, which normally ended with the imposition of an annual tribute over the Italians, they scouted the area, a policy they followed prior to the invasion of Bavaria a year later. They were quick to exploit a neighbor's internal problems, launching raids on populations in disarray. Moving quickly on horseback and using bows as their main weapon, they seemed unstoppable. They were interested in loot, not possession of lands.[24]

As Liutprand, the Italian bishop of Cremona, wrote, they were "fond of prey, daring, unaware of the all powerful God, not ignorant of every type of

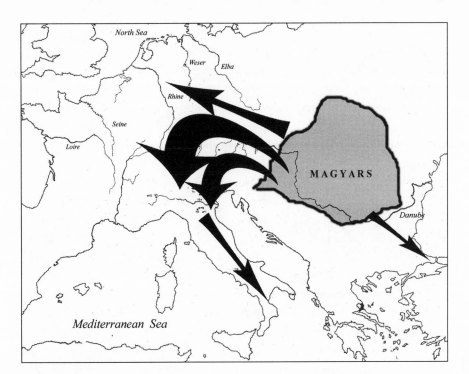

Figure 9.3   Major Magyar Raids 900–955

crime and murder and only eager for thefts."[25] Their violent passage through Italian lands was like the rampage of wild beasts.[26] What they left behind, say contemporary sources, were cities and fields without any living beings, houses and churches afire, and a multitude of captives in chains.[27] The sources write about the sudden appearance of the horsemen as springing from the earth's bowels, preceded by storms of arrows, and their terrible war cry *hui! hui!* as a prelude to the capture or slaughter of any individual who did not find safety.[28] And local authorities were usually powerless to stop the attacks, as they were never preceded by signs that an invasion was coming. Surprise was their most effective element[29] (Figure 9.3).

The Magyars would return time and again to Italy, looting the peninsula from the Alps to its tip. Similar was the situation in the Germanic lands and parts of modern Switzerland and France. In 917 they captured Basle and, taking advantage of the fact that the Rhine had frozen, passed into Alsace and Lorraine. In 924 they pillaged Provence. Around 925 they sacked St. Gallen, the richest Benedictine monastery in Europe, and in 942 they went as far as Spain, spreading terror in the Muslim lands of Córdoba.[30] They organized at least thirty expeditions against western lands in the period 898–955, not counting those carried out in French lands, a continuation of German or Italian campaigns.[31]

In appearance their raids seem similar to those of the Vikings. Both shared the element of surprise and ferocity, but the Vikings were also after land. This was never the case with the Magyars. Moreover, unlike the Vikings, Magyar raids always meant wanton destruction and bloodshed,[32] creating the most macabre impressions in the minds of the people who suffered. A Magyar leader named Bulcsu, divulged a German source with obvious exaggeration, hated the Germans so much that he drank their blood as if it were wine and ate their flesh after roasting it on a spit.[33] The only way to stop the onslaughts was to pay an annual tribute, the solution adopted in Italy and in the German lands. Other tactics—surprising them in small groups or when crossing a defile, laden with loot, were cosmetic solutions; these could never lead to a crushing defeat.

The invasions began at the beginning of spring and would last until fall, when they would finally return to their lands. They may have advanced not with one army alone but, according to a source, divided into several smaller hosts (a source says seven, each with 30,000 men, an obvious exaggeration). As they moved into enemy territory, the Magyars avoided fortified places, protected their camps with encampments of wagons, took control of the communication network (roads and passes), and then wreaked havoc on soft targets, often compelling local authorities to come to terms with them by paying tribute. Pacification did not work in the long run, for they would return the next year.[34] If a western army met them in a pitched encounter, the westerners would have won, but that did not happen, for the Magyars studiously avoided face-to-face combat. If compelled to fight, the Magyars, armed with bow, sword, and spear, would disorder the enemy ranks with storms of arrows; when the enemy came to grips, they would turn their horses away, enticing the enemy to pursue. If the enemy did, a nasty surprise waited. The Magyars would turn their horses and attack the pursuers, now split into small groups, enjoying numerical superiority and the order and cohesion that the pursuers had just lost. As for most armies, the Magyars' main target was the opposite leader to deprive the host of their "thinking head." They were often successful. In 907 they killed Liutpold of Bavaria, in 908 Burckhardt of Thuringia, in 910 Gosberto of Klettgau, in 937 Ebbo of Chateauroux, and later Gottfried of Marania and Duke Everard at Lubiana.[35]

According to a Byzantine emperor, the Magyars deployed into the traditional center and two wings in squadrons of about 1,000 riders. The right wing moved to attack the enemy center, showering it with storms of arrows before withdrawing to redeploy on the left of the Magyar battle line. As the right wing withdrew, the left moved forward. Again the goal was the enemy center, and again the Magyars would withdraw before redeploying on the right. Harassment of the enemy's center may have caused him to move forward in pursuit of the Magyars. At that moment the Magyars either feigned withdrawal or attacked if they thought that they could inflict the killing blow to a disordered, confused enemy.[36]

The main opponent of the Magyars in German lands was the state of Saxony, but even King Henry I had avoided in 924 the threat of a new Magyar attack by paying tribute in exchange for nine years of peace. Henry was not idle during those years. He favored the construction of obstacles, castles, and fortified walls, even for monasteries, to slow down any invasion and trained the army to avoid the usual Magyar stratagem of feigned withdrawal: do not follow them in disorder; advance as a block; never be enticed to lose order by the appearance of enemy defeat. Moreover, he gathered a standing army, recruiting even thieves and bandits and training them as soldiers on horseback.[37] It brought results. On 15 March 933 Henry's soldiers defeated the Magyars at a place called Riade; in 938 his son Otto I (936–973) defeated them again near Wels on the River Traun, compelling the plunderers to avoid Saxony for the moment. But it was not the end, which came in 955 at the Battle of the Lechfeld with Otto leading the army.

At the Diet held before Riade (933), Henry forcefully exposed the danger hanging over the German lands. They had no more gold or silver to give to the Magyars unless they despoiled churches and monasteries of their sacred vessels. If the Germans had been successful against the non-Germanic people on their borders, bringing them under control, there was no reason why they should not try the same approach against the Magyars. When the Magyars arrived to ask for the annual tribute, Henry sent them away empty-handed. A legend says that instead of money he sent a dog whose ears and tail had been cropped. It was the equivalent of a declaration of war. Quickly, the Magyars, who had already sent two expeditions, one to Italy and one to the Balkans, assembled another army to launch against Saxony. They expected help from the Slavic population along the way, as had happened in 906, but this time the Slavs, afraid of Saxon reprisals, refused to join.

In the German region of Thuringia the Magyars divided their army into two expeditions, one advancing from the south, the other from the west. However, one of the armies soon met disaster. Faced by an improvised army of Saxons and Thuringians, the Magyars fell, their leaders killed, many slaughtered, the rest taken prisoner or escaping only to die of hunger and cold.[38] The other Magyar army had stopped to besiege an unknown town, where they had heard that the wife of the Thuringian lord was the sister of King Henry and the owner of a great treasure in jewels and gold. The siege did not last long. The night following the siege, an army led by King Henry arrived in the neighborhood, camping in a place called Riade. Cornered, the Magyars tried to withdraw. During the night they recalled groups that were foraging and looting nearby areas and began a withdrawal. It was too late. By now Henry's army was close, yet the king still feared that the enemy would escape. So he resorted to a trick. He sent forward a smaller contingent of Thuringian foot soldiers together with a few cavalrymen as a screen for his main army. The ploy worked in part. The Magyars realized that the main body of the German army was following and tried to escape. Many did; others, a minority it seems, fell prisoner. Happy about his victory, Henry used the tribute money for grants to the churches and alms to the poor.[39] The Magyars' casualties had been minimal, but the victory had great meaning for the Saxons: the king finally had stood up to the invaders, had shown to be a forceful defender of his people, and had proved that good preparation and careful tactics could lead his army to victory. Moreover, while Henry remained alive, no Magyar army dared to cross the borders of either Saxony or Thuringia.[40]

It was a momentary respite. With the accession of Henry's son, Otto I (936–973), the Magyars reappeared on German lands, and although they suffered reverses in 938 in Saxony and in 944 on the River Traun near Wels, they launched a major expedition in the German lands in 955, probably attracted by the news that there had been a civil war there in the previous months. Crossing Bavaria, they arrived in Suabia; some proceeded to the Black Forest, but the majority stopped near Augsburg, which was placed under siege.[41] King Otto was ready, however. Starting with a small contingent, by the time he reached the Magyars he had gathered an army of about 3,000–4,000 horsemen.[42] It had been difficult, for troops had to be left on the eastern frontier to confront a possible threat from the Slavs. Otto moved toward Augsburg, likely from a northwest direction on terrain that lessened the danger of a Magyar ambush[43] (Figure 9.4).

The Magyars' siege seemed deadly ominous to the citizens of Augsburg. The fortifications built previously to sustain any Magyar attack had deteriorated, but under the heroic leadership of their bishop, Ulrich, they engaged in frantic repairs of the walls while women held processions on the bishop's

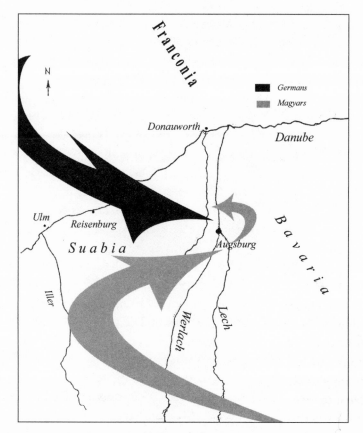

Figure 9.4   The Lech Campaign 955

orders to plead for God's help.[44] On 9 August the Magyars delivered their attack, which for a moment Augsburg's citizens were able to contain. News of Otto's arrival from the northeast saved the city from further attacks. The direction of the emperor's arrival spelled trouble for the Magyars, who had a large army but likely smaller than that of their opponent. Otto marshaled his troops along the obvious route that the Magyars would take if they retreated toward their lands. Also worried that they might try an alternative route by marching west toward Lorraine before moving in the direction of the Carpathian Basin, it is likely that he must have instructed Bruno, the archbishop of Cologne and viceroy of Lorraine, not to join him but to be on guard in case the Magyars chose that route. Meanwhile, groups of soldiers were alerted to guard every place and river east of Augsburg that fugitives could use to escape. Clearly, Otto had in mind not defeat but total destruction of the opponent's armed forces. His plan worked amid dangers and difficulties when the two armies met on the flat terrain of the Lechfeld.

On 9 August Otto's troops fasted and took oaths of mutual peace and practical support to each other when battle was joined.[45] Then next day, 10 August 955, they moved toward Augsburg under a heavy summer sun, advancing in a column of eight main battle groups, the standard of St. Michael leading the way. Bavarians manned the first three battle groups; Franks were the main element of the fourth; the fifth was the royal unit with Otto's Saxons; the sixth and seventh were Suabians; and the eighth Bohemians and the baggage train.[46] In spite of all precautions the German army was surprised by the Magyars. After lifting the siege of Augsburg, the Magyars had crossed quickly to the Lech's right bank, moved north, and recrossed the river north of where a Lech tributary, the Werlach, joined the main river at Augsburg.

It is likely that the Germans were not ready for the attack (Figure 9.5). They were deployed in marching position with the eight battle groups separated from each other. They expected the opponent to come from the south; instead they found him at their back on the north. The Bohemians suffered greatly and were routed, and the baggage train fell to the Magyars. The Bohemians' flight toward safety, where the two Suabian units stood, brought chaos among those who, the Bohemians hoped, could save them. The Magyars' success ended here. Wasting time to loot the baggage instead of inflicting the killing blow, the Magyars met the fourth battle group, the Franks, led by Duke Konrad. They stemmed the Magyars' rush, held them in check, and together with the other battle groups the Saxons, led by Emperor Otto and the three Bavarians units, routed the enemy[47] (Figure 9.6).

As the Magyars went down to defeat, they must have realized that Germans were poised on their eastern route of escape and that the Lorraine troops were on the west; their escape would not work because the enemy was on horseback. Some of those who did not fall on the battlefields sought refuge in huts and houses nearby. They met their ends as the Germans put such hiding places to fire. Others drowned in the waters of the Lech or were caught downstream and slaughtered. Among them, three leaders had tried to escape in a boat on the Danube. The Bavarians caught and hanged them all. The major German losses were Dietpold, the brother of the bishop of Augsburg, Ulrich, and Duke Konrad, who, burdened by the hot August day, had taken his helmet off and fell victim to an arrow that pierced his throat.[48]

After the Battle of the Lech, Magyar attacks against western Europe stopped. Not much later, when Christianity came to Magyar lands, the people

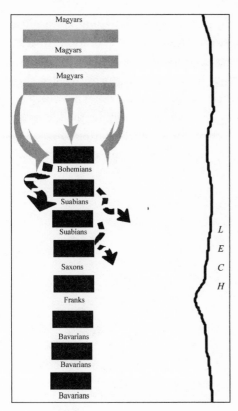

Figure 9.5
Lech Campaign 955:
The Magyar Attack

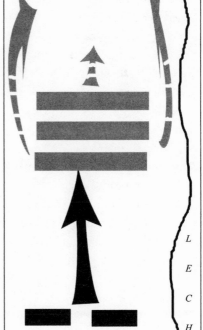

Figure 9.6
Lech Campaign 955:
The End of the Battle

inhabiting the Carpathian Basin would play a key role as a bulwark against eastern incursions into one of the most important strategic locations in central Europe. The Battle of the Lech was even more important for the future of the German lands. The disappearance of the Magyar threat signaled that the Saxon Dynasty was now the true heir to the Carolingians. That development served to lessen internal conflicts that had been plaguing the Germans for years. It is not surprising that Otto would look at the patron saint of 10 August, St. Lawrence, as the protector of his dynasty and of the imperial crown.

Chapter Ten

The Norman Conquest of England

HAROLD GODWINESSON, the forty-five-year-old king of England, knew that William, duke of Normandy and pretender to his throne, was coming. He awaited the arrival and had mustered a fleet to intercept the invader at sea. If that failed, he had spread his soldiers along the southern coast of England. But William did not appear, and the time for an invasion seemed unlikely (September had come); he sent his soldiers home on 8 September. His army had run short of supplies and men were needed for the fall harvest. The problems had not ended for the English king. One of his brothers, Tostig, had risen in rebellion against him and, although defeated, sought refuge in the north, where he would join forces with a new pretender to the throne, a much more dangerous enemy, the Norwegian Harold Hardrada. Hardrada—the bravest soldier in Europe, people said—had landed with an army of 300 ships' at the head of Vikings who in the past had ravaged the land and whose presence was still clear, for Viking blood ran in the veins of Harold himself.

As he had shown in his strike into Welsh lands, Harold quickly gathered an army and force-marched north between 18 and 20 September. He covered the 180 miles in a few days. On 24 September 1066 he was at Tadcaster, about 12 miles southwest of York and close enough to the Norwegian army. Just a few days earlier the Norwegians had inflicted a bloody defeat to Earls Edwin and Morcar, who had supported Harold in the north. In a brilliant action, Harold pushed forward and surprised Hardrada and Tostig at Stamford Bridge. Both fell on the battlefield together with many other soldiers, but wisely Harold did not continue the fight to the finish, allowing the survivors, now reduced to only twenty-four ships, to sail back to Scandinavia.

Harold's campaign had been masterful in strategic and tactical terms. His response had been immediate; his decision to attack was appropriate, not only because surprise was on his side but also because the enemy host must have suffered losses even in the victory at Fulford Gate against the northern earls. But Harold's army suffered casualties at Stamford Bridge; recovery time had been minimal, for he was informed that the enemy he feared most had landed in England on 28 September and was now about 57 miles from London. Harold reacted with his usual speed and force-marched to London, where he arrived on 5 or 6 October. He rested there five or six days before marching the 57 miles to meet the new enemy on the southern coast of England.

The Arrival of the Normans

What we know about William's bid for the English throne comes mainly from William or from sources using the information that the Norman court had spread. There is nothing from Harold, probably because of an oath he had taken to be William's steward in England and to facilitate passing the throne to the Norman duke once the legitimate king, Edward the Confessor, had passed away. In 1051 Edward had promised the throne to William, and when Harold appeared a few years later on French shores, probably pushed by adverse currents or a tempest, he owed a debt of gratitude to William, for the duke had forced his freedom from the lord who had taken Harold hostage on the coast. William had befriended Harold, taken him on a military campaign, and probably forced from him the oath that would eventually strengthen William's claim to the English throne. An oath gained in this manner was invalid, but Harold's decision not to defend his action helped create a climate in which William looked like the honest defender of his rights sanctioned by an oath taken over religious relics. The Norman duke was skillful in exploiting this advantage. He called the secular powers around him to regard his claim as just and proper. He even received the blessing of the pope, who sent him the banner of St. Peter to be unfurled once he decided to move against Harold.

Diplomatically, then, William's preparations had been masterful. Even more so were the material arrangements despite some hesitation among his Norman subjects. Expectation of rich rewards from a man noted for generosity made Normandy the new frontier of European adventurers in search of gains and glory. They came from Flanders and all parts of France, especially Brittany. Some may have come from southern Italy, where Normans had established principalities before moving on to Sicily and displacing the Mus-

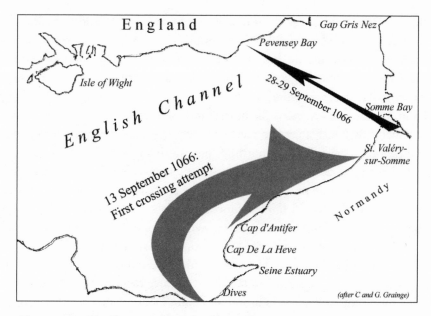

Figure 10.1   The Normans Cross the Channel

lims there. In the end, about 6,000 soldiers gathered around the duke. But men had to be taken to English shores, and William needed a large fleet, which was prepared in a rather short time using nonseasoned wood for most of the ships. By the day of the invasion he must have had more than 700 ships to carry his men and probably 2,000 horses.

Assembling ships and men was only part of the problem. Even providing supplies seemed minor compared to the decision as to when to cross the channel, some 60–90 miles wide. The army was ready by the end of August at Dives, but days and weeks passed—almost a month—and the fleet did not move.[2] The problem was to find a south wind to help the crossing. Finally, the time seemed to come around 13 September, but the crossing had not yet begun when unfavorable weather pushed the ships northward along the Norman coast. Some ships were lost, and some soldiers must have died. As the fleet rested at St. Valéry, near the Somme estuary, William buried the casualties secretly so as not to discourage his men[3] (Figure 10.1).

The weather remained unfavorable for two more weeks with the fleet remaining off St. Valéry. It changed on 28 September when a high-pressure system brought clear, sunny skies and a favorable southerly wind. The day for crossing had finally come. As the fleet left the French coast with the afternoon tide, William ordered the ships to stop not far away from land to make sure they were deployed in an ordered formation. They remained there until a signal from a lantern and the sound of a trumpet instructed them to move across the channel. He did not want to arrive at England at night given the obvious dangers that darkness would create. When the fleet finally started moving again, his ship outdistanced the others, and for a while he feared that he had lost them. By 8 A.M. they had reached Pevensey, where they landed.[4] Harold and his men were still in the north, or just starting their trek back south.

In his typical careful way, William first thought about defense and built a precut wooden castle near Pevensey. Later he erected another at Hastings. But this was not all. He had limited time at his disposal, for supplies could run short and he could not trust the insecure and dangerous supply line across the water.[5] Unlike his usual strategies of attrition and delay, he would seek confrontation in the open field. He moved with the utmost ferocity and destruction across the lands near his landing. It was an area that belonged to the Godwinessons—the land of the king and his family. Honor demanded that Harold should react and move against those who were destroying his patrimony.

Harold really did not need extra stimulus. He understood warfare as a matter of lightning surprise, even if speed sacrificed numbers and mass. His recent experiences against the Welsh and the Norwegians told him that was the right approach. The king force-marched against the Normans, although many soldiers had not joined his army yet. He seemed not to have been preoccupied with the fatigue evident among the men, who had already marched to London and were to march 57 miles from London to Hastings. Nor did he seem concerned about the obvious heavy casualties that his host must have suffered at Stamford Bridge. Surprise was clearly on his mind (Figure 10.2).

The Armies at Hastings

The main evidence depicting the soldiers at Hastings is the Bayeux Tapestry, woven probably in England a few years after the encounter. A considerable contingent of the Saxon army, identified as household troops, or *housecarls* (professional soldiers in the service of lords), wore helmets and hauberks similar to the Normans, but the rest had heavy leather jerkins, trousers, and legs protected by leather or cloth thongs and leather boots. Some of the household troops were armed with two-handed axes, swords, and spears, the last two common in the Saxon army. The household troops were not a standing military force. Although any connection to the soldiers settled on the island by the Danish king of England, Cnut, should not be discarded, it seems clear that by

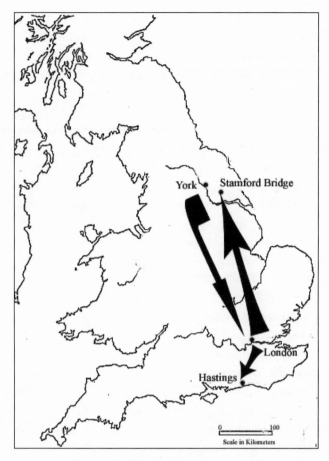

Figure 10.2　Harold's Route to Hastings

the time of the invasion housecarls were neither a standing army nor a law-bound guild.[6] They may have received some kind of monetary pay, but their allegiance to King Harold and the other great lords was based on the lordship bond, that is, military obligations that arose out of the ties of men in the household of Saxon lords, earls, bishops, and local magnates.[7] Although one can say that they were particularly well trained for war, this does not necessarily mean that the rest of the Saxon army was of inferior quality or that the household troops were superior to the *thegns*, the social and military elites of the Anglo-Saxon kingdom.[8] This is a period when fighting must have been second nature to most. Tied to the land, they must have been physically able to do well in a conflict where spear, sword, and axe—physical power—were the primary weapons.

We do not know how many of Harold's host at Hastings were household troops, but we must assume that their number was considerable, though the harsh battle at Stamford Bridge and the forced marches must have taken a toll. Most of the army, in any event, served because of the military obligation tied to land tenure. To raise the royal army, or *fyrd*, land was assessed by a unit called hide, initially a parcel of territory able to support a family. Every five hides of land had to provide a soldier for military service and to work on fortresses and bridges.[9] We do not know the proportion of soldiers serving on the basis of lordship bonds to those serving on the obligation of land tenure. It is likely that those wearing hauberks and holding two-handed axes, as well as some of those fighting with a spear, may have been part of the household troops, the rest being part of the regular *fyrd*. There was also probably a sizable contingent of Danes come to support Harold. In terms of total numbers, the Saxon army had between 6,000 and 8,000 troops, roughly identical to or slightly larger than the Normans.[10]

The Norman host was different. Whereas the Saxons used horses to travel but not to fight, the Norman host was perhaps 30–35 percent horsemen. During the battle the horsemen used their lances in a variety of motions: throwing it like a javelin, striking downward with the arm raised, hitting with the lance held with an arm relaxed at the side of the rider, and tucked under the armpit.[11] Moreover, they had a considerable number of archers, probably about 15 percent, whereas practically no archers were present among the Saxons. Had they been left behind in Harold's rush to the battlefield? Normans also were better equipped in defensive armor (though artistic license among the Bayeux Tapestry's weavers may explain this). A typical knight of the eleventh century would have a knee-length mail hauberk (armor for the body and arms) weighing about 11.4 kilograms, slit back and front, a conical helmet with nose protection, some kind of protective cloth leggings, a lance of about 4–5 meters in length and made of ash or applewood, normally with a leaf-shaped head of various length, a sword, and a kite shield.[12]

The Norman army was not a feudal force, that is, men who owed military service to William because of having been granted a fief, exclusively. Normandy became the new frontier as soon as William laid claim the throne of England. It attracted soldiers from many parts of the continent in search of loot and glory. Certainly many were mercenaries. The household troops of William and the other great lords served because of pay and bonds of fealty, not dissimilar to the status of some soldiers in the English army.[13]

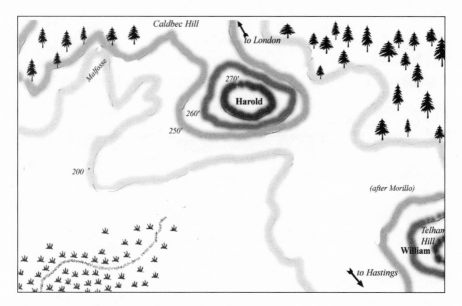

Figure 10.3 Saxons and Normans at Hastings 1066

The Battle

As R. Allen Brown wrote in 1981, "Almost everything about the Norman Conquest is controversial amongst English-speaking historians."[14] Yet the fundamental lines of the encounter seem clear.[15] The battle, which went from around 8–9 A.M. until darkness, is best understood if divided into stages.

When on 14 October 1066 Harold and his men came out of the forest, where they must have rested during the night, there was a surprise waiting for them (Figure 10.3). He saw the Normans appearing on Telham Hill, about 2 miles away. A day earlier scouts had warned the Normans about the arrival of the king's army. William had prepared for the next day's ordeal by attending mass and taking communion. He had also ordered his men to keep ready for battle in case Harold attacked them at night. Now the surprised Saxons saw William's forces marching toward them in the distance.

It seems unrealistic to argue that Harold, surprised, was compelled to remain in a defensive position on the hill because his intention had been offensive, not defensive. It would have been suicidal, unless exploiting the element of surprise, for an army of infantry to attack a balanced enemy of missile units, footmen, and horsemen on the plain between two hills; the cavalry would have easily turned their flank or hit their rear. Without the element of

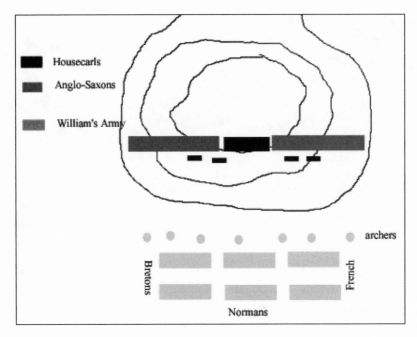

Figure 10.4   Hastings 1066: The Initial Deployment

surprise, the best choice was to remain on the crest of the ridge of Caldbec Hill and wait there for the Normans to attack. It was a logical solution that Harold refined by sending a fleet off the coast to ambush the Norman forces if they attempted to go back to France.

The location was perfect for defense. It allowed most of the army to deploy more deeply than one rank; the approach from the south, the Normans' route, would be difficult as an attempt to strike from the west (swamp) or east (woods). In other words, the Normans had one choice: to attack frontally by moving on terrain that nullified the rushing power of their horses and favored the men fighting on the higher position. It was no surprise that the battle would last the whole day, the Anglo-Saxons steady like blocks of stone, the Normans rushing continuously uphill to be beaten back (Figure 10.4).

William lined up his soldiers in three battle groups, each subdivided into three main units. He kept the center for himself and his Normans, the right wing for the French troops, the left for the Bretons. In the first lines he deployed his archers (it is unlikely that he had crossbowmen). Behind them at a certain distance were the footmen, then the cavalry after the infantry. The deployment made clear the duke's plan: let the bowmen cause casualties and disorder, strike with the footmen to increase the disarray, and drive them off the ridge with a cavalry charge. It did not work that way.

The archers caused little damage to the Saxons, lined up tightly in a shield wall; when the infantry moved forward, they found soldiers in the first rank who were stiffened by the presence of household troops in the center and likely along the whole line. Moreover, several Saxons, armed with deadly two-handed axes, the weapon of the Danes, must have caused terrible casualties among the attackers, who failed when the horsemen took the place of the footmen. Disaster almost struck the Norman line at this stage. The left wing, discouraged by the heavy losses and the stubborn resistance of Harold's men, retreated and gave the impression they were abandoning the battlefield after word spread that William himself had been killed.

It was a moment of peril for the Normans; several Saxons followed the Bretons as they withdrew. But the rush forward could be translated into a killing blow only if the whole Saxon line attacked, not just a few elements from the right wing. Moreover, once they left the security of the ridge, the pursuing Saxons were open to a Norman counterattack. When the news of his demise reached William (probably his horse was killed under him, the first of three he lost during the day), he stood up on his horse, raised his helmet, and forcefully shouted, "Look at me! I am alive, and will be the victor, with God's help!" William's gesture rallied his men on the left wing; the center cavalry and foot, in combination, cut down any Saxons who had left the ridge.

The failure of William's left wing had given the Saxons a great opportunity to end the battle if they had attacked all at once. It is unknown why they did not. Stephen Morillo suggests that it was a moment of crisis for the Saxons, who may have lost two of their leaders, Earls Gyrth and Leofwine, Harold's brothers.[16] It may also have been the case that Harold, confident in his position's strength, felt he would win because he had more men than William. And if it is true that he had mustered only a third of his army at the beginning of the battle,[17] he may have been waiting for reinforcements to arrive. He could wait and accept losses; the Normans, stranded in enemy land, could not. Certainly William made no headway in the hours that followed.

The battle became a tiring sequel of Norman attacks from cavalry and infantry, intermingled with arrow showers, successful Saxon defensive stands, and Normans regrouping after rushing uphill. This may have spelled trouble for the Normans if the Saxons were numerically superior, and casualties among those attacking uphill must have been high. But two major developments interrupted the natural flow of battle. Twice the Saxons were tricked into following the Normans down the ridge after William's men effected a feigned withdrawal.[18] There is no reason to doubt that this would have happened or that the Normans would have been incapable of effecting it. The rushes down the ridge must have depleted the Saxon forces. Even more crucial was the work of the archers. They started to shoot arrows in a parabola, hitting the rear ranks, not the first ranks, who must have been well protected inside their shield wall. One of these arrows, the Bayeux Tapestry shows, hit Harold's eye, which must have taken the king out of the fight. The Normans' final rush up the ridge must have come soon thereafter, for darkness started to envelop the battlefield. Their leaders killed or incapacitated, their king dead on the ground and his face so crushed that he could not be recognized, weakened by their losses, and with no hope for relief, the Saxon line gave way, some on foot, some on horseback if they could find a horse. Many remained on the battlefield, their sight obscured by the blood of their wounds; others died in the forest in their desperate search for safety. The Normans suffered heavy losses when a group of knights, their sight diminished by the impending darkness and in a rush to come to grips with the fleeing enemy, fell into a ravine while pursuing the Saxons.

There were several reasons why the Saxons lost. The encounter came too soon after the victorious campaign against Hardrada; Harold should have gathered a stronger force; his battlefield position was too static to be successful against a sophisticated army combining foot, horse, and missiles; he should have exploited the wavering of the Norman line at the beginning. Instead he had suffered twice, actually three times, the illusion of following the Normans down the ridge. One must also take into account the determination of William to win; his brilliant preparation of the campaign; and his steely nerves on the battlefield. It was not a victory of the cavalry against an outmoded infantry. William's success was based on the proper chemistry of all forces at his disposal. Probably the most important contingent was the archers, although the sources, probably for social reasons, tended to minimize their role.

The final conquest of England took time and effort, although probably the most serious obstacle came when William fell ill to dysentery. The greatest Saxon loss at Hastings was the destruction of their leadership. From then on, no major leader would emerge to stop the Normans. Toward the end of the Norman invasion of England, the main military problem for most soldiers was how to defend or take a castle.

Chapter Eleven

The War Against Walls

THE CASTLE IN MEDIEVAL TIMES soared over the landscape, tow-
ers spreading right and left, its power exemplified by fortified gates. The castle
as symbol was part defense, part protector and oppressor of people nearby.
Social superiors inhabited these symbols of subjection, where punishment was
meted out to commoners and peasants who failed to comply with their law-
ful duties. Every year at the same time, armed men swarmed from them into
the countryside to make sure that not an ounce of what was owed to the lord
was wasted, hidden, or pilfered. The castle was the symbol of safety, but also
the seat of evil, abuse, and oppression.

Fortifications and How to Bring Them Down

During the period from the tenth century to 1300, fortified places proliferated
throughout Europe, the castle emerging as the most dramatic and effective
form. There were at least four categories of castle ownership: some belonged
directly to the sovereign; some were held directly by the main lord of the region
(duke, count, baron); some were entrusted by sovereigns or lords to vassals; and
some were the private property of individual families.[1] One French king, Philip
Augustus, held about 100 fortified places, forty-five in Normandy alone. There
were forty-nine royal castles and 225 others belonging to the lords of the kingdom at the time of Henry II Plantagenet in 1154 in England. Sixty years later
royal castles had almost doubled, to ninety-three, although the places held by
barons had decreased to 179.[2] In Italy the proliferation of castles (*incastella-
mento*) spread quickly until the whole landscape was marked by fortified
places—castles, fortified villages, or strongly fortified cities. It is no surprise
that the fortification of urban centers was a priority in Italy. They could be
erected atop fortifications built during classical times; it was a necessity for a

civilization characterized by strong urban concentrations; it was mandatory given the fractured nature of conflict, neighbor against neighbor, city against city. By 1300 Italy was by far the most urbanized place in Europe, counting at least five cities with a population between 50,000 and 100,000, eight between 25,000 to 50,000, and fifteen between 10,000 and 25,000. Except for Muslim Spain, which had two populous cities in Córdoba and Granada, large urban concentrations in the rest of Europe were few, except for Paris in France and Ghent and Bruges in Flanders, the latter with about 50,000.[3]

Castle-building was not the sole prerogative of the sovereign but spread to every corner, showcases for the power of local lords vis-à-vis the people in their dominion, a visual statement of strength against neighbors, tacit defiance against sovereign power. This meant that many times castle-building was against the ruler's interests. Yet even powerful kings like the Ottonian Dynasty in tenth-century Germany were only able to slow the process, never stop it.[4] The development took strength from several factors. Fortified places sapped the sovereign's drive for centralization, for he always had to contend with the old regional ideals of autonomy and independence; they were places in Europe with the menace that the new invaders, Vikings and Magyars, brought against the land; it was an efficient method to stay on guard in areas under constant peril like the Muslim-Christian frontier in the Iberian Peninsula and in the Near East; they could be the launching pad against "new enemies," the heathen Slavs in the East; they were repositories where local laws were drafted; and they were centers of administration, bureaucracy, and cultural development.

Initially, during the tenth and the eleventh centuries, castles were built over a motte, a mound in the form of a cone, about 5–6 meters in height and 30 meters in diameter at the base, perhaps 10 meters at the top. In its simplest form, a ditch surrounded the base of the motte, a wooden palisade defending the top, which was the defenders' living quarters and the place where the most effective defense could be engineered.

The construction followed certain guidelines. Initially the castle may have been just the keep, a fortified building square in shape (but round or multi-cornered from the end of the thirteenth century).[5] Its location might be artificially prepared, as in the case of a motte, or a naturally strategic site, like a hill or a rock formation or nearby a watercourse. The builders' intent was clear: control the surrounding countryside, make a strong stand in case of attack. This often meant that each castle might cover an area equal to one day's ride.[6]

From the mid-twelfth century on, timber castles became less fashionable, replaced by stone and brick.[7] Also by that time square towers were dropped in favor of round and semicircular shapes. The new form provided less obstructed views for defenders; was more difficult to undermine and target to missiles; and could be reinforced with smaller masonry pieces. The new constructions of the thirteenth century became more complex and visually stronger.[8] By the end of the thirteenth century, castles were mainly stone constructions with merlons (alternating raised portions of the defensive wall), machicolations (stone replacement of timber hourds), barbicans (outer enclosure with small gate), and drawbridges. All these elements made defense more effective and counter-attack possible. Towers became cylindrical or prismatic, built at shorter intervals, which led in some cases to the abandonment of the keep as the primary defensive structure. Walls were reinforced as a measure against sapping. The plan became simpler, ideally based on a concentric format that allowed the establishment of more defensive lines of access.[9]

How to Conquer a Castle

At its simplest, the siege meant overcoming the lines of defense that prevented access into a city or castle. The most effective tactic was to surround the place, cut it off from reinforcements, food supplies, and, if possible, water until exhaustion, despair, or illness forced the besieged to surrender. Yet this was a process rarely used in medieval times, for it required time, a luxury that few medieval armies had, as soldiers served a limited time before rushing home to look after their families and lands, especially at harvest. Moreover, unless the place was poorly defended, besiegers had to muster a great numerical advantage to succeed.[10]

The first line of defense, unless the walls were built on the natural defense of a perpendicular rock surface, was a ditch, which was filled, if possible, with water. On the opposite side stood a wall very close to the ditch to prevent the attackers from exploiting the terrain for their siege engines. The top of the wall would have a walkway, the allure, on which soldiers were posted. The wall battlement was crenelated by alternating merlons, that is, raised portions of the wall about two meters high, with embrasures, lower wall sections—the former to protect the defenders, the latter to allow them to strike the attackers with all sorts of objects (arrows, bolts, stones, boiling water, burning naphtha). Although potentially a murderous weapon, boiling oil must have been used rarely because of its scarcity in northern Europe and its cost. Moreover, the battlement and eventually the lower levels would have loops of various size and shape from which an archer could direct arrows while safe inside the protective wall. The next defensive line, after the initial ditch and wall, could be another ditch, the outer bailey, protecting the wall of the inner bailey. Inside the wall of the inner bailey stood the citadel, where the men sought refuge in their last stand against invaders.

Over the course of time the wall defenses were strengthened by a protective wall, roughly a meter high from the embrasure level, and by the addition of one or two wooden shutters that would be raised when the defender needed to throw an object against the attackers. Yet a problem remained: the defender would have no line of sight once the attackers had reached the base of the wall. The solution to the problem was to build shelves projecting from the wall summit, the so-called hoardings and brattices of wood and machicolations of stones. The hoardings would have holes on the floor so that objects could be dropped onto the attackers. Naturally the problem of visibility was solved by the use of round or polygonal towers instead of square ones.

The weakest point of the defensive line was the gate. The large opening, without a stone wall, could become the road through. In the ancient Near East, particular care was given to the line of approach to make sure that the least defended side of the attacker—his right, where no shield was held—was open to missile fire. But this would not have been enough if the gate did not have special defenses. Besides the drawbridge and ditch, the attackers would face a gate built with wooden planks strengthened by metal bars and flanked by projecting towers on both sides. If the gate was smashed, the next obstacle was the portcullis, a grated obstruction that would have been lowered to present another obstacle or to isolate the first group that smashed through the gate. The attackers would then be isolated between the first portcullis and a second, lowered in front. So-called "murder holes"—openings on the roof and on the sides—allowed defenders to launch arrows or other objects at the trapped men.

The besiegers' first task was to render the outer ditch ineffective by filling it with rocks, brushwood, sand, or earth so that siege engines could be pushed next to the wall. But before this was done the wise commander would weaken the barrier with siege engines to open a breach in the defense. The most efficient artillery engine was the trebuchet.[11] The trebuchet reached its highest form of sophistication around the thirteenth century. It consisted of a giant sling suspended to a beam that pivoted around an axle dividing the beam into a long arm to which a sling was attached, and a short arm that held ropes at the beginning and eventually a counterweight. That enormous sling could have a devastating impact against fortifications.[12]

The trebuchet had undergone three developmental stages by 1300. As Paul E. Chevedden explains, in the initial form the traction trebuchet used men pulling ropes to launch missiles; the hybrid trebuchet combined the power of a pulling crew with gravity; the third type used only the force of gravity, captured through a counterweight (counterweight trebuchet). The traction machine was used in China around the fourth century B.C. It seems to have developed into the hybrid form in the lands of Islam during the conquests of the seventh and eighth centuries. Finally, in the early twelfth century in the West we see the transformation to the counterweight trebuchet.[13]

The destruction caused by the machine increased through each stage. The most powerful traction trebuchet constructed in China needed about 250 men to launch a stone weighing between 54 and 60 kilograms a distance more than 77 meters. As shown during the crusaders' 1218 siege of Damascus, the missile could weigh as much as 185 kilograms, that is, about three times heavier than the rock of a traction trebuchet, but still almost half the 300 kilograms missile launched by the counterweight trebuchet. Moreover, accuracy had improved greatly. Any new development in the artillery was met by changes in fortification structures, especially by 1300. In the Near East, walls were thickened and towers became larger. Towers were spaced at shorter intervals to shorten the stretches of wall between towers. This process initiated the final fortification developments of the Middle Ages. (The next would come when gunpowder became effective.)[14]

Trebuchets remained costly, hard to maintain, and difficult to carry from siege to siege, requiring large crews. For most of the period 900–1300 other forms of artillery were used: generic stone throwers, mangonels, and ballistae, some dating to the Roman era. We are not certain whether the mangonel was used before the fourteenth century, although the name is used earlier, possibly referring to a generic stone thrower. The mangonel consisted of two wooden posts to which were attached two elastic ropes made of human hair that pulled a wooden arm, its extremity shaped like a giant spoon. When the arm was released, the stone was launched against the fortifications.[15] Mangonels and similar engines (the trebuchet, for instance) could be used to throw other objects like dead horses, diseased corpses, and live humans. In one case the envoy of a besieged castle was thrown back within the city walls, his sin to have been the spokesman for unacceptable terms of surrender.[16] The ballista was similar to a giant crossbow, launching a bolt or giant arrow, which could be lethal.[17]

Stone bombardment started a race and counter-race between attackers and defenders. What the besiegers destroyed during the day was repaired at night. It was a system that had a history in the ancient Near East. If bombardment was ineffective, the attacker had another option: move rams near the city's walls or a gate, fairly easy to batter down. The ram, which appeared in the ancient Near East around 3000 B.C., was a strong timber, usually with an iron tip, pushed by men and suspended on chains under a canopy.

If the artillery or ram failed, the attacker could go over or under the walls. Assuming that the ditch had been filled, ladders with hooks at the top and belfries (assault towers that reached the height of the walls) could be pushed against the fortifications. The interiors of belfries had platforms connected by ladders so that a steady stream of attackers could follow once a bridgehead was established on the enemy battlements. However, this did not guarantee success; the allure (i.e., the passageway), protected against an outside attack, had no protective wall on the inside, and so attackers were exposed to a new missile attack after conquering the allure.

Defenders could counter the attack in several ways. Whatever pulled the towers (whether human teams or draft animals) toward the city walls became a target. Naturally the attackers devised methods to limit the dangers. Towers were pushed from the inside, and rams were protected by a testudo (turtle), a roof suspended over the weapon. Yet even these precautions were not enough: incendiary arrows torched the towers and ram turtles before they came within effective range. The attackers answered by using fireproofing such as hides.

Going under the walls was done by digging tunnels, begun at a certain distance from the fortifications and continued until they reached the foundation. The aim was not so much to infiltrate the stronghold but to weaken the walls. As the attackers dug beneath the fortifications, they built a wooden structure to prevent the wall from crumbling; the cavity was filled with brushwood or other combustible material, the idea being that the collapse of the wooden structure would cause the fortified wall to collapse.[18] Defenders countered with a tunnel of their own to meet the enemy before damage could be done. Yet tunnels presented serious risks to both attackers and defenders. If they met while digging a tunnel, both sides could suffer serious casualties. Moreover, success was never certain, and in any case offensive efforts could be countered by a determined defender. Individual castles, even the most sophisticated, could not resist a determined siege. They would eventually fall due to treason, starvation, or fatigue. Castles built in clusters were more formidable.

In spite of the primacy of fortifications during this period, the most important military development was the emergence of the knight and the civilization he inspired.

Chapter Twelve

The Way of the Masters:
Men on Horseback

BERTRAN DE BORN (CA. 1140–1215) could hardly wait for the coming of spring, when pavilions and tents and armed soldiers and warhorses spread through the countryside. Bertran picked up his lute and started singing a piece he had written to express his yearning for war. What a delight it was to see soldiers compelling people to run away with the belongings on their back! What a pleasure to admire a host besieging a castle! What a treat to see a lord be the first to move into the breach to taste the blood of the enemy! Compared to these things, sleeping and eating and drinking were less fun. "Lords," he sung, "pawn all your belongings, your castles, villages, and towns, so that you can afford to wage war against each other." De Born was a minor noble from Aquitaine but his song captured the violence and excitement that was the stated creed of the knight.[1]

At the Origin

Eventually the Latin word *miles* (plural *milites*) became synonymous with *noble*. It was not so at its origin. It referred to a soldier in the general sense, but then around the tenth or eleventh century it became identified with a soldier fighting on horseback. It was, however, a new type of horseman: his armor, weapons, and function on the battlefield had no equivalent in the western territories of Europe. Thus *miles*—that is, "knight"—and the ethos surrounding his persona tended to differentiate him from footmen and common cavalrymen. Several European languages made this distinction: *chevalier* (knight) and *cavalier* (horseman) in French, *Ritter-Reiter* (German), *caballero-jinete* (Spanish).[2] The knight's supremacy over civilians and common soldiers was a practical efficiency (the heavy cavalryman was usually superior in battle) but might also be seen as a conspiracy among the lords and those who sang their praises—the intellectuals of the time.

The knights first appeared as the strongmen of castellans. They maintained order in the dominion, sharing the benefits of exploitation over nonnobles living in the territory and anybody passing through. The division of power between the lord and his knights, on one hand, and the rest of the population (peasants, merchants) on the other implied an important social revolution: it singled out some individuals (lord, knight, vassal) as the ruling elites. At the beginning clergymen, but not necessarily the high prelates (they were closely tied to the secular aristocracy), contrasted this development, but in the end the Roman Church too came in most cases to accept the new warriors as beneficial to Christendom.[3]

Chivalry was the term applied to the role and system of values that these new horsemen, the knights, shared first in the lands of the Carolingians. Chivalry was based on three concepts: bravery, or the ability to use physical force to achieve a military or nonmilitary goal; loyalty to the lord and other knights; and liberality, or scorn of material wealth (though riches were essential to greatness in many contexts).[4]

The origin of chivalry is shrouded, although most today think that the new way of fighting on horseback and the new ethos came into being at the end of the ninth century, with the year 1000 being the watershed.[5] According to one school of thought (the great medieval historian Georges Duby, among others), the decline of the king's authority in the lands of the Carolingian descendants led to endemic disorder. Eventually the castles mushrooming over the land became the basic structure of the political and social system. The soldiers serving the castellans took advantage of the political unrest, which transferred power from the center, the royal court, to the periphery. Originally from the lower ranks of the aristocracy, or even from a much humbler background, household soldiers started to impose hegemony over the mass of peasants and lower social orders, charging taxes and exactions of every kind. It was a process that separated them from the masses and brought them close to the lords, dividing society between those who carried weapons (*milites*) and those who did not (*inermes*). It was a radical change from the past, which had split people between freemen and nonfreemen, that is, social status.[6]

Dominique Barthélemy, among others, sees the development differently. There was neither a social crisis, says the French scholar, nor the creation of a new class. What happened was a slow process in which the new warriors on horseback, not necessarily from humbler social strata, became mixed with the older aristocracy. In other words, nobility, aristocracy, cavalry, and political and social power are the expression of a similar development. A recent survey of the topic by Jean Flori, who has investigated the problem for years, has argued instead for a synthesis of various views. The heavy horsemen and chivalry, the institution that defined them as a group, that emerged at the turn of the eleventh century were the product of a slow but progressive phenomenon combining elements, some from the late Roman period, others from the contemporary worlds of politics, culture, religion, ethics, and ideology.[7]

Being a *miles* did not mean being a vassal, that is, an individual who had been granted lands in exchange for military service. Initially many knights were soldiers in the court of a great lord who provided a livelihood and the accouterments necessary to fight on horseback. Naturally the people selected combined physical vigor and fighting skill with fealty and homage to the lord.[8] The profession of knighthood attracted those who could find the weapons, armor, and horses necessary; as such, it became the refuge of the younger sons of a lord to whom the future may have seemed financially bleak (by custom, only the firstborn son inherited most of the father's lands). As Duby claims, knighthood was the profession of youth in search of adventure, prestige, and fortune, which they expected to receive from war or sometimes from marriage to a rich woman. Initially it attracted not only the sons of the lower nobility but also better-off peasants who owned the instruments of a heavy cavalryman. This was the case of Guigonnet of Germolles, a rich peasant of the twelfth century. Guigonnet had his living quarters not in a tower or a fortified manor or castle, like the nobility, but in an agricultural center, where the products of the land—wheat, wine, fruits—were gathered. What distinguished him from the other peasants was his higher standard of living. Probably he did not work the land with his own hands anymore; he had subordinates to do that. Moreover, he spent time hunting like the aristocrats and belonged to religious organizations, where he met social superiors. But the most important aspect of his life was that at times he wore the knightly weapons and armor that he owned, rode his strong horse, and joined the other knights.[9]

Guigonnet is obviously the exception, even at the emergence of knighthood. A more typical person is William the Marshal. The fourth son of a minor Norman noble living at the court of King Henry I of England, William was sent to his maternal uncle in Normandy for his education, becoming a knight in 1167 at the age of twenty-two (he was born around 1145). His exploits on the battlefield and at tournaments attracted the attention of King Henry II, who became his patron, entrusting him with the education of his children.[10]

William was called "the greatest knight of the world," although his beginnings were modest. When he attended his first tournament, he was a poor man without land or fief; he did not even own an appropriate horse. It was a grim start that changed to dazzling success during the next fifteen years. At a tournament held near Eu in 1170 he captured ten knights and thirteen horses. Paired later with another knight, Roger de Gaugi, he succeeded in capturing 103 knights during ten months of tournaments. William and his comrades freed some of the defeated, but the majority had to pay a ransom (besides losing their weapons and horses). As it suited the mind-set of the period, William went to fight in the Holy Land. When he returned, he married the rich Isabel of Pembroke at the age of fifty, finally achieving what he, the poor son of a nobleman, had sought all of his life: financial wealth besides knightly glory and military success.

Although Duby tends to downplay the violence engendered by the rise of the knight, he maintains that the period around 1100 saw an increase in the violent behavior of warriors associated with the castles that had spread throughout France. The knights were the "first knives" (*premiers couteaux*) in enforcing the law of the local lord.[11] Dominque Barthélemy, by contrast, argues that brutality was less common; when it happened it was considered normal for the period.[12]

There is no doubt as to the preeminence of the knight and the tendency of every castle owner to surround himself with a retinue of heavily armed horsemen and footmen. The lord's men carried two goals: resolving personal vendettas and imposing justice. Their main task was to keep the social equilibrium stable by making sure that the rights of individuals were not trampled. Of course, their sense of justice and ethics was distorted by the conviction that the powerful had to retain primacy. It was necessary to force the peasants into a state of subjection, taking away their earthly possessions by violence (if they were subjects of an enemy lord) or imposing heavy taxes (if they lived on the lands of the knights' master). The knights were the defenders of law skewed in favor of their own social group. It is an unfair system to modern eyes, but it was within the legal and ethical mores of the time. Also, if their oppression was excessive or cruelty unjustified, they could expect some kind of punishment: relatives might refuse to support them, their allies might denounce them, their vassals might become disorderly. Moreover, knights also performed social duties that benefited the whole community: they acted as police *ante litteram,* preserved order in the territory, or supervised the construction of new roads and villages.

Yet the evidence of intense violence during the eleventh and twelfth centuries is overwhelming. During the First Crusade enemies were beheaded, their heads thrown over the walls of a besieged town or fixed on lances to terrorize their comrades; bodies were dug up to take any material possessions buried with them; captured soldiers were impaled.[13] This did not happen exclusively in the Holy Land, where religious fury and blindness typified both sides; such violence was also present in the struggles among Christians in Europe. For instance, in Flanders the two brothers of a knight named Bonifacius murdered his wife and child and forced him to leave his castle, but he returned, killing one of the murderers and forcing the other to flee. In the Bruges area, murders were commissioned with a pay of 10,000 marks.[14]

Fighting on horseback with lance, sword, and heavy armor did not necessarily make a knight out of a soldier, even during the early period. Other mounted and nonmounted soldiers coexisted in the immediate retinue of the knight (the "lance") or as independent or semi-independent units of mounted sergeants, or *routiers.* The retinue of a knight changed with time and location. In 1100 Robert II, Count of Flanders, promised to provide 1,000 knights, each with three horses, to King Henry I of England, suggesting that the knights were accompanied by other men who may have fought with them besides taking care of the horses. The religious Order of the Knights Templar listed three horses for each member. In 1268, when Charles, Count of Anjou, moved into Italy to take the southern peninsula from the successors of the Normans, he ordered each knight to bring four horses, suitable armor and weapons, as well as a squire (*armiger*) and two other retainers (*gardiones*). Each member of the "lance" performed different functions on the battlefield. The squire, who was not necessarily a young man, acted as a light cavalryman, the others as footmen with bows or crossbows and spears. Later on, larger retinues became common.

Sergeants were also common in the armies of the middle period of medieval warfare. In 1187 the count of Hainault sent Philip Augustus 110 of his best knights together with eighty sergeants equipped like the knights. In 1194 the king of France could count on the recruitment of 240 sergeants from St-Denis, 300 from Sens, Laon, and Tournai, 500 from Beauvais, and 1,000 from Arras. Generally their wages were between three and four sous a day, well below the five to seven sous given to knights. When the loot taken at Constantinople in 1204 was divided, their share was double the share of foot sergeants but half that of knights.[15] Mounted sergeants were not identical to squires but of mixed social origins. Some came from the lower ranks of nobility, holders of small fiefs who could boast neither prestige nor financial means. Others may have originated from the ranks of the bourgeoisie, or even the peasantry, who had training in arms, become supporters of a lord, and learned how to fight on horseback.[16] Their role on the battlefield varied. At times they lined up with the knights; sometimes they fought as a separate unit; sometimes they were given instructions to carry out a specific mission. At the Battle of Bouvines they were grouped as a light cavalry to soften up the enemy for the knights. Toward the end of the battle, 3,000 were given the task of crushing any remaining resistance.[17] However, by the second half of the thirteenth century sergeants on horseback disappeared from the French armies; the mounted men were usually divided between knights and squires. The term *knight* was replaced by the generic term *man-at-arms*.[18]

The *routiers* fought from horseback but were different from knights and mounted sergeants. The term *routiers*, probably originating from the Latin *rumpere* and meaning "members of a detachment," constituted groups of adventurers, men known for their wild behavior and not constrained by the ethical rules of knighthood. They were usually referred to as *Brabançons*, one of the places of their origin, although they must have come from other regions as well.[19]

In conclusion, during the ninth and tenth centuries, the notion of freeman as soldier was abandoned for a concept in which military duties of individuals were measured by landownership or loyalty to a higher lord. Under Charlemagne this meant an obligation to provide the ruler with one or more soldiers, or even a portion of a soldier by combining with other smaller landowners. Eventually the profession of soldier moved away from that arrangement. On the assumption that all territories belonged to the king, land was granted to great lords (vassals) and from them to lesser lords (valvassors) in exchange for military service for a certain number of days every year. This was the feudal system and became prevalent in France, most German lands, England, and northern Italy. Vassals provided knights, but there were also knights originating from the large or small courts of the lords whose military duties were rewarded with stipends, benefits, and weapons. Sometimes they even came from the peasantry. Finally, fighting next to the knights were sergeants and *routiers*.

When the knights first appeared, around the eleventh century, the term *knight* was not synonymous with *nobleman*. It applied to any heavy cavalryman regardless of social background. What counted was the function of the individual on the battlefield. By 1300, however, a major change had taken place. Society had become stratified, and moving up from one's station in life became increasingly difficult, even impossible. By then it was normal for knights to hold a fief in exchange for military service. Moreover, the word *knight* became equivalent to *nobleman*. As this took place, the mystique of knighthood began to lose its allure. One did not need to be a knight to be a heavy cavalryman or a man of high social standing. One's status as a noble guaranteed both, and the most common characterization of the heavy cavalryman was the man-at-arms.[20]

How to Train a Knight

Fighting as a knight involved expense that became greater over time. In the twelfth century the knight's basic equipment (horse, helmet, hauberk, and sword) required the annual revenue of 150 hectares. Three centuries later it cost the yearly income of 500 hectares.[21] The horses alone of Gerard de Moor, Lord of Wessegem, amounted in 1297 to 1,200 *livres tournois* (the livre was worth twenty sous).[22]

The investiture ceremony also became more complex. According to Jean Flori, initially we have no evidence of the existence of a particular induction ceremony into the order of knights.[23] It is likely that recruitment was a simple act: a lord giving the required equipment to selected individuals. However, as we move into the twelfth century, things started to change. The rite of induction (*adoubement*) emphasized not only the professional aspects of the people chosen but also their social status. The process eventually became synonymous with entry into the nobility, but by the fourteenth century the induction was no longer essential. The well-known French leader Bertrand du Guesclin was dubbed in 1356 at the age of 34. And around 1300 one noble out of three was inducted; by 1500 it was one out of twenty.[24]

Originally it seems that knights arrived prepackaged in the sense that a warrior, already known for his military prowess and skill on horseback, became a knight when he was given a sword, probably after a brief ceremony consisting of a buff on the back of the neck with the palm of the hand. With the passing of time the preparation for knighthood and the ceremony changed. By the middle of the thirteenth century, the sons of knights and noblemen were sent to serve at the court of a relative or another lord of military prestige. There they were trained in arms, serving as squires until they were considered ready to enter the order of knighthood. The knight's preparation involved professional training, during which young men were taught the skills and values of a warrior, together with exercises to strengthen physical vigor and improve stamina. Becoming a knight was a rite of passage to adulthood and eventually nobility (by the fourteenth century what had been an occupation open to talented men had become a caste). The ceremony acquired a sacred character. The initiated might spend the night in prayer in a chapel; when morning came, he was dubbed by touching his left and right shoulder with the flat side of a sword, which had been placed on the altar while ritual passages and blessings similar to the consecration of kings were performed.

The consecrated man adopted honor as his central value. Honor required that his status could never be challenged unless the challenge was defeated swiftly by force. It involved certain behavior toward women and the rest of society. The knight had to avoid insulting and using manipulations against peers and proclaim undying love and dedication to the wife of a lord. This ideal, which separated men of the court from commoners, was praised in poems, songs, and chivalric accounts performed at court. It was propaganda, which the knights' lifestyle reinforced through adventures, wars, hunts, and tournaments in which bravery and fearlessness were sanctified and exalted. Although the Catholic Church initially condemned this lifestyle, in the end it came to terms. In reality there was already originally an "osmosis," as Duby writes,[25] between the order of knighthood and the upper clergy, because prelates and religious institutions were also among the most important providers of warriors. At the same time ecclesiastics would try to make the chivalric ethics Christian, as when knights provided the main force to regain the Holy Land from the Muslims or pushed the Christian frontiers east of the Elbe among the pagans. The knight became the *miles Christi* (knight of Christ), consecrated by the ceremonial induction and principles dear to the Church—defense of women and children, liberality, service to the Church—mixed with secular aims—shedding the enemy's blood, military bravery, glory, courtesy, and honor. But the osmosis between laity and clergy was never complete. Friction always existed, for the very concept of courtly love was at odds with religious principles. The Christian concept of knighthood in the Church was never a perfect match with the secular world.

Training for war did not end with entry into the knight's order. It continued throughout life in actual conflicts and exercises and games, especially hunting and tournaments. The tournaments of the late thirteenth to the fifteenth centuries give a false impression. They became sanitized events, held in a fixed rectangular area, normally among heavily armed knights who were protected with thick jousting armor and blunt-tipped lances, not the deadly points used in combat.[26] At the beginning the games had been different.

Tournaments were a French creation attributed to a Loire lord named Geoffroy de Preuilly who died in 1066, but the first mention of their existence is around the beginning of the twelfth century. Tournaments increased in popularity, arranged in French territory about every fifteen days. In England, where they were forbidden for a time, King Richard (the Lionhearted) had to relent, allowing them with certain restrictions. It was necessary, he thought, as tournaments trained young men for war. Tournaments acquired such prestige that the greatest lords tried to form all-star teams of the greatest knights. Victory on tournament day would bring prestige to the lord who had assembled the team.

Tournaments were held in open fields and woods, but also in villages. The participants (knights, squires, archers, and other footmen) were divided into fairly even teams, and the event took place over several days. The first phase was dedicated to the formation of the groups; the second to skirmishes and individual duels; the third and final day to a collective clash between the contestants, quite different from the individual matches of later tournaments. It involved all weapons—lances, swords, maces, hatchets, bows, crossbows. Although the goal was not to kill the opponent, casualties were inevitable.

Tournaments and war could be highly rewarding. The Crusaders who attacked at the Battle of Doryleum cried, "Be of one mind in your belief in Christ and in the victory of the Holy Cross, because you will all become rich today, if God wills."[27] And the Crusaders in the *Chanson d'Antioche*: "Out there on the grass, we shall either lose our heads or else become rich in fine silver and gold, that we shall no longer have to beg from our comrades." And "see how the gold and silver glitter in the meadows! The man who gets that will never be poor again."[28] The promise of wealth was a main attraction for many knights to wage war in the Holy Land. "Anyone who was poor there [in Europe] became rich [in the Holy Land] through God's favor. Anyone who had only a few shillings there has countless bezants here. Anyone who had not even a village there, has a city here, thanks to God. Why go back to the West, when we can find all this in the East?"[29]

The Ideology of Knighthood

Chivalry was surrounded by a set of ideals that was constantly being reinforced. When the Church came to terms with the institution, knights became the "knight of Christ." In the meantime, an intense propaganda campaign devised vehicles to glorify actions through heraldry, personal appearances, and the works of poets, writers, and artists. It was a process that made knighthood an institution, a cultural model and ideology that would endure beyond the Middle Ages, a model for later generations of aristocrats.[30]

The early use of painted symbols and coats-of-arms on shields and horse vestments is debatable, but most agree they appeared by the second half of the twelfth century.[31] They became a splendid visual statement of identity and greatness, of the preeminence and ancestry of an aristocratic line, though heraldic signs were favored by ordinary knights more than great lords. It is also certain that the need for identification in tournaments, less so in battle, may have been a stimulus for their use. Heraldic signs were a perfect vehicle during a period of social transition, when new families were coming to the fore. Popular when patronymics were being adopted, they stated identity and social class, which extended from the individual to his family and from his family to the class they belonged to.

Initially the symbol, usually derived from an animal or plant or abstract geometric signs, was not permanent and could be dropped in favor of a new one. For instance, Richard the Lionhearted, who was probably the first English monarch to use a heraldic sign, adopted two lions facing each other, but in 1195 that was dropped in favor of three lions over a red background.[32] It seems that heraldic signs started to become permanent between 1120 and 1140. By the thirteenth century, heraldry spread to all kinds of noble and nonnobles—clergymen, women, corporations, cities, and so on. As time went by, heraldic symbols followed strict rules and underwent changes. Quartering became popular by the end of the thirteenth century. The division of the shield into quadrants allowed the blending of paternal and marriage-based heritage. The most common geometric symbols are the chief (broad horizontal band), the pale (a vertical line on the center of the shield), the bend (a diagonal line), the chevron (similar to a military stripe), the cross, and the saltire (cross of St. Andrew). With prohibitions on one color over color and metal over metal, the colors became gules (red), azure (blue), sable (black), vert (green), purpure (purple), tenne (orange), and *murrey* (reddish-purple). Gold was rendered with yellow and silver with white.[33]

The greatness of knighthood was conveyed in manuscripts. The drawings therein are often an assault on the imagination, with stunning hues, elegant lines, and engrossing messages.[34] The knights' gestures, words, and visual magnificence embodied the greatest ideals of the elites—and how beneficial this hegemony was for society as a whole! Were knights not symbols of military bravery, champions of religion, defenders of women and children? In the process all negative elements of knighthood were ignored.

The most important propaganda was the epic poem, or chanson de geste.[35] Originating probably from an oral tradition or the barbarian chants that Charlemagne ordered preserved during his reign, the chansons de geste became, starting in the twelfth century, testimonials to the bravery and greatness of the knight. Eventually three main types developed. One group of poems was associated with the Crusades; a second described the conflicts among nobles or against the centralizing action of the king; a third became dominant by the end of the thirteenth century and related stories of adventures and heroic actions. Initially they were recited by performers visiting the castles of the nobility. The poems were shorter in the beginning but became longer as time passed. The *Chanson de Bertrand du Guesclin*, on the famous general of the Hundred Years War, has 24,000 verses.

The Knight in Battle

J. F. Verbruggen has shown that, in spite of the propaganda, the knight experienced fear and panic.[36] Confesses Fulcher of Chartres, at Doryleum in 1097 in the Holy Land, "We [the Crusaders] were all herded together like sheep in a sheepfold, trembling and frightened; eventually we were totally surrounded by the enemy."[37] And Baldwin of Boulogne openly admits, "We feigned bravery but feared death." But fear could also be the stimulus for the greatest bravery: "If we flee we'll be killed! We might just as well die trying to defend ourselves, rather than while trying to escape."[38] Yet there is no doubt that bravery was an essential quality.

We can dismiss the old view that portrays knights as disordered rabble, each fighting for vain glory, unaware and uninterested about the rest of the army, although it is clear that such individualism never disappeared. It became evident in a much later period, during the Italian Renaissance. Baldassare Castiglione, who established the prototype of the true gentleman in the early sixteenth century, advises his readers that it is wise for the nobleman to fight within sight of his lord so that his bravery can be seen and eventually rewarded. Yet the evidence available presents a more variegated picture. The approach toward the enemy, discipline on the march and in battle, order kept during the actual encounter, the ability to perform complicated maneuvers— all point to a sophisticated understanding of the art of war. The Order of the Knights Templar, for instance, had very strict and detailed instructions on how to operate while moving toward the enemy. The instructions given by

Richard the Lionhearted during the march from Acre to Jaffa were motivated by a careful analysis of the dangers that soldiers experienced while moving toward the enemy. It was an example followed by Baldwin III in 1147 as he left Jerusalem to approach Bosra. When the time came to camp, it was normal to fortify the location to avoid surprise attacks. During the siege of Acre in the Holy Land, King Guy of Lusignan fortified his camp, afraid of an incursion by the forces of the Muslim leader, the great warrior Saladin.[39]

Orders before and during a battle were given by trumpets and banners. The trumpets might indicate the time to attack; banners, depending on the way that they were held, instructed soldiers that a particular order was intended— to begin or to stop an attack or to strike camp at the end of a march.[40] Of particular importance was the leader's standard. Protected by elite soldiers, the standard was indicative of the morale status of the host. As long as it stood tall, it said to all the soldiers that hope for victory was still high in their leader's heart; if it dropped and was not picked up and raised again by another knight, it suggested acceptance of defeat. At Hattin in 1187 this situation was understood by Saladin. As the knights of Guy of Lusignan charged, pushing back the Muslim army, the Muslim general's son saw his father's face become sad and pale, but he soon recovered and encouraged his men to counterattack, forcing the crusaders to withdraw. "We have won," shouted the young man. But he was wrong: the knights came back, charging again and again until they were forced to withdraw, prompting the young man to scream, "We have driven them off!" But his father dismissed the enthusiasm of his son saying, "Not yet. Their standard is still up." It was only later, when the crusader standard finally went down, that Saladin sprang off his horse and, weeping with joy, knelt to the ground, thanking God.[41] When possible, and in the case of small units, the orders could also be relayed by voice. During the attack on Constantinople during the Fourth Crusade, two of the bravest men of each battle were instructed to shout "Spur!" to command riding forward quickly or "Advance at a walk!" if the intention was to proceed slowly.[42]

Before the final preparations for battle, new warriors might be elevated to knighthood, apparently without the complex ceremonies typical of the rite. On 11 June 1302 at the famous Battle of Courtrai, such was the case for the Fleming Pieter de Conine and his two sons, together with about thirty leading citizens from Bruges. At Mons-en-Pévèle, another well-known clash in the French attempt to subdue Flanders, King Philip the Fair of France knighted 300 squires.[43] Knightly armies were divided into several battle groups, or "battles," of various numerical strength. They could include the vanguard, the main battle, the rearguard, two wings, and at times even more battle groups. At the Battle of Ascalon in 1099 the knights deployed into nine main units— three in the vanguard, three in the middle, and three at the rear; the second line supporting the first but also preventing any encirclement, the third line covering the rear and supporting the first two.[44] The leader usually fought in the front ranks, which had not always been the case among the Romans.[45]

Although most armies around 1000–1200 relied on heavy cavalry, infantry forces may also have been present. As regards the cavalry, each battle was divided into smaller units, or "banners" (*bannières*) or *conrois*, made up of a leader with his relatives and vassals. At times, two or three smaller banners joined in a single *conroi*, between twenty and twenty-four knights.[46] As they prepared for battle the knightly line was shallow (between two and four ranks deep) and very tight, so much so that a battlefield 1 kilometer wide might accommodate 1,500 or 2,000 horsemen.[47] The literary and chronicle sources of the time repeat similar images in describing the knights. They were "formed up in such close ranks, as though they were welded together. . . . It was impossible to drop a plum, except on knights in shining armor." As they rode forward, "there is no space where a glove can fall." They advanced "in such close formation that the wind could not blow between their lances." Of course literary license must have played a role in such descriptions.

It is likely that attacks were carried out by section (one to three *conrois* at a time), each withdrawing to regroup after the initial clash. The knights moved slowly at the beginning, making sure to keep their line, but as they arrived closer to the enemy they rode as fast as possible to bring the greatest possible effect against the opposing line. Before contact the enemy would arrange their shields to deflect or minimize the lance's power. When the knights overpowered the opponent, the other members of the knights' retinue, squires and footmen, would intervene to kidnap the living for ransom or, if dead, to spoil them of weapons and armor.[48]

If the lance broke after the clash, it was necessary to go to the sword or mace. But the sword needed more space, giving credence to the belief that whereas the original thrust was a collective effort, the rest of the encounter devolved into disorder, where the skill and bravery of the knight were key. Even more likely, the riders would withdraw and regroup behind a screen of footmen, allowing the next section to move forward.

It has been suggested that the main goal of the knight was to unseat the opponent, opening the way for soldiers, squires, and footmen. The knight rarely targeted footmen if they were on the field. If footmen became a target, the tactical goal was to disorder their ranks, isolate individuals, and kill them one by one.[49] In that case the lance was not an appropriate weapon, and the rider must have used sword and mace.

Knights also fought dismounted, a method wrongly associated only with the English armies of the Hundred Years War. For instance, the king of the Romans, Conrad III, and his knights dismounted during a battle in the Holy Land in 1148. The Anglo-Norman knights also fought dismounted at the Battle of Tinchebray (1106), where King Henry I and his retinue stood in the footmen's middle. At Brémule (1119), Henry I again instructed his cavalry to dismount and fight on foot, an example followed at Bourgthéroulde (1124), where the Norman knights lined up with their archers to stiffen the footmen's courage.[50] When this happened, common military wisdom dictated to stay put after deployment, because normally the line that advanced to combat faced a handicap. It may have made tired the advancing line, which would begin the battle in weaker physical condition.[51] That is what happened to the French at the Battle of Agincourt in 1415.

Chapter Thirteen

The Way of the Commoners: Soldiers on Foot

DEPLOYED IN SERRATED RANKS, their bodies embraced by thick armor, their lances slightly diagonal, they advanced first slowly and then, as the target got closer, spurred their horses toward impact. The rhythmic, frenetic sound of the animals raising clouds of dust, the din of the trumpets, the cries of the approaching mass, the light bouncing over their armor and steel points brought terror. If one was a footman, standing still and keeping the spear, pike, or bow ready to confront the charging knights must have taxed the soul to the extreme. Only few infantrymen were able to do so: the knight was supreme. Not that footmen were discarded. Footmen took the field alongside their social superiors and were more numerous, and at times they became masters of the battlefield. Yet much more often they were confined to a supporting role, and in almost all cases they were ignored or despised by knights and those who recorded the events.

At times foot soldiers did not take the field with their masters.[1] But that was the exception, not the rule. Battles between knights usually involved considerable numbers of footmen, although a foot force of 10,000 must have been the upper limit, even among the most notable hosts of infantrymen in Switzerland and Scotland.[2] Some infantrymen were squires; others were foot soldiers (bowmen, crossbowmen, spearmen) who supported their lord by being a point of reference during the clash or by spoiling the fallen of their weapons or taking them prisoner. When the Guelph army of Florence (the supporters of the Papacy against the Ghibelline supporters of the empire), met the Ghibelline army from Arezzo at Campaldino on 11 June 1289, the Florentine host numbered about 10,000 footmen and a little more than 1,000 cavalrymen. The army from Arezzo had about 800 knights and 8,000 infantrymen.[3] Verbruggen considers unreliable most of the figures found in a chronicler of Hainault, Gilbert de Mons, who mentions 30,000 and 60,000 for certain campaigns, but reliable when Gilbert's figures are much smaller. In 1172 the count of Hainault marched against the count of Namur at the head of 1,500 picked foot soldiers; three years later Baldwin IV led 200 knights and 1,200 foot to a tournament; and in 1180 he complied with a request for help from the French king by dispatching 3,000 infantry.[4] The French kings normally did not deploy large contingents of foot soldiers, although in most cases, as in the rest of western Europe, those fighting on foot were always more numerous than those on horseback. The communal force at the Battle of Bouvines numbered 3,160. Louis IX had 1,600 footmen when his knightly army moved against the count of Brittany in 1231.[5]

Footmen were used in several roles, in rather thin lines, probably two or three deep. If bowmen or crossbowmen, they could open the battle or remain poised to protect the flanks. Crossbowmen would kneel on the ground behind a large shield, shooting while a comrade held a shield and helped recharge the weapon and, in extreme cases, defending with a spear against enemy attacks. Bowmen must have lined up fairly close to one another without the protection of a shield. This made them easy prey if the enemy came close enough. At times, however, dismounted knights were inserted into the line to stiffen the resistance of the footmen and to increase the psychological determination of the light troops. This happened at Bourg Théroulde, where the Norman knights dismounted to fight alongside their archers.[6] But during 900–1300 missile units were small[7] and thus less likely to decide the outcome.

Spearmen also could be used in several roles. They may have deployed on the first line, spears stuck in the earth to protect the horsemen's deployment or more likely behind the first line of knights, becoming the rallying point for horsemen who withdrew and regrouped in the rear. A most interesting deployment was tried by Richard the Lionhearted at the Battle of Jaffa in 1192. The king, with a select group of knights, took refuge in a circle of spearmen, their weapons stuck in the ground under the protection of their shields, with a kneeling crossbowman and a loader for every two spearmen.[8] Footmen could also perform a variety of other functions. They could follow knights at a close distance to assail the unhorsed enemies. They could also help their masters to remount, or provided a fresh horse or lance. Invariably, however, footmen were an accessory to the knight, who remained the determining factor on the battlefield. Footmen could be a match for a warrior on horseback only in specific situations.

Successes experienced in the fields were the product of a specific type of footman or terrain that worked against the horseman. The men who gathered to defend the freedom of the Lombard communes (independent or semi-independent city states) against Emperor Frederick Barbarossa, or those who fought for the Flemish cities, were not the normal lower classes typical of most infantry. They came from the middle strata or lower-middle strata (artisans and so on) of the city's population. They had ideals to defend, freedoms to protect, and economic interests to pursue. In other words, they were unlike the normal footman, who was forcefully taken from his meager surroundings, a man who had little to defend. The higher social standing of the footmen in Flanders is also shown by his equipment (he had to provide it), which could be quite expensive. For instance, at Zierikzee in 1304 some citizens of Bruges lost expensive equipment, amounting a small fortune for some.[9] But even if paid by the city or guild, a spirit of solidarity typified these soldiers. It also mattered how they were lined up on the battlefield.

One weakness of medieval armies was fragmentation. They acted in separate units, often too small to make a difference. Even the basic fighting knightly unit, the *conroi*, had about 20 men and in many cases less. It is true that more than one *conroi* advanced together, but the reality is that the battle was like a series of a movie scenes tied together only by the final clash. It worked for the knights, but not the footmen. Small blocks of infantrymen are usually not effective. Only mass achieves results, but this scheme was rarely used. Moreover, continuous training in the art of war was denied to the infantryman. Assembled when needed and disbanded soon after a campaign ended, they lacked the cohesion and practice that comes from continuous experience. The knight was a professional fighter, constantly training or fighting in the belief that secular power and religion were on his side. So it is remarkable that infantry armies were able to achieve great successes against knightly armies.

Legnano: The Lombards Against Barbarossa

The great empire of Charlemagne eventually split into two areas of influence: One centered around the French king, the other around the German territories and the Holy Roman Emperor. The main worry of the emperor was containing the Magyars in the Carpathian Basin, a problem solved when the Magyars fell at the Battle of the Lechfeld in 955. Eighty years would pass before the emperor had to bring another large force against them. The other concern was the Italian lands, an endemic problem never solved to the emperors' satisfaction in spite of the fact that they crossed the Alps in twenty campaigns between 936 and 1137.[10]

After the defeat of the Longobards by the Franks and of the Muslims and Byzantines by the Normans, the Italian peninsula was divided into three main political areas. The Normans and their successors controlled most of the south; the Holy Roman Emperor was the overlord of most of northern and central Italy; and the pope carved a substantial temporal state in the center of the peninsula but also at the upper margins of the south and lower margins of the north. Theoretically, then, emperors remained the overlords of much of Italy, but their claim became weaker and weaker. The emperors' feeble enforcement of sovereignty sucked German resources during the times of Frederick Barbarossa (1152–1190) and his grandson Frederick II (1220–1250), the offspring of the marriage between Frederick's son and the last descendant of the Normans.

When Charlemagne displaced the Longobards from northern Italy and replaced them with Franks or Italian nobles loyal to him, the kings of Italy, located in Pavia, entered a period of irreversible decline until sovereigns only in name. At the same time the towns forcefully asserted independence from king and emperor. As the power of kings and emperors waned, cities fell under the control of local noblemen and bishops, with the cathedral becoming the focus of religious, social, and political life. Eventually power shifted from secular lords and bishops to lay magistrates, called consuls, who were elected by citizen councils.

The commune, as these semi-independent cities came to be called, was an urban government typical of at least three areas in Europe: northern and parts of central Italy, the Rhine region, and Flanders, but the development in Italy was unique. Elsewhere cities, as they fought for independence, did not extend supremacy outside their walls. In Italy the communes claimed control over the surrounding countryside and inevitably over the region's weaker cities. They were an administrative, political, and territorial entity that acted as a magnet for most of the aristocrats who moved from the countryside. The commune, a city-state in the manner of the polis of ancient Greece, was based on the belief that the citizens should take an oath for the defense and interests of the community. This did not mean that all inhabitants had the same rights. Initially the magistrates came from the aristocracy, but eventually they were representative of several social groups: nobles who had come to live in the city, burghers (lawyers and notaries), merchants, artisans and craftsmen, and professionals. Excluded were women, the poor, and anybody not belonging to the guilds, which separated managers and workers from the *senza arte nè parte* (those without a skillful occupation and without guild membership). The unemployed, and underemployed, besides those who did not have a specialized occupation or belong to a guild, were excluded.

As Bishop Otto of Freising, maternal uncle of Emperor Frederick Barbarossa, eloquently describes, the beautiful land of Italy had turned, through intermarriage, the natural "crude, barbarous ferocity" of the children of the Longobards into the "Roman keenness and gentleness," retaining at the same time "the refinement of the Latin speech and their elegance of manners." However, the beautiful cities had become "so desirous of liberty that, avoiding the insolence of power, they are governed by the will of consuls rather than rulers." The consuls represented the nobles and all the major social groups of the city, that is, the great nobles (*capitanei*), the lower nobles (*vavassores*), and the commoners. Their desire for liberty and their economic accomplishments made them unwilling to recognize the authority of their prince, the emperor: "they scarcely if ever respect the prince [emperor and king of Italy] to whom they should display the voluntary deference of obedience or willingly perform that which they have sworn by the integrity of their laws, unless they sense his authority in the power of his great army." Yet the communes never submitted to imperial authority for very long and "frequently receive[d] in hostile fashion him [the emperor] whom they ought to accept as their own gentle prince, when he demands what is rightfully his own."[11]

The most powerful of the northern communes was Milan, which had extended or kept trying to extend its supremacy over most of the fertile plain of Lombardy. But Milan was only one of many communes, each certain of its right to freedom and independence from all, including the emperor, unless subordination involved only token homage. It was a situation that no emperor, holding at the same time the crown of king of Italy, could accept. In appearance, the task of enforcing the imperial rights seemed easy. After all, how could cities stand the might of the empire when they were often fighting each other, whereas the imperial ruler could rely on both German and other Italian cities and feudatories to support his claim? Yet it was not easy. The defeat of one commune might lead to the founding of other, more dangerous ones. Moreover, fighting the communes meant confronting the holder of the Papal See. Popes had an obvious interest in weakening the imperial crown, which claimed lordship over lands that the pontiff considered to belong to the Patrimony of St. Peter. And the cities were never completely isolated, for Milan was able to assemble most into a league, the objective of which was to defeat the emperor's claims. In 1164 a league was formed among the Venetian cities of Vicenza, Padua, and Treviso. Three years later the coalition became quite strong with the addition of Milan, Brescia, Mantua, and Cremona, as well as cities along the Po River in the Emilian territory, Ferrara, Modena, and Bologna. This diplomatic and military alliance, called the Lombard League, formed new versions, in 1185 and 1195, making the emperor's task almost impossible. It was an alignment revived on a grand scale in 1226 against Barbarossa's grandson, Frederick II.

The communes' defiance came to a head during the reign of Frederick Barbarossa, who led several expeditions into Italy from 1154 to 1184. Born in 1125 or 1126, Frederick was younger than thirty when Barbarossa, as the Italians called him (because of his red beard) was elected king of Germany in 1152. A sharp, energetic, intelligent man, although he never learned Latin well, Barbarossa was of medium height with a rather powerful neck, broad shoulders, and strong legs, energetic and known for his ability as hunter, rider, and swimmer.[12] He was a pious individual who at times could be gentle and humane but also cruel and ruthless when challenged. Rarely deterred by failure, he would avoid diplomacy and compromise, preferring brutal enforcement.

Barbarossa led six campaigns into Italy for several reasons in 1154–1555, 1158–1162, 1163, 1167, 1174, and 1184. The country was rich and had an ideal climate. Moreover, it continuously challenged imperial authority. Also, in Italy he had received the iron crown of king at Pavia and was invested as emperor by the pope in Rome. The imperial expeditions assembled the troops either at Augsburg or at Ratisbon and then crossed the Alps, normally through Brenner Pass. The expeditions began in August or September, though at times in early spring or even during the months of November, December, and February. The troops' return took place during good weather from May to September.

After entering Italy, the imperial army stopped on the Roncaglia Plain in Lombardy, where the Italian vassals were called to join the host and where the emperor waited for the rest of the German armies that had not started out with him.[13] At Roncaglia the emperor placed a shield on a long pole and ordered a herald to summon all the princes to join the imperial host together with their vassals. It was an order that extended to both secular and religious lords. Those who refused were punished by the confiscation of their fiefs unless the lands had been bestowed on them in perpetuity.[14]

Barbarossa's armies were typical feudal hosts. The soldiers could be summoned by using the right of *bannum*, the royal prerogative of calling all citizens in case of extreme danger, with punishment or heavy fines meted out to those who failed to answer the emperor's call. The *bannum* meant that everyone had to come, not just the knights but also burghers and free peasants and footmen, some of them "more accustomed to agriculture than knighthood," as described by a contemporary.[15] The knights came from a variety of sources: household troops at the imperial court and at the lesser courts of the lords of the land, laymen, bishops, and abbots. Each magnate was required to fill a certain quota depending on the extent of his dominion or based on arrangement sanctified by tradition. Some of the knights came also from a nonfree group, the *ministeriales* (knight-serfs), but all of them, whether free or nonfree, enjoyed the resources of a fief, sometimes quite small, or were supported by a lordly court. The imperial army was a combination of forces. Their service was limited (forty days), and usually did not fight outside the borders of their territories. In case of campaigns against external enemies, participants served because of traditional ties with the emperor, the lure of loot, or financial compensation. A 981 document, indicating the effects of Emperor Otto II's expedition to Italy, indicates that of the 6,000 *loricati* (chain-mail soldiers), 1,400 came from Bavaria, 1,100 from Lorraine, 900 from Alemannia, 800 from Franconia, and about 1,500 from Saxony. In the 1124 campaign to France the forces at the emperor's disposal included not less than 300 horsemen from Poland and Bohemia.[16]

The Italian communes were able to raise strong armies, 1,000 soldiers or more in some communes.[17] In 1298 Bologna could count on 1,600 knights, but not all would be required for every campaign. When needed in Florence, the call to arms was divided among the city's six sections (*sesti*), although only a small number of sections were bound to participate. The requirement to serve applied to knights (nobles) and to citizens enjoying certain economic means. The latter were defined as "knights for the commune" (*milites pro commune*). The members of these groups had to provide a warhorse for military use. In 1162 Pisa armed 300 *milites*. If at the death of the original *miles* property was divided among his heirs, as the laws of inheritance allowed in the Italian cities, the heirs had to combine their resources to deploy a heavy cavalryman. At the Battle of Montaperti in 1260, two-thirds of the Florentine army was composed of soldiers assembled on that basis. The commune was responsible for the upkeep of the warhorses during the year, whether at war or during times of peace, and the owner was compensated if it was injured or killed. He also received pay during a campaign.[18] Besides those fighting on horseback, all citizens or subjects of the commune, whether living in cities or as peasants in the countryside, were required to serve as footmen from the age of fourteen (more commonly eighteen) to sixty. They received pay during service.[19] Communal armies included nobles, burghers (urban middle classes), lower classes, peasants, and, by the middle of the twelfth century, mercenaries. Already in 1124 Fiesole hired strangers to help in its struggle against neighboring Florence. By the end of the century, a mixed force, both horse and foot, of Lombards, Germans, Catalans, and Spaniards served under the new dynasty of the Angevins in Naples. At their strongest they may have numbered 2,500 cavalry and about 20,000 infantry. Moreover, the features of what will typify the mercenary warlords—called condottieri in the following centuries—started to appear very early; this meant hiring a body of soldiers accustomed to serving under a particular leader for a regulated contract specifying rates of pay and equipment. However, the core of the communal armies remained the city's subjects for the cavalry and the infantry.[20]

The main symbol of the citizen armies was the *carroccio*, a wagon that combined religious and patriotic elements. Its first appearance was at Milan in 1039, when one was constructed at the urging of the archbishop, Heribert. The wagon, always pulled by white oxen, had a pole on top holding the cross or the figure of a patron saint (St. Ambrose in Milan) or the flag of the city (a red cross on a white field for Milan). It deployed in battle with the army's standard, protected by a small elite force, normally infantry. It was a rallying point during the battle and during times of peace was a symbol of the city during ceremonies, processions, receptions for a foreign dignitary, and oath ceremonies.[21]

Reconstructing Legnano is very difficult. Sources are poor and contradictory on every aspect. Yet a few facts seem clear. The battle began unexpectedly between scouting cavalry units of both sides; it continued with a long clash of about six hours between the imperial cavalry and the infantry of the Lombard League; it ended when the Lombard cavalry, routed in the first fight, regrouped and with the help of new arrivals defeated the imperialists[22] (Figure 13.1).

The main goal of the Lombards was to prevent the arrival of reinforcements from Germany to the imperial army located at Pavia. The Lombards moved to intercept the emperor, who had gone personally to greet the reinforcements at Como before they joined the rest of his troops. Legnano was well located strategically to achieve such a goal. The town was about 15 miles north of Milan and thus between the emperor's point of departure, Como, and his point of arrival, Pavia.

It is clear that not all the troops of the Lombard cities had arrived, as some joined the battle toward the end. In all probability the Lombards had

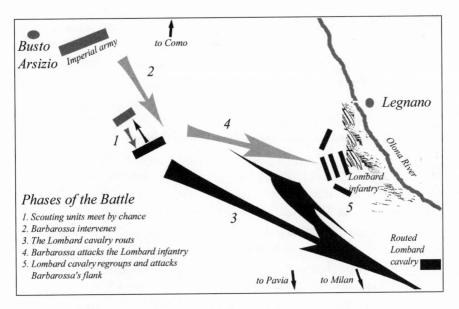

Figure 13.1   Legnano 1176

10,000–12,000 men at their disposal, including foot and horse. They were numerically superior to Barbarossa, who led a larger cavalry contingent.

While most of their army deployed near Legnano, about 700 Lombard cavalrymen scouted the area north to report on the emperor's movements. Scouting was also on Barbarossa's mind, for he too had sent ahead a scouting contingent of about 300 cavalrymen. The two sides met unexpectedly about 5 kilometers from Legnano. The clash favored the Lombards initially, as they could count on more men. But Barbarossa, not far away with the rest of the army, came to the relief of his cavalry. The outcome could not be but favorable to the emperor. The Lombard soldiers were routed and fled toward their army, but the rest of the cavalry was routed too. The fugitives stopped about 900 meters away from where their infantry had deployed.

Instead of continuing his pursuit of the enemy cavalry, Barbarossa decided to destroy the Lombard infantry, which had deployed in a strange position with a ridge at its back. The ridge prevented easy flight, which meant that the Lombards had no choice but to fight or die. The struggle lasted probably six hours. One after another, four of the Lombards' infantry lines were compelled to withdraw, but the fifth, grouped around the *carroccio*, resisted all attacks. Made up of people who had an economic and juridical stake in the independence of their cities, their morale strengthened by the symbol of their land, the Lombard infantry defended its position. They never passed over to the counterattack, yet they stubbornly stood their ground.

The battle might have ended in a draw if Barbarossa had decided to end his futile efforts. The cavalrymen, who had regrouped and were strengthened by fresh arrivals, probably from Brescia, counterattacked. It was not difficult to defeat the imperial forces. While the Lombard infantry pinned Barbarossa's troops, the Lombard League's cavalry moved against the imperial flank. It was a complete defeat. The emperor's standard-bearer was killed in front of his leader; the rest of the soldiers, abandoning arms and even horses, rushed to safety north and south of the battlefield. Barbarossa himself seemed to have fallen, for no one knew where he was. He was safe, however, and later reappeared in Pavia.

Legnano was a humiliating defeat for the emperor, who afterward had to accept most of the terms, which emphasized the freedom and the actual, if not theoretical, independence of the communes. It also meant the end of Barbarossa's dream of reestablishing the empire that had reached such greatness under Charlemagne. When his grandson Frederick II tried to reestablish real imperial authority, his effort also ended in failure.

The battle is fascinating. It would be wrong to claim that it was a victory of infantry against cavalry. The cavalry inflicted the killing blow. Yet Legnano does show how effective footmen could be if they were schooled well and supported by cavalrymen. And as we see in Flanders in 1302, infantry could defeat an army of horsemen outright.

The Day at Courtrai: The Humiliation of the French Knights

The deployment in a single large battle, careful choice of terrain, confidence in the rightness of their cause, the realization that defeat meant death, and the use of a murderous and efficient weapon were the keys to the great Flemish victory at Courtrai on 11 July 1302.

The confrontation between the Flemings and the French King, Philip the Fair, became inevitable after the Bruges Rebellion of 18 May 1302.[23] The Flemings had massacred more than 300 French (many still asleep) in the early hours of the morning. The struggle began with the armed invasion of the French king into Flanders to jail the count of Flanders, Guy of Dampierre, for having supported the king of England in the past war against France. Although many Flemings sided with Philip, many others chose to stand against the occupation. Among the most vocal and enterprising were the burghers in many Flemish cities, strengthened by the support of a few nobles as well as by peasants from the countryside around the urban centers. All of them feared the French—the men of Bruges because of an earlier massacre against them, the nobles who valued their ancient rights and independence, and the better-off peasants because of the additional taxation burdens of foreign troops. Victory meant salvation, defeat death.

Punishment of the rebels had to come immediately, because the Flemings had brought 334 French personnel, who had taken refuge in the Courtrai castle at the rebellion's outbreak, to the edge of surrender.[24] The numerical strength of the armies is not clear, although most historians would agree that the Flemings outnumbered the French if we count only those who fought after the initial missile skirmish. Philip assembled a considerable army, usually understood as a knightly army, although at least half were foot soldiers. The French host numbered about 3,000 knights and at least the same number of infantry. The day of the battle they faced between 7,400 and 11,000 Flemings, all on foot, including the few knights that had joined the burghers and men from the countryside.[25] The Flemish troops came from Bruges, the countryside around the city (these were the so-called Francs de Bruges), together with others from West and East Flanders, that is, people from the lands near the sea and from Ypres.[26] They included also about sixty aristocrats and urban patricians,[27] such as Guy of Namur, William of Jülich, and John of Renesse, the natural leaders of their forces.

The Flemings' numerical superiority would have meant little against a charge by 3,000 French knights across flat, unencumbered terrain, but the area they had chosen, in the proximity of the French garrison in the castle at Courtrai, contained many advantages to people fighting on foot (Figure 13.2). The Flemings lined up their troops next to the city of Courtrai in a reverse-L formation, or semicircle in the form of a half-moon, as the Italian chronicler Giovanni Villani wrote a short time after the encounter.[28] Its front, facing south, was at most about 800 meters wide,[29] and its side, facing east, was about 400–500 meters.[30] It was a brilliant choice of terrain. The waters of the Lage River anchored their right and a monastery their left. Their rear was protected from any nasty surprise by the River Lys and because the only bridge connecting the river with the other side was demolished. Moreover, the area on the opposite bank was unsuitable for horses, with extensive swamps. With their rear secure, the Flemings made sure that their deployment would be as safe as possible on the flanks and in the front. On their right, the city of Courtrai and the Lage Vijver made any encirclement impossible; on the front, the French would find the Grote Beek (the Great Brook), which, though fordable, prevented a direct charge. The situation was repeated on the Flemish left,

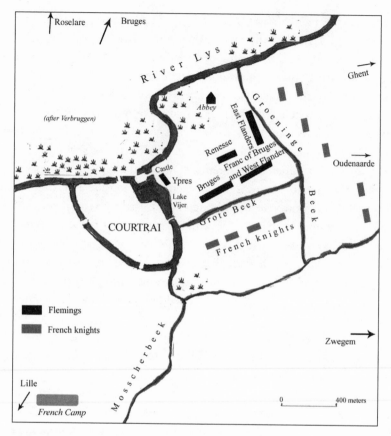

Figure 13.2   Courtrai 1302

where the Groeninge Beek ran to join the Grote Beek at an angle before continuing its course. The Groeninge was not an impossible obstacle, but it was
troublesome enough to make any direct charge impossible unless the horses
first crossed the brook and then regrouped on the opposite bank. And this was
not all, for the Flemings in front of their deployment may have dug ditches,
hidden with dirt and branches after being filled with water from the creeks or
the river. The register of expenses of the French leader, Robert of Artois, shows
that the French bought a map of the ditches of the area,[31] although the map
may have indicated only those that existed before the encounter, probably
channels for agricultural purposes. The Flemings also lined up a group of soldiers to face the castle in case the French forces decided to mount a sortie from
within in combination with their forces on the battlefield. Finally, a reserve
under John of Renesce was set up behind the front line.

The Flemings chose to stand in a manner that would certainly cause great trouble to any charging cavalry. At least part of the infantry was armed with the *goedendag* ("good day"). As the French sergeant from Orléans, Guillaume Guiart, who fought at Flanders, describes, the *goedendags* were "long, heavy shafts reinforced with iron" with "a long, sharp, iron point." They could "strike without moving [because of their long reach] by stabbing... [the] enemy in the belly."[32] No doubt, the *goedendag* was a fearsome weapon that, as shown in the Courtrai Chest at New College in Oxford, included a heavy steel head of a semi-oval format with a spiked tip, combining spear and mace. Held with two hands, it was an ideal weapon to bring down a horseman and then crush his armor. The Fleming footmen were so fearsome because they combined the *goedendag* with another staff weapon, the pike. Pikemen took their place on the first line, two hands on their weapons, which was either stuck on the ground or pushed against a foot in a diagonal direction to disorder the knights' initial charge. Then the men armed with *goedendags* would come forward, their long, formidable weapons having the advantage over the shorter blades and maces of the French cavalrymen. In any case, any horseman who fell would be helpless.

The obvious weakness of the Flemish deployment was the impossibility of retreat. Boxed in as they were between the River Lys, the Lage River, and the two brooks on the left and front, disaster would have been inevitable if they were forced to flee. It was a weakness, however, that they turned to their advantage. The Flemings had no alternative but to stand still and die fighting on the spot.

When the French arrived at Courtrai on 26 June, they realized that the enemy had chosen an almost impregnable position. They hesitated, and different plans were proposed at the council of war held before the battle. Raoul de Nestle emphasized the dangers. If the French were compelled to retreat, the two brooks that they had to cross could cause havoc among the ranks. Godfrey of Brabant discouraged any immediate assault: let them be without food and drink under the summer sun, delaying the attack one day to further weaken their bodies. But the majority insisted on immediate action. The grand master of the crossbowmen, Jean de Burlats, suggested opening the clash with his men from a distance (the Flemish had few missile units). Then the cavalry would move ahead against the disordered line.

The French divided their host into ten battles, about 300 knights each. Two were left in reserve midway between the four, to face the enemy on the front across the Grote Beek, and the four positioned on the left of the Flemish line as they stood across the Groeninge Beek, three of them in front and the fourth slightly behind. The decision spelled disaster from the outset. The French met the massed power of the Flemings with a fragmented attack, with no possibility of retreat and little likelihood that the reserve could be launched to save the situation. Yet when the battle opened around noon, the superior firepower of the crossbowmen from across the brooks portended a good beginning for the French forces. They easily outshot the Flemish missile units, compelling them and the front lines of the infantry to withdraw. It would have been logical for the French to continue shooting, as intended in de Burlats's plan, but the French commander, Robert of Artois, ordered his missile units to stop their action and the cavalry to move to the attack. Probably, the process seemed to last too long; probably, as some said, the knights did not want to share the glory of victory with their humble infantry; probably, they thought that the enemy was at the breaking point.

Crossing the brooks was not an easy matter. In their rush, the French cavalry ran over some of the crossbowmen. And apparently they left behind their infantry support. A few knights fell into the muddy waters, but on the whole the advance was successful, although the French must have spent time reorganizing their ranks after the crossing, each battle in three lines and each line containing only one rank of knights, as Ferdinand Lot claims on the basis of what was customary during this period.[33] The attack across both brooks met a wall that did not flinch, although the leader of the four battles on the left of the French line, Godfrey of Brabant, seemed to have initial success. He broke through the Flemish front ranks and knocked down, but did not kill, one of the enemy leaders, William of Jülich, before the Flemings closed in and killed him. The loss of Godfrey was followed by that of the commander of the French left wing, Raoul de Nesle, depriving Artois's army of two leaders after the first clash. By the end of the encounter only one French leader survived. When Robert of Artois realized that the situation was desperate, he called the reserve, which never arrived, so he led a second charge. He reached the standard of the Flemish host, tearing off part of it, but met his death after his horse was felled, covered with wounds. The Flemings seemed to have given way only in the center, where the line angled to follow the course of the Groeninge. Some of the footmen fled in panic, but the Flemings repaired the situation when the reserve under John of Renesce came forward to push back the French. It could not be otherwise if one takes into account the power of a determined army of 7,000–12,000 footmen against a knightly army of at most 2,400 horsemen (about 600 had been kept in reserve). Of these 2,400 only the first group of battles, about 1,600 men, were involved in the two initial charges. The third line never charged, it seems,[34] and followed the survivors in retreat as they streamed to safety across the brooks.

Until this moment the battle had followed the usual course, but the Flemings changed the rules. Instead of remaining fixed, they counterattacked, initiated by the Flemish center that had been relieved by Jean of Renesce's reserve. The other parts of the Flemish line followed. Under normal circumstances many knights could have saved their lives, but a combination of terrain and determination by their enemy brought chaos to their ranks. Many fell into the ditches and the brooks, where they drowned; others, brought down by the Flemish infantry, met their death under the sharp spear points or the crushing heads of the *goedendags*. By the end of the day, at least a third of the French knightly army had perished. Their bodies were stripped; between 500 and 700 golden spurs, a symbol of knighthood, were placed in the Cathedral of Our Lady in Courtrai; flowers paved the streets of Bruges, while the fleur-de-lis, the symbol of the French crown, was carried through the mud as the crowds shouted, "On with the lion, and down with the lily."[35] The Flemish casualties amounted only to a few hundred.[36]

Bouvines: The Making of the French Monarchy

Much more typical was the Battle of Bouvines on 27 July 1214 between the King of France, Philip Augustus, and an Anglo-German-Flemish army led by Emperor Otto IV. The confrontation was caused by the attempt of the Plantagenet King of England, John, to recover the territories of Normandy and Anjou, which Philip had occupied in 1203–1204.

The campaign started in the manner of all wars of this period (Figure 13.3). As Georges Duby eloquently states, war "was a seasonal adventure, an enterprise of depredation, a sort of secular and bold harvesting. Conducted much as a cautious farmer works, it warily unfolded under any pretext, in the midst of the web of continually rekindled quarrels endlessly opposing rival powers, all sharing the same rapaciousness."[37] The ideal goal was the defeat of the opponent and a cornucopia of wealth. If this was impossible, then the goal was to compromise. But in all cases the bloodshed should be minimal among the knights. The footmen did not count. They were better left dead than alive. But leaving one's wounded peers on the ground was not considered proper for people who lived by the ideals of the tournament and sought financial gain by keeping prisoners alive. Inevitably someone would pay handsomely for a prisoner's freedom.

The logical end of every campaign should have been the battle, but large pitched battles were a rarity during this period, as it presented many dangers,

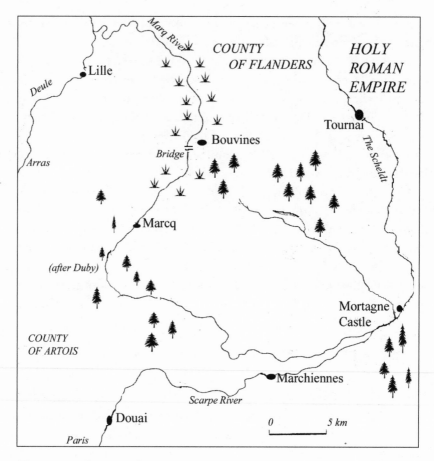

Figure 13.3   Bouvines Campaign 1214

and the outcome was never certain. Four generations of counts in Anjou fought only six battles during the tenth and eleventh centuries. In Flanders, where recourse to war was a chronic occurrence, there were only three battles over a 150-year period. William the Conqueror was involved in only two major encounters, Val-des-Dunes and Hastings. Before Bouvines the Capetian kings of France had experienced a major clash only at Bremule in 1119.[38] Yet the two sides would meet in battle, with God deciding the champion of right. Victory at that time was believed to be the expression of God's will to reward the just ruler and to punish those who did not follow divine rules. The man behind the invasion of France was John Lackland, the king of England— "bluntsword," as they mockingly called him. It did not matter that John was trying to regain lands that were rightfully his or that he hoped to convince

Emperor Otto IV and the Flemings and French subjects to take up arms against the king of France. King John remained the personification of evil, the man who ravished all the beautiful women of his realm, whether daughter of nobleman or commoner, and who stole from the Church. The pontiff had excommunicated him, joining the leader of the northern army, Emperor Otto, whom the pontiff had also excommunicated.

King John launched his attack against the French king from two fronts. On 14 February 1214 he landed at La Rochelle, while in the northeast Emperor Otto IV started to move from the imperial lands into Flanders. But John went nowhere. The French king's son, Louis, easily routed him on 2 July at La Roche-aux-Moines near Angers. In the meantime, King Philip moved forward to intercept the emperor. Philip was of two minds as to whether to seek the ordeal of battle. From the south, where Peronne stands, he moved to Douai and then crossed the River Marcq at Bouvines, with the only bridge. From there he moved into the lands of Ferrand, the count of Flanders, who had taken the side of King John and was a commander in the imperial host. As he entered the lands of the count, Philip destroyed and looted everything for his army. He stopped at Tournai, the gateway to Flanders, on the imperial lands' border. There, after a heated council of war, he decided to arrest his march, for the terrain was becoming unsuitable for his mounted knights. Better to withdraw to a safer position near Lille on the other side of the Marcq, where the terrain was favorable and where the imperial advance would have to move through difficult marshes on both sides of the river.

Of the two contenders, Otto seemed more intent on battle, and he forced Philip to accept a confrontation. As Philip turned toward Tournai, the emperor marched from Valenciennes to the Mortagne Castle, an area nominally part of the French domain. The two sides missed each other, but on 26 July they were separated by about 10 kilometers. Philip ordered his troops to withdraw toward Bouvines. But he had taken precautions and sent a detachment of lightly armed horsemen under the command of the *burgrave* of Melun and the duke of Burgundy to scout the enemy army. The emperor must have been informed of these movements, for as Philip moved in a southwest direction toward Bouvines, he would strike north and then northwest, crossing a wooded area to reappear just south of Bouvines. Meanwhile, the French detachment under Melun kept shadowing him while Brother Guerin, a knight of the religious order of the Templar who had joined the scouting detachment, turned back to inform King Philip of the position and movement of the imperial army.

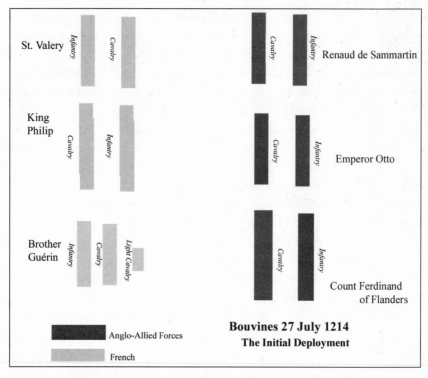

St. Valery

King
Philip

Brother
Guérin

Renaud de Sammartin

Emperor Otto

Count Ferdinand
of Flanders

Bouvines 27 July 1214
The Initial Deployment

Anglo-Allied Forces

French

Figure 13.4   Bouvines 27 July 1214: The Initial Deployment

The French order of march from Tournai was carefully crafted. Wagons carrying the weapons of the foot soldiers and the Oriflamme, the sacred banner that symbolized the presence of Saint Denis at the side of the king, opened the way, protected by foot soldiers, then the king, then after him the knights and light horsemen, and finally the rearguard. By the morning of 27 July, the footmen and the king had passed through Bouvines and started to settle on the opposite bank. It was a hot day, and the king had taken off his armor to rest in the shade of a tree, eating bread dipped in wine. He would have preferred to fight another day, but it was here that Brother Guerin reached him. Otto, he informed the king, was proceeding at full speed toward Bouvines, either to force a pitched battle or to surprise the French forces in the process of crossing the river. Philip had no choice but to accept the encounter. He hastily suited up, entered a chapel for a short prayer, jumped on his horse, and ordered the troops who had just crossed the river to recross and deploy for battle. It was almost noon, and soon the peace was broken by the sound of trumpets and shouts inciting the knights to battle—"To arms, barons! To arms!" (Figure 13.4).

The French ruler was fifty-three, elderly for the time. He had been anointed at fourteen, a few months before the death of his father, Louis VII. Like all rulers of the time he had engaged in many military campaigns, but not necessarily in pitched battles. In 1190 he had been in the Holy Land, and although he had failed to reconquer Jerusalem, he had proven his military skill during the siege of Saint John of Acre. When he returned to Europe, he was blind in one eye and prone to fits of temper. Yet according to one flattering portrayal at the time, Philip remained a handsome man who enjoyed good food and drink.[39] At Bouvines he had no less than 1,300 knights, a similar number of mounted sergeants, and 4,000–6,000 footmen.[40] The host was sharply divided between the infantry (members of the lower classes whose destiny on the battlefield was of little concern to the sovereign) and the knights (members of the upper class and the only ones for whom the chroniclers would show concern and respect). The sergeants occupied a role between; they fought on horseback with some prestige.

Multiple loyalties, as Duby writes, tied the knights together, some of them being the king's drinking companions. Many were related by family bonds; all were part of different levels of the vassalage system; several had struck personal friendships during the campaigns together; and many came from the same region.[41] The majority of French participants were from nearby regions: Artois, Picardy, Soissonais, Laonnais, and Thiérarche.[42] The knights were supported by 150 mounted sergeants from the abbey of St. Médard at Soissons, with a similar number from Champagne, unless the Champenois present at the battle should be considered as heavily armored knights.[43]

Philip's soldiers hurriedly deployed at Bouvines, probably choosing to face north. The intent was to force the imperial army to stand in a southerly direction, so the sun would shine in their faces and obstruct visibility. At least this is what William the Breton, who was an eyewitness, says.[44]

Although there is an element of uncertainty as to the numerical strength of the French line and their position on the battlefield, we can make a reasonable description. Philip, with his standard of golden fleur-de-lis on a blue field, took the center with 175 knights and 2,150 footmen. The left wing, where the two brothers, cousins of the king, Robert, Count of Dreux, and Pierre of Courtenay, Count of Auxerre, stood, had about 275 heavy horsemen and more than 2,000 infantry. Among the units there the dismounted knights and footmen under the command of Thomas de St. Valery, Lord of Gamaches, played an important role during the encounter. The right wing, led by Guerin, was the strongest battle group. It deployed about 150 mounted sergeants in the first line, at least 490 knights in the second, the strongest in the first row, and about 2,000 soldiers on foot in the third. According to this calculation, the number of knights comes to 940 and thus is lower than the 1,200–1,300 attributed to the French. We do not know where the rest, about 260 knights, were assembled.[45]

The infantry on the left wing deployed behind the cavalry. We are not certain, but it seems likely that on the right the footmen were placed in the second line behind the heavy horsemen. The light cavalry deployed ahead of the knights. The center, where the king stood, was a comedy of errors. Initially the cavalry stood in the first line, waiting for the arrival of the infantry with the Oriflamme, which had been taken across the river. The ones who had to take the center of the line (the others on the left and right of the French line must have been already on the battlefield), arrived late and hurriedly moved in front of the knights. They would not remain there long; soon attacked by the imperial troops, they were forced to withdraw behind their knights. Finally, along the whole front from right to left there must have been pockets of crossbowmen who played an insignificant role during the encounter.

The commander in chief of the imperial army, Otto IV, emperor of the Holy Roman Empire and king of Germany, led an army motivated by pay or by personal enmity against the French crown. Otto was between thirty-two and thirty-nine years old (we do not know whether he was born in 1175 or 1182) and thus younger than Philip. He took the field having been excommunicated by the pope and legally deposed as emperor. "Arrogant and stupid but strong,"[46] he took position in the center, where the imperial standard, a golden eagle over a dragon, stood high on a wagon. His army was likely more numerous than Philip's, about 1,500 knights and 7,500 footmen.[47] The allied center was manned by a modest number of knights (about 175) in the first line and about 3,500 footmen in the second (roughly equal to the French in knights but stronger in footmen). The right, led by a personal enemy of Philip, Renaud of Sammartin, Count of Boulogne, had 175 knights and 1,500 very strong footmen; among them were the renowned Brabançon mercenaries, who by the end of the battle were reduced to 400 or 700. The allied right was numerically smaller than the French left wing, which had at least 275 knights and more than 2,000 infantry. The allied left was strong. Led by Ferrand, Count of Flanders, 1,200 knights were in the first line. The 2,500 footmen were in the second line, although they seemed not to play any role because they were not fully deployed at the time of the clash or because they stood too far from their first line. The French had on their right at least 490 knights, and approximately 2,000 footmen and 300 light cavalry.[48]

The deployment of the armies shows that each was placing trust in the power of the horsemen. The footmen were to provide a wall behind which the knights could repair after each charge. The terrain was a plateau east of Bouvines and the Marcq River, the French right poised on the marshes that enclosed the left and right bank of the Marcq, the allied left near the marshes.[49] Protecting the flanks was more important for the French, who were outnumbered, and so their cavalry lines seem to have deployed thinner than normal on the right, where the allied knights outnumbered them more than 2:1.

The clash began around noon and continued for three or four hours along the center and right, longer on the left. The first to experience the pressure, excitement, and terror of the conflict was the French right wing, expertly led by Guerin, who had been appointed to the Senlis episcopal see but was not yet consecrated. Guerin was sixty-one at the time and had a distinguished career in the Holy Land as a member of the Order of the Knights Templar. Unexpectedly he sent only 150 mounted sergeants to open the hostilities against a considerable line of Flemish and German knights. The imperial leader, Count Ferdinand of Flanders, looked in disbelief at the daring and arrogance of the French sergeants; instead of countering with a charge of his own, he ordered his men to stand. Guerin's intent was to disorganize the enemy ranks before he moved his knights forward. It did not work that way: 150 men could do little. They were pushed back easily, with only two men killed. But somehow the men from Soissons caused disarray in the allied line; some of the enemy horsemen abandoned their post to pursue them.

In the skirmish the men from Champagne, probably mounted sergeants instead of knights, moved forward. The result was a small disaster for the allied soldiers who abandoned their line. They were either disabled or taken prisoner. At this stage the count of Flanders sent the rest of the line forward. As William the Breton describes, it is likely that the "full" attack meant individual forays by units, not a collective clash. Although one is tempted to doubt the veracity of the winners, it seems clear that the French knights, although inferior in number, were more successful than Ferrand's troops. Some of them were able to pierce the enemy line and then regroup, attacking them again on the reverse. The allied infantry must have been deployed at a distance. The French troops would have found it impossible to effect such a maneuver. The end came when Count Ferdinand was struck to the ground and injured with many wounds, falling prisoner "half-dead" and unable to continue. It was the end for the left wing of the imperial army. With the leader in enemy hands, the survivors fled the battlefield. The fight had lasted three hours and typified medieval warfare. War was the business of knights fighting against their peers; the encounter would follow a staggered pattern, unit after unit; and once the leader fell or was taken prisoner, there was only defeat.

Fighting in the center differed from the pattern of the right wing. Here the infantry on both sides was involved, the allied scoring a success and the French failing to stand, mainly because of the behavior of their own knights. Again, the main goal was to kill the leaders or take them prisoner. Foot soldiers with the Oriflamme had already crossed the Marcq when Philip Augustus, convinced that battle was inevitable, ordered them to move back across. When the infantry reached the battlefield, the knights, their king among them, had already deployed in the first line and pushed aside the footmen as they tried to displace them from the first line. It was a comedy of errors that Otto's men exploited. In a clever combination of cavalry and foot soldiers, they pushed back Philip's infantry, placing the life of the king himself in jeopardy. Armed with long spears, some with hooks, they brought down some French knights, the king among them. The battle raged around the sovereign. He would have died if not for the bravery of those around him. The standard-bearer of the fleur-de-lis desperately waved it to call for help; another knight offered his horse to the king; and with great effort a screen developed in front of the ruler, withdrawing from the first line. One of the knights was killed with a weapon unusual for the time. As he laid helpless on the ground, an allied soldier dug a long and slender knife with three sharp edges through the eye slit, reaching the brain of the French knight.

When the allied troops were forced back by the action of the French knights, probably in combination with their own dismounted sergeants (ignored in William the Breton's account), the main goal changed. Now the quarry had become the emperor, not Philip. Twice the French tried to capture Otto. First a man caught his horse's bridle, but, obstructed by the crowd of bodies and animals struggling near the emperor, he made no headway. A French knight then extracted his knife and hit the emperor in the chest. The blade found no room through Otto's well-protected chest. The French soldier tried again, but instead of hitting the emperor he struck the horse, which bolted back, falling dead not far away. His life in great danger, Otto decided to leave the battlefield while the symbol of imperial power, the golden eagle over a dragon, fell into enemy hands. But the victory of the French had not been reached without serious danger for some. One of the bravest, who had penetrated the thickest enemy line, was saved when reinforcements from the left wing arrived, inflicting the killing blow to the allied center. Thomas of St. Valery had come at the head of fifty knights and 2,000 foot men (an inflated figure).

St. Valery's arrival from the French left wing may suggest that the struggle there had finished. It was not so. The allied right kept fighting even after its center and left had gone down to defeat. Because of the nature of the clash, the French could spare St. Valery to help the center. The allied right benefited greatly by the presence of an exceptional leader, Renaud de Dammartin, Count of Boulogne, and by the daring innovation of an unusual defensive tactic carried out by the long spears of the famed Brabançon mercenaries, and by other mercenaries under the command of the Earl of Salisbury. Here, as in the center, both foot and horse combined for an effective manner of fighting, although primacy was left to the knights. Renaud deployed his mercenaries in a circular or semicircular formation, two men deep, with an exit probably at the back. He used the circle as a protective curtain for the approximately 175 knights on the right. The horsemen could rest and reorganize ranks after each charge, certain that the French would not dare to break the circle of long spears. But nothing worked. The joint commander of the allied right, the Earl of Salisbury, fell prisoner after the bishop of Beauvais hit his head with a bludgeon, not a sword, for any clergyman was forbidden to shed blood. Several of the other knights, seeing the center crumble, left the battlefield in small groups.

At the end of the day only six knights had remained at Renaud's side, and the brave leader fell into French hands when his horse fell and trapped his right leg. Now only between 400 and 700 foot soldiers remained on the battlefield. Philip sent St. Valery to destroy them. St. Valery had fifty knights and a large number of foot soldiers. While the infantry pinned the Brabançons, the knights must have destroyed the mercenaries. The fight on the left shows that good, well-trained infantry could play an important role, especially in defense. The struggle centered around the leader, and the action of the knights was in a staggered fashion—charge, redress the ranks, rest, and charge again.

Since the battle had begun around noon and ended about an hour before sundown, it must have lasted longer than the three hours that brought the allied left to defeat, for Philip ordered only a limited pursuit of the enemy as darkness was falling. In the allied army, 131 knights had fallen prisoner, with around 170 killed. We have no figures for the foot casualties, which must have been especially heavy among the Brabançons. In the typical manner of the time, they were disregarded and forgotten.

Infantry and Cavalry

There is no doubt that under certain conditions infantry can whip a knightly army. However, the type of footman who could resist the onslaught of the knight was rare in Europe. He was the product of environments in which commoners enjoyed a certain degree of prestige and personal independence. It is not a surprise to find them only where great communal or societal bonds existed, as among the Scots, the Swiss, the Italian burghers of the twelfth century, and the urban Flemings of the late thirteenth to early fourteenth centuries. That is where the power of the aristocracy had declined or was checked by a strong middle class. But even this was not enough to create an effective infantry. Training and performance on the battlefield had to be coupled with strength of intent and awareness that the struggle was for personal interests. In other words, footmen had to undergo continuous training and practice in war, much like the knights.

Even if these conditions were met, it would be suicidal for an infantry to face a knightly army on flat terrain, where the horses ruled and where the flanks and rear of immobile footmen were in constant danger. The terrain had to be such that horses would have difficulty. Even at Courtrai all this would not have meant victory if Robert of Artois had let his crossbowmen continue their work for longer. Thus the future of the great foot armies of northern and central Italy and of Flanders would be bleak. In 1382 French forces, after a victory near Courtrai, burned the city in revenge for the loss eighty years earlier and took back the golden spurs that the Flemings had displayed in the Cathedral of Our Lady at Courtrai.

Heavy cavalry remained dominant on the battlefield during the Middle Ages until the very end, despite the brilliant English victories at Poitiers, Crécy, and Agincourt. It was matter of efficiency and, most important, social primacy. Yet it is clear that a good army, as the crusaders would show in the Holy Land, needed heavy cavalrymen and a substantial number of infantrymen, including missile units.

Chapter Fourteen ~

The Crusades, or God at War

IT IS THE MORNING OF 20 JUNE 1128. Soon the forces of William Clito of Flanders will meet the army of Thierry of Alsace. The prize is control over the county of Flanders. The light began to chase away the darkness, but Clito's first task is to make peace with God so that the celestial forces will be in his favor. He kneels in front of the Abbot of Oudenberg and confesses his sins, promising to be a just ruler and a faithful defender of the church and the poor. Then he approaches his knights and asks them too to plead for God's forgiveness and protection. They also cut, as a sign of contrition, their long hair, the symbol of their depravity, according to the church; they shed the clothes that mark the greatness of their lineage and cover their bodies only with a simple shirt and hauberk. It is only then that the time for battle arrives.[1]

This ritual is repeated over and over before the battles of this period, making the object of killing and winning some kind of trial where God reveals His will. If this belief was the norm in the struggles between Christian princes, it became even more important and necessary if the enemies were those who did not believe in Christianity. The theoreticians of the faith had always found it difficult to justify violence against other Christian princes, and the solution often proclaimed of a just war was an invention that could not stand scrutiny. In the war against Muslims or the heathens of eastern Europe this was not the case. The warriors proceeded certain in the holiness of their cause, finding even more powerful rituals to show that God favored them. At Antioch, Syria, for instance, in 1198 the prologue to the final battle developed around the discovery of the Holy Lance.

Famished, surrounded by thousands of enemies, and plagued by illness, the few crusaders left in Antioch had little hope of surviving the inevitable

Muslim onslaught, but the justness of their cause and the prospect of victory loomed large once a poor man of doubtful character revealed that Jesus had visited him with St. Peter and St. Andrew. Yes, he had been assured that the crusaders would win if they marched to battle with the Holy Lance that had pierced Christ's body while on the cross. Some of the leaders did not trust the man's words. Yet after some hesitation and after a similar vision by another individual they decided to dig in the Church of St. Peter where the man had been told that the Holy Lance was hidden. They dug from morning to evening. They found nothing, and despair entered their souls as a new group kept digging. But the young man who had claimed that he had been visited by Christ, disrobed, took his shoes off, and, praying, jumped into the pit. Soon a shout of joy broke his prayers. He had found an old, rusty spear point—the Holy Lance. The crusaders would take it with them to the battlefield despite the feeling that the whole story had been concocted. It raised the morale of their small army, becoming an effective motivation during the forthcoming fight.[2]

The Laws of War

In the eleventh century, when society was sharply divided into warriors (*pugnatores, bellatores*) and the unarmed population (*inerme vulgus*), the Catholic Church tried with the proclamation of the Truce of God and the Peace of God to introduce a more humane approach to warfare. War among Christians should be waged, the Church said, only between Monday morning and Thursday evening, and never during Advent and Lent. It was a law that in reality could never be enforced, similar to the attempted prohibition of crossbows and longbows. The Church also maintained that children, women, clergymen, old people, agricultural workers, and the poor should be spared. It was a law that seemed to count only for subjects. If any member of those groups belonged to the enemy's dominion, then he was legitimate prey, whether commoner or knight. But there was a difference: knights would be spared; common soldiers would be slaughtered on the battlefield or in the lands nearby.[3] At best, such rules applied to Christians, not to heathens or Muslims.

According to Robert C. Stacey, law theorists, theologians, and princes distinguished between four types of war during the medieval period. Three applied to open battle, the fourth to siege warfare.[4] Placing a city under siege followed norms that went back to at least the third millennium B.C. Briefly, they maintained that if the besieged resisted, the opponents, once they had penetrated the city, could dispose of the defenders and their property as they desired. It normally translated into mass slaughter for the soldiers, slavery and rape for the rest, pillage and fire for the living quarters. In the medieval period this was the rule. Yet there were various ways to limit the horrors of massacre. If the city fathers agreed to surrender when the enemy herald came to their walls proclaiming the siege, their lives might be spared and their property untouched. That being the case, the leader in charge of a city found himself in a situation where any choice was fraught with danger: if he resisted, he placed the lives of all in jeopardy; if he surrendered, his lord would consider his decision an act of treason. This meant that at times the person in command of a city required a contract from his lord stating that his obligation to resist was limited to a certain length of time or to the arrival of a relief army within a certain period since the siege had begun. The contract allowed the besieged to negotiate with the besieging army that if no relief arrived within the stated time, they would surrender the city in exchange for their lives and property. At times, however, the lives of the soldiers were spared as long as they promised not to take up arms against the winners in the future; the civilians were massacred.[5] This had been the case during the siege of Milan in the sixth century when the Ostrogoths slaughtered all civilians but let the enemy soldiers go free.

The endless conflicts of the period 900–1300 between feudal lords subject to the king or emperor fall into the category that jurists called *guerre couverte* (covert war). The participants had to follow strict rules given the conflict's private nature. Killing the enemy in battle was allowed, but plunder, burning property, or taking prisoners for ransom were forbidden. Also forbidden was spoiling the enemy of lands or displaying one's banner during the conflict.[6] Rules limiting the impact of war were applied also to the *bellum hostile*, the conflict between two Christian sovereigns. The armies moved to the encounter by displaying the leaders' personal banners, which meant that the laws of war superseded the laws of peacetime. Plunder and spoil were permitted with the understanding that the soldiers should receive a share of the loot. Theoretically, according to the Peace of God, this also meant that certain categories should remain immune from ravage. Yet women, children, clergymen, and the poor could become casualties. In many cases the combatants exacted blackmail and extortion not only on the lands of the enemy but on one's own territories.[7] Normally those victims would be at the bottom of the social ladder.

The last type of conflict was a war without limits, the *guerre mortelle* (mortal war), a rare occurrence between Christians but the norm against non-Christians and in civil confrontations, although in most cases the harshest rules were not applied if knights confronted knights in battle. Knights had to follow a specific code of conduct, which meant that shedding the blood of peers was not the goal. It was to render him unable to defend himself and thus become a prisoner for ransom. Cannon fodder, to use a modern expression, were those at the bottom of society or those who did not believe in the right God. This time the banner unfurled was the color of blood, red, no distinction being made between those who fought on the field and those who were civilians. The blood of both could stain the soldiers' swords. In his attempt to bring the Saxons to bay, Charlemagne waged a thirty-year campaign marked by plunder, deportation, mass slaughter, and slavery, until finally the Saxons accepted Christianity. The Saxons' slaughter was a blueprint for the pagan Slavs east of the Oder when the Teutonic knights and their followers struck eastward.[8] The crusades witnessed even worse cases of massacres and intolerance.

Christianity and Islam

During its origin Christianity was a pacifist religion that forbade any involvement in war to the faithful, but Constantine's acceptance of the creed with his Milan edict of 312 started to change that attitude. As the Council of Arles (313) stated, serving in the army during peacetime was obligatory for the faithful since the Roman Empire was by then the defender of peace and a propaganda engine for Christian religion. Yet killing in war was still considered a sin. We have to wait for St. Augustine for another change. At times war, he said, could be just, and being a soldier was what God envisaged for the good Christian. The next major evolution took place with the emergence of the barbarian kingdoms and their acceptance of Christianity. The key transition took place in France, where the Merovingians' acceptance of religion as promulgated by Rome made the state a defender of the truth against the heresy of Arianism, a competing form of Christianity. The stemming of the Muslim advance at Poitiers in 732 and the Frank kings' decision to become the champions of the papal claims against the Longobards in Italy strengthened the Christian acceptance of the idea of war. It could not be otherwise because, as the popes extended their territorial possessions in Italy, it made little sense to criticize the business of war when the head of the clergy himself was engaged in aggressive confrontations. New, however, was that war could be understood as a defender of the faith in general and as the proper tool for the territorial claims of the papacy. It was easy, this being the situation, to justify war against the new invaders of the Christian kingdoms, Vikings and Magyars, wreaking havoc in the Christian lands. Now war was the proper instrument to stop the onslaught of the new heathens and to turn them into loyal believers of the Christian creed. As Jean Flori eloquently says, "War was not considered anymore as an absolute evil but as a necessary evil to protect the Christians and their churches from an even worse evil."[9]

It is likely that the initial manifestations of the idea of a holy war against Islam originated in Spain. After a brief period of Christian successes in the Iberian Peninsula, the Muslims counterattacked, regaining some of the lands they had lost in previous decades. In 1000 they even looted the sacred sanctuary of Compostela, one of the most treasured holy places of the Middle Ages. For the first time in the history of Christianity, several monks took up weapons against the attackers. They died, but their sacrifice was not in vain, for a myth rose around their end. A few decades later, news spread that the monks had reappeared in a French church announcing that their martyrdom had opened to them the gates of Paradise.[10] The important novelty was that the use of weapons had spread from laymen to clergymen if the cause of war was considered "holy." A few decades later that concept, coming from several sources, was embraced on a large scale.

The popes played a key role in the campaign against Muslims. The crusade became a likely goal when Pope Urban II (1088–1099), a Frenchman from a knightly family, advanced the idea from the pulpit in the French town of Clermont in 1095. The lure was that by freeing the Holy Land the crusaders, now considered the "warriors of Christ," would receive an indulgence that remitted their sins and that if they died in their mission they would be admitted into Paradise. Pope Gregory VII had already played with the idea of a crusade about twenty-one years earlier. He had said that 50,000 men were ready to march with him to free the Holy Sepulcher and the Byzantine Empire from the impending collapse at the hands of the Seljuk Turks. Gregory's idea was translated into fact by Urban's words. The times had changed. The speaker was a member of the class that controlled Europe, the knights; the plight of the Byzantines, now pushed increasingly out of Asia Minor, had become serious; the western European states enjoyed a period of economic vitality after the financial darkness of the early Middle Ages; probably the East could become an area of material gain and personal salvation for the people who were already on top of western society. Urban's plea was directed to his peers, not the poor, the disadvantaged, the sick, or the common clergymen. "You are not allowed to join the knights in their quest of freedom of the Holy Land," Urban II warned the monks of Vallombrosa in his letter of October 7, 1096.[11]

The Crusades were also different from the Muslim holy war, the Jihad. The prophet Muhammad had been the emissary of Allah and had fought at the side of the early Muslim converts, sword in hand. Yet the Prophet's ultimate goal had been the conquest of new territories, not the conversion of the people residing there. Only later the ideas of conquest and conversion were combined. At this time, Muslim rulers were well known for their tolerance of non-Muslims, Christians or Jews, as long as they obeyed the laws of the state and did not engage in proselytization. Urban's goal was different in the sense that he planned to free the Holy Land and eventually convert the people residing there.

Once the idea of crusade was launched there was no way to limit it to knights. A skillful propaganda machine came into play with stories that the holy sites were used as stables for animals or converted into mosques and that the pilgrims visiting the land were abused and humiliated by Muslims. It was propaganda that mixed truthful points and the memory of awful deeds and fabrications; a Muslim visiting the West would have found more animosity there than a Christian in Jerusalem or Bethlehem. Like Pandora's box, once the pope and clergymen preached the idea of a crusade as a beneficial enterprise for the knights, the idea could not be limited to them. Popular preachers, Peter the Hermit above all, spread their fiery words from city to city and from hamlet to hamlet insisting that it was the duty of every Christian, rich and poor alike, to go to the Holy Land and regain the lands that the Christians had lost. At the same time their preaching responded also to the desire to hurt non-Christians in the western territories. The "enemies of Christ," they said, were not only the people in the faraway places in the East but also their neighbors in the West. Pogrom after pogrom against Jews spilled blood in the Rhineland, at Cologne, Spier, Worms, and Mainz. No place was safe, especially for the rabble led by a petty lord named Emich of Leisingen. Even when at Mainz, Jews sought refuge in the palace of the bishop, who had defended them, their safety did not last long. The mob compelled the bishop to flee and then slaughtered the poor souls who had taken refuge in his residence. The situation during the pogroms was so hopeless that at times mothers killed their own sons and daughters before pushing the daggers into their own heart since at times the only choice was either death or baptism.[12]

Thousands upon thousands of disadvantaged in Europe moved by land toward Palestine, some pillaging and occasionally murdering those who were reluctant to offer them food and places to stay: the "crusade of the poor" preceded the "crusade of the knights" to the dismay of popes and rulers (Figure

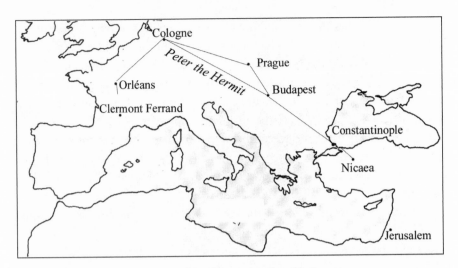

Figure 14.1   The First Crusade 1096–1101: The Crusade of the Poor

14.1). It was in many ways an expedition combining resentment toward the people who dominated them at home and the hope that by flocking to the walls of Jerusalem they would witness the final fight between Christ and the Antichrist. But the poor never reached their destination. Most of them found death in the lands of Asia Minor. As Anna Comnena, daughter of the Byzantine emperor, writes, the pilgrims became the victims of Turkish swords: "when the scattered remains of the slaughtered men were collected, they made not merely a hill or mound or peak, but a huge mountain, deep and wide, most remarkable, so great was the pile of bones."[13]

The goal of the crusade involved a process of double liberation—freeing the holy sites while at the same time giving religious freedom back to the faithful oppressed by the Muslims. War became mixed with the idea of pilgrimage. Visiting the lands where Christ once had been was mandatory for believers in His creed. It was the duty of every knight to pursue that goal. The crusade was transformed from a religious endeavor into a mission to restore the honor of Christianity, using in other words the same phrases that knights might employ to justify the conflicts against each other. The lure of riches for many knights economically disadvantaged in their own lands was another siren calling them eastward. And though this was true for some, the economic benefits for most were meager. Many would return home empty-handed in a more ruinous condition, for moving by land and especially by sea was very expensive for any man fighting as a knight.

The truth is that the idea of crusades, which would continue for centuries even after their failure in Palestine, was a project torn by conflicts. People who theoretically were pacifist were engaged in wars of destruction and unbelievable cruelties. Regaining the Christian lands or converting new people to Christianity were successful in the Iberian Peninsula and in the East against the Slavs but failed in the place where the major focus resided. The Byzantines, the orthodox Christians of the East, who were one of the reasons for the initial drive, came out of the movement more resentful than at the beginning. Especially after the Fourth Crusade and the capture of Constantinople the break between the Christians of the West and those of the East became irreversible. The expeditions, intended to free the Holy Land from non-Christians, became for many the first manifestation of Western colonialism. The Italian maritime cities like the republics of Venice and Genoa benefited from the enterprise. In the end the failure of the drive eastward also encouraged other European powers to seek alternative routes to the Far East now that the land across the Hellespont had fallen firmly into non-Christian hands. Finally, while the crusader conquest failed, new enemies appeared from the East, the Mongols, who would ravage both Christians and Muslims, and then the final push by the Ottoman Turks in their destruction of the Roman Empire of the East.

On the whole, priority on why so many persons, warriors, their vassals, and faithful traveled to Palestine must be given to religious motivation. It was typical of the mental baggage of the period to believe in such an enterprise. Both clerical and nonclerical propaganda endlessly proclaimed that it was the duty of every Christian to regain the land of Christ. In the process, the enemy was demonized and presented in the worst light possible. Material motivations were also present, but they were secondary to spiritual ones. Another reason for the endless source of recruitment in the West was the exotic nature of the East, with all the allure that such idealizations have constantly played in western minds.

How Many Crusaders Went Eastward

Jean Flori distinguishes eight separate Christian Crusades.[14] Other historians count a minimum of seven to a maximum of nine. There were at least three different phases in the western campaigns against the Muslims.[15] The first phase, ending in 1147, was characterized by the success of the western armies in the First (1096–1101) and Second Crusades (1147). In the second phase (Third Crusade, 1187–1197) the Muslims, led by Salâh-al-Dîn (Saladin), counterattacked, inflicting serious reverses to the invaders, who had set up four principalities from the southeastern reaches of Asia Minor to the Gulf of Aqaba. The third phase (Fourth Crusade, 1202–1204; Fifth, 1217–1219; Sixth, 1221–1229; Seventh, 1248; and Eighth, 1280), all in the thirteenth century, ended in 1291 when the last crusader stronghold, Acre, fell in Syria.[16]

Crusaders came from all parts of Christian Europe, even from Spain, although the Church exempted them from serving in the Holy Land, for they had a crusade at home. Certain parts of Europe were represented more often than the rest. This is especially true of France, specifically the Ile-de-France/Champagne and Normandy, Flanders, and the Italian peninsula in the south and north. Fewer participants in all the Crusades seem to have come from the German lands and from England, although large English contingents from the island and from Poitou were present in at least three crusades (1187–1190, 1245–1248, and 1287–1290).

The numerical strength of the Crusades was initially a matter of wild guesses and strong debates, ranging from a minimum of 120,000 to a maximum of 360,000 in the First Crusade. In the twentieth century the reverse was true for a while, with people claiming that the knights were not more than 5,000. It would have been impossible to raise more knights in the West, and larger numbers would have created unsurpassable logistical problems; the figures found in the medieval sources were mainly allegorical or symbolical and as such not representing reality.[17] Jean Flori has taken a different stand. First of all, he argues, such authors assume that all knights had to be nobles, which would limit their number, while in reality practically anybody who could afford or came to own a mount and the armor could fight as a knight. Logistical problems would have been (and actually were) enormous. Yet, argues Flori, we should not dismiss immediately all medieval guesses, for they still contain a certain amount of truth.[18]

The First Crusade seems to have been the largest numerically. Jonathan Riley-Smith assigns 43,000 men to it after the capture of Nicaea, a figure that does not include the "crusade of the poor" destroyed by the Turks. Jean Flori proposes a much higher number: 90,000–120,000, of whom 10,000–15,000 would have been knights. We are less certain about the numerical strength of the Second Crusade. although 70,000 may be acceptable after rejecting as fantasy the Byzantine estimate of 900,000 for the army led by Conrad III. The sources assign 100,000 soldiers to the Third Crusade, which Flori decreases to roughly 30,000, arguing that medieval estimates should be interpreted as one for every three. The organizers of the Fourth Crusade, which ended with the pillage of Constantinople, not with confrontation in the Holy Land, had con-

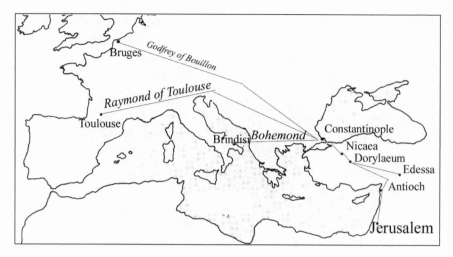

Figure 14.2   The First Crusade 1096–1101: The Crusade of the Knights

tracted for the transit of 4,500 horsemen, 9,000 squires, and 20,000 footmen with the Venetians, although many crusaders in the end chose to reach the Holy Land on their own, not trusting the aims of the carrier. The Seventh Crusade of 1248 seems to have been the smallest. It started with an army of 15,000–20,000 warriors, of whom 2,500–2,800 were knights. Muslim sources maintain, however, that they were much more numerous, 37,000 in all, of whom 7,000 were knights.[19]

The First Crusade

The knights arrived in Asia Minor soon after the massacre of the poor (Figure 14.2). They reached Constantinople by different routes, some at least partially by sea, others by land. It included mainly warriors from the lands of the French, Normans and Franks, with Norman contingents from southern Italy. The "Franks," as the Muslims called the crusaders regardless of their ethnic or geographical origins, picked up where the crusade of the poor had left. At the beginning, the crusade of the knights seemed to have done the dirty work for Byzantine Emperor Alexius Comnenus in clearing most of Asia Minor from the menace of the Seljuk Turks; in reality the suspicions of the emperor on the goals of the crusaders (and he was not mistaken) made the relationship between Byzantines and westerners quite strained. Very soon, in a mixture of violent threats, single-mindedness, and arrogance, the crusaders would push aside the half-hearted support of the emperor and pursue their own goals.

The campaign in Asia Minor had begun with the rather easy capture of the city of Nicaea, near the shores of the Black Sea, and then with the bitter victory at Doryleum, where the crusaders, faced by the hit-and-run attacks of the Turks, had finally found a way to rush them, with their heavy knights remaining masters of the battlefield and breaking Seljuk hegemony in Asia Minor. But the cost was bitter, including several casualties. Even worse was the march from the heart of Asia Minor to Syria's northern shores. Their way lost at times, slowed down by the presence of pilgrims (old people, women, and children), and underestimating the difficulties of scorched terrain or intense cold, they suffered exhaustion, hunger, and above all thirst. Several died along the way; others turned back toward the shores of the Black Sea. Those who continued suffered incredible torments. Pregnant women, says Albert of Aachen in his chronicle, "their throats dried up, their wombs withered, all the veins of the body drained by the indescribable heat of the sun and that parched region, gave birth and abandoned their own young [probably stillborn], in the middle of the highway in the view of everyone." Men collapsed in droves along the road. Prize dogs, necessary companions of their knightly masters during the hunt, were killed by their owners' hands. When the travelers finally reached a river, they ran to the waters in a confused mob. Many died there, for they drank excessively.[20]

On 21 October 1096 the crusaders finally saw Antioch's walls cutting the clear sky. After the stunning wave of Muslim conquest in the seventh and eighth centuries, which had pushed the Byzantines to the western side of the Taurus Mountains, the Byzantine emperors had staged a strong counterattack in the tenth century, regaining control of Asia Minor and of Syria's northern shore. In 969 their troops had entered the ancient city of Antioch, but when the crusaders reached its walls in 1096 the city had fallen again to the Seljuks after a period of Byzantine dominance for more than a century. The problem was that the Seljuk Turks had taken over where the early Muslim armies had left off and after the battle of Mantzikert (1071), where they had inflicted a stunning defeat to the Byzantines, again had pushed the imperial forces to their capital on the Hellespont. For the moment, however, the crusaders had again, after the capture of Nicaea and their victory at Doryleum, pushed the Turks back, and now they faced the first great city of Syria: Antioch.

Antioch was a town with a great past (Figure 14.3). Under the Romans it had counted 200,000 inhabitants, although now its population barely reached 40,000, among them many Nasârâ, the Arab term for the followers of the Nazarene, that is, the Christians. Its ruler, an old man with a long white beard

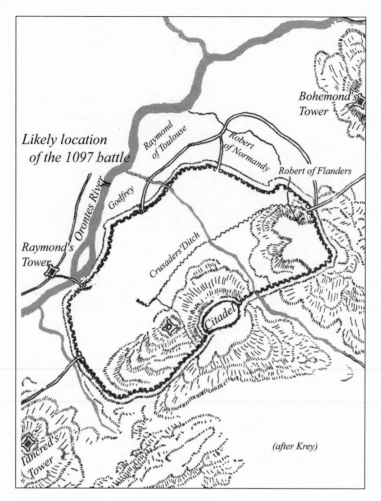

Figure 14.3   Siege of Antioch 1096–1097

named Amir Yâghî Siyân, was fair and judicious; however, as the Franks were approaching, he had expelled all the Christian male residents for fear of treason, assuring them that no ill would fall upon their women and children during the forthcoming siege, a promise that he would keep. Antioch was strongly fortified with a wall of about 12,000 meters in circumference and 360 towers erected on three different levels.[21] It stood between the Orontes River on the western side and Mount Silpius on the eastern side. At the highest point inside the city walls stood the citadel.

Antioch withstood the siege for seven months. It fell in June 1097, betrayed by an Armenian armorer who let the crusaders scale the city walls from a rope suspended out the window of the tower where he lived. From there the cru-saders quickly opened one of the gates, and while the rest of them flooded into the city, panic spread among the Muslim troops. Some sought refuge in the citadel; others, their leader Amir Yâghî Siyân among them, fled through the gate, opposite the one from which the assailants had come. Siyân did not last long. Desperate for having left the city he ruled and the members of his household in the hands of the Franks, he fainted, falling from his horse. The encouragement of the other fugitives to jump back on his horse were to no avail until worried about their own safety, they abandoned him there. Siyân "was at his last gasp when an Armenian shepherd came past, killed him, cut off his head and took it to the Franks at Antioch."[22]

Taking the city did not solve all the problems that the crusaders were fac-ing. The day after their conquest the army of the leader of Mosul, the Atabeg Karbuqa, appeared near Antioch's walls. By then the crusaders were facing not only the swords of a much more numerous enemy but also starvation, illness, and a beastly state of health. When they had first reached Antioch's neighbor-hood, they had been amazed by the abundance of fruits and food available, but then as the months passed, their supplies had run out and their forays into the surrounding areas declined, for they often ended with several dead at the hands of Muslim skirmishers. The weather had become horrible, cold and rainy, a surprising twist for the crusaders, who hardly expected a climate sim-ilar to northern Europe. Famine ravaged their ranks, with bread, goat intes-tines, a horse head, or a chicken reaching unbelievable prices if found. They were reduced to plucking unripe figs and cooking them together with the hides of cattle and horses that they would have discarded in the past.[23] When Karbuqa launched his first assault against the city walls on 9 June, they repulsed it with great difficulty, suffering again losses that they could not afford. At night several crusaders, the *funambules,* because of their way of escape, hung ropes from the walls and escaped from the city toward the sea, about 15 miles away.

Desperate, the crusaders tried to strike a compromise with Karbuqa; they even offered to become his vassals, but Karbuqa refused. Victory seemed cer-tain: he had thousands of men under his command, and the crusader knights, reduced at most to 1,000 men and probably 3,000 foot, were caught in a vice, having to contend with the Muslims in the citadel and his own army in the plain. And not all the knights had horses, for some animals had become casu-alties of war or had been eaten as food. After twelve days without food, writes a Muslim source, "the wealthy ate their horses and the poor ate carrion and leaves from the trees."[24] But Karbuqa's situation was not the best. His delay in reaching the city before it fell (he had tried in vain to take another town from the crusaders) had robbed the Muslims of certain victory. Moreover, his arrogance and scorn and contempt of other army chiefs was breaking the cohesion of his army, encouraging treacherous behavior among his subordinates. At the same time an event boosted the crusaders' morale when it was claimed that the lance that had transfixed Christ's body had been found, hidden underground in the Church of St. Peter in Antioch. There were crusaders who did not believe in the seriousness of the find, but in the end the leaders accepted it as a sign of God's will. The man, who had first claimed the vision from Saint Andrew, Saint Peter, and Christ himself, had also been assured of victory if the army marched to battle with the Holy Lance.

The crusaders fasted for three days (the little food they had was given to the horses), went in procession from one church to the other, confessed their sins, attended mass, and took communion of the body and blood of Christ. On 28 June they streamed in small groups through the city gate nearby a mosque. Karbuqa, who may have been engaged in a chess game at the time, was told, "Go up to the city and kill them one by one as they come out; it is easy to pick them off now that they have split up." "No, wait until they all have come out and then we shall kill them," he answered.[25]

The crusaders numbered less than 1,000 knights, probably as few as 700, and not more than 3,000 foot[26] (Figure 14.4). They left 200 men in the city around the citadel, worried about a sortie by the defenders. The rest were deployed in five divisions, each including knights and footmen. The soldiers moved across the Orontes River to line up in the nearby plain amid the prayers of bishops, priests, clerics, and monks who followed them with crosses in hand. Other clergymen stood on the city walls holding sacred objects and praying.

Strangely enough Karbuqa did not move to the attack, not even when he could take advantage of the element of disorganization present at deployment. The crusaders were divided into five battle groups. In the first stood a thin line of foot soldiers to protect the rest from a sudden enemy attack and certainly during deployment. Then three divisions came with Hugh de Vermandois anchoring the right on the Orontes, Godfrey of Bouillon in the center, and the Bishop of Puy, Adhémar, and Raymond of Aguilers holding the Holy Lance on the left. Each division deployed the knights in the first line and the foot soldiers behind them. On the rear, in reserve, stood the knights and the footmen under the command of Bohemond.

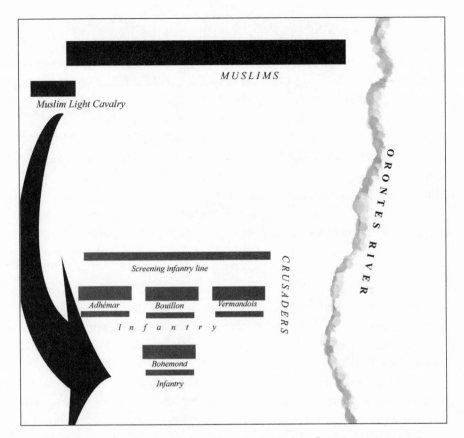

Figure 14.4   Battle of Antioch 1097: The Initial Clash

The crusaders' position seemed hopeless when they stared at the thousands of enemies in the distance. The situation became worse when units of the Muslim light cavalry turned their left flank and attacked the rear of the foot soldiers of the division under the command of Adhémar. The infantry responded by adopting a circle formation and thus refusing flanks and rear to the Turks. Still they would have fallen in defeat without the help of the knights detached from their own division (probably with some from the center and right under the leadership of a knight named Rainald). In their rush to help and in a manner not unusual in medieval armies, they trampled even some of their own infantry before striking the enemy. Faced by the much heavier soldiers, some Turks fled to safety toward the south; others in the north, where their main line stood, put fire to the dry grass to impede the crusaders' pursuit.

The defeat of the Turkish attack on the Crusaders' rear must have discouraged the enemy host. It turned into a rout when the crusader knights struck in the traditional staggered motion, first the right wing, then the center, and finally the left. A reputable Arab historian, Al-Athîr, bitterly notes, "The Muslims were completely routed without striking a single blow or a single arrow."[27] The crusaders suffered few casualties; heavy were those of the enemy footmen.

The Battle of Antioch is an excellent example of the sophistication of medieval armies with their combination of foot soldiers supporting the knights, the use of a frontal infantry screen to avoid any nasty surprise, the skill of the foot to assume a sophisticated defensive formation (the circle on their rear), the use of a reserve, the possibility of detaching units to support a formation in trouble, and the formidable impact of the charge of the heavy cavalry. The crusader victory at Antioch was made possible also by the dissensions that plagued the Muslims at the time. The people living in the region seemed unable to confront the will to win of the Crusaders or to face the fear that the advance of the Franks caused in their midst. Most cities in Syria and Palestine gave up without a fight, fearful as the Crusaders approached their walls of a worse fate if they resisted. And they were right, for a reputation of cruelty and abominable behavior preceded the Crusaders. At Antioch, after taking the city, they put all males to the sword and took women and children as slaves. When later they took Jerusalem, they spared neither Muslims nor Jews. The Jews who had taken refuge in a temple found death when the Franks put the place to fire. The Crusaders saw their God as a punisher, forgetting that the basis of Christianity meant forgiveness and the rejection of violence. It was a violence that soon the Muslims would adopt in later confrontations.

There is no better example of the ferocity of the invaders than mentioning the myth that arose out of their conquest of Ma'arra, a town near Antioch. After a bitter siege, that city fell. A group of soldiers led by a Norman named Tafur (his soldiers are sometimes referred as Tafurs), who once had been a knight but who now commanded a body of infantry, may have committed acts of cannibalism and roasted an enemy on the spit before a battle.[28] Raoul of Caen says, "Our soldiers boiled the adults, placed the children on spits and would eat them after roasting them." Albert of Aix adds, "Our men would eat not only Turks and Saracens but also dogs." Although cannibalism may have been in part the result of starvation among the Franks, it was also the kind of behavior that spread the utmost fear among the enemy, making difficult any form of compromise between Christians and Muslims. As an anonymous

Figure 14.5   Crusader States After the First Crusade

Muslim poet from Ma'arra wrote, "I ask myself whether this is the place where savage beasts roam or where is my house, the place I was born."[29]

Strengths and Weaknesses of Both Sides

Lack of unity was the main reason for the Muslim downfall during the First Crusade, although they were still able to field strong armies (Figure 14.5). Yet they were unable to stop the Crusaders, whose success surpassed any dream. In a very short time, the Crusaders were able to understand and find effective countermeasures to a type of warfare to which they had not become accustomed in Europe, even if one had fought against Muslims in Spain or Sicily. Their best weapons were the massed charge of heavy knights, the ability to bring down most of the fortified cities in the area, and the fear caused by their reputation for cruelty. This is not to say that infantry played no role. Even at Antioch about 3,000 footmen fought side by side with mounted soldiers. Civilians played an important role despite the fact that their presence must have slowed the armies' march. They were the source of auxiliaries, without which the success of the heavy horsemen would have been impossible; they kept alive, in moments of distress, the religious fervor and thus the military enthusiasm of the whole host; and from them came the Tafurs, the men that terrorized the enemy with their reputation for cannibalism.[30] Also from them, or from the union of Christians and Muslims, came the mysterious Turcopoles, who provided light soldiers, probably both foot and horse, to the crusader states established in the East. But the Turcopoles seemed never to have been in numbers large enough to be a match for the Muslims' light soldiers.

The Muslim armies were an amalgam of different troops coming from all corners of the land dominated by Islam—heavy cavalry from Persia, archers from Armenia, Syria, and Persia, infantry from the Daylami on the Caspian Sea. The dominant ethnic groups in the armies of Syria and Palestine were the Seljuk Turks. In the armies coming from Egypt we find native African infantry, among them many from the southern lands of Egypt, ancient Nubia, together with Berbers, Bedouins, and North African light cavalry. Eventually, however, when Saladin united the forces of Syria and Egypt, Kurds and Turks became predominant in the Egyptian Muslim army. But the most feared elements were the Mamluks, Turkish slave soldiers who were masterful at shooting while riding.[31] Despite the variety of soldiers, the main strength of the Muslim armies resided with their mounted archers.

The tactical and strategic approaches of the Muslims were different from western warfare. Continuing a tradition from the ancient Near East, they made the ambush their preferred approach. If this was impossible, they tended to attack the enemy while on the march, an easy task for an army with thousands of light cavalry operating in wide, unprotected terrain. This approach compelled the crusaders to move in serried bodies. True, this formation made them an easier target for Muslim arrows, but it also prevented them from becoming disorganized and allowed them to adopt quickly the proper formation for a charge.[32] If possible the Muslims tended to avoid a pitched encounter, and if that could not be avoided, they used a tactical approach to which the westerners were unaccustomed. The goal was to delay the face-to-face confrontation as long as possible and, if necessary, move to the flanks and rear of the opposing host using the advantage of their agile horses and large numerical superiority. The battle would begin with wave after wave of mounted archers whose projectiles, it seemed to the Crusaders, darkened the sky more than rain or hail. The objective was not so much to cause considerable casualties (the armor of the Crusaders withstood most arrows at a distance of 80 and even 60 meters), but to disorganize the enemies, creating a nervous strain that might force them either to move to the attack in a moment when their morale was low or to begin a reckless pursuit. If pursuit was the choice, the Turks were masters of the feigned withdrawal, known in Europe (e.g., the Normans at Hastings in 1066) but not normally used. When the Crusaders' mounts had spent most of their energies in pursuit and their lines had become disorganized, the Turks would move in for the kill, using spears, maces, and swords. That approach was facilitated by the greater mobility of their armies (their horses were more nimble, though less strong, than the Crusaders') and by the fact that they could hurt their adversaries from a distance by using the bow, which was not a weapon widespread in the armies of the Crusaders. Yet this sophisticated war machine had both strategic and tactical flaws.

Rarely Muslim armies took the field for long periods. The rule was that although conflict was possible during most of the year, the soldiers tended to return home during the winter to seek the affection of their women and look after their lands. Not even Saladin was able to keep his soldiers under arms every time he needed them. Moreover, the Muslim chain of command was in disarray during the First Crusade, and their heavy reliance on horses and bows hid several problems. Their horses needed vast grazing lands, which meant that their use was not without limits; their bows operated well only in good weather, as rain tended to ruin them. Made from horn and sinews and glued to a hardwood stave, their composite bows required seasoning before use. This meant that it was difficult and sometimes almost impossible to repair them during a campaign. Their worst enemy being rain, the mounted archers had few options if compelled to fight in bad weather: they could fight at the risk of ruining their weapons; they could engage in face-to-face combat with swords, spears, maces, or clubs, at a disadvantage against the Crusaders; or they could flee the battlefield.[33] But one can assume that no rain clouds darkened the sky and that the Latins would not launch their attack from less than 100 meters. Anything farther would have given the Muslims more shooting opportunities. Theoretically, according to some, the arrows struck from a composite bow could reach a distance of 600 meters, but in reality the killing range was much less against armored soldiers like the knights. We have examples during the First Crusade of Western soldiers looking like porcupines after an encounter with the Muslims. Several arrows were fixed into their body, but none caused serious injury unless the range had been less than 60 meters. Charles R. Bowlus argues that foot archers could be effective only starting at that distance against a well-protected enemy. Shooting from horseback must have lessened the range considerably. Assuming then that the knights serried their ranks and began their charge at about 100 meters from the enemy line, and that they would take about ten seconds to cover the distance, it meant that an archer, assuming that he had no natural frontal protection and limited to about seven seconds per shot, could discharge his arrows only once during the charge with three seconds remaining to flee. If he stood for another strike after the first, he would become an easy target for the assailant.[34] Knights were trained to use the utmost discipline during a charge. As Liutprand, Bishop of Cremona, writes, repeating Emperor Henry I's instructions to his cavalrymen against the Magyars, a people also relying on archery like the Turks, "When you begin your charge no one should attempt to ride ahead of the others, even if he has a faster mount, but each of you should cover one another with your shields and take the first enemy arrow. Then you should impel yourselves onward vigorously at a full gallop, so that he cannot launch a second arrow before feeling the wounds inflicted by your arms."[35] Finally, the crusader shield, unlike the round, smallish Turkish shield, was suited, thanks to its kite shape, to withstand the arrow of any archer. All this meant that if the knights were able to bring the enemy to close quarters, their chances of triumph were high.

Yet crusader armies had serious handicaps from the beginning. They increased with the passing of years and with any renewed crusade. After 1101 the supply line, which ran from Constantinople to northern Syria, was truncated. From then on the only contacts with the West had to come by sea. The Italian seafaring republics of Pisa, Genoa, and Venice performed excellent work in communication between the warriors and pilgrims in the Holy Land and Europe; yet they could never carry sufficient weapons and men to continue the fight against the Muslims. Moreover, although the Normans of southern Italy and the subjects of the German emperor in the north and the pope were among the most fervent supporters of the enterprise, the prime motivation for the Italian sea republics was economic gain, which came to fruition when the Fourth Crusade became the tool for the Venetians to appropriate the riches of Constantinople.

Crusader war conformed in many ways to the type of feudal wars among peers waged in the West. As John France says, it was war by committee:[36] too many leaders, too many divergent objectives, too many participants who, although part of the same army, were divided by ancient hostilities and old memories. For instance, the Crusaders' strategic plans veered between securing a stronger basis in the East by the conquest of Damascus, and penetration into Egypt, which promised abundant riches. Torn between these opposite goals, they were unable to achieve either, and in the end, with Saladin's emergence during the Third Crusade, they were crushed between the two poles. Often internal rivalry split the participants of the same crusade: Provençals against the rest in the First Crusade, French against Germans in the Second Crusade, Richard the Lionhearted against Philip Augustus in the Third Crusade.[37] The problem was that the crusaders, being at an astronomical distance from the West and taking the means of transportation into consideration, had to rely on their own resources in the states that they established from Asia Minor to the Sinai Desert. This meant at one point the rather meager total of 2,000 knights at the most: 100 from the short-lived principality of Edessa, about 200 from Tripoli, 700 from Antioch, and 1,000 from Jerusalem; and not all of them could be asked to serve at the same time. After the Battle of Ascalon (1000) Godefroy de Bouillon had only 300 knights and about 2,000 horsemen at his disposal.[38]

When the Muslim counterattack began around 1147, it was only a matter of time before the entire crusader power apparatus in the Near East began to crumble. It is a credit to the resilience of the Crusaders that their hold in the East lasted until the end of the thirteenth century. The last to fall was Acre on 18 May 1291 after forty-four days of siege.

The Military Orders

His health was precarious all his life, his mode of living austere and deprived of all luxuries, his physique debilitated, but he compensated for his frailty with devotional works that became the *vademecum* of many people of his age. St. Bernard of Clairvaux (1090–1153) was the son of a knight from Dijon who at the age of twenty-two, followed by his brothers and several other noblemen, entered the Order of the Cistercians, preferring a life devoted to Christ to one of endless tournaments and violence. His main goal was the Holy Land, and in seeking this goal he was able to rise over the religious hatreds of his age. In 1144 he even went to Germany to persuade King Conrad III to stop his persecution of the Jews and to dedicate his martial efforts to the defense of the

Holy Land. For the holy sites were uppermost in St. Bernard's mind. Although he always kept reservations about the knightly business of killing, he also put forward in a treatise written in the 1130s, *De laude novae militiae* (Praise of the New Knighthood), a justification for the military orders that had emerged toward the end of the previous century. The members of those orders were the new epitome of what a Christian knight should be, he wrote. Devoid of the vanity and of the material desires of everyday life and the killing of other Christians, the new clergymen dedicated their life to the defense of Christianity in the East. If they killed, he said, they killed for Christ; their homicides were done to erase evil.

It was a program reflected in the several orders that flourished between the twelfth and thirteenth centuries in three regions, Syria and Palestine, the Iberian Peninsula, and the Baltic.[39] Their birth was in the Holy Land, but as difficulties increased there, they spread also to eastern Europe (the objective here was to subjugate the heathen Slavs) and in the Iberian Peninsula, where the enemies were the Muslims who still held parts of the territory. While the orders in the East and Spain aimed at the defense or, if possible, the conquest of territories from the Muslims, the war in the Baltic regions was one of both conquest and conversion, although the atrocities committed against the heathen Slavs were much harsher than those in the Holy Land.

The first such order was founded in 1119 at Jerusalem by the knight Hugh de Payns and a few others of his comrades. The poor knights of Christ, as they were called, were given a section of the al-Aqsa Mosque, the same building identified as the remains of the Temple of Salomon. The statutes of the new order, the Templars, were approved by the Council of Troyes in 1120. Other orders followed soon. The Hospitallers of St. John, founded in 1070 to care for the pilgrims who had become ill or who were initially in poor health, became a military order around 1130–1136. The Order of St. Lazarus was formed at the time of the capture of Acre in 1192, and the Teutonic Order developed out of the German hospital in Jerusalem in 1199.

The orders included chaplains, but generally their members were laymen who had taken religious vows. Only the chaplains were priests. They were divided into two groups of soldiers: knights and sergeants-at-arms. The equipment of the two groups was similar, although knights had three or four mounts, sergeants only one. Moreover, unlike the knights, the sergeants could fight not only on horseback but also on foot. They were joined at times and for a short period by pilgrims to the Holy Land, and on occasion they hired auxiliaries and mercenaries from the surrounding areas. Their main military task in the East was the defense of castles, some of them amplified or built new by the orders. Safed, for instance, counted 80 knightly brothers, 350 auxiliaries, 820 servants and workmen, and 80 slaves.⁴⁰ But normally the brothers' contingent was much smaller. They also took part not only in the defense of the castles and strongholds but also in the pitched clashes of the period, although in relatively small numbers. Highly praised for their fervor and courage, they often suffered heavy casualties in the field. At the Battle of Cresson in May 1187, the Templars lost 80 brothers, and later that year only 33 Templars and 26 Hospitallers survived the defeat at Hattin. They left 300 men each on the field.⁴¹

The orders' last stand in the Holy Land was at the obstinate defense of Acre in 1291. Most of the survivors were massacred. Whoever succeeded in fleeing sought refuge in Cyprus. As all orders left the Holy Land, they regrouped elsewhere: the Hospitallers first in the island of Rhodes; chased away by the Turks, they resettled at Malta; the Teutonic Knights transferred their goals from Palestine to the Baltic. The case with the Templars was more complex. Hated not only by Muslims but also by Christians, they were tainted, probably unfairly, as trying to establish their own state within a state. Some of the animosity resulted from the order's success and power, their subordination only to Rome (not to local authorities), and their apparent wealth, for they had many convents in Europe that acted as retirement places for the old brothers, locations of recruit for new young ones, and repositories of funds before their transfer to the order in Outremer, that is, the Holy Land. In 1307 Philip the Fair, King of France, arrested its members, getting hold of their possessions and accusing them of all kinds of misdeeds, including witchcraft and lustful behavior. Five years later, in 1312, Pope Clement VII, pressured by Philip, abolished the order.

PART FOUR

The End of the Middle Ages, 1300–1453

Chapter Fifteen

The Hundred Years War:
A Matter of Contradictions
and Resilience

EDWARD III'S CRÉCY CAMPAIGN in 1346 started in a manner reminiscent of the 480 landing of the Persians on Greek territory. Then, as Herodotus says, the Persians' Greek puppet, Hippias, was overcome by a coughing and sneezing fit that made one of his teeth fall into the sand. Hippias tried to retrieve it in vain. "This land is not ours!" he exclaimed. "My tooth has taken the only share of it that will come to me."[1] And Edward, as he landed at La Hogue, stumbled and fell, bumping his nose on the beach. The blood flowing from his nose scared his men. This was a bad omen; better for their king to return to his boat. "Why?" rebutted the king. "It is a very good sign for me. It shows that this land is longing to embrace me."[2] He was right. For a long while that land—France—embraced the English dream, but at the end it jilted them all.

The Hundred Years War, which became known by that name for the first time in the nineteenth century, was a conflict between the kings of France and of England and took place during 116 years, from 1337 to 1453. Hostilities lasted for fifty-five years; the other sixty-one years were characterized by truces, momentary respites, sharpening the weapons, monetary exactions, and a spirit of resentment and revenge that was never dormant.

Bloody battlefields were not the only feature. Even more pervasive and destructive was the Black Death, which arrived in 1348; by the time it petered out (the plague never disappeared but returned at intervals) between one-third and one-half of the European population had perished from it. As the great Italian writer Giovanni Boccaccio says about Florence in *Decameron*, "Those who recovered from the plague were few, the rest almost all within three days from the appearance of the symptoms, sooner or later, died, and in most cases without any fever or other attendant malady." Shocking episodes became the norm. Boccaccio saw two hogs that, after coming into contact with the rags of a poor man who had died of the disease, succumbed almost immediately, as if poisoned by touching the clothes.[3]

And to define the conflict exclusively as an English-French struggle is inaccurate. While England presented a united front, with forces drawn from a population of about 4 million (and occasionally from friendly French domains), France's 16 million subjects enjoyed the fruits of a wealthier land that was nevertheless torn by internal conflicts, pitting rich against rich, and rich against the poor and the disadvantaged. France alternated between the slaughter of its own subjects and confrontation with forces marching behind the standard of the Plantagenet king invading from across the English Channel. Nor were the commoners or the great lords of the land uniform in their support of the French Valois kings. Some, like the men from Guyenne, the Aquitainian area bordering on the Atlantic, had recognized the sovereignty of the kings of England for quite a while; others, like the great lords of Brittany, Burgundy, and Flanders, saw war as a chance to restate their own ancient claims of sovereignty or of whittling away at the prerogatives of the sometimes powerless and weak king in Paris. So it is not shocking to realize that defeat more than victory marked the French armies. More shocking, by the end of the conflict, the French, not the English, emerged as the winner.

As the confrontation continued, society changed irreversibly. The control exercised by the kings of England and France increased at the expense of the great lords of the land. The two countries, together with the eventually triumphant Aragonese and Castilian sovereigns in the Iberian Peninsula, extended their sovereignty over their kingdoms, something that others, the Italian rulers, for instance, were unable to do. That may explain the cultural achievements on the peninsula as well as its political irrelevance at the end of the fifteenth and early sixteenth centuries, when it faced the unified states of France, Spain, and the Spanish-dominated Holy Roman Empire.

By the time the war ended, a new military world had emerged: permanent armies, a more realistic role for the heavy cavalry, an increasingly more effective infantry, the increasing reliance on mercenaries, the deployment of larger and larger armies, the stunning introduction of gunpowder, and the obvious frailty of the old castles against the new artillery. True, most of these developments would become dominant only decades after the end of the Hundred

Years War, but the signs were evident when the English finally abandoned their dreams of establishing rule in most of France.

The Contradictory Nature of the War

The Capetian Dynasty that had ruled France since the tenth century ended in 1328 when the last of the three sons of Philip the Fair died without a direct male heir. The claimants to the throne were Philip of Valois, son of Philip the Fair's brother; and the Plantagenet king of England, Edward III, whose grandfather had been Philip the Fair (his mother, Isabelle, was Philip's daughter). Dynastically, Edward was closer to the throne but encountered an obstacle in the Salic Law of the French kingdom, which excluded women and their descendants from claiming the throne. It was no surprise when the French barons disregarded Edward's claim in favor of the Valois, who assumed the name of Philip VI (Figure 15.1).

Obviously the choice did not please Edward, who referred to Philip as "that man who claims to be the King of France." Yet for the moment he paid homage to the newly chosen king, for it was the duty of the lord of Guyenne, in the northwest region on the Atlantic, to give fealty to his overlord, the king of France. The accommodation soon fractured under the stress of old claims and hatreds. The kings of England entered a potentially ambiguous territory starting with William the Conqueror in 1066; they had become kings of England while holding territories in France, which made them vassals of whomever held that king's crown. The situation gave rise to a series of conflicts that only increased when Eleanor of Aquitaine married Henry II of England, bringing even more French territory under the control of her husband and their heirs. The crisis seemed to have been solved in 1259. At that time Henry III renounced his claim to most French lands except for Guyenne. Yet the issue of control over Guyenne control led to new conflict when on 24 May 1337 Philip confiscated the territory from Edward III. Edward had to accept the takeover or challenge Philip's legitimacy to the throne of France (to which he himself was potentially closer because of his mother). He sent a defiant letter on 7 October, and a few years later, in 1340, he proclaimed himself king of France. England's claim was based on dynastic succession in addition to the important political and economic interests in Aquitaine, Flanders, and Scotland, where the French had meddled by raising the Scots' expectations for independence.

As Christopher Allmand argues, the war is understood best if divided into four phases: 1337–1360, a period of reversals for the French; 1360–1396, when

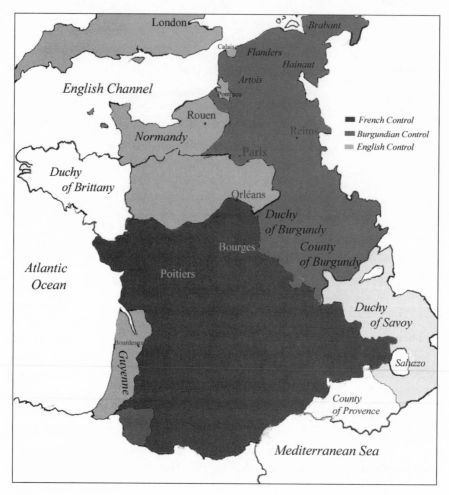

Figure 15.1   France in 1429

the French recovered some of the territories they had lost; 1396–1422, a difficult phase of instability for the French kingdom and one of triumph for the
English cause; and 1422–1453 when the English, after initial success, were
compelled to abandon their dream of continental supremacy.[4] The conflict
began in 1340 when the French fleet was obliterated at Sluys. The reverse
spelled doom for the French, for command of the sea would allow the English to cross the channel at will. Yet there were no further gains for Edward.
The threat posed by Scotland and the expense of military campaigns led to a
lull, which did not last long. Hostilities switched to a new theater, Brittany,
where England and France fought to establish hegemony; in 1341 a struggle

was initiated among rival claimants to the throne upon the death of the local duke. It was an opportunity for the English to establish a client state on French lands and to control another bridgehead (besides Guyenne) for invading the continent. An attack could now be engineered from multiple directions—Brittany, Guyenne, and possibly Flanders (considering the ancient hostility of the Flemish burghers toward the French and the defense of their economic interests that tied them closely to the English).[5]

When a peace conference called by Pope Clement VI at Avignon in 1344 ended with no settlement, hostilities renewed on a larger scale in the French territory. In July 1346 Edward III landed in Normandy with an army of some 15,000 men. He advanced, burning and looting towns like Caen, from which he immediately dispatched loot to the coast for shipment to England. Then he moved toward Paris before changing his mind. He then veered north, crossed the Seine River, and tried to find a way to cross the next major obstacle, the Somme.

The English king's campaign could not go unopposed. Avoiding a direct confrontation with the English was useful, for in the long run attrition might compel their withdrawal; yet inaction meant that the enemy troops, in the classical manner of a *chevauchée,* brought misery to peasants and burghers (which could be acceptable to the French king and his councilors—after all they were just commoners!) but also poverty to the kingdom (which was unacceptable because it reduced the tax base). In the end Philip responded by recruiting a large army to shadow the English. Edward was in great danger now and decided to move toward the safety of the coast. But the Somme's bridges were well-guarded. The solution was to cross at the Blanche-Taque ford, where a column of two men wide could advance. But on the opposite riverbank a large contingent of French soldiers appeared. It is proof of the strength of the English army that they forced a passage, although with heavy losses. Across the river they settled nearby Crécy on terrain that protected them against the French cavalry while also enhancing the deadly combination of their longbowmen and dismounted men-at-arms. By the end of 26 August 1346, Philip's army, which had foolishly rushed to the attack, was crushed. Many knights were left dead on the battlefield.

Another disaster followed this unexpected defeat. Edward laid siege to Calais, an ideal location for another bridgehead on French territory. It took him longer than expected to bring the city to its knees. After eleven months of resistance, Calais, hopeless of receiving any support from the outside, decided to surrender, but Edward imposed humiliating conditions. "Choose six of your most distinguished citizens," he said, "have them bring the city keys bareheaded and barefoot, with a cord around their neck." It was a demeaning request that Calais could not accept. Six citizens did come with the keys, but not in the submissive posture that Edward had demanded. He became angry and ordered the envoys to be executed. When the queen and the knights begged him to be merciful, he rescinded his order, but most of the inhabitants of Calais were forced to leave their city, which was repopulated with Englishmen and their French supporters. Calais would remain in English hands for about two centuries.

Difficulties in raising the necessary finances led to another lull, more beneficial to the French than to the English, but another calamity fell on French shoulders. When Philip died in 1350, he was succeeded by his son, John the Good, a man of good intentions but of political and military mediocrity. In his search for financial support he even debased the currency, angering practically everybody in the kingdom. And then a new claimant to the throne came to the fore, Charles the Bad, King of Navarre. It was obvious that Edward and Charles the Bad would reach an agreement against John the Good. And then Edward's oldest son, also named Edward but better known as the Black Prince, a nickname first used in Tudor times because of the colors of his attire, entered the picture. The Black Prince had already distinguished himself at Crécy at the age of sixteen. In a new foray into French territory he became one of the leaders of a three-pronged attack: the Black Prince from Bordeaux striking into the north-central area; Henry, duke of Lancaster, from Normandy; and Edward III from the north.[6] The attack failed, but the Black Prince succeeded in amassing loot. When pursued by a French army, he turned on it near Poitiers on 18 September 1356. The French command again launched its soldiers against a well-protected English force of dismounted men-at-arms and longbowmen. John the Good and his men were certain of success (their army was about double the English host), but the day ended as at Crécy, with huge casualties for the attackers and few losses for the English. John the Good was taken prisoner, and his own son, Charles Dauphin (heir to the throne), saved his own skin by fleeing the battlefield.

At Poitiers France seemed to have reached a new low point, but there were other problems. In 1348 the Black Death had arrived in French lands; the sailors of a Genoese ship had been infected while in the Near East. In a year at least one-third of the French population perished. The pestilence appeared in England, with a similar rate of casualties. But that was not all. Between periods of violence and truce, the civilian population must have wondered whether peace was preferable to war. When the armies stopped meeting on the battlefield, bodies of unemployed soldiers, the so-called *routiers*, roamed the countryside, famished, eager to pillage and to use violence against anybody, now that their wages had stopped. They made no distinction between enemies and supporters of the crown. The target was the civilian, regardless of allegiance. It was a pernicious situation that lessened the financial base of the kingdom: a poor, oppressed population could hardly meet the increasing taxes that the conflict required. Anarchy followed, in which unemployed soldiers, first in small groups, then in larger contingents, became the masters of the countryside. According to a *routier* quoted by a chronicler of the time, Froissart, they were happy "when our thirst of adventure brings us to find a rich abbot or prior, or a rich merchant or a convoy of mules carrying golden cloth or silk or leather or spices. . . . We grab everything and if the prey is a rich individual, then we shall ask a rich ransom. The peasants fear and respect us bringing wheat and flour and the best wines, and meat, beef, sheep, goats, chickens to us and oats to our horses. We dress like kings; our lifestyle is fascinating and rewarding."[7]

Not even lords seeking refuge behind their castle walls were safe from the *routiers*, for they may have been surrounded by the despised Jacques Bonhomme, the symbol of the rioting peasants.[8] On 21 May 1358 the peasants of a few villages in the Beauvaisis rose against their lords. This idea quickly spread through France, especially in Picardy, Isle-de-France, and Champagne. The resentment of years of subjection unleashed the peasants' hatred against those who had controlled them from time immemorial. As Jean de Venette writes in his *Chronique latine* about the Jacquerie, as that type of revolt was called, they marched in one instance to the chateau of their lord, took him prisoner, and killed his pregnant wife and his children in front of him before dispatching him; then they sacked the castle and set it on fire. Well-to-do burghers, knights, their women, their children's hands around their necks, fled as far as possible from the ravages of the peasants.[9] Anarchy and violence spread to all corners; the fields went uncultivated; villages made churches into strongholds, surrounding them with moats and placing war machines atop the bell towers. As the first signs of Jacquerie spread, the villagers would leave their houses, seeking refuge in churches, hoping that the peasants would not gain access, some trusting their defensive works, others nourishing the hope that the assaulters would not shed blood in a holy site.[10]

Even the burghers of Paris rose up against the king, requesting representation in the royal council, a demand that seems reasonable to modern eyes but which was revolutionary and treacherous to the ruling class at the time. The Parisian leader, a man named Etienne Marcel, abandoned his legitimate king and took the side of Charles the Bad, pretender to the crown, opening the gates of Paris. But the Parisians rose in revolt and massacred him and fifty-four of his comrades on 31 July 1358: their corpses, stripped of their garments, were left for days to rot in the streets so that everybody could see and reach his own conclusions about the danger of siding with the crown's enemies.[11]

Intensive negotiations followed the disaster at Poitiers. Finally the parties reached agreement on 24 October 1360 by the Treaty of Brétigny. Aquitaine, Ponthieu in northeastern France, and Calais were to remain under the sovereignty of England; the ransom to be paid for John the Good was agreed upon, at least for the moment. But the most important clause, Edward's formal renunciation of his claim to the crown of France and John's forswearing of his overlordship over Aquitaine, was never ratified, spelling trouble for future relations. By 1360 England seemed to have triumphed while France was barely hanging on. The English strategy of attack, placing France on the defensive, seemed to have worked to perfection. The climax at Brétigny was deceptive, however. During the next twenty years, France was revived and posed a formidable challenge to the English.

The English triumph in the first phase was due to the internal weaknesses of the French, the administrative talent and leadership of Edward III, and the daring of the Black Prince, the first to receive the title Prince of Wales. In the second phase, 1360–1380, the reverse was true. Talented war managers among the French arose thanks mainly to the wisdom and cunning of the new ruler, Charles V, the first heir to the French throne who had enjoyed the title of Dauphin (i.e., heir to the throne), based on his lordship over the Dauphiné, conquered in 1349 under Philip VI. Charles was the son of John the Good and Bonne of Luxembourg. Born in 1338, he had taken part in the Battle of Poitiers, fleeing once the French side came to defeat. He had become regent after his father had been taken to the Tower of London. His physical frailty and self-effacing character were deceptive. He was clever and astute, a great administrator despite of his age, a connoisseur of wise councilors. In 1364 the king's crown was his after his father died in London. Charles restored the broken finances of the kingdom, developed the marine force, organized an efficient army (in which mercenaries played a leading role), and invested in the manufacture of artillery (which had first appeared with the English at Crécy), thereby initiating a century-long process that would make French guns the most effective by the start of the Italian wars of the Renaissance in 1495.

As his performance at Crécy had shown, the new king was not a gifted military commander. For that he relied on Bertrand du Guesclin, a Breton knight of modest origin with a checkered background (he had also been a *routier*). The new commander, eighteen years older than the king, lacked the brilliance and daring of the Black Prince. He preferred ambushes and skirmishes to pitched battles. His command was also blessed by his important defeat of the other pretender to the crown, Charles the Bad of Navarre, at Cocherel, in southeastern Normandy, on 16 May 1364. A wonderful complement to Charles the Wise, du Guesclin experienced victories as well as defeats, falling prisoner a few months after Cocherel, against the Bretons at Auray in southern Brittany, and later at Nájera in Spain on 3 April 1367 against the Black Prince, now in the twilight of his career. But Charles, who never lost his confidence in du Guesclin, paid his ransom as quickly as possible, supporting him in good and bad even after Nájera, where the normally cautious du Guesclin had imprudently deployed his soldiers with their backs to a river.

One of the most serious problems Charles faced was the *routiers*, the unemployed soldiers ravaging his lands. A solution was found for the moment when du Guesclin took them to Spain to meddle in the succession crisis of the throne of Castile. As was typical, du Guesclin mixed success with failure when faced by the Black Prince, who had come to support another pretender to the Castilian throne. But in the end the Spanish campaign was positive for the French; their man gained the throne.

Although the theater had shifted from France to the land across the Pyrenees, peace did not return to Charles's domain. The problem rested with Aquitaine, where the Black Prince, heavily in debt, tried to impose a more stringent and probably illegal taxation upon the lords of the land. The Aquitainians knew how to play the game, for now they saw their champion in the French king; they asked him to intervene. Charles, being the overlord in Aquitaine, could not refuse. The march toward new hostilities was quick: in December 1368 Charles agreed to discuss the complaints of the Aquitainians; in June 1369 Edward answered by reassuming the title king of France; in November Charles confiscated Aquitaine. War had restarted, although the people of the time, crushed between the English, French, and *routiers*, must have thought that hostilities never ceased.

Because of the English inability to inflict the killing blow and of French resilience, the war dragged out. Gestures of peace followed offensive strikes. But now the French avoided pitched battle. After all, how many more casualties could even the populous land of France endure? Quick raids into English territories, especially Aquitaine, offered a long frontier and endless routes of attack. Yet with a young, inexpert Dauphin on the throne, the future looked bleak. So the French limited their strikes into enemy territories, where they brought death, chaos, and poverty. This time success bred success: in 1371 Charles the Bad of Navarre, probably worried by the efficacy of the French strategy, finally came to agreement with the king of France; the duke of Brittany was chased out of his territory by people who detested the English; in 1372 the English fleet trying to bring reinforcements to the continent was defeated by the Castilian-French counterpart near La Rochelle; and French and Castilian ships reappeared on the English coast, sacking villages.[12] The English crisis became more serious when in 1371 the Black Prince died, followed by his father, Edward III, a few months later; a ten-year old, Richard II, rose to the throne.

By the end of 1377 the French had reconquered most of their territories while the English were facing serious internal problems: in 1381 the peasants rose in revolt, and in the years that followed influential segments of the population, like the Lollards and John Wycliff, started to question the futility of this war. But France had its own problems. It had recovered many territories given up at Brétigny, but the English still controlled the main ports on the Atlantic—Calais, Cherbourg, Brest, Bordeaux—and several strongholds in the interior. Moreover, both Charles V, never in good health, and du Guesclin died in 1380 (the king was only forty-two years old) and the throne fell to a boy, twelve-year-old Charles VI, with real power resting with his feuding older relatives. Disorder reigned in certain lands, squeezed by the heavy taxes that Charles V imposed to support his war effort. At Rouen, the Maillotins, with mallets in their hands (hence their nickname), chased the tax collectors sent by the king. Moreover, in spite of their victory against the Flemish at Rozebeke on 27 November 1382, the French saw England reconquer many coastal regions and methodically advance toward the interior. Yet both sides were tired of war and in 1396 agreed to a twenty-year truce, cemented by the marriage of Richard II to Isabella, one of Charles's daughters. It was a fragile compromise, and war soon returned.

The French success in the second phase had been ephemeral. By the end of the third phase, in 1422, they found themselves on the brink of collapse. While rule was legally in the hands of Charles VI, a decent man but often incapable (he was afflicted by periodic bouts of madness), real power rested with his uncles—Charles, duke of Anjou; John, duke of Berry; Louis, duke of Bourbon; and especially Philip the Bold, duke of Burgundy. The struggle for hegemony among these kingmakers was fierce and ruthless. At one time it ended in murder when the men of the king's cousin, John the Fearless, son of Philip the Bold, assassinated the king's brother, Louis of Orléans, in the Rue Vieille-du-Temple in Paris. While the internal struggle for power continued among the supporters and enemies of the powerful duke of Burgundy, the situation was unsettled in England, where Richard II was deposed and then murdered in 1400. His successor, Henry IV, began his reign with a tactless gesture: he sent Isabella, the murdered king's wife, back to France without her dowry. Moreover, in spite of the truce signed in 1396, low-level hostilities poisoned relations between the two powers. The English continued to raid the Norman coast; piracy by both sides infested the English Channel; France kept meddling in the affairs of Wales and Scotland against the English crown; and English forces moved to the continent to support one of the various claimants to power, in this case the duke of Burgundy.[13]

Full hostilities did not break out until Henry V became king of England in 1413. Henry, along with the Black Prince, was the most gifted English commander of the war. And unlike the Black Prince, he combined military skill with a long-term vision of taking permanent English control of the continent. Only his sudden death on 31 August 1422 saved the French. Although great men do not necessarily make history, their presence, especially when leadership fell to few individuals, could change the tenor of a conflict. A man of great ambition and iron character, Henry V sat on the English throne, while France languished under a mad king, ripped apart by faction.

Again the English were masters of the battlefield, although their great victory at Agincourt on 25 October 1415 came out of a strange campaign by Henry V that should have ended in disaster. After landing on the French coast on 14 August 1415 and taking the city of Harfleur, Henry moved across Normandy, placing his army of about 6,000 in serious jeopardy. He was tracked down by a much larger French army and caught between the road to the seacoast and the interior of France. But French leadership again showed its frailty in the pitched encounter at Agincourt. English longbowmen, intermixed with dismounted men-at-arms, routed the French host, benefiting by a careful deployment, protection on the flanks, and a terrain rendered muddy by a violent storm. By the end of the battle many French noblemen were dead on the field.

Unlike his predecessors, Henry's aims were clear. He had come to France to stay, to become its legitimate ruler, and to leave the entire kingdom firmly in the hands of his dynasty. He pursued these goals ruthlessly and efficiently.

Most French territories in the north quickly fell to the English. They were stopped only at the Loire River, a line that could be broken if Orléans, later placed under siege, were to fall. On 20 May 1420 the Treaty of Troyes stated that upon the death of Charles VI the French crown would become Henry's. For the moment, waiting the demise of the mad king, the English ruler assumed the title of regent. The capital, Paris, was under his control, as well as Reims, where the kings of France were consecrated.

The astonishing English conquests were interrupted when dysentery, contracted at the siege of Meaux, killed Henry in 1422, to the rejoicing of his French opponents. Now that he had disappeared, a French song at the time trumpeted: "From the land of France those English are all rejected / And there is no longer any talk of those tailed English [English monkeys], / May the entire lineage [of Henry V] be cursed."[14] The French crown now fell officially to Henry's son, Henry VI, then only a few months old, which meant that the men in power were Humphrey, duke of Gloucester, Cardinal Beaufort in London, and the infant king's uncle, the duke of Bedford, in France.

King Charles VI of France had died soon after Henry V. The French heir to the throne, Charles VII, claimed that he was the true king of the land, but in reality his hold was tenuous, resting on the hope that Orléans would not fall into English hands. Otherwise, his enemies would spread into the remaining loyal territories south of the Loire. For the moment, as Orléans seemed on the verge of collapse, the English and their French supporters had nothing but hatred for the "self-styled Dauphin," that "little king of Bourges," the unofficial capital of his quickly disappearing kingdom.

Then a young peasant woman of seventeen years changed the course of the war in a land dominated by men and social divisions. The appearance of Joan of Arc in 1429 gave confidence to the defeated cause, seemed to bring God to the defense of the French claim, and was instrumental in lifting the siege of Orléans. As the contemporary Christine de Pizan wrote during the year of her success, "In the year one thousand four hundred and twenty-nine the sun once again began to shine."

The English failure at Orléans opened the last phase of the war. About two months later the French defeated the English at Patay, taking prisoner a prestigious commander, John Talbot. Unflinching in the belief of her mission, Joan convinced the vacillating king to reach Reims, where it was customary to anoint the rulers of the realm. At the ceremony in Reims two of the symbols of kingship were missing: the orb and the scepter of the crown, left in enemy hands at St. Denis, on the outskirts of Paris. But the chrism of the Holy Vial, which legend said a dove had carried to St. Remi to anoint the founder of the Merovingian kingdom, Clovis, was present there. The journey to Reims was not without danger, for the city was in enemy territory held by the duke of Burgundy; 12,000 soldiers accompanied the king and the Maid. The duke of Burgundy, probably worried less by the soldiers than by his wavering support of the English cause, caused no problems during the journey. The anointment was a public statement of great psychological importance, for it announced to French subjects that Charles VII, not Henry VI, was the legitimate ruler. The Holy Vial showed that God had chosen him.

Joan would not remain long on the scene. Her military presence was not as crucial as it had been earlier, and Charles almost abandoned her. On 24 May 1430 the Burgundians captured the Maid nearby Compiègne and sold her to the English. A week later an ecclesiastical court, controlled by the English, declared the woman "a witch, a soothsayer, a false prophetess," a person "guilty of impudence and totally forgetful of decency and what is seemly for her sex." She was burned at the stake in the market of Rouen. It was a hollow and bitter victory for the English cause, for English hegemony over the territories that Henry V had conquered was slipping away. The cause was not yet the enemy's supremacy on the battlefield but the serious financial problems afflicting the land: the Parliament in London was increasingly reluctant to support a war across the channel that brought headaches more than gains; subjects in Normandy resisted the heavier taxes imposed by the duke of Bedford; and then the duke of Burgundy decided to make peace with Charles, opening the gates of Paris. The "little king of Bourges" became King of France.

Success followed success as the French army underwent a small revolution. The French were able to exploit the military resources of their kingdom in full. While a relief force sent by the English met defeat at Formigny on 15 April 1450, the Norman towns kept falling to Charles VII's troops. By August 1450 the English had been expelled from Normandy. They had been there for thirty-three years. Only Guyenne remained, but that region too fell to French arms when the eighty-year-old Lord Talbot and his relief force were defeated at Castillon on 17 July 1453. Lord Talbot's end was a melancholic symbol of the failure of the English cause. At Castillon, where Talbot had fallen from his horse, the French rushed over his body, hacking it to pieces. Guyenne became part of the French state. The Hundred Years War ended. For the English it faded into the bitter War of the Roses. Whereas peace returned to France, the English endured bitter civil war.

The Winning Ways of English Strategy and Tactics: Chevauchées, Crécy, and Agincourt

The English hosts combined good organization with clear strategy and deadly tactics. It meant that they retained the initiative. Their strategic aims went through four stages. Initially up to 1360 they were based on the *chevauchée*; in the middle period until the end of the fourteenth century the English were on the defensive, which meant the abandonment of sudden and savage raids into enemy territory; with the accession of Henry V their approach was based on permanent settlement in French lands; the last stage, after Henry V's death in 1422, was defensive until the final triumph of the French under King Charles VII.

In 1339, after his *chevauchée* around Cambrai, Edward III wrote to his son in England, "The Monday, on the eve of St. Matthew, we passed out of Valenciennes, and on the same day they [the fires] did begin to burn in Cambrésis, and they burnt there all the week following, so that the country is clean and laid waste, as of corn and cattle and other goods."[15] He should have added "empty of people," for destruction and mayhem were the aims of all *chevauchées*: fear, death, material destruction, and finally battle at a time and place best suited to your own men. It cut the heart from the French population; commoners had nothing to hope from the marauders. Noblemen could pay ransom and call on the canon of chivalry uniting both friend and foe. During the Crécy campaign a group of knights and squires sought refuge from the English soldiers, and when the besieged communicated their names to their noble peers among the English their lives were spared. Upon hearing their identity the English commander was delighted. He could save the lives of peers and make a fine haul of valuable prisoners, enough to bring in 100,000 moutons.[16]

The *chevauchée* strategy brought the French to their knees with two humiliating defeats at Crécy in 1346 and at Poitiers in 1356. *Chevauchée* began with a relatively small but mobile army, for most of the soldiers were mounted. They included men-at-arms and longbowmen together with smaller numbers of assorted infantrymen. The raids' mobility should not be exaggerated. For instance, the army of Edward III in 1346 marched 10–12 miles a day and even when pursued may have moved no more than 15 miles in a day. The Black Prince's famous *chevauchée* of October–November 1355 averaged 10 miles a day, although in one case it made a journey of 25 miles in 24 hours.[17] Valuable as they had been, the times of the *chevauchées* reached an end by 1359–1360. In the next phase, the French turned the tables on the English, organizing their own raids into English-held territory.

If we move from the field to the operational and tactical domains, the superiority of the English continued, with brief interruptions, throughout the war until Joan of Arc's relief of Orléans in 1429. It was based on a defensive deployment, with longbowmen at the side or in front of dismounted men-at-arms.[18] It started with deadly arrow volleys against the advancing enemy before they made contact with the English men-at-arms. There the attackers faced dismounted horsemen and the archers, hitting their flanks with swords, daggers, and clubs. The approach had been used in the aftermath of the Norman Conquest but eventually was abandoned in favor of the conventional charge of mounted men. Yet the vicissitudes of the conflict with the Scots in the later part of the thirteenth and early fourteenth centuries caused the English to rethink their tactical disposition. It was an idea nourished by the experience in the clash against the Scots, especially at the Battle of Falkirk in 1298 and Bannockburn in 1314. The new approach was honed at Boroughbridge in 1322, Dupplin Moor in 1332, and especially at Halidon Hill in 1333, all against the Scots. The combination of dismounted men-at-arms and a large body of longbowmen opened the small engagement of Morlaix in Brittany in 1342 and was perfected at Crécy in 1346.

The Crécy campaign gives the impression that Edward's overall goal was unclear except to cause havoc in the French lands (Figure 15.2). Finally, he decided to land in the Cotentin, for Normandy, as one of his advisers assured him, was one of the richest countries in the world.[19] Also, it is likely that he may have intended to contact Flemings sympathetic to the English cause. But much more important was the building of a strategic and tactical model that brought death and destruction to the French. His advance through the French countryside and towns brought his army rich loot, destruction and humiliation to the enemy, and a realization among the enemy's own people of the powerlessness of their sovereign: the English "ravaged and burnt, plundered and pillaged" the "good, fat land of Normandy."[20] Their army of about 4,000 men-at-arms, 10,000 longbowmen, and a large number of troops from Wales and Cornwall marched in three columns very close to the sea, where the English fleet must have provided logistical support. The softer targets, that is, locations that offered minimal resistance either for lack of manpower or for their weak fortifications, fell one after the other to the English, who proceeded "robbing, pillaging and carrying off everything they came across."[21] Barfleur, Cherbourg, Valogne, Saint-Lô, and Caen capitulated to Edward's army, and

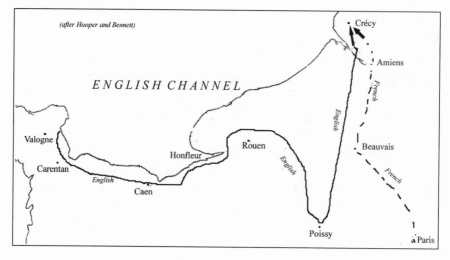

Figure 15.2   Crécy Campaign 1346

its horrible violence, for "in an army such as [the one that] the King of England was leading it was impossible that there should not be plenty of bad characters and criminals without conscience."[22] The English even made a foray
near the heartland, Paris, burning Saint-Germain-en-Laye, Saint-Cloud,
Boulogne, Bourg-la-Reine, and Montjoie, a favorite castle of the French mon-
archs. It was a humiliation that Philip Valois could not endure long. He
decided that he had to confront the enemy in the field and hastily gathered a
large army, which took time to organize.

The defiant march of the English troops must have increased morale and
sullied the confidence of Philip's men-at-arms. Edward overcame physical
obstacles like the Seine and the Somme, then inflicted serious losses on the
French when they met. But in the last stages Edward gives the impression of
being cornered, for he seemed to have engaged in a desperate flight to avoid a
face-to-face conflict. After the crossing of the Somme Edward may have
decided that pitched battle was the answer. The choice of the battlefield is testament to the skill of the English king and his councilors. They decided to
make a stand on a ridge about 1,800 meters long between the villages of Wadicourt on the left and Crécy on the right, parallel to the French line of advance
along the road from Abbeville. The ridge rose sharply on the right, about 100
feet, and gently on the left. Toward the middle of the ridge were terraces that
seem to have provided a natural physical obstacle to the French and were thus
not necessary to man. The right of the English army on Crécy was strong,

benefited by the sharp incline and by a river, the Maye, that flowed along its flank, as well as by the wooded area that ran from the center toward the right. The left was less protected where the incline was nonexistent; the fields at the back were open, except for the village of Wadicourt.[23] It is strange that the French decided to attack the strongest side, the right, instead of the left, unless people arriving along the road had the impression that this was the easiest, as it was the closest.

The three columns of Edward's army converged at Crécy on the noon of 24 August 1346. He had traveled about 335 miles in 32 days with an average of 10 miles a day. Instructions to survey the ground were given, the deployment was discussed, and then the soldiers settled for the night after polishing armor and getting weapons ready for combat. As the morning of 25 August broke, the king rose early and made his peace with God, asking His help for victory: he knelt on the altar that had been prepared and took communion with most of his men, or at least the leaders. Then the troops were ordered to deploy according to the previous day's instructions; all the horses were led into a park on the edge of the wood on the back, for all had to fight dismounted. The king himself would take his post where a windmill stood on the highest point of the ridge, allowing an excellent view of the battlefield (Figure 15.3).

The deployment envisaged three "battles," two of which were on the right and left of the line; the third, led by the king, was in a central position, a little behind the other two. The battle on the right was under the command of the king's son, Edward of Woodstock, the Black Prince. He was only sixteen, but his brilliance and daring presaged future military exploits. His father surrounded him with some of the most experienced commanders of his army. The battle on the left was entrusted to the earl of Northampton, who had fought with distinction at Halidon Hill in 1333 and might have been the inspiration for Edward's defensive battle plan. Each battle, or at least the two forward battles, had large groups of longbowmen, lined up on the flanks, with some in front of the men-at-arms during the initial phase. The actual deployment of the archers has been a matter of controversy.[24] Regardless, we can assume that they were located on the flanks of the battles in ways that maximized the number of weapons they could bring to bear upon the enemy; the rise of the ground may have allowed some of the rear ranks to shoot effectively. Taking into consideration that the French knights' target would be the men-at-arms for questions of prestige and honor, not the rabble of commoners, the bowmen could be effective on the flanks of the attackers.

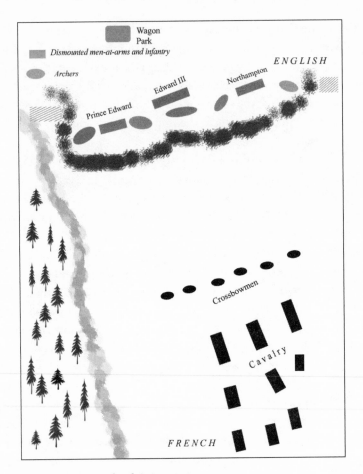

Figure 15.3   Battle of Crécy 1346

The numerical strength of Edward's army at Crécy has also been controversial. The majority of historians and contemporary sources say that they
were vastly inferior to the French. One of the lone dissenting voices was the
distinguished French historian Ferdinand Lot, who assigned 12,428 men to the
English and 12,000 to the French.[25] Contamine thinks that the French were at
most 19,000.[26] However, there is no doubt on their numerical superiority,
though we should discount exaggerations.[27] Froissart seems credible when he
lists the English: 800 men-at-arms, 2,000 archers, and 1,000 light troops in
the right battle, 500 men-at-arms and 1,200 archers on the left, and 700 men-
at-arms and 2,000 archers in the king's battle.[28] This gives a numerical strength
of 2,000 men-at-arms and 5,200 archers, a proportion 2.6 longbows for every

dismounted horseman. We probably have to raise the number of ordinary foot soldiers to 3,000–4,000,[29] which would give a total strength of a little more than 10,000. As for the French, they were superior in men-at-arms, probably with as many as 8,000–9,000 and 3,000–5,000 crossbowmen. Moreover, a large array of low-quality volunteers came with the army, probably for loot. Others from Rouen and Beauvais arrived a day later in time to be mercilessly cut down by the English.

The French were at a distance of about 18 miles the morning of the battle. Philip, like Edward, rose early and attended mass with his leaders at the Abbey of St. Peter in Abbeville. Then he divided his troops into at least eight or more battles in pursuit of the English. He did not advance recklessly, as is some-times argued, for Froissart says that he sent four knights in advance to scout the location and disposition of the English troops. When they came, they warned him about the strong defensive deployment of the adversaries. "They have no intention to retreat," one of the knights warned. "It may be worth-while stopping, reorder the troops which are tired instead of facing fresh and rested enemies, and then study the best approach to defeat the enemy later."[30]

The king seems to have agreed with his scouts, but when he gave the orders to delay the attack until the next day, he was ignored. Confusion brought the French army to its demise. Hesitant, the king changed his mind, directing the troops to their doom. The French army surged forward in "no order or for-mation."[31] As they arrived on the battlefield, the French crossbowmen in the vanguard, with orders to open the battle, begged their commanders to let them rest at least for while. They were tired, they complained, and had little desire to open the battle immediately. It was a reasonable request, for they had marched since the early morning on a warm August day. The count of Alençon dismissed them as cowards. It also seems that when the crossbows were deploying for battle, a thunderstorm struck, damaging their weapons' strings. Yet they advanced as ordered. Whether their bolts failed to reach the English archers is debatable. The crossbow's range matched or surpassed that of the longbow, although it is likely that the ridge gave the English arrows extra distance. The impact of rain should not be dismissed; the English avoided damage to their bowstrings by placing them beneath their helmets. Yet the French did not have their *pavises*, large protective shields, for the carts transporting them had not arrived. This meant that they were more vulnerable. Moreover, the likely use of bombards by the English may have demoralized the French crossbowmen after the initial advance, when they approached the English line with three shouts. Finally, it is likely that they were numerically inferior to the English archers, for they had suffered losses in the encounters before Crécy. In all probability, they were less than the 15,000 given to them by Froissart or the 6,000 by modern authorities.

The failure of the crossbowmen and the tendency of some to retreat enraged the knights of the French battle. Crying treason, they ran down their own missile units, killing any who did not seek safety. It was four o'clock in the afternoon. Mowing down the crossbowmen, the knights then moved against the English line. The long ride to the battlefield, the effort spent against the crossbowmen, the problematic terrain (soft after the thunderstorm), and the pits that the archers had dug in front of their locations spelled disaster for the French cavalry. The arrows seemed to cover the sky as they met the English men-at-arms. When they fell to the ground, Welsh and Cornish *coutilliers* dispatched them with long knives. After all, these commoners had no interest in ransom, for the proceeds would go to their lords, not them.

The French carried fifteen charges and the battle lasted until evening. The charges were not continuous but launched piecemeal as various battles arrived to the field. The confusion caused by this approach continued throughout the day. As darkness fell, the French lost contact with their leaders and wandered aimlessly among their opponents.[32] The battle's length favored the longbowmen, allowing them time to retrieve their arrows (between twenty-four and forty missiles were in a quiver) and rest.

The best French effort was against the right wing that was led by the Black Prince. The situation there seemed to have been so dangerous that the English called for help. Some was provided by the earl of Northampton from the English left, which suggests that the French attack there was mild, and some (only twenty knights) by the prince's own father, who had first answered, "Let my son gain his spurs," the symbol of knighthood.

British casualties were minimal, although one estimate of two knights and a squire and a few Welshmen is suspect. The writer describing the battle was correct in saying that the "whole army is intact and unharmed."[33] As darkness enveloped the battlefield, 1,542 French men-at-arms and squires laid dead; Edward sent men to count the next morning.[34] More commoners died the next day when a force from Rouen and Beauvais appeared unexpectedly.

Casualties could have been much higher if Edward had not forbidden his men to pursue the enemy. The lateness of the hour and a belief that the enemy could still marshal a large force must have convinced him that prudence was the proper course. In the spirit of the times the casualties among the commoners were not counted; such disregard continued before his advance to Calais, when

Edward instructed that only the bodies of the chief noblemen be picked up and buried in consecrated ground.[35] It is also indicative of the concept of two nations—commoners and aristocrats; chroniclers remembered the behavior of old King John of Bohemia. Blind in both eyes, he asked his men to guide him to the battle, for he wanted to strike a blow with his sword. Obediently his knights tied all their horses together by the bridles and led him against the English. All of them were found dead, their horses still fastened together.[36]

King Philip Valois escaped with his life, although he had two horses killed under him. His standard-bearer met his end in front of the sovereign. Apparently an arrow lightly hit Philip on his face. The French king had been a poor commander (his words were not obeyed), but he did not act the coward. After the battle he must have suffered shock. He gave the impression of seeking death. At one point he had to be restrained. And instead of moving toward Abbeville, where he could regroup, he rode to Amiens, about 45 miles away. From there he asked for a three-day truce to bury the dead; he executed for treason any Genoese crossbowmen that he could lay his hands on; he finally moved to a chateau 35 miles north of Paris. He remained there until October and was joined by his son John,[37] who followed him on the throne before falling prisoner to the Black Prince at the Battle of Poitiers ten years later, in 1356.

About seventy years later the French fell at Agincourt on 25 October 1415; it was a trap similar to their defeat at Crécy. King Henry V, who rose to the throne upon the death of Henry IV in 1413, was a man of iron will, daring, inventive, and certain of his right to the crown of France. Yet the campaign that led to victory is difficult to explain in rational terms (Figure 15.4). The troops under the king's command were too few to pursue any effective long-term policy in France. They were too few to conquer Normandy, too few to bolster the English defense in Aquitaine, and too few to challenge the French on an open field. Initially he must have landed on 14 August 1415 at Chef-de-Caux on the Normandy coast with about 10,000, enough to besiege and take Harfleur, but again not enough to pursue the logical options open to Henry afterward. Moreover, the ranks of the English troops had been ravaged by dysentery, an illness typical of sieges, at Harfleur, and he had been compelled to post 900 men-at-arms and 1,200 archers in the newly conquered city. This meant that at Agincourt (Azincourt in French) he had no more than 1,000 men-at-arms and 6,000 longbowmen at his disposal.

The conquest of Harfleur was an acceptable goal for the moment, and there was no reason to remain in France. The road to Normandy was open,

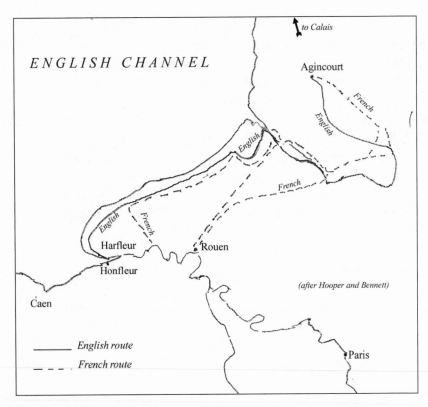

Figure 15.4 The Agincourt Campaign 1415

but 7,000 men with no siege train could not hope to conquer a region stud-
ded with fortresses, likely strengthened by the addition of 800 French men-at-
arms and 400 missile units during the late spring. The route southwest toward
Guyenne and to the east toward Paris were full of dangers and blocked by
French forces. The most logical choice would have been to return to England.
But strangely Henry must have decided to cross Norman lands in a northerly
direction to show how powerful he, the legitimate king of France, was and
how weak was the impostor in Paris. The biggest obstacle northward was the
River Somme. For a while he followed its course southeast until he was able
to cross upstream from Amiens.

The sickly, mad king of France, Charles VI, or his advisers, had not been
inactive. Besides strengthening the fixed positions in Normandy, a large army,
slowly perhaps, under the command of the great aristocrats of the realm had
gathered around the monarch, who had moved to Rouen. The figures given
by contemporaries are wild. Likely it did not count more than 9,000 men-at-

arms and 4,000–5,000 missile units, still larger than the 7,000 English and vastly superior in men-at-arms (nine French against one English). The French decision to pursue a pitched encounter had been arrived at with hesitation. According to one source (Enguerran de Monstrelet), it was only on 20 October that the royal council, gathered at Rouen, decided to seek victory in the field with a vote of thirty in favor and five against. The French army that was tailing the English received the order to bar the road to Calais on Thursday, 24 October 1415, and the engagement took place a day later.

It was here that a chain of errors, idiotic bravery, and the vicissitudes of nature combined in a historic episode. The terrain could not have been better for the English host, as it was in the shape of a funnel or corridor along the cover of woods right and left. It minimized the numerical superiority of the French. The night was spent under a storm that rent the sky with lightning and thunder. In the darkness the event must have terrified the English yet strengthened their resolve. Caught in a cage among people who wanted to destroy them, they had no choice but to fight to the finish. Safety meant breaking the French line through the northeast in the direction of Calais.

When the troops woke up, the terrain was a quagmire, though the sky was clear (Figure 15.5). It was not a problem for men fighting on foot or for dismounted riders. The English deployed about 1,500 meters from the French line. They waited in a defensive stance, but when the French did not advance they moved to within bowshot distance.

Initially the French seemed to have a good plan of attack: open with a duel of missile units and follow up with waves of men-at-arms, some on horseback, some dismounted. In reality, when the battle began the French missile units had disappeared. It is a mystery, but according to some they were behind the first line, which made no sense if true. Likely certain of their victory, the French had no time to line up their missile units ahead of the battle front once they began attacking the English line. After all, had not the French men-at-arms ridden over their own crossbowmen at Crecy? The moment of confrontation came when the English archers, now in close position to the French, started to shower them with arrows. Yet the French deployment was not necessarily reckless. Most of the men-at-arms, the memories of Crecy and Poitiers fresh in their minds, had dismounted. The first line was all of dismounted warriors except for two small squadrons at the flanks; during combat the second line eventually merged with the men who preceded them. The third line, on horseback, as well as the two contingents at the flanks of the first (maybe 1,000 men-at-arms, but in reality far fewer—160 according to a

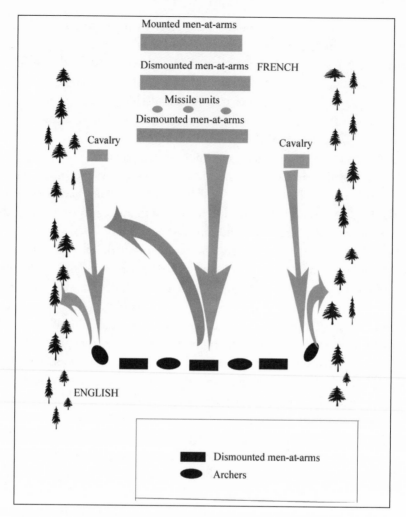

Figure 15.5   The Battle of Agincourt 1415: The Initial French Attack Fails

French source, Jean Le Fevre). The English line was now deployed with dismounted men-at-arms intersecting archers protected by spikes in front.

It is no surprise that 160 horsemen could do little against the archers; nor is it a surprise that the horses may have refused to impale themselves on the sharp stakes.[38] The attack of the dismounted men-at-arms of the first and second line had potential, but burdened by heavy armor and in muddy terrain, their energy must have been sapped; showers of arrows decimated their ranks. And the more they advanced, the closer their ranks to the bows; they became an easier target for the English. But the key to the English success was in the longbowmen. They made the French line of advance a killing field. And as the French attacked the English men-at-arms in a face-to-face confrontation, the English archers left the safety of the stakes and moved in for the kill, assaulting the Frenchmen with swords, daggers, and maces. Men went down at the first hit or were sprawled helplessly in the mud.

With the first and second lines destroyed, with many dead or taken prisoner, the outcome was still in doubt, for the third line had not yet advanced. In the meantime, the English rear line felt threatened, mistaking groups of ravaging peasants in search of loot for enemy soldiers. Henry ordered the slaughter of all French aristocrats who had been taken for ransom. It was a cruel but logical decision in light of the threat to his rear. When the third French line advanced to contact, it was easy to dispose of them. The battle lasted only about four hours. Begun around 10–11 A.M., it ended at 3–4 P.M., before vespers.

"Never since Christ was born has anyone done so much damage to France," wrote a French chronicler. The casualties must have been over 1,500, likely more, among them the flower of the French aristocracy—about 600 members of the nobility. Many were taken prisoner and shipped to England pending ransom. The official English figures counted only twenty-five dead, but 500–600 is more likely, most of them archers deployed on the right wing.

It is hard to pinpoint a single cause for the French defeat. Various elements came into play: the choice of terrain, the mud, the French idiocy of not using their own missile units, the misplaced confidence in their men-at-arms, the superiority of a defensive formula where dismounted men-at-arms stiffened the archers' resolve, the archers' decision to leave their protective screen and attack the enemy on the flanks.

The key was English organization. England undertook changes in structure, composition, and military strategy.[39] The army which had been based on feudal obligations had become a contract host of paid volunteers. At its heart was the indenture system, contracts between the king and captains, normally coming from all the ranks of the nobility, to wage war for a certain period of time, usually six months, at a certain pay. Although not all recruits signed an indenture contract if the king himself led the army, it was understood that most of the soldiers were administered along the same lines. After 1370 indenture became the main method of raising an army, and by Agincourt in 1415, even though the king was the leader, all the soldiers had been contracted by indenture.[40]

The indenture system was an ideal method to exploit the military resources of English society. Recruitment could be tailored to fit the expected duration

of the campaign, the theater, and the financial resources of the crown. Moreover, the army could be subject to periodic review, which assured that its fighting potential was always at a peak; it could be efficiently assembled for campaigns of great breath and duration. Finally, it allowed the aristocracy,
especially those of limited financial resources, to engage in a calling particularly suited to their class without worrying about the financial implications.
In the long run the number of knights declined. Yet war offered social mobility to the lower ranks and financial gains to younger aristocrats.[41] Service
enticed many because it was a way to make a living. Aristocrats, often involved
in endless disputes with neighbors, could receive a letter of protection from
the king, which ensured their interests while they served overseas. For commoners the enticement could be a pardon for some past criminal offense. For
instance, several thousand soldiers at Crécy and Calais in 1346–1347 had been
issued pardons.[42]

Compensation depended on the activity performed on the battlefield. All
would receive a certain pay, scaled from the highest for knights down to the
other soldiers. The man-at-arms would receive a bonus payment, a *regard*,
probably to cover costs of expensive items like plate armor. If his horse was
killed in battle, he was paid an equivalent value. It was a system that did not
always work to the advantage of the cavalryman, for compensation involved
only the main horse, not the rest of the animals in his retinue. Finally, the division of loot (material acquisitions or ransoms) increased the soldiers' compensation, although at least a third of its value had to be given to the sovereign.[43]

Those changes accompanied the formation of mixed retinues of men-at-
arms and mounted archers. The mounted archer was not necessarily from the
lower ranks of society. Closing the gap between the aristocracy and the rest of
the army gave soldiers esprit de corps. For some the process was disreputable.
As Sir Thomas Gray wrote with distaste, "Young fellows who hitherto had
been of but small account . . . became exceedingly rich and skillful in [this]
kind of war . . . many of them beginning as archers and then becoming
knights, some captains."[44]

The "tactical revolution" of the English army, Andrew Ayrton remarks,
involved the emergence of a paid army, the use of the indenture system for
recruitment, the combination of mixed groups of men-at-arms and mounted
archers, and the establishment of an effective method of taxation.[45] In the fifteenth century the proportion of expeditionary corps of English soldiers on
the continent normally involved an even higher ratio of mounted archers to
men-at-arms, at times with an extraordinarily high rate of 19:1 in 1429 and 12:1

the year after, but on the whole the most common rate remained 3:1.[46] Yet by the second quarter of the century, after the relief of Orléans by Joan of Arc, the French finally were able to solve the problem of facing and defeating the English armies on the continent.

French Armies: From Disaster to Triumph

For most of the conflict the English remained superior to the French. They showed that their hit-and-run strategy, the *chevauchée*, was effective and that their strength was unmatched in pitched encounters. They constantly placed the French on the defensive and brought the whole of France under assault. At times the Valois seemed powerless vis-à-vis the ambition of the English royal house and the treachery and greed of their own great lords. Their country, Philippe Contamine says, was like a heavily contested frontier.[47]

French manpower remained overwhelming in numbers. This was the case at Crécy and at Poitiers, and it remained so throughout the war. At Agincourt they dwarfed the English host. Yet the image of large French armies and smaller English armies should be revised. At the siege of Calais in 1347 the English summoned 60,000 men, 32,000 of which were soldiers, the rest support troops. The truth is that despite a population one-fourth that of the French, Edward III was able to marshal forces at the beginning of the conflict in a much more effective way than Philip Valois.[48]

The core of the French army remained the men-at-arms, who did not always fight on horseback. This was the case with the majority of horsemen at Poitiers and at Agincourt. Infantry of all types was numerous among the French in the early days of the war. In 1339 the army deployed between 12,000 and 14,000 men-at-arms and 30,000 footmen, a proportion of about 2.5 infantry to one horsemen. The same year, the projected invasion of England, which did not take place, listed about 4,000 men-at-arms with 15,000 foot sergeants and 5,000 crossbowmen, a proportion roughly of one horseman to almost four generic infantry and about 1.25 missile units.[49] By the 1350s, however, except for the crossbowmen, who remained in the hundreds and sometimes in the thousands, the rest of the army was made up of men-at-arms. The dramatic decline in the infantry must have been in part the result of the Black Death, which wiped out at least one-third of the French population, in part Valois's inability to muster enough resources, and in part the realization that large hosts with mediocre infantry contingents were not effective.[50] This meant that the French army was defined by horsemen and crossbowmen, although at times, especially after 1350, they experimented with lighter horsemen. The host was mobile, for the Italian crossbowmen from Genoa came to the battlefield on horseback. When hostilities began, the Genoese dismounted.

The French used different manners of recruitment. In the beginning they relied on the feudal obligations of people from eighteen to sixty; the *arrière-ban* was called seven times between 1338 and 1356. At times the age was lowered to fifteen, as when John the Good called to arms his subjects after Edward III landed at Calais,[51] although in this case the lower age probably referred to squires, not men-at-arms. Recruitment began with a royal proclamation or individual orders to feudatories, demanding one to be at a certain place at a certain date. Attention was given to assembling supplies and the requisition of wheat, oats, bacon, calves, steers, sheep, wine, vinegar, and *verjus*, an acidic concoction made by pressing unripe grapes and used as seasoning. Everything had to arrive by the fixed date. Merchants were given special safe-conducts and sometimes armed escorts to support the soldiers with their goods. Once troops arrived, marshals and their lieutenants would inspect them and their equipment, estimate the value of their horses (the state would reimburse the value of one mount per owner), and disbursed an advance, representing between fifteen days to a month of wages. Finally, the combatants were allocated to one of the various battles.[52]

The *arrière-ban* was ineffective. It took too long to assemble the troops; it suffered from endless delays and exemptions; and command, once on the battlefield, was fragmented among the various lords. One of the problems was the small size of most contingents, sometimes as small as two to nineteen men-at-arms. Moreover, the men were thrown together with people from different areas, often under the command of unfamiliar individuals, a situation not ideal to developing esprit de corps. Also, there was no consistency in the size of the battles "which could range from a few hundreds to thousands." In 1340, for instance, the royal host included twelve battles, led by the king, the duke of Normandy, the count of Flanders, the duke of Burgundy, the count of Armagnac, the constable, and the marshals of France. But if we take into consideration that the normal battlefield deployment included three battle groups in the first line with one in reserve, this may have meant that eight battles remained idle, unless they combined with the battles in the first line.[53] In other words, there were not enough men on the edge of the fight and too many somewhere else.

The French armies during the reign of Charles V were different in structure and strategic and tactical aims. The military reforms had begun under the reign of Charles's father, John the Good. In 1350 the king instructed his feudatories to organize not the small contingents of the past but larger ones (twenty-five to eighty men-at-arms). In 1355 he repeated those instructions with financial rewards commensurate to the size of the contingents.[54] But the turning point came in 1364 with the ascension of Charles V to the throne. He initiated extensive fortifications, constructing or reconstructing castles and urban walls, demolishing decaying or unsuitable walls, and requiring local populations to serve as guards and lookouts in their neighborhood strongholds. As Contamine claims, castle-building, in decay during the previous period, saw a revival.[55]

Strong defensive obstacles were essential in Charles's new approach to war: avoid pitched battles; abandon the countryside to the ravages of the English *chevauchées*; find safety behind fortifications; hit back by harassing the enemy; launch mobile, quick strikes into enemy lands. The only ones to suffer were peasants on both sides, but the king's aims were clear: "Let the English advance into our lands: they will bring ruin to themselves in pursuit of their goals; and all this without us meeting them in battle."[56]

Charles V also tried to establish a permanent army. The backbone was the men-at-arms and crossbowmen, the latter from the usual recruiting grounds in Italy, Gascony, and Spain. To those we must add a small number of foot or horse troops raised in the urban communities, including a few archers, sergeants, and *pavisiers*. Charles also paid attention to the artillery, which played an important role in the siege of Saint-Sauveur-le-Vicomte in 1375.[57]

Although he did not use the *arrière-ban*, the king did issue general summonses of men-at-arms and crossbowmen in times of military duress, in 1369, 1373, 1375, 1378, and 1380, on the basis of his authority as the feudal overlord, recruiting not just in towns, but also in the countryside. His host became an army of volunteers, paid from the central finances of the kingdom, if they were horsemen, or by the localities of origin, if they were footmen. But the king managed from the center. It was a new and more efficient way to conduct war.

His troops were recruited on the basis of *lettres de revenue*, that is, they were hired for a specific period of time and regularly paid. It was a system similar to the English indenture.[58] Moreover, little mention is made of the awkward division of the battles. The *routes* were usually associated with the feared and despised soldiers ravaging the land in times of peace. There was also a tendency to standardize the strength of the *routes* with about 100 men-at-arms, which meant that they were large enough to play an important role if deployed in conjunction with other *routes*. Finally, several soldiers were kept permanently in service and stationed at strongholds throughout the kingdom.[59] As Christine de Pisan wrote, heavy horsemen, which suffered reverses in the past, were revived and became a strong element.[60]

Charles V's reign, as Contamine portrays in his analysis of a contemporary poem, showed the organization of war at its best. Armed conflict was a constant. April heralded spring and the beginning of war; personal ties were crucial in the life of a soldier; regular pay and fair distribution of loot were mandatory to keep discipline; the army also needed the support of specialists like artillerymen, engineers, miners; and finally the royal war council was essential to managing the conduct of the conflict and provided clear goals.[61]

It was an ideal situation that did not last long after Charles V's demise in 1380. In a sense, the reforms may have been too radical for his successor, Charles VI, a decent man when sane. But he was plagued by bouts of mental illness, and political power devolved to factions, the Armagnacs and the Burgundians. The road to the destruction of the Armagnacs at Agincourt in 1415 was paved with bad decisions, lack of strategic clarity, and selfishness. The weakness of the central authority is shown by the renewal of the *arrière-ban*, which had been abandoned under Charles V. Yet the sudden disappearance of the practically invincible Henry V in 1422 and the ineffective rule of Henry's successors allowed some respite. But by 1429 even the last French defensive line, the land south of the Loire, seemed on the verge of collapse. The turning points were the inspirational drive of Joan of Arc in 1429 and peace with the duke of Burgundy in 1435.

The forces involved in the siege of Orléans also reflect how the French army was becoming more effective. Crucial was the 1422 elevation of a new king, Charles VII (1403–1461). In the period 1410–1420 the French army counted two men-at-arms for every crossbowman, whereas the English had three archers for every horseman.[62] At Orléans the two largest groups of soldiers were the men-at-arms and the crossbowmen.[63] The men-at-arms were protected with plates of steel and armed with lance, sword, dagger, mace or hatchet, several horses, and two servants, the "valet," who would enter the fray if required, and a youth, the page. The equipment of the man-at-arms could be an expensive burden, although by the middle of the fifteenth century expenses were taken up by the crown. The crossbowmen and archers were less protected. Other soldiers included sergeants, armed foot soldiers, artillerymen, miners, and surgeons.[64]

The Orléans army was organized more properly than the army of Agincourt. Yet it was not yet the impressive war machine of the last years of the Hundred Years War. That army would rise from the later 1430s to the end of the 1440s with the major changes implemented between 1445 and 1448.[65] The Orléans army was essentially still an army of *routiers,* with all its problems of ill discipline and disloyalty. Moreover, the presence of non-French elements, especially Spaniards and Italians, was a main characteristic. In this sense there was a gap between the soldiers and the civilian population that became more serious when the contract signed in the *lettres de revenue* ended. What the French needed was a host with ties to the land they defended at the disposal of the crown when needed. In 1445 Charles VII, under the advice of his councilors, established a permanent army of 6,000 soldiers and 3,000 support troops. Each company was under the command of a captain and included about 600 men: 100 men-at-arms, 200 mounted archers, 100 *coutilliers* (foot infantry whose main weapon was a long and deadly knife), 100 valets, and 100 pages. The basic administrative unit was the lance of a man-at-arms and his retinue of five troops. In battle, however, all men-at-arms were grouped together as units; the same applied to the other soldiers of each lance.[66] The lances were usually located in the interior, called together during an offensive campaign. They were the backbone of the French armies during the conquest of Normandy and at the Battle of Castillon.

The establishment of the permanent army reflected the ethnic nature of the kingdom. In 1448 measures were implemented in the countryside and among the feudatories compelled to serve the king. In the countryside Charles tried to create a counterpart to the English archers who had tormented the French host. He required each parish (and later each fifty to eighty households) to support a missile man, the *franc-archer,* who would train with a bow or crossbow during days of rest. The *franc-archers,* who received a pay of seven *tournois* a month, may have numbered as many as 8,000 at the siege of Caen and at Castillon. On the whole, however, the experiment was not fruitful in the long run. Feudatories were unreliable because they were unable to support the cost of war at times. A census of their holdings was taken and then, when called to serve the king, they were to be provided with wages equivalent to those who served in the companies of ordinance, that is, fifteen *tournois* a month.[67]

Taking into account the artillery, the French army of the 1440s was a powerful war machine that included men who received regular pay and were directly responsible to the king. It is no surprise that they would win the war. But England's internal conflict and disenchantment with the war would not explain everything. The French had to contend with armies better equipped and better led than their own. After Henry V, power fell into the hand of an infant and his relatives. And the English were never able to muster enough manpower in places they had conquered, like Normandy. But Charles VII led a skillful administration of his kingdom, a newly recovered spirit among the nobility, a great effort to develop artillery and a longbow tradition, and an army of professionals paid by from the royal coffers and controlled by the sovereign.

The end of the Hundred Years War coincided with the "cultural waning" of the Middle Ages. War was far different from that of the early fourteenth century. New features included the use of mercenaries and artillery. But the weapon of the future would not be the longbow or field artillery but the pike. Like the longbow, the role of women on the battlefield, heralded by Joan of Arc, would find no place in a world dominated by men.

Chapter Sixteen

The Maid of Orléans and Women at War

As the call for the Third Crusade (1187–1197) came to various corners of the West, "a great many men sent each other wool and distaff, hinting that if anyone failed to join this military undertaking, they were fit for women's work." Mothers and wives urged their husbands to go, "their only sorrow being that they were not able to set out with them, because of the fragility of their sex."[1] The same year a few hundred Templars were killed by thousands of Muslims in a clash in the Holy Land. It was reported that a Muslim warrior who had witnessed the great acts of bravery of a Templar "cut off the man's genitals, and kept them safely for begetting children so that even when dead the man's members—if such a thing were possible— would produce an heir with courage as great as his."[2]

The two anecdotes are a stunning contrast of the way women and men were considered in regard to warfare: war was for men. Women rarely engaged in face-to-face combat during the medieval period. Yet this did not mean that they were absent or that they were not influential.

What Contemporaries Thought About Women Warriors

According to Megan McLaughlin, women in warfare elicited little comment until the end of the eleventh century. This is the case of Richilde of Hainault, captured during the Battle of Cassel in 1071. An important change took place afterward. The woman who practiced war abandoned her feminine characteristics: she had "unsexed" herself.[3] That view was never dropped during the Middle Ages.

In all cases the appearance of women was rare among western chroniclers. More often they are found in Muslim accounts of the Crusades, but the veracity of such stories is suspect. Mentioning women was a way to show how spiteful the Christian warriors were. Regardless, it is clear that women played a role in emergency situations, as when the husband was dead or absent. Sometimes they assumed a leading role regardless, as with Mathilda of Tuscany and Eleanor of Aquitaine in France and during the Second Crusade in the Holy Land. In 1081 the Longobard Princess Sichelgaita, dressed in handsome armor, took part in the siege of Durazzo, rallied her husband's men, and chased their enemies, spear in her hand.[4] In the twelfth century Helvise, Countess of Evreux, rode to war with armed men and was a source of inspiration for her courage and behavior. Toward late fourteenth century Thomas III, Marquis of Saluzzo, wrote how his grandmother, Richarda Visconti, carried out the most ferocious acts of war while her husband languished in prison. It was said that the sister of Bertrand du Guesclin, Julienne, was so carried by the desire of defending a castle under siege that she pushed away the ladders of the assailants from the walls in spite of the fact that she was a nun. Froissart mentioned Countess Jeanne de Monfort taking part in the Breton clashes of the Hundred Years War, mounted on a fine horse, sword in her hand, dashing bravely into the fray.[5]

It is no surprise that a noblewoman would participate in combat in certain situations. Her environment conditioned her, for it is not unlikely that she received training in riding a horse to battle and holding a spear or sword. As Christine de Pisan, born in Venice but eventually married and widowed in France, writes, the wife of a great nobleman "ought to have the heart of a man, that is, she ought to know how to use weapons and be familiar with everything that pertains to them, so that she may be ready to command her men if the need arises. She should know how to launch an attack or to defend against one, if the situation calls for it. She should take care that her fortresses are well garrisoned."[6]

Although aristocratic women participated in the Crusades, commoners seemed to have played an ancillary role.[7] As such they performed humble but necessary tasks such as removing lice from soldiers' heads or washing clothes. Actually the washwomen were the only women that the Roman Church allowed during the First Crusade, and only as long as they were physically unattractive for fear that the troops would have sexual relations with them. The ecclesiastical prohibition was hardly obeyed, for all types of women took part in the crusades. Every time an army marched, several females would join the troops as sutler or servant, but the most numerous were prostitutes. Unmentioned in victory, they took the blame for defeat, for they embodied sin among soldiers who had left their homelands to fight a holy cause.[8]

The emotional support provided by women workers and prostitutes translated into battlefield support. In an 1382 campaign a Flemish woman carrying the flag fell at the end of a conflict won by the army of Charles VI. In 1396 we find a Frisian woman, dressed in blue and fighting in a frenzy, in an encounter between Frisia and Hainault.[9] In 1428, during the early stages of the siege of Orléans, "the women . . . were of great support, for they ceased not to carry very diligently to them [the French soldiers] that defended the rampart [south of the bridge over the Loire], several things necessary, as water, boiling oil and fat, lime, ashes and caltrops."[10] Another commoner named Jeanne Hachette behaved splendidly at Beauvais in 1472.[11] Such examples were fairly common in the Holy Land. At the Battle of Dorylaeum in 1097 women ran through the battlefield, providing water to the soldiers, an enormously important task in the scorching heat. At the sieges of Antioch and Jerusalem in 1123 they brought stones and water to the troops. They were also employed in filling the moat with fascines and earth, sometimes dying in the enterprise, as one woman did during the siege of Acre. Her body pierced by an arrow, she begged in her dying moments that her body be thrown into the ditch to finish the work she had begun.[12] That was not the only reported female casualty. We find women killed at Dorylaeum (1097) and at the siege of Antioch (1101), in the 1001 campaigns against the Turks, in defending a crusader fortress (1126), at the battles before the founding of the First Latin Kingdom (1186–1187) and before the founding of the Second (1189), and at the siege of Acre (1190).[13] Yet there is only one major example of a woman engaged in war, for women, like Jews and clergymen, were excluded from face-to-face combat.[14] That woman was Joan of Arc.

Joan revived French fortunes in the Hundred Years War and played a leading role in several strategic decisions. She exhibited unwavering strength despite the doubts and uncertain minds of the other leaders. Moreover, she became a powerful myth in French history. It began early, wavered during the Wars of Religion, and again became dominant from the end of the eighteenth century through the writings of Voltaire and then Michelet. She became a saint in 1920 after her canonization in 1909.

Not the Distaff but the Sword

Like most women of the period, Joan learned "to sew linen cloth and to spin."[15] She was born on 6 January 1412 in the village of Domrémy in the Duchy of Bar, between Champagne and Lorraine. Her parents, Jacques D'Arc and Isabelle Romée, were wealthy peasants. A woman who had known Joan since childhood said "Joan was a good, simple and sweet-natured girl" who "went often and of her own will to church. . . . I have heard the priest who was there in her time say that she came often to confession. Joan [also] busied herself like any other girl; she did the housework and span and sometimes—I have seen her—she kept her father's flocks."[16] It was an assessment repeated many times during Joan's rehabilitation trial. "She was very devout towards God and the Blessed Virgin, so much so that I myself who was young then, and other many young men, teased her," confessed a man at the trial.[17] This did not mean that she shied from revelries. She had danced and sang at the Ladies' Tree, a customary meeting place of young boys and girls during Springs Sunday.[18] Her young life, however, must have had an atmosphere of foreboding. A disturbing dream had afflicted her father when she was young. In his dream he had seen her run away from home with men-at arms. He had not forgotten that dream and often told her brothers, "Truly, if I knew that that must happen which I fear in the matter of my daughter, I had rather you drowned her. And if you did not do it, I would drown her myself."[19] Yet Joan had decided at age thirteen or thereabouts, after hearing the first voices, that she would keep her "virginity as long as it pleases God."[20]

She was in the garden around noon when, as she revealed at her trial, she heard a voice that made her very afraid initially but that later she believed to come from God initially and then from an angel. The voice promised that it would help and guide her. From then on almost every time that she heard the voice it was accompanied by a great light. The voice instructed her that for her soul's salvation she had to be good and had to go to church often. The voice also encouraged her to go to the Dauphin at a time when the king of England claimed to be the legitimate holder of the French crown. But Joan, being a maid and knowing nothing of riding or fighting, must have hesitated and went instead to one of her uncles. She remained in his house for eight days until she begged her uncle to guide her to Vaucouleurs. She went to Robert de Baudricourt, captain in the town of Vaucouleurs, and explained the mission.[21]

"Sir captain," she said to Baudricourt when she was finally in his presence, "it has been a while that God has instructed me to go the Dauphin who is and should be the true king of France. He will give me a body of troops with whom I shall defeat the English who are besieging Orléans. I shall make sure to take him to Reims, where he will be crowned king."[22] But Baudricourt had no time for her, twice refusing her request; but on the third try she convinced him to send her to the Dauphin, dressed as a man-at-arms with a sword and in the company of two noblemen and a valet.²³ The voyage of the small group was replete with danger, for they had to cross territories in English hands; in the end they safely reached the Dauphin at Chinon.

It was not very difficult to convince the Dauphin. The French situation at Orléans was desperate, and seemingly the Dauphin was impressed when Joan for the first time in his presence addressed him directly in spite of his ordinary attire: "the counsel of his voice," she would say later at the Rouen trial, had told her that he was the man she was looking for. Another factor in convincing Charles may have been Joan's revelation of a royal sign, about which we know nothing in detail. Yet Joan had to go through another ordeal before the court accepted her vision's veracity. She was interrogated on her beliefs and examined to make sure that she was a virgin, that is, "a true and entire maid in whom appeared no corruption or violence." The examination of the "secret parts of her body" was carried out by two noblewomen of the suite of the queen of Sicily, Yolande of Aragon, the Dauphin's mother-in-law.²⁴ Later Joan revealed that she would last only a year and that she had been entrusted with four missions: "to expel the English; to have the King crowned and anointed in Reims; to free the Duke of Orléans from English hands [the duke had been captured and taken to England]; and to raise the siege which the English had laid to Orléans town."²⁵

In mid-1428 the English had a choice: strike toward Anjou and then Touraine and Poitou, or conquer Orléans and from there move toward Berry, breaking the Loire line of the kingdom that they disparagingly called "the kingdom of Bourges." Both targets were important, but attacking Anjou meant further antagonizing the mother-in-law of Charles VII, whom they hoped to turn to their cause.²⁶ On 12 October 1428 a large army moved toward the city under the command of the count of Salisbury, a man with a good military reputation. However, he probably made a mistake in besieging the city; as the events unfolded, neither he nor his successor at the head of the English troops had enough men to establish a tight blockade.

Orléans, which had a civilian population of about 24,000 with a garrison of 2,400 soldiers,²⁷ extended over about 37 hectares of terrain encircled by fortifications about 2,590 meters long (Figure 16.1). The five gates were protected by towers at each side. The rest of the walls had a total of 28 more towers and a small castle, the Chatelet. The south side of the city rested on the right bank of the Loire River, and the bridge connecting the city to the left bank was protected by a strong fortification, Les Tourelles, which in turn was shielded by the rampart of Les Augustins. The French garrison could rely on strong artillery, with guns placed atop most towers.²⁸

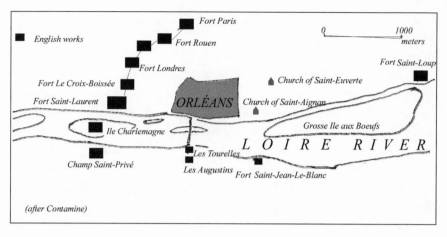

Figure 16.1   Siege of Orléans 1429

Facing an obstinate defense, Salisbury decided to isolate it, prevent the arrival of external support, and reduce the city by force or negotiation. But the first task was to disrupt the link tying the city to southern France. Less than two weeks after his arrival, Salisbury's men captured Les Augustins and then Les Tourelles, cutting supply from the south. The victory was bittersweet for the English. While Salisbury stood on the tower of Les Tourelles a cannonball from the city struck a window, displacing an iron bar that cut his face in half. He lasted eight more days, eventually being replaced by John Talbot. That Salisbury was hit is an example of the accuracy of the French artillery, for he had been injured from a distance of about 500 meters.[29] In another case an artillery shot hit an English boat on the river from a distance of almost 1,400 meters,[30] although in this case the height of the city walls and a smaller caliber must have determined the long distance covered by the shot. Especially successful was a *culverineer*, a native of Lorraine, who killed, the *Journal of the Siege of Orléans* claims, many Englishmen. Adding insult to injury he pretended to have been hurt by an English shot, leaving the walls on a stretcher only to come back soon perfectly healthy in charge of his culverin (an artillery piece longer than a cannon but of the same caliber).[31]

The siege continued, broken by sudden attacks, sorties, and the building of fortifications by the English, who were trying to establish a tight blockade and prevent any contact with the exterior. The besiegers reinforced the original French rampart, Les Augustins, now in their own hands, at the head of the bridge over the Loire. They also built forts on the west of Les Augustins, the

Champ-Saint-Privé, and on the east the Saint-Jean-le-Blanc. The perimeter of English defenses on the left bank covered about 2 kilometers. They also tried to surround the city on the right bank by erecting six ramparts east and north, the Saint-Laurent, the Croix-Boissé, London, the Colombier, Rouen, and Paris at about 600 meters from the city of walls and thus generally safe from large artillery shots. They also protected river access by building a fort on the Ile Charlemagne west of the bridge. The besiegers' fortifications on the left had only a fort, the Saint-Loup, about 2 kilometers from the city. This meant that the Burgundy Gate, which stood on the eastern side of the city, remained the best road of access to the besieged, especially after the troops of the duke of Burgundy abandoned the siege following a disagreement with the English. Yet the English fortifications west and north of the city remained easy to break through. They were too far from each other and vulnerable to French infiltration after the project of tying each fort with a ditch was abandoned.[32]

At least initially, the more successful policy was instead to starve the defenders. They destroyed the twelve mills that the city used near the Loire. Yet even then the defenders found a solution, building eleven mills within the ring of fortifications using horse power instead of water. Regardless of the English forts, food supplies always seemed to pierce the defensive curtain. On 3 January 1429, 400 sheep and 154 swine entered the city.[33]

After hesitating a while Charles VII decided to help his city by ordering an army assembly at Blois. A contingent under Charles of Bourbon left that city for Orléans on 11 February 1429. When news of their approach reached the troops stationed in the city, it was decided to send a contingent to meet them and to intercept an English convoy of herrings that had been sent to Talbot. The French plan ended in disaster because of the defensive posture assumed by the English and dissensions among the French troops. Bourbon decided to fight dismounted, thus assuming a defensive posture, while the constable of Scotland decided to strike the English, who had withdrawn behind a park constituted by their carriages. It ended in defeat for the French, routed and pursued, although the English suffered losses when mounted units struck back when they left their defensive positions.[34]

The new failure seemed to have disheartened the French even more. They initiated negotiations for a truce or peace, leaving the issue of control until the legitimate king was clarified. Talbot refused: he who "beats the bushes leaves to others to capture the birds."[35] However, Talbot's refusal must have enraged the duke of Burgundy, who was at the side of the English. He ordered his men to leave the siege, leaving the eastern side open. It was from there, by exploit-

ing the waters of the Loire, that French reinforcements started to arrive beginning on 24 April. Five days later Joan of Arc, riding a white horse, entered the
city through the Burgundy Gate. She carried her white standard, the figure of
"Our Lord holding a fleur-de-lis in His hand."[36] The crowd pressed around,
trying to touch her or her horse; the idea that a maid would save Orléans from
the English had spread quickly throughout the land.[37]

It was news that did not please the English. The men who had come with
Joan were nothing but "miscreant pimps," Joan nothing else than "the Armagnacs' whore," words that deeply hurt Joan, making her cry.[38] She was eager to
break the siege, especially after the Bastard of Orléans, who had been sent
away for help, arrived with reinforcements on 4 May; but the Bastard was
reluctant to pass to the offensive, especially after he knew that the fearsome
John Falstaff was joining Talbot's troops. But none could squash Joan's desire
to fulfill her mission. Rather angrily she directed these words to the "Bastard,
Bastard, Bastard, in God's name I command you that, as soon as you know
that Falstaff is come, you shall make it known to me, for if he passes without
me knowing of it, I promise you that I shall have your head taken off."[39] But
even after this outburst Joan could not rest quietly. She went to bed on a mat-
tress, but as her faithful companion, Jean d'Aulon, recounted at the retrial, he
was just beginning to doze off (he slept in the same room as Joan) when the
Maid suddenly sprang from her bed with great noise. When he inquired what
was the matter, she replied, "My voices told me that I must attack the English." While he was arming the Maid, excited noises and cries came from outside. The English were causing great harm to the French, they heard. The
Maid left the room immediately before d'Aulon could follow her, found a
page in the street, ordered him to give her his horse, and quickly galloped
toward the Burgundy Gate, where most of the noise came from, outdistanc-
ing d'Aulon, who finally had also come to the street. In spite of the shock of
meeting a severely wounded Frenchman and of the Maid's assertion that she
never saw French blood without her hair standing on end, the Maid passed
the gate and reached the fracas. Her arrival gave courage to her kind, and soon
they were pushing away the assailants and conquered the fort of Saint Loup.[40]

The capture of Saint Loup opened a new phase in the siege of the city.
Now, stubbornly led by Joan of Arc, the French moved on 6 May to displace
the English from the southern end of the bridge on the Loire's left bank. The
first to fall was Les Augustins, which protected the approach to Les Tourelles
and thus the bridge. Joan inspired the men remaining on the battlefield from
morning until the evening. At the end Joan, who usually fasted on Friday, was

so exhausted that before falling asleep she dined in her customary way, dipping bread into wine. But her mind was set on breaking the siege even after a knight suggested that they be happy with what they had achieved so far and wait for the reinforcements that Charles would now certainly send.

On 7 May Joan woke up early in the morning, summoned all the captains, and decided with the agreement of the other leaders to continue the attack on the southern end of the bridge and to conquer the fortification of Les Tourelles. That day the clash began in the morning and lasted until the end of the day. It seemed that the French attack was going to fail, and the Bastard of Orléans decided to withdraw his troops. Joan begged him to wait, and after withdrawing for a short time in prayer, she returned and led a final strike that ended with the capture of Les Tourelles. Joan's behavior was especially remarkable because during the assault an arrow had struck her body above the breast; she had shed a few tears and continued her leadership, sword in hand.

After their failure to hold Les Tourelles the English broke the siege, withdrawing toward places that they held near the Loire, but the French pursued and took Jargeau, Meung, and Beaugency. At Jargeau Joan showed her ability to withstand danger. While on a ladder to gain entry into the city, the defenders threw a stone on her helmet, making her fall to the ground. She picked herself up immediately, crying to the soldiers, "Up, friends, up! Our Lord has doomed the English. At this very hour they are ours. Be of good cheer!" It was the encouragement that the French needed to displace the adversaries from the town.⁴¹ But the greatest French success, after the relief of Orléans, was their victory at the Battle of Patay on 17 June 1429, where they captured John Talbot and compelled Falstaff to withdraw to the safety of Paris with a depleted army.

Now that the immediate threat on the Loire had been defeated, Joan intended to fulfill another duty. Insistently and stubbornly she finally succeeded in convincing the king to go to Reims, the traditional place of consecration for French kings. In spite of crossing territory under the control of the duke of Burgundy, Charles, accompanied by Joan and a fairly large army, arrived safely at Reims, where his coronation took place on 17 July 1429.

The rest of Joan's story is less exciting from a military viewpoint. At St. Denis, a suburb of Paris, she experienced her first defeat while attempting to capture the French capital. A crossbow bolt also wounded her leg. As the new year came Joan campaigned in the area north of Paris, again with limited success. Finally, on 23 May 1430 the Burgundians captured her in a sortie out of the besieged city of Compiègne. They released Joan to the English for a sum of money. Practically abandoned by Charles VII, she was taken to Rouen in front of a tribunal chaired by Frenchmen but controlled by the English. Joan was convicted of heresy and condemned to "perpetual imprisonment." But when she began to wear male clothes again, she was considered to have abjured her recantation and was burned at the stake in the Vieux Marché of Rouen on 30 May 1431.

The Court of Inquisition that condemned her at Rouen found Joan to be "a witch, a soothsayer, a false prophetess . . . impudently and totally forgetful of decency and what is seemly for her sex." But the trial was carried out in an atmosphere of unfairness and hatred. Persons who tried to keep the interrogation proper were silenced, dismissed, or not called to testify. Clearly the Maid's destiny had been marked before her trial for a variety of reasons—the hatred of her adversaries, the resentment that she was a woman who had stood against men, and the astonishment in people's mind that a woman could behave like a man in her attire and in her role on the battlefield.

Joan was a simple and uneducated woman. Jean II, duke of Alençon, said,

> In the conduct of war she was most skillful, both in carrying a lance herself, in drawing up the army in battle order, and in placing the artillery. And everyone was astonished that she acted with such prudence and clear sightedness in military matters, as cleverly as some great captains with twenty or thirty years of experience; and especially in the placing of artillery, for in that she acquitted herself magnificently.[42]

There was no doubt that the young woman was a courageous individual. She stood in the front lines, never seemed to hesitate in her mission, and had the courage to stand against males who were older and of higher social class. She revealed unusual poise and courage under fire and was an inspiration. As Christine de Pisan wrote, "In the year fourteen hundred and twenty-nine" the sun came out again for the French and "good times anew came with its shine." Joan, maintained the contemporary poet Alain Chartier, "raised [all] spirits towards the hope of better times."[43] Yet in spite of Joan's great story she remained an exception in the role of women on the battlefield. A much more crucial development of the Hundred Years War was the emergence of larger and larger groups of mercenaries.

Chapter Seventeen ~

"Waging War Gives Me Bread . . . Peace Destroys Me"

THE CASTLE OF MONTECCHIO STOOD about a mile from the Umbrian city of Cortona in central Italy. Two monks had just crossed the gate when they met the great John Hawkwood, the English mercenary captain, who for about sixty years ravaged the lands of Italy with his company of adventurers. The soldier stood straight as a pole, staring with amusement at the two clergymen.

"God, may grant you peace, sire!" wished the monks. "And God may deprive you of your alms!" retorted the captain to the astonished and now fearful Franciscans.

"Why do you address us this way?" complained the monks.

"Do you think that your wish of granting me peace makes me happy? It is like wishing that I die of hunger! Do you not know that waging war gives me bread and that peace destroys me? You make a living by begging, I by war."[1]

Franco Sacchetti, the son of an Italian born in Dalmatia in 1332, reported this event in a short story in *Trecentonovelle*, written after 1392. He had personal experience in the affairs of state. After settling in Florence in 1363 he had served as ambassador of the Florentine Republic to Bologna and covered the office of *podestà* (nonnative chief magistrate) in various Tuscan towns. He knew well his times and the way of the mercenary warlords, the condottieri, for whom the most desirable way of life was continuous war. Many shared Sacchetti's pessimistic view in Italy and elsewhere, but his view did not always reflect reality. Mercenaries could also be trustworthy and essential because ordinary citizens refused to serve or were incapable of standing firm on the battlefield. Sacchetti is correct, however, when he assumes that the fifteenth century saw an ever-increasing number of mercenaries whose interest was in the never-ending presence of war.

The World of Mercenaries

Two of the major characteristics of the Hundred Years War was the standardization of military service on the basis of monetary payment and the increased reliance on mercenaries. Mercenaries were different from ordinary soldiers. They did not fight for their own land. They fought for another master, often brought along their women and children, and even household items, and were specialists that performed some of the less common and more difficult functions needed in an army. Money defined their status. Yet that aspect did not set them apart from other soldiers, for eventually practically all would receive compensation for service. What made them different was that they fought for a lord or a king who was not their own. This did not mean that all mercenaries in France and Italy were ethnically different from the rest of the population. Italy was divided into so many states that a soldier from Lucca, for instance, only a few kilometers from Florence, might have been considered a mercenary if he fought for Florence or any other city-state. The same applied to Bretons, whose land today is part of the French domain.

Sacchetti (and later Niccolò Machiavelli in a much more powerful vein) harshly criticized the mercenaries' conduct, yet hired practitioners of war became the most dominant element of the conflicts in Europe. The process, begun much earlier, followed two main characteristics: fighting alongside the regular soldiers of a state; and fighting as a substitute for citizens who for one reason or another devoted themselves to tasks different than those on the battlefield. In the tenth century a Venetian recruited mercenaries in Lombardy and Tuscia. In 992 Count Fulk of Anjou sent a combined army of mercenaries and his own subjects to support the cause of Conan of Brittany. Even a Pope recruited mercenaries in Germany to fight against the Normans of southern Italy during the time of Henry III.[2] Frederick Barbarossa resorted to their service in 1166 and 1174 in his Italian campaigns, after receiving limited support from his feudatories.[3] Although the Lateran Council forbade their use in 1179, the decree fell on deaf ears. Men fighting for money for a state not their own are found all over western Europe by different names—*aragonenses, navarii, bascoli* in the Iberian Peninsula, *ribaldi, masnadieri, fuorusciti* in Italy, *milites stipendiarios* in England, *routiers* in France, and Brabancons all over the continent, whether they came from Brabant or not.[4] In at least one case their actions, begun as temporary support of local forces, were so successful that they established a state of their own. This was the case of the Normans in Italy, who founded a southern kingdom by displacing the Muslims in Sicily.

The impression that they came from the disadvantaged classes is inaccurate. True, many originated from the poorest parts of Europe—Scotland, Switzerland, Romagna. But leaders and sometimes the rank and file came from the lower nobility. Bertrand du Guesclin originally was a *routier*, that is, a French mercenary. Although several mercenaries fought on horseback at the beginning, the most common type was the footman fighting with a staff weapon (the bill and later the pike) or with the crossbow, which Italians from Liguria and Spaniards from across the Pyrenees treasured. The most famous of all mercenaries were the followers of the condottieri (mercenary warlords) in Italy. Mainly on horseback, they dominated warfare on the peninsula and refined the style of warfare that had been prevalent during most of the Middle Ages. At the same time they pointed the way to the future.

The Condottieri: The Case of the Honeyed Cat

At Padua, near the church of a great medieval holy man, St. Anthony, stands a striking equestrian monument whose visual power is not diminished by the daily indignity of swarms of pigeons. The monument is the work of Donatello, the early Renaissance artist who indicated the road to the future in sculpture, as would Brunelleschi in architecture and Masaccio in painting. The work is particularly important as it represents a revival of the tradition of the great Roman equestrian monuments, of which Marcus Aurelius is a stunning example (Figure 17.1).

The subject of the Padua monument is Erasmo da Narni, nicknamed Gattamelata (Honeyed Cat), a famous leader of mercenaries.[5] Born in 1370 at Narni, an Umbrian town in central Italy, Gattamelata disappeared in 1443, well-respected by the subjects of the Republic of Venice, which he had served with great honor. By then he was a shadow of his better days, for in 1439 he had suffered a stroke, a month after his capture of Verona in 1439. Physically he had always cut a dashing figure. He was a tall man, over 2 meters tall, quite different from other mercenaries whose names suggest smaller stature like Micheletto Attendolo or Piccinino. Light brown hair and brown eyes highlighted his light complexion. In spite of his consuming involvement in war, he had tried to lead a normal life, fathering six children, one boy and five girls, all of them marrying well, above their grandfather's station in life, a baker by trade.

Gattamelata distinguished himself early in life for his ability in siege operations. After serving in different mercenary companies and for different states,

Figure 17.1   Italy in 1454

he ended up with the soldiers of Pope Martin V, against whom he had often waged war in the past. His move was not treacherous, for the condottieri were required to serve faithfully during the term agreed by contract but were normally free to pass even to the enemy once their contract had expired. He ended his career as faithful commander of the soldiers of the Republic of Venice.

Gattamelata's reputation was indeed high during his career, and the great honors given him by Venice—the erection of the equestrian monument, his burial in the Church of St. Anthony, and the respect owed to his children— are a reflection of that. He was a soldier who had the reputation of never allowing sacking, looting, devastating fields and peasant dwellings, or raping and abusing women, children, or mothers. He seems also to have been the

kind of condottiere who was not shy about avoiding a ferocious pitched battle, as when he met another famous condottiere, Niccolò Piccinino, at the
River Sangonaro, near Imola, in 1433 and again at Monte Canino in 1438.
Venice treasured not only his daring but also his wisdom of sparing the troops
when necessary to fight another day.

It had not begun and will not continue that way during Gattamelata's times
and later. Foreign mercenaries would be the dominant aspect of the Italian military landscape between 1340 and 1380.[6] The Italian peninsula was an ideal place
for the endeavors of unemployed soldiers who had arrived there either in the following of a great lord or on their own. The emergence of small states, inevitably
competing for territorial and commercial supremacy, provided employment for
experts in the organized violence of war. But it was not just a matter of an abundance of employers in Italy; the peninsula was the wealthiest region in Europe.
Moreover, financial success went hand in hand, north of Rome at least, with a
change in values of the ruling groups of the Italian city-states. Many chose the
life of merchants to that of war, which meant that they had the resources for hiring outsiders to wage war for conquest or defense. This dovetailed with the
deliberate policy of separating the lower classes from the business of government.
Using the disadvantaged was dangerous for two reasons. If too successful, they
could become an internal threat; but their elimination from participation in
government inevitably meant that their performances were lukewarm if forced
to serve. It was safer and more efficient to rely on foreigners who could at least
be dismissed and sent home when not needed. The facts showed this to be a false
conviction. Mercenaries would breed like weeds and poison the political life of
the city and the balance of power among the states.

The Growth of the Mercenary Community

The Angevin conquest of southern Italy brought many French troops in the
1260s. And they must have arrived in considerable numbers during Henry VII
of Luxembourg's expedition in 1310. After Henry's death in 1313 German,
Flemish, and Brabantine troops found themselves in Italian territory without
employment or money. The process continued in 1327 with the arrival of
Louis of Bavaria and in 1333 with that of John, King of Bohemia. In 1347 it
had been the turn of Louis I, King of Hungary, when he arrived in Italy to
claim the crown of the Kingdom of Naples, after Queen Joanna I murdered
her husband, brother of the Hungarian sovereign.[7]

Two foreign condottieri, the German Werner von Urslingen and the Provençal Fra Moriale, left a legacy of efficiency combined with terror. Urslingen,

the feared *duca Guarneri*, as the Italians called him, sported this device on his breastplate: "Duke Werner, head of the Great Company [of mercenaries], enemy of God, enemy of compassion, and enemy of mercy." He appeared in Italy in 1339 and formed his company in 1342. As would be typical of all mercenary companies, Urslingen would serve different lords from Milan to the king of Hungary against Joanna of Naples and Cola di Rienzo against the pope. He was, contemporaries said, the man who "first devised this plague of [mercenary] societies."[8] That belief was not quite accurate. Michael Mallett shows instead that before the German mercenary leader, the Catalans of William della Torre and Diego de Rat had formed their own societies.[9] It is indicative of the times that Urslingen, the same man that pillaged, looted, and killed so many (after taking Anagni by storm he massacred most of its inhabitants), would end his career by entering the Church.

Montreal d'Albarno (Fra Moriale) was a knight of Rhodes and a Franciscan friar who had been defrocked but who still called himself "Fra Moriale, captain of war and standard-bearer of the Church."[10] He led a company of French, Germans, Burgundians, Swiss, and Italians, including notaries, lawyers, money-changers, musicians, merchants, and prostitutes. Fra Moriale, former member of an order, the Franciscans, that chose poverty as a way of life, was a man for whom money was the ultimate idol and whose brother, a banker residing at Perugia, wisely invested likely with the same rapacity of other usurers.[11] After terrorizing most of Italy, the end of Fra Moriale showed that, after all, his understanding of other human beings was quite poor. He believed in the promise of the man who briefly held sway in Rome, Cola di Rienzo, whom Fra Moriale despised and wanted to kill, because, he said, Cola was a man of words, not of action. When Fra Moriale moved toward Rome with forty other condottieri, he was betrayed by his maidservant and apprehended by Cola, who executed him in 1354. The words that the mercenary warlord addressed to the Roman populace, while moving toward the place of execution, reversed what had been the aim of his life of rapine: "Romans," he said, "I am dying unjustly. I am dying because of your poverty and my riches." As he placed his head on the chopping block, he made the sign of the cross and kissed the block. But then he seemed to hesitate, either out of a desire to delay his end or to make sure that the executioner would cut his head cleanly. He tried a few other positions until satisfied. In the end the executioner proceeded: he "found the juncture [of the neck]. The iron was set: at the first blow Fra Moriale's head leapt forward and fell. A few hairs from his beard remained on the block."[12]

The Great Company, which Fra Moriale had led, continued its existence until 1361, when it was defeated by the White Company, largely English mercenaries. Eventually, John Hawkwood would take command of the company. He would be the most famous of all foreign mercenary captains, for he combined the ruthless methods of those groups with faithful service to his later and main patron, the Republic of Florence. He also brought the English manner of fighting to the Italian battlefields—dismounted men-at-arms deployed among groups of missile units. In the end Florence honored his memory (he died in 1394) by a large fresco in the cathedral, painted by one of the great artists of the early Renaissance, Paolo Uccello, in which the figure of the condottiere sits on horseback in a surrealistic, pale-green light.

Hawkwood and his men were not the last foreigners to enter Italy. While he was active, probably the most ruthless of all companies appeared on Italian soils. Composed mainly of Bretons but also of Gascons, they arrived at the service of Pope Gregory XI, who left their management to a most cruel man, Cardinal Robert of Geneva. Their task was to subdue the rebellious cities of Romagna in north-central Italy. They fulfilled their task in a shocking manner in which their violence, bloodshed, and pillage surpassed all others. When the citizens of Cesena surrendered, trusting the cardinal's promise of mercy, the Bretons instead engaged in a three-day slaughter of all, men, women, children. In the end the corpses were left in the streets, a horrible feast for wild dogs.[13]

Although foreign mercenary captains predominated for most of the fourteenth century, Italians were never absent from the ranks of the looters, both as leaders and as followers of the self-styled companies of adventurers. The main break, however, came in 1378 with the formation of the Company of St. George, made up exclusively of Italians, under the command of Alberico da Barbiano. Barbiano silenced the Bretons by defeating them in 1379 in the Battle of San Marino. Afterward, Italian companies proliferated. By the mid-fifteenth century foreign companies had practically disappeared from the Italian scene. Michael Mallet suggests three main reasons for the supremacy of Italian mercenaries.[14] It is likely that at a time of economic difficulties in the aftermath of the Black Death foreign mercenaries may have found better possibilities of employment across the Alps, although economic problems must have ravaged every region in Europe. Also, dislike and hatred of foreign soldiers seemed to have become rampant in Italy among the populace, which is understandable, but also among intellectuals representing the people in power. By the mid-fifteenth century a certain amount of political stability arrived on the peninsula with the emergence of five major states: the Duchy of Milan, the Republic of Venice, the Republic of Florence, the States of the Church, and the Kingdom of Naples. All this took place in the midst of the forceful and illegal establishment of several signori (despots) in Romagna and in central Italy. Normally they were people who made a living as professional soldiers since they controlled usually quite poor territories.

Italian companies were not less ruthless than foreign mercenaries, although the employer usually kept a certain degree of control over them. The contract, the *condotta*, was somehow similar to the indenture in England or the *lettre of revenue* in France, but with a major difference. English and French practices referred mainly to subjects of their realms. The *condotta* was a contract between the state and soldiers who were the subjects of another territory. The contract specified the length of the service, the type of pay, the size and quality of the company, and any additional bonuses.[15] Although it came under the leadership of one person, the company was made up of various *condotte*, each contributing several soldiers. Each leader of a *condotta* brought several soldiers with whom he was also tied by contract. The company of Micheletto Attendolo, one of the great captains of the fifteenth century, included 87 minor companies, each with a hierarchical structure, for a total of 561 lances and 187 condottieri—on the whole 1,122 mounted soldiers. In all there was a condottiere for every six men. Each *condotta* was made up of several lances. In Attendolo's case this varied from companies as large as fifty lances to as small as twenty-five lances. The numerical consistency of the lance changed over time, but in the case of Attendolo's troops it meant two men-at-arms and a non-fighting page. When the time came for deployment the companies were grouped into larger battle groups.[16] The size of a company varied, although they seem to have become large by the fifteenth century, as was the case with Attendolo. Niccolò Piccinino signed for a company of 4,000 horses (2,000 lances) and 1,000 troops for the king of Naples, Alfonso the Magnanimous, during the period September 1442 to January 1444.

The process of hiring mercenaries was difficult, for a wise ruler needed not only a sizable army but also to avoid clever captains joining his rivals' forces.[17] In the fourteenth century mercenary captains and their followers were hired only for a limited time, usually from one to six months; in the fifteenth century the *condotta* was much longer, at least a year with an option for renewal. Moreover, whereas in the early companies the condottiere was just a peer among peers (i.e., there was a democratic aspect to the group), in the fifteenth century mercenary societies were structured like a pyramid, with powers diminishing from the top to the bottom and with the leader enjoying full judicial and contractual authority. He decided what to distribute to his employees, normally a fifth of ransoms, looting, or any other gain. In turn, lower leaders divided their portions with immediate followers.[18]

In the large and most powerful states mercenary units constituted the majority of troops. This was the case in Naples, where household knights were the nucleus of the army while the rest had been hired all over Italy.[19] This was also the case when Venice tried to stop Charles VIII's retreat to France at the Battle of Fornovo in 1495.[20] In the smaller states mercenary companies might be the only available troops for offensive operations. In defense, as during a siege, one could always rely on the city-dwellers besides the hired troops.

The armies of the fifteenth century were noticeably larger and included mercenaries belonging to various *condotte*, all under a main leader, and the *lance spezzate*, mercenaries not part of a *condotta* but hired directly by the state. Yet the armies were still relatively small. As Michael Mallett argues, very rarely they could count on more than 20,000 soldiers.[21] The army that King Alfonso envisaged in 1446 had on paper an initial roster of 1,000 foot soldiers and 3,000 horsemen that could be increased to 9,000. In reality he could rely on 6,000 horsemen and 2,000 infantry at the most.[22] Although they had some artillery and field firepower besides archers and crossbowmen, mercenary companies were fighters on horseback with some support by footmen.

At the time of his arrest in Rome, the Provençal Fra Moriale angrily addressed his jailers when they approached him with a cord, that is, a symbol of torture. "Didn't I say that you were rustic villains?" he screamed at them, contempt in his voice. "You want to put me to the torture; don't you see I am a knight? How can you be so despicable?" Even when they hoisted him a little, he repeated, "I was chief of the Great Company, and because I am a knight I wanted to live honorably." What he added to those words may sound strange to modern ears: "I took ransom from the cities of Tuscany; I taxed them. I robbed towns and captured people."[23] In other words, the fact that he was a knight compelled him to live in a honorable way, which meant that he felt no blame in pillaging towns and depriving people of their property.

The knighthood that Fra Moriale claimed as his was a statement familiar among the condottieri. In reality most came from a noble background, although a few, like Gattamelata and Niccolò Piccinino, had humble origins. They were the exception, not the rule. Some condottieri were displaced political exiles; a common method to rid political opponents was to exile them. This implied that they belonged to the urban patriciate. Some actually came from feudatories, like the Malatesta, the Montefeltro, the Orsini, the Colonna, and Alberigo da Barbiano, who for the lower roles in their company used some of their own subjects. The majority, however, were from the lower ranks of nobility. Mario Del Treppo, author of a detailed study of the Attendolo's company in the earlier stages of the fifteenth century, found that about forty condottieri came from aristocratic families out of the 430 for which he could establish a social connection. On the whole, the sample analyzed by Del Treppo showed that the condottieri in Attendolo's service were a mix of feudal nobility, urban patriciates, and minor property owners. Moreover, by this time, foreigners were a modest percentage of the warriors. There were only ten people coming from the Balkans (Slavs, Greeks, and Albanians), who had their roots in southern Italy, and sixteen from the other side of the Alps, of which the most numerous group were the Germans, with six.[24] The predominance of Italians was also the case in the army of Alfonso the Magnanimous. For instance, the *condotta* of the Italian Borso d'Este, who served Alfonso, counted forty leaders of ten lances or more out of fifty-four captains; in Naples, where the king was Aragonese, Spanish soldiers were always present.[25] Del Treppo's sample also shows that mercenaries had their roots in cities that enjoyed a strong connection with the countryside like Bologna and Arezzo, not from large commercial centers like Venice and Florence. Moreover, many of the condottieri of each company were tied together by family, personal loyalty, or common goals. This was the case with Attendolo. This would also be the case with Giovanfrancesco Gonzaga, the leader of the Venetian army at Fornovo in 1495. The only exception was Naples, but this is no surprise, for the town's military tradition had been established among the town's nobility.[26]

Companies, once formed, rarely disappeared, although in a few cases they did end in catastrophic defeat, like Attendolo at Caravaggio. Even in peacetime, a central command structure was kept, for companies had a type of central administration that continued during lulls.[27] Companies were elastic formations that decreased or increased membership according to war and the captain's reputation. They could be inherited, be the outcome of marriage, or were formed by the lord of a small and relatively disadvantaged state as a way to increase revenues.

The wages they received at the moment of signing were not the only rewards that successful captains could expect. Besides ransoms and looting, the state that employed a brave and faithful condottiere usually rewarded him in other ways—the granting of a fief, marriage in a leading family of the state he had served, an extra financial bonus, the respect of the community, which at that time translated to material gains, and, probably the most treasured of all, public esteem. They could even carve out a state for themselves. This was what Cesare Borgia intended in the early sixteenth century, although Borgia himself cannot be considered a condottiere. But the most famous example of success remains the Sforza family, which at the disappearance of the Visconti dynasty became the rulers of Milan, one of the five great Italian city-states during the fifteenth century.

Although rewards could be considerable, punishment for poor service or suspected betrayal could be harsh. For some the ultimate punishment was death, as in the case of Carmagnola, executed by the Republic of Venice for fear that he was going to pass to the service of his old employer, the Duchy of Milan. Other punishments could consist of fines, withheld payments, or dismissal if the state feared no reprisal.

One of the great minds of Western civilization, Niccolò Machiavelli, did a disservice to posterity when he condemned condottieri as unreliable, untrustworthy, and inefficient. Machiavelli was the heir to a tradition that in the early fifteenth century already had a prestigious exponent in the figure of the humanist Leonardo Bruni. Moreover, Machiavelli was also the spokesman of a large group of intellectuals who condemned key aspects of the times—mercenary soldiers and life at court. Machiavelli was wrong and partisan at times, but the greatest culprits for the survival of his assessment of the condottieri must be found among successive writers and historians who repeated the Florentine's statements without subjecting them to effective analysis. Today the tendency seems to be the reverse, with historians claiming that Machiavelli was inaccurate and that the condottieri were reliable. On the whole, the revisionist view is accurate. However, picturing the condottieri as effective soldiers would be as inaccurate as Machiavelli's view. True, the immediate future was not the formation of national armies but rather armies of mercenaries around a nucleus of soldiers drawn from the state's subjects. This was the case of the army of Alfonso the Magnanimous in Naples, the Venetian army at Fornovo, and the army of the King Charles VIII of France when he invaded Italy at the end of the fifteenth century. There is also no doubt that many condottieri were faithful and honest servants and that their adaptation to the new rhythm of warfare was more immediate and enterprising than among the states' subjects. Their independence on the battlefield was limited by the presence of civilian commissioners attached to their armies. Machiavelli's claim that condottieri conflicts ended in few or no casualties is also nonsense. Their encounters could be bloody indeed. Yet pitched battles must have been rare. For instance, in twenty-five years of the Attendolo company there were only twenty-five condottiere casualties out of 512 captains, that is, an average of one a year. Of the seriously wounded, only four were forced to leave the company. If one adds that thirty-one of the 512 deserted,[28] the picture does not seem very bloody. And there were examples to doubt the honesty of a few condottieri. Astorre dei Manfredi defrauded King Alfonso of Naples of a large sum that he had received. He never arrived to serve the sovereign. It is no surprise that Alfonso paid advances only when the condottiere he was hiring had given him some form of security in hostages or, preferably, lands. Territories and castles had no legs; hostages could escape.[29]

The war practiced by condottieri is best defined by skirmishes, sieges, and complex movements in the hope of catching the enemy in a weak position. Pitched encounters did take place, but they were the exception. The risk was too great for the condottiere and the state he served. Losing would open the state to the enemy, with limited possibility of defense, whereas cunning, industry, and attrition could bring adversaries to their knees.[30] Moreover, the eternal distrust between employers and employees prevented decisive actions. It was an attitude that contrasted sharply with future developments. Swiss infantry and the French and Spanish armies of the second half of the fifteenth century and early sixteenth century adopted a different approach. The main goal was not to outsmart the opponent but to destroy him totally. Armies would rely on strong foot forces and eventually on gunpowder. But the future owed strategy and professionalism to the old breed of mercenaries. It is no surprise to find, even when condottiere armies were disappearing, that mercenaries were increasing in number and that the overall command of an army was often entrusted to a condottiere. This would be the case with the French armies during the early stages of the wars of the Renaissance in Italy. Gonzaga, who had led the Venetian army against the French at Fornovo in 1495, would command the French against the Spaniards at the Garigliano in 1503.

The great Italian Renaissance historian Francesco Guicciardini summarizes the tactical approach of the opposing conceptions of battlefield confrontations. At Fornovo in 1495 the Venetian by squadron army, mainly mercenaries, still expected to confront the enemy squadron with a full-scale clash at the end. The Venetian mercenaries also intended, in spite of the prohibition of their leader, to take prisoners for ransom. What happened on the battlefield shocked them. It was not a matter of ordered strikes of squadron after squadron. The enemy attacked them with all the might of its cavalry as a whole, the deadly advances of their support infantry, sparing no life. It was a form of battlefield war to which they were unaccustomed.

Chapter Eighteen ~

New Weapons, New Men, New Ideas

T HE MEDIEVAL WORLD GREW FROM the ruins of the late Roman Empire. In the roughly 1,000 years from the collapse of Rome in the West to the end of the Hundred Years War and the fall of Constantinople in 1453, at least four different stages are evident. During the first period, roughly 476–800, various barbarian kingdoms were established in most of Europe. The most successful was the Frankish kingdom in Gallia, with its blend of old-world Rome, and the new Germanic heritage. The barbarian kingdoms operated in an atmosphere of constant conflict that settled only with the emergence of Charlemagne.

Chronologically parallel to the formation of the barbarian states in the West was a new threat to the remains of the Roman Empire, the emperors of Constantinople: the emergence of the Muslims. Starting from the bleak landscape of the Arabian Peninsula, the Muslims overran, in a rather short period, Syria, Iraq, Persia, Egypt, and North Africa before crossing into Spain. They brought a new system of warfare, an unflinching belief in their mission, and a dislike of Christians.

The third stage, 800–1300, began among fears of new invaders, Vikings from the North, Magyars from the East. Yet once their invasions were muzzled (the Magyars were compelled to stop in Hungary) or redirected toward less unsettling limits (the heirs of the Vikings settled in Normandy before crossing, as Normans, into England), the borders of the West became safe. War was endemic internally, but now the western powers began a counterattack against the enemies at their borders, Slavs and Muslims, and across the Mediterranean in their doomed quest to preserve the Holy Land.

The final stage, roughly 1300–1453, saw the emergence of new soldiers, new weapons, and new ideas. Some of the changes were already evident by the end of the period; others were a blueprint of the future.

Medieval warfare emphasized different aspects according to the period, geography, and the historical environment. Yet three values were primary: religion, personal honor, and profit.

The Infantry of the Future

The Hundred Years War seemed to say that future warfare would belong to dismounted men-at-arms and longbowmen. It was a promise that never materialized, although the English kept the bow for a very long time. The crossbowmen did prosper for a longer time on the continent. The future of the infantry would be, however, the sturdy Swiss pikemen and troops armed with handheld firepower.

The Battle of Morgaten in 1315 of the Swiss against the Austrian troops is usually understood as marking the first encounter of the new association of Swiss cantons and as an example of the superiority of their infantry on the battlefield. Morgaten, in which Swiss mountaineers defeated the cavalry of duke Leopold of Austria, and the Swiss defeat at Arbedo in 1422 are instead the beginning and end of a period in which their style of fighting was quite different from their tactical behavior in the second half of the fifteenth century. At Morgaten the Swiss benefited from terrain that was narrow and forested on both sides—unsuitable to their cavalry opponents. They also enjoyed the element of surprise and the use of weapons, halberds and bills, that were extremely effective against men on horseback. At Arbedo in the lands of the duke of Milan, a Swiss contingent held very well initially against the cavalry of the mercenary leader Carmagnola, but when the Italian mercenaries, aware of the failure of their attack, decided to fight dismounted, it was a different story. The Swiss were close to being destroyed and likely would have been if the mercenaries, seeing in the distance a group of foragers, had not mistaken them for a relief contingent.

Both Morgaten and Arbedo show the ferocious reputation of the Swiss infantry and the fear that it generated in its adversaries. Yet their weapon of choice, the halberd, could not allow the type of formation that typified future armies. The halberd, an elongated axe, needed, like a bill, a wide space to be efficient, for it had to be swung in a circular motion, which prevented the close-rank deployment of later Swiss infantry. After Arbedo, however, the

Swiss weapon of choice was a long pike; the core of mountaineers were intermixed with urban dwellers, grouped according to villages, cities, and cantons. They deployed in very large squares, the core of which were soldiers
holding pikes about 5.5 meters long, protected on the flanks by skirmishers
armed with crossbows and later firearms and preceded sometimes by missile
units, crossbows and bows, and always by halberds or two-handed swords to
break the front of the enemy formations. It was also a very bloody way of
warfare, where the aim was to kill the enemy regardless of status, not to take
him for ransom. That was the system that destroyed the creative armies of
the duke of Burgundy in the space of ten months, at Grandson on 2 March
1476, at Murten about three months later (22 June), and at Nancy on 5 January 1477. At Murten the Swiss battle order included three infantry battle
groups, divided into vanguard, main battle, and rearguard, with a small cavalry contingent. The front of the line was occupied by the vanguard, with
the cavalry protecting its left flank. Then came, in a staggered formation, the
main battle of about 10,000 men and behind that a smaller rearguard. Disposed in the form of an elongated quadrilateral with a triangular shape at the
top the main battle massed 10,000 men in very close ranks in a small area
(only 60 by 60 meters).[1]

The Swiss pikemen would terrorize the European battlefields at the end of
the fifteenth century and the initial part of the sixteenth, especially during the
Italian Wars of the Renaissance. Most European states hired or imitated them.
After the Burgundian War, infantry became practically synonymous with people holding a pike. At the same time, however, they were joined by troops
sporting firearms, and crossbows tended to disappear. Arbedo was a set-piece
on how to confront the unbeatable pikemen—dismounted soldiers armed
with swords and eventually small shields. What later would be effective, as
Italians and Spaniards would show in 1503 at Cerignola, was to pound the
large Swiss squares with firearms, add to their disorder with terrain obstacles,
and then penetrate their ranks using bucklers and swords.

The infantry's success did not mean that the cavalry lost its prestige on the
battlefield, only that the horsemen's action was limited to cavalry opponents
or to harassment and pursuit. Malcolm Vale argues that the prejudice against
the lower classes, conservatism in military affairs, and the cavalry's adaptation
to the new weapons with lighter and better-designed armor meant that the
horse would still play a leading role on the battlefield.[2] The prestige did not
fully disappear until the introduction of more deadly forms of firepower.

Those Un-Christian Weapons

Missile power reappeared in the form of gunpowder. Like all devices that brought death to men-at-arms from a distance, gunpowder weapons were greeted with dismay and obstinate condemnation. And it did not help their associations with Muslims or, even worse, heathens. But what had been greeted with hostility became the darling of any power engaged in conquest or defense.

The formula for gunpowder is found in *Wujung Zongyan,* a Chinese work of 1044. But the Chinese used it for visual and emotional effects—smoke and incendiary and explosive bombs.[3] The first to adopt gunpowder to the battle-field were Asiatic people, with the invention then moving slowly westward. Mongols used it on a large scale in their attempted invasion of Japan between 1274 and 1281, but already much earlier, in 1241, they seem to have experimented with it at the Battle of Sajo in Hungary. From the Mongols the invention passed to the Muslims with various appellations for saltpeter from "Chinese snow" to "Chinese salt." Finally the gunpowder formula found its way in 1267 into the work of Roger Bacon.[4]

Its use on western battlefields appears in several documents during the first half of the fourteenth century, although never in such an amount as to decide a battle—at Metz in 1324, at Cividale in the northeastern corner of Italy in 1341, and at Crécy in 1346. In sieges from 1325 to 1425, however, gunpowder weapons left their mark. They could breach a wall faster and more effectively than other artillery pieces. Yet several problems plagued the introduction of the new weapons—inadequate equipment, high cost, unsatisfactory gunpowder, and difficulty in siting and carrying the new weapons to the battlefield. A radical change took place in the 1380s when lower prices for gunpowder were accompanied by a better manufacturing formula and continuous experimentation in the design and carriage of weapons. Especially important, says Bert S. Hall, were changes introduced in the manufacture of gunpowder during the fifteenth and sixteenth centuries. Siege artillery was certainly impressive in the English conquest of Normandy between 1410 and 1425 and played leading roles in the Hussite Wars in Bohemia after 1419, in the last stages of the Hundred Years War, and finally in the siege of Constantinople of 1453.[5]

While the English had kept the upper hand in the use of siege artillery before the 1440s, supremacy passed into French hands. Artillery did not bring final victory to Charles VII and his army but certainly was instrumental in accelerating the end of the conflict. French superiority was in the higher level of organization of the new weapons thanks to the revolutionary changes brought by the treasurer of France, Jean Bureau, and his brother Gaspard, master of the artillery. The changes brought by the brothers went hand in hand with the king's establishment of a permanent army. In the end the period saw the foundation of a royal artillery, including an organized system of personnel, arsenals, and magazines, "all geared toward providing a large, reliable supply of siege guns and supporting firearms wherever and whenever the king might demand them."[6] Results came quickly in the conquest of Normandy in 1449–1450 and in subduing the last English Aquitainian hold in Guyenne between 1451 and 1453.

Thanks to the combined operations of four armies and their artillery, the French passed from one success to another in Normandy, where the English were making their last stand along the coast and the cities and ports of Cherbourg, Caen, Harfleur, and Calais. French guns battered and conquered Harfleur in December 1449; on 12 August of the following year Cherbourg fell. Meanwhile, on the battlefield the English experienced defeat at Formigny on 15 April 1450, where the English flanks had been battered by two culverins until the English, desperate, tried to rush the guns and became easy prey for a French counterattack. The only major city and port remaining in English hands was Calais, a sad reminder of their previous primacy in the region.[7]

The conquest of the remaining territory in Aquitaine, which the English had kept for 300 years, was more complicated and needed two different offensive phases. Bordeaux, deprived of the hope of any relief by the expert siege craft of the Bureau brothers, decided to surrender, and on 30 June 1451 French troops entered the city. Two months later, on 20 August, Bayonne, a key strategic location south of Bordeaux, fell to the French. But the French were soon unwelcome in the region, and Bordeaux expelled them as the English sent a relief army under the command of the great John Talbot. It is ironic that the final defeat of the English at Castillon on 17 July 1453 came with a reversal of roles. The English decided to attack the French, who had assumed a defensive stand behind the fortifications of a camp protected by trenches, earth parapets, log walls, and various artillery pieces. Talbot foolishly exposed his men to certain defeat on a field encumbered by obstacles, caught on the flank by French guns. As a French eyewitness says, "The artillery . . . caused grievous harm to the English, for each shot knocked five or six men down, killing them all." Talbot met his end on the battlefield. It took his servant of forty years almost a day before deciding what mutilated body was his old master's.[8] On 17 July 1453 the last major battle of the Hundred Years War was fought on French soil. It was the epilogue of the English dream of establishing a strong presence on the continent. The combination of weakness and conflicting aims at home and a renewed stronger French army possessing a new destructive weapon had brought defeat.

In spite of the performance at Formigny and Castillon gunpowder weapons were not a crucial element in most other battles of the Middle Ages. Hand firearms were even less so, although they spread quickly among the armies of the day, as in Lombardy. At the battle of Caravaggio on 29 July 1448 the *scoppectieri*'s shots covered the whole battlefield with smoke so dense that the soldiers could hardly see each other.[9] At an attempted relief of the siege of Marignano in 1449 Milan seemed to have sent several *scoppectieri*, which prompted the besieging general, the famed condottiere Francesco Sforza, to instruct his men to rush the firearm soldiers quickly, giving them no time to either shoot or recharge. Then the men holding firearms, he predicted to his troops, would turn into "fearful sheep."[10] It would take some time for hand firearms to play a decisive role. The first time they helped decide the issue on the battlefield was during the next period, the Renaissance, in 1503 at Cerignola, one of the great encounters of the early stages of the Italian wars.

Siege artillery became more effective in the last stages of the Hundred Years War. The later medieval fortifications, tall and relatively lean, were no match. They would collapse as ball after ball hit their walls. In reality not even stronger walls, like Constantinople's, could withstand the power of the new weapon. The solution to the new threat would come later, with the construction of the bastion. Yet it took time, and from the second half of the fifteenth century onward the battlefield changed. The relatively small armies of the early Middle Ages became increasingly larger. Much larger armies were only one aspect of the military changes following the Middle Ages. More important was the adoption of different levels of permanent armies. France, the Italian states, and Burgundy were the most effective examples.

Turks and Mongols

While the Iberian Peninsula fell into Christian hands, the story was different in eastern Europe. One key to the Crusaders' defeat in the Near East had been the contribution of the Seljuk Turks, who eventually established ruling dynasties in Iraq, Syria, and Asia Minor. After adopting Islam in the early 900s, this nomadic Asian tribe conquered Baghdad in 1055. In 1071 they inflicted a severe defeat to the Byzantines at Manzikert, often regarded as the first sign of the inevitable collapse of the Roman Empire of the East.

Invaders from the East did not stop with the Seljuks. An even more formidable invasion came with the Mongols, who originated from the desolate plains of modern Mongolia and combined a kaleidoscope of religions that included adherents to Buddhism, Nestorian Christianity, and Islam. Joined by Turkish tribes, they spread across China, the Middle East, and eastern Europe under the leadership of Genghis Khan (ca. 1162–1227), whose birth name was Temüjin (blacksmith). In 1235 Peking and northern China fell to Genghis's men, and later southwest Asia. In 1258 Persia and Iraq came under the rule of the Mongols; their spread into the Middle East was stopped when the troops of the Mamluk Sultan of Egypt defeated them. In the meantime, filtering through the plains on the northern shores of the Black Sea, they arrived in Europe. In 1237 they attacked Russia; Kiev fell in 1240. From there they advanced into Poland and Hungary; after initially crossing the Danube, they withdrew from the area, never to return.

Most of the rulers of the various khanates, into which the Mongol Empire was divided, converted to Islam between 1300 and 1377. However, this did not mean that the wars against their religious comrades stopped. The descendant of a vizier of the great Genghis Khan's son, Timûr Lang (Tamerlane), surpassed his most ruthless predecessors in ferocity and cruelty. Born in 1336 south of Samarkand in Transoxiana (the land beyond the River Oxus, corresponding to modern Amu Darya), Tamerlane soon became the subject of praise and vilification. For some he was not the descendant of a vizier but the son of a shoemaker.

Tamerlane followed in the footsteps of Genghis Khan. After establishing a secure basis in Central Asia, he moved west. In 1380 he invested Afghanistan, Persia, Fars, and Kurdistan in a series of lightning strikes. In 1393 he was in Baghdad, capturing Mesopotamia and erecting a pyramid made of skulls at Tikrit, the birthplace of Saladin and, centuries later, of Saddam Hussein. In 1395 he arrived in Moscow, occupying the city for about a year and leaving horrible signs of his conquests everywhere he went. When he invaded northern India, 80,000 inhabitants of the region lost their lives. In 1400 he was in Syria, subjecting Aleppo to three days of plunder and destruction and erecting mounds with the 20,000 heads of decapitated Muslims ten cubits high and seven meters in circumference and destroying the great schools and mosques of the previous rulers. In 1401 Damascus was destroyed by fire, all but the walls of the great Umayyad Mosque; he carried the gifted scholars and craftsmen of the great city to Samarkand. Moving from Damascus to Baghdad to avenge the death of some of his supporters, he set up a macabre landscape of twenty towers with the skulls of the people he had slaughtered in revenge. In 1402 he moved into Asia Minor, defeating the army of the Ottoman Turks (their name derived from the founder of their dynasty, Osman I, 1299–1326) and at Ankara on 21 July captured Sultan Bayazid I. He took the sultan prisoner and chained him, like an animal, in a cage pulled by two horses. When Tamerlane died in 1404, his body was carried to Samarkand, where his tomb stands. The Mongol Empire slowly withered away after Tamerlane.[11]

The Mongols' defeat of the Turkish Sultan Bayazid I at Ankara only temporarily weakened the hold that the Ottoman Turks had established in Asia Minor by the early fourteenth century. Thanks to the military contributions of the Ghazis—men whose aim in life was to enforce their view of Islam—they settled within the borders of the Seljuk Empire in Asia Minor. The original place of the Ottomans was most likely Mongolia. In their move westward they mixed with people of various ethnic groups, especially Iranian tribes. By 1000 they are found northeast of the Caspian Sea, from where they constituted a continuous menace to the cities on their south—Bukhara, Samarkand, and Merv. Their expansion followed the usual modus operandi: establishing a great reputation as raiders and mercenaries before moving into Transoxiana by conquering Bukhara in 999. From there they expanded westward preceded by the reputation of a very effective military machine. Once in Asia Minor, they eroded the power of the Byzantine Empire, reducing it to a small player across the Hellespont and southern Greece. And in a series of successful campaigns they crossed the Hellespont and conquered most of the Balkans and what are today the states of Romania and Bulgaria. The neighboring states of Walachia, Bosnia, and Serbia (the last one defeated in two major battles, both at Kosovo, in 1389 and 1446), were reduced to the status of vassals (Figure 18.1).

The conquest of Constantinople in 1453 came as a shock to the rest of Europe. Yet by then the Byzantines maintained an empire in name only. During the siege the city population was 40,000–50,000, manned by 5,000 Greek soldiers and 2,000–3,000 foreigners, mainly Italians, Genoese most of all, who were much more effective than the resident Byzantine soldiers in defending the city. The fall of Constantinople was meaningful only for the psychological impact among Christians and as a matter of prestige for Ottomans, who renamed the city Istanbul. The real adversaries of the Turks, however, were not

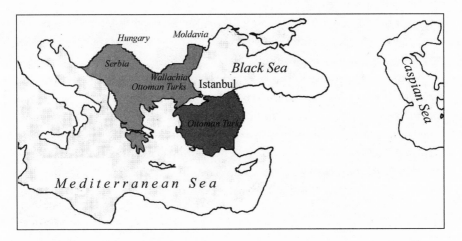

Figure 18.1   Ottoman Empire 1492

the Byzantines but the Italian cities of Genoa and Venice, which had important commercial interests in the eastern Mediterranean. It was thus no surprise that much more important was the sea war between the new rulers of Asia Minor and the two Italian states; the Turks concentrated on building a strong fleet. During the rest of the fifteenth century and most of the sixteenth century, Europeans witnessed a gradual reduction of the power of Venice in the eastern Mediterranean and an expansion of Turkish dominance from the Balkans to most of the North African coast. In the process the Turks created a great empire that would last until the end of World War I.

The efficiency of the Ottoman army was based on a state that combined a strong military tradition with tolerance and fairness toward its subjects. They were also skillful in raising powerful military contingents by deliberately recruiting among the Christian people who they defeated. For instance, the famous janissaries were young Christian children who had been educated and indoctrinated into Muslim traditions and religion since their capture at an early age. Finally, they were able to master the culture and civilized behavior of the areas they conquered. In this sense their settlement in the three great cities of Samarkand, Merv, and especially Bukhara must have provided a great laboratory for their cultural upbringing.

Unlike most other nomadic people, the Turks in the end were able to combine light troops with soldiers who could be used for hand-to-hand clashes. A typical Turkish action involved an initial harassment by light cavalry to draw the enemy toward a fortified position manned by soldiers skilled in face-to-face combat and eventually armed with firepower. Their discipline and experimentation is evident in the fact that the Turks were among the first to effectively deploy gunpowder weapons.

By the end of the Middle Ages and the beginning of the Renaissance, changes in the battlefield and in the management of war paralleled changes in mental attitudes. A new concept of the individual, and the way the individual shaped and was shaped by history, appeared alongside new values and a new approach to life. But by then a new period in history started to dominate the West, first in Italy, then in France, and later in most of the West and in the new worlds dominated by the European powers.

Notes

Chapter 1

1. Jordanes xlviii.
2. Based on Jordanes xlix but also on Michael A. Babcock, *The Stories of Attila the Hun's Death: Narrative, Myth, and Meaning* (Lewiston, N.Y., 2001).
3. E. A. Thompson, *A History of Attila and the Huns* (Oxford, 1948), p. 151.
4. Jordanes l.
5. Jordanes xxiv.
6. Claudio Azzara, *Le invasioni barbariche* (Bologna, 1999), pp. 26–27.
7. Code Théodosien, XIV, 10, 4.
8. On the process see the exciting ideas put forward by Patrick Amory (*People and Identity in Ostrogothic Italy, 480–554,* Cambridge, 1997), who develops the model of ethnogenesis presented by Austrian and German scholars like Reinhard Wenskus and Herwig Wolfram.
9. Azzara, *Le invasioni barbariche*, pp. 30–36.
10. Ibid., p. 48.
11. Ammianus xxi.4.11.
12. After E. A. Thompson, *Romans and Barbarians: The Decline of the Western Empire* (Madison, Wis., 1982), pp. 15–19.
13. Herwig Wolfram, "The Shaping of Early Medieval Kingdoms," *Viator* 1 (1970): 9.

Chapter 2

1. Procopius V.1.12.
2. Procopius V.1.25.
3. Philippe Contamine. *War in the Middle Ages,* trans. Michael Jones (Oxford, 1984), pp. 86–97.
4. Walter Goffart, *Barbarians and Romans, A.D. 418–584* (Princeton, 1980), pp. 58–102.
5. Giovanni Tabacco, "La storia politica e sociale. Dal tramonto dell' Impero alle prime fondazioni di Stati regionali," in Ruggiero Romano and Corrado Vivanti, eds., *Storia d'Italia, Vol. 2: Dalla caduta dell'Impero romano al secolo xviii* (Torino, 1974), pp. 21–26.
6. Jordanes lvi.
7. Procopius V.1.26.
8. Patrick Amory, *People and Identity in Ostrogothic Italy, 480–554* (Cambridge, 1997), pp. 48–49.
9. Ibid., pp. 40–41.
10. Herwig Wolfram, *History of the Goths,* trans. Thomas J. Dunlap (Berkeley, 1988), pp. 8, 300–301.
11. Ibid., p. 300.

12. Amory, *People and Identity*, p. 108.

13. Wolfram, *History of the Goths*, pp. 302–303.

14. Ibid., pp. 302–306.

15. Procopius VIII.30.1. See also Thompson, *Romans and Barbarians*, pp. 77-91.

16. Ibid. VII.1.12.

17. Ibid. VI.29.34.

18. Ibid., p. 303.

19. Wolfram, *History of the Goths*, p. 305.

20. Ibid., p. 304.

21. John Haldon, *Warfare, State, and Society in the Byzantine World, 565–1204* (London, 1999), p. 100.

22. Ibid., p. 120.

23. Ibid., pp. 128–138.

24. Ibid., pp. 128–131.

25. Ibid., pp. 128–131.

26. Ibid., pp. 193–197.

27. Ibid., p. 192.

28. Wolfram, "The Shaping of Early Medieval Kingdoms," p. 12.

29. "Patterns of Political Activity of the Armies of the Roman Empire," in W. E. Kaegi, Jr., *Army, Society, and Religion in Byzantium* (London, 1982), pp. 4–35.

30. Procopius V. xxviii.27–29.

31. Ibid. V.15.

32. Ibid. V.14.17.

33. Ibid. V.11.26.

34. Ibid. V.11.28. Cf. Wolfram, *History of the Goths*, p. 344.

35. Wolfram, *History of the Goths*, p. 344.

36. Procopius V.14.12–14.

37. Thomas Hodgkin, *Italy and Her Invaders*, vol. 4 (Oxford, 1889–1899), p. 146.

38. Procopius V.14.17.

39. Ibid. V.16.

40. Wolfram, *History of the Goths*, p. 344.

41. Procopius V.16.11.

42. Hodgkin, *Italy and Her Invaders*, vol. 4, pp. 133–134.

43. Procopius V.17.19.20.

44. Ibid. V.18.

45. Ibid. V.19.

46. Ibid. V.19.14.

47. Ibid. V.21.

48. Ibid. V.22.

49. Ibid. V.23.

50. Ibid. V.23.26.

51. Ibid. V.23.

52. Ibid. V.25.15–17.

53. Ibid. V.27.3–10.

54. Ibid. V.27.11–14.

55. Ibid. V.27.15–20.

56. Ibid. V.27.21–23.

57. Ibid. VI.4.19; VI.5.1–2.

58. Ibid. VI.13.16–18.

59. Ibid. VI.10.1.

60. Ibid. VI.10.8.

61. Ibid. VI.10. 13.

62. Ibid. VI.2.37.

63. Ibid. VI.10.12–20.

64. Ibid. VI.21.38–40.

65. Ibid. VI.22.17–22.

66. Ibid. VI.30.27.

67. Ibid. VI.1.27.

68. Ibid. VII.6.1.

69. Hodgkin, *Italy and Her Invaders*, vol. 4, pp. 709–711. On the battle at Taginae, see Procopius VIII.28–33.

70. Hodgkin, *Italy and Her Invaders*, vol. 4, p. 713.

71. Procopius VIII.32.7–8.

72. Procopius VIII.31.6.7.

73. Ibid. VIII.31.9–10.

74. Wolfram, *The History of the Goths*, p. 360.

75. Procopius VIII.31.17–21.

76. Ibid. VIII.32.1.

77. Ibid. VIII.35.22–29.

78. On this see A. Cameron, *Procopius and the Sixth Century* (Berkeley, 1985), p. 189 ff.

79. Ibid., p. 190.

80. Ibid., pp. 200–201.

81. Ibid., pp. 193–194.

82. Procopius VII.30.19–24.

83. Ibid. VIII.34.7.8.

84. Ibid. VI.21.38–40.

85. Ibid. VII.17.15–21.

86. Ibid. VI.20.17–21.

87. Ibid. VI.20.17–33.

Chapter 3

1. Ubaldo Pizzani, "The Influence of *De Institutione Musica* of Boethius up to Herbert d'Aurillac: A Tentative Contribution," in Michael Masi, ed., *Boethius and the Liberal Arts: A Collection of Essays* (1981), pp. 119–121.

2. The physical portrayal of Alboin and the general appearance of the Longobards is based on Paul the Deacon (see ii.28 for Alboin's height, iii. 29, iv.23, 38) and on István Kiszely, "On the True Face of the Longobards in Italy," *La cultura in Italia fra tardo antico e alto Medioevo. Atti del Convegno tenuto a Roma 1979*, vol. 2 (Roma, 1981): 887–892, who reaches his conclusions on the examination of 870 skeletons.

3. Paul the Deacon ii.8. The mountain may correspond either to Monte Re or Monte Matajur.

4. Kiszely, "On the True Face of the Longobards in Italy," pp. 889–890.

5. Ernesto Sestan, "I longobardi," in Ovidio Capitani et al., *L'Italia dell'alto Medioevo* (Milano, 1984), p. 71.

6. J. M. Wallace-Hadrill, *The Barbarian West, 400–1000* (London, 1966), p. 45.

7. Paul the Deacon ii.7.

8. Ibid. ii.7.

9. Ibid. i.2.

10. Kiszely, pp. 888–892; Marc Rotili, "La civiltà dei Longobardi negli insediamenti protoitaliani," *La cultura in Italia fra tardo antico e alto Medioevo. Atti del Convegno tenuto a Roma 1979*, vol 2 (Roma, 1979), pp. 933–946.

11. Kiszely, "On the True Face of the Longobards in Italy," p. 889.

12. Ibid.

13. Ibid.

14. Ibid., p. 888; Paul the Deacon ii.26.

15. Procopius viii.33.2–3; Sestan, "I longobardi," pp. 72–73; Neal Christie, "Invasion or Invitation? The Longobard Occupation of Northern Italy, AD 568–569" *Romanobarbarica* 11: 94.

16. Paul the Deacon iii.5–7.

17. Kiszely, "On the True Face of the Longobards in Italy," p. 888.

18. Paul the Deacon ii.6.

19. Sestan, "I longobardi," p. 74; Ernesto Sestan, "La composizione etnica della società in rapporto allo svolgimento della civiltà in Italia nel secolo vii," in Ernesto Sestan, *Italia medievale* (Napoli, 1968), p. 30.

20. Sestan, "I longobardi," p. 74.

21. Ibid., pp. 74–75.

22. Arianism was the main heresy of the fourth century. It denied the unity of Father, Son, and Holy Spirit: R. P. C. Hanson, *The Christian Doctrine of God: The Arian Controversy*, pp. 318–381.

23. Gian Piero Bognetti, "Longobardi e Romani," in *L'età longobarda*, vol. 1, pp. 91–92.

24. Paul the Deacon ii.26.

25. Ibid. ii.26.

26. Christie, "Invasion or Invitation? The Longobard Occupation of Northern Italy, AD 568–569," pp. 79–108.

27. Paul the Deacon iii.1–4, 8.

28. Paul the Deacon ii.28, 31; iii.34.

29. Christie, "Invasion or Invitation," p. 98.

30. Sestan "I longobardi," p. 78.

31. I have followed Paul the Deacon ii.28, but Annalisa Bracciotti ("Il ruolo di Peredeo nell'assassinio di Alboino," *Romanobarbarica*,13, 1994–1995: 99–123) presents a different version, based on the *Origo gentis Langobardorum*, in which Peredeo is the originator of the plot and Helmichis its executor.

32. See also Tabacco, "La storia politica e sociale," pp. 40–41, 60–62; Sestan,"I longobardi," pp. 75; 79–81.

33. Tabacco, "La storia politica e sociale," p. 63; Gasparri Gasparri, Stefano. 1984. "L'Italia meridionale contesa tra bizantini, longobardi, franchi saraceni," in Ovidio Capitani et al., *L'Italia dell'alto Medioevo* (Milano, 1984), pp. 195–197. For the *fara* see Gian Piero Bognetti, "L'influsso delle istituzioni militari romane sulle istituzioni longobarde del secolo VI e la natura della 'fara,'" in *L'età longobarda*, vol. 3 (Milano, 1966–1968), pp. 1–46.

34. Gasparri, "L' Italia meridionale," p. 196.

35. Ibid., pp. 196–197.

36. Ibid., p. 196.

37. Sestan,"I longobardi," p. 80.
38. Tabacco, "La storia politica e sociale," pp.65–66.
39. Sestan, "I longobardi," pp. 76–77.
40. Paul the Deacon iii.16.
41. Sestan, "I longobardi," p. 71.
42. Marco Balbi, *L'esercito longobardo, 568–774* (Milano, 1981), pp. 14–16.
43. Tabacco, "La storia politica e sociale," p. 63.
44. Ibid., pp. 45–56.
45. Ibid, p. 56.
46. Balbi, *L'esercito longobardo*, p. 16.
47. Tabacco, "La storia politica e sociale," pp. 68–69.
48. Ibid., pp. 69–70; Balbi, *L'esercito longobardo*, p. 18.
49. Balbi, *L'esercito longobardo*, p. 32–50.
50. For instance, see Sestan, "I longobardi," p. 79.
51. Ibid., pp. 112–117.
52. Tabacco, "La storia politica e sociale," p. 44.
53. Ibid., p.61.
54. Ibid., p. 44.
55. Sestan, "I longobardi," p. 116.

Chapter 4

1. Ian Wood, ed., *Franks and Alamanni in the Merovingian Period: An Ethnographic Perspective* (San Marino, 1998), p. 38.
2. See, among many, H. J. Hummer, "Franks and Alamanni: A Discontinuous Ethnogenesis," in Wood, *Franks and Alamanni*, pp. 11–14.
3. Ibid., p. 10.
4. Ibid., p. 13.
5. C. E. V. Nixon, "Relations between Visigoths and Romans in Fifth-Century Gaul," in John Drinkwater and Hugh Elton, eds., *Fifth-Century Gaul: A Crisis of Identity* (Cambridge University Press, 1992), pp. 73–74.
6. Hummer, "Franks and Alamanni: A Discontinuous Ethnogenesis," p. 13.
7. Ralph Whitney, *Roman Aristocrats in Barbarian Gaul: Strategies for Survival in an Age of Transition* (Austin, Texas, 1993), pp. xii–xiii.
8. Ibid., p. 145.
9. Hummer, "Franks and Alamanni: A Discontinuous Ethnogenesis," pp. 13–14; I. Wood, *The Merovingian Kingdoms* (London, 1994), pp. 33–35.
10. Wood, *The Merovingian Kingdoms,* p. 40.
11. Ibid., pp. 64–66.
12. Fredegar iv.74.
13. 200,000 *solidi* according to Fredegar iv.73.
14. Paul the Deacon iii.13.
15. Wood, *The Merovingian Kingdom*, p. 64.
16. Frank Siegmund, "Social Structure and Relations," in Wood, ed., *Franks and Alamanni*, p. 83.
17. Gregory ii.27.
18. Ibid. ii.40.

19. Ibid. ii.42.

20. Procopius vi.25. Modern experiments have shown that an axe of about 1.2 kilos (a handle of 40 centimeters and a head of 18 centimeters) would rotate one time at a distance of 4 meters, twice at 8 meters, and three times at 12 meters. The weight of the iron head could vary from a minimum of 300 grams to a maximum of 900. Philippe Contamine, "La fondation du Regnum Francorum," in André Corvisier, *Histoire militaire de la France I: Des origines à 1715* (Paris, 1992), p. 12.

21. Ibid., 12–13.

22. Agathias ii.5.

23. Contamine, "La fondation du Regnum Francorum," p. 13.

24. Ibid., p. 14.

25. Bernard S. Bachrach, *Merovingian Military Organization, 481–751* (Minneapolis, 1972), p. 124.

26. Bernard S. Bachrach, *The Anatomy of a Little War: A Diplomatic and Military History of the Gundovald Affair, 568–586* (Boulder, Colo., 1994), pp. 119–148).

27. Bachrach, *Merovingian Military Organization*, p. 124; Contamine, "La fondation du Regnum Francorum," p. 18.

28. Bachrach, *Merovingian Military Organization*, p. 125.

29. Contamine, "La fondation du Regnum Francorum," pp. 15–16.

30. Bachrach, *The Anatomy of a Little War*, pp. 119–148.

31. Agathias I.7.9.

32. Ibid. I.7.8; I.15.24.

33. Ibid. I.16.1.3.

34. Procopius VIII.26.14–17.

35. Agathias I.19.1–3.

36. On Leutharis's march, ibid. II.2.2–4; II.3.

37. Ibid. II.1.1–2.

38. On the battle, ibid. II.5–9.

39. Ibid. II.4.10; II.5.2.

40. Ibid. II.9.11–12.

41. Ibid. I.20–22.

42. Ibid. I.21.6.

43. Ibid. I.22.6–7.

44. Einhard I.1.

45. Ibid. III.22–26.

46. Ibid. II.15; IV.30.

47. Philippe Contamine, "L'espace carolingien," in André Corvisier, *Histoire militaire de la France I: Des origines à 1715* (Paris, 1992), p. 25.

48. Einhard II.9.

49. Contamine, "L'espace carolingien," in Corvisier, *Histoire militaire de la France* I, p. 23.

50. Einhard II.13.

51. Contamine, "L'espace carolingien," in Corvisier, *Histoire militaire de la France* I, pp. 25–26.

52. Einhard II.6.

53. Ibid. II.7.

54. Contamine, "L'espace carolingien," in Corvisier, *Histoire militaire de la France* I, p. 27. Also Jean François Verbruggen, "L'armée et la stratégie de Charlemagne," in Helmut Beumann et al., eds, *Karl der Grosse. Lebenswerk und Machleben*, vol 1 (Düsseldorf, 1985), pp. 420–436;

Bernard S. Bachrach, "Charlemagne and the Carolingian General Staff," *Journal of Military History* 66 (2002): 313–357.

55. Verbruggen, "L'armée et la stratégie de Charlemagne," p. 420.

56. Timothy Reuter, "Carolingian and Ottonian Warfare," in Maurice Keen, *Medieval Warfare: A History* (Oxford, 1999), pp. 25–28; Bernard S. Bachrach in K. Raaflaub and N. Rosenstein, eds., *War and Society in the Ancient and Medieval Worlds: Asia, the Mediterranean, Europe, and Mesoamerica* (Washington, 1999), pp. 287–288.

57. Verbruggen, "L'armée et la stratégie de Charlemagne," p. 426.

58. Ibid., p. 421; Contamine, "L'espace carolingien," pp. 28–29.

59. Verbruggen, "L'armée et la stratégie de Charlemagne," p. 423.

60. Bachrach in Raaflaub and Rosenstein, p. 288.

61. Ibid., pp. 283–289; Contamine, "L'espace carolingien," pp. 27–28.

62. Contamine, "L'espace carolingien," p. 28.

63. Ferdinand Lot, *L'art militaire et les armées au Moyen Age en Europe et dans le Proche Orient*, vol. 1 (Paris, 1946), p. 98.

64. Reuter, "Carolingian and Ottonian Warfare," in Keen, pp. 28, 30.

65. Bachrach in Raaflaub and Rosenstein, p. 294.

66. "Charlemagne and the Carolingian General Staff," *Journal of Military History* 66 (2002): 353.

67. Contamine, "L'espace carolingien," p. 30; Verbruggen, "L'armée et la stratégie de Charlemagne," p. 435.

68. Contamine, "L'espace carolingien," pp. 29–30.

69. Verbruggen, "L'armée et la stratégie de Charlemagne," pp. 428–429.

70. Contamine, "L'espace carolingien," p. 28.

71. Bachrach in Raaflaub and Rosenstein, p. 283.

72. Verbruggen, "L'armée et la stratégie de Charlemagne," pp. 420–421; Contamine, "L'espace carolingien," p. 31.

73. Verbruggen, "L'armée et la stratégie de Charlemagne," p. 424.

74. Contamine, "L'espace carolingien," p. 31. On Carolingian weapons see also Simon Copeland, "Carolingian Arms and Armor in the Ninth Century" *Viator* 21 (1990): 29–50.

75. See Bachrach, on Charles Martel's and Charlemagne cavalry, in *Armies and Politics in the Early Medieval West* (Great Yarmouth, Norfolk, 1993).

76. Contamine, *War in the Middle Ages*, pp. 183–184.

77. Verbruggen, "L'armée et la stratégie de Charlemagne," p. 436.

78. Ibid., pp. 431, 433.

79. Ibid., p. 433.

80. Ibid., p. 434.

81. Ibid., pp. 433–436.

82. Contamine, "L'espace carolingien," pp. 23–24.

83. On this and what follows see Roger Collins, *Charlemagne* (Toronto, 1998), pp. 141–159; and Robert Folz, *The Coronation of Charlemagne 5 December 1970*, trans. J. E. Anderson (London, 1974), pp. 234–244.

84. Folz, *The Coronation of Charlemagne*, pp. 144–150. The act of proskynesis is at the year 801 of the *Annals*.

85. Einhard II.28.

86. Folz, *The Coronation of Charlemagne*, p. 145.

87. Ibid., pp. 132–150.

88. Wilfried Hartmann, "L'incoronazione dell imperatore il 25 dicembre 800," in G. Alteri, et al., *Carlo Magno a Roma*. Catalogo (Roma, 2001), p. 61.

Chapter 5

1. Quoted in Muhammad Hamidullah, *The Battlefields of the Prophet Muhammad* (Hyderabad, 1973), p. 19.

2. Kurt Raaflaub and Nathan Rosenstein, eds., *War and Society in the Ancient and Medieval Worlds: Asia, the Mediterranean, Europe, and Mesoamerica* (Washington, 1999), p. 309.

3. Patricia Crone, *Slaves on Horses: The Evolution of the Islamic Polity* (Cambridge, 1980), p. 18.

4. Aikaterina Christophilopoulou, *Byzantine History*, vol. 2, trans. Timothy Cullen (Amsterdam, 1993), pp. 31–33.

5. Fred McGraw Donner, *The Early Islamic Conquests* (Princeton, 1981), p. 12.

6. Ibid., p. 20.

7. Ibid., pp. 11–20.

8. Ibid., pp. 16–18.

9. Crone, *Slaves*, pp. 22–26.

10. Donner, *Early Islamic Conquests*, pp. 52–53.

11. Ibid., pp. 55–62.

12. Ibid., pp. 75–82.

13. Ella Landau-Tasseron, "Features of the Pre-Conquest Muslim Armies in the Time of Muhammad," in Averil Cameron, ed., *The Byzantine and Early Islamic Near East* (Princeton, NJ, 1995), pp. 299–316.

14. Ibid., pp. 299–316.

15. Ibid., p. 331.

16. Ibid., p. 314.

17. Muhammad Hamidullah, *Le Prophète de l'Islam*, vol. 1 (Paris, 1959), p. 162.

18. Landau-Tasseron, p. 316.

19. Ibid., pp. 324–330.

20. Ibid., pp. 330–334.

21. Hamidullah, *Le Prophète de l'Islam*, vol. 2, pp. 636–637.

22. Ibid., vol. 2, pp. 636–637.

23. Ibid., vol. 2, p. 638.

24. Ibid., vol. 2 pp. 635–638.

25. Ibid., vol. 2, pp. 635–640.

26. Analysis of battle based on the information contained in William Muir, *The Life of Mohammad* (Edinburgh, 1923), pp. 214–237; Hamidullah, *Le Prophète de l'Islam*, vol. 1, pp. 144–150; and especially Hamidullah, *Battlefields of the Prophet Muhammad*, pp. 13–21.

27. Muir, *The Life of Muhammad*, p. 221.

28. Ibid., p. 216.

29. Ibid., p. 221.

30. Ibid., p. 221.

31. Hamidullah, *Le Prophète de l'Islam*, vol. 1, pp. 144–146.

Chapter 6

1. Leone Caetani, *Studi di Storia Orientale*, vol. 1 (Milano 1911), pp. 133–138, 369–371; Donner, "Centralization," pp. 341–343.

2. J. Koren and Y. Nevo, "Methodological Approaches to Islamic Studies," *Der Islam* 68 (1991): 87–101.

3. Frank McGraw Donner, "Centralized Authority and Military Autonomy in the Early Islamic Conquests," in A. Cameron, ed., *The Byzantine and Early Islamic Near East* (Princeton, N.J., 1995), pp. 337–360.

4. Donner, *Early Islamic Conquests*, pp. 267–271.

5. Ibid., pp. 96–98.

6. Kaegi, Walter Emil Jr., *Byzantium and the Early Islamic Conquests* (Cambridge, 1992), pp. 29–30.

7. Ibid., pp. 45–46.

8. Benjamin Isaac, "The Army in the Late Roman East: The Persian Wars and the Defence of the Byzantine Empire," in Cameron, *The Byzantine and Early Islamic Near East*, pp. 125–156, 150–151.

9. Donner, *Early Islamic Conquests*, pp. 111–119.

10. Kaegi, *Byzantium and the Early Islamic Conquests*, p. 58.

11. Ibid., pp. 93–95.

12. Ibid., p. 90.

13. Donner, *Early Islamic Conquests*, pp. 117–118.

14. Ibid., pp. 119–127.

15. Donner, *Early Islamic Conquests*, pp. 126–127, and Donner, "Centralized Authority."

16. The topographical view of the terrain is based on the lucid analysis provided by Leone Caetani, *Studi di Storia Orientale*, vol. 3 (Milano, 1910), pp. 508–539.

17. John W. Jandora, "The Battle of the Yarmûk: A Reconstruction," *Journal of Asian Studies* 19 (1985): 13.

18. Caetani, *Studi di Storia Orientale*, vol. 3, p. 600.

19. The wadi is an irregular course of water the strength of which depends on the seasons.

20. Ibid., pp. 514–515.

21. Kaegi, *Byzantium and the Early Islamic Conquests*, p. 132.

22. Jandora, "The Battle of the Yarmûk," pp. 13–16.

23. Alfred Morabia, "Recherches sur quelques noms de couleur en arabe classique," *Studia Islamica* 21 (1964): 98.

24. Kaegi, *Byzantium and the Early Islamic Conquests*, pp. 126–127.

25. Ibid., p. 174.

26. Ibid., p. 140.

27. Ibid., p. 145.

28. See Whitby on "recruitment" in Cameron, *The Byzantine and Early Islamic Near East*, p. 121.

29. W. Treadgold, *Byzantium and Its Army* (Stanford, Cal., 1995), pp. 206–219.

30. Donner, *Early Islamic Conquests*, pp. 157–173.

31. 'Abd Al-Husain Zarrinkûb, "The Arab Conquest of Iran and Its Aftermath," in R. N. Frye, ed., *The Cambridge History of Iran,* vol. 4 (Cambridge, 1975), pp. 1–56.

32. Donner, *Early Islamic Conquests*, p. 173.

33. *The History of al-Tabarî, p.* 2228.

34. Zarrinkûb, "The Arab Conquest of Iran and Its Aftermath," pp. 8–9.

35. Donner, *Early Islamic Conquests*, pp. 205–209.

36. Zarrinkûb, "The Arab Conquest of Iran and Its Aftermath," p. 10.

37. Donner, *Early Islamic Conquests*, p. 221.

38. Zarrinkûb, "The Arab Conquest of Iran and Its Aftermath," p. 10.

39. Donner, *Early Islamic Conquests*, p. 205.

40. Zarrinkûb, "The Arab Conquest of Iran and Its Aftermath," p. 10.

41. Ibid., pp. 10–11.

42. *The History of Al-Tabarî*, p. 2288.

43. Ibid., p. 2293.

44. Ibid., p. 2295.

45. Ibid., p. 2287.

46. Ibid., p. 2309.

47. Ibid., p. 2286–2303.

48. Ibid., p. 2309.

49. Ibid., p. 2312.

50. Ibid., p. 2319.

51. Ibid., p. 2320.

52. Ibid., p. 2336–2337.

53. Zarrinkub, "The Arab Conquest of Iran and Its Aftermath," pp. 11–12.

54. Ibid., p. 25.

55. On *topoi* see Albrecht Noth, *The Early Arabic Historical Tradition. A Source-Critical Study*, 2nd ed. (Princeton, N.J., 1994).

56. Hugh Kennedy, *The Armies of the Caliphs: Military and Society in the Early Islamic State* (London, 2001), p. 4.

57. D. B. Hill, "The Role of the Camel and the Horse in the Early Arab Conquests," in V. J. Parry and M. E. Yapp, eds., *War, Technology, and Society in the Middle East* (Oxford, 1975), p. 42.

58. Ibid., pp. 42.

59. Ibid., pp. 41–42.

60. Donner, *Early Islamic Conquests*, p. 222.

61. Whitby, pp. 123–124.

62. Donner, *Early Islamic Conquests*, pp. 223–224.

63. Ibid., p. 234.

64. On banners and battlecries, see Martin Hinds, "The Banners and Battle Cries of the Arabs at Siffin, A.D. 657," in M. Hinds, *Studies in Early Islamic History* (Princeton, N.J., 1996), pp. 97–142.

65. Kennedy, *The Armies of the Caliphs*, pp. 168–182.

66. Ibid., pp. 175–178.

67. Ibid., pp. 168–171.

68. Ibid., pp. 171–173.

69. Claude Cahen, "Les changement techniques militaires dans le Proche Orient médieval et leur importance historique," in Parry and Yapp, eds., *War, Technology, and Society in the Middle East*, pp. 114–115.

70. Donner, *Early Islamic Conquests*, p. 231.

71. Raaflaub, pp. 311–312.

72. Kennedy, in Cameron, *The Byzantine and Early Islamic Near East*, pp. 361–378.

73. Kennedy, *The Armies of the Caliphs*, pp. 4–5.

74. Raaflaub, pp. 314–318.

75. Christophilopoulou, *Byzantine History*, vol. 2, pp. 44–45.

Chapter 7

1. This portrayal of the Berbers is based mainly on three sources: Al-Bakrâ (1068), Ibn Battûta (fourteenth century), and James Richardson (1845–1846).

2. Jamil M. Abun-Nasr, *A History of the Maghrib* (Cambridge, 1971), pp. 6–8.

3. Ibid., pp.2–3.

4. 'Abdulwâhid Dhanîn Tâha, *The Muslim Conquest and Settlement of North Africa and Spain* (London, 1989), p. 55., thinks instead that the conqueror of Egypt realized from the very beginning that the control of the coast was necessary to safeguard supremacy in Egypt.

5. Pedro Chalmeta, *Invasión e Islamización* (Madrid, 1994), pp. 76–77.

6. Ibid., pp. 80–82; Tâha, *The Muslim Conquest and Settlement of North Africa and Spain*, pp. 56–58.

7. Chalmeta, *Invasión e Islamización*, pp. 81–83; Tâha, *The Muslim Conquest and Settlement of North Africa and Spain*, pp. 58–60.

8. Chalmeta, *Invasión e Islamización*, pp. 83–85; Tâha, *The Muslim Conquest and Settlement of North Africa and Spain*, pp. 58–62.

9. Chalmeta, *Invasión e Islamización*, pp. 85–86.

10. Ibid., pp. 83–85; Tâha, *The Muslim Conquest and Settlement of North Africa and Spain*, pp. 58–62.

11. H. T. Norris, *The Berbers in Arabic Literature* (London, 1982), pp. 47–48.

12. Robert Brunschvig as quoted in Norris, *The Berbers in Arabic Literature*, p. 48.

13. Chalmeta, *Invasión e Islamización*, pp. 86–87; Tâha, *The Muslim Conquest and Settlement of North Africa and Spain*, pp. 65–66.

14. Tâha, *The Muslim Conquest and Settlement of North Africa and Spain*, pp. 68–69.

15. Ibid., p. 71; Norris, *Berbers in Arabic Literature*, pp. 49–52.

16. Norris, *Berbers in Arabic Literature*, p. 52.

17. Ibid., p. 51.

18. Ibid., pp. 52–53.

19. Tâha, *The Muslim Conquest and Settlement of North Africa and Spain*, p. 71; Chalmeta, *Invasión e Islamización*, p. 91.

20. Tâha, *The Muslim Conquest and Settlement of North Africa and Spain*, pp. 71–72.

21. Ibid., pp. 73–76.

22. E. A.Thompson, *Romans and Barbarians: The Decline of the Western Empire* (Madison, Wisc., 1982), pp. 156, 158, 159.

23. Ibid., p. 164.

24. Chalmeta, *Invasión e Islamización*, p. 72.

25. Ibid., pp. 67–94.

26. Ibid., pp. 68–69.

27. Ibid., pp. 70–71.

28. Ibid., p. 71.

29. Ibid., pp. 71–72.

30. Ibid., p. 123.

31. Ibid., pp. 121–129.

32. Quoted in Ibid., p. 133.

33. Ibid., pp. 132.

34. Ibid., pp. 134–137.

35. Ibid., pp. 142–144.

36. Ibid., pp. 142–144.

37. Ibid., pp. 151–152.

38. Ibid., p. 170.

39. Tâha, *The Muslim Conquest and Settlement of North Africa and Spain*, p. 95.

40. Tâha, *The Muslim Conquest and Settlement of North Africa and Spain*, p. 98; Chalmeta, *Invasión e Islamización*, pp. 180–181.

41. Tâha, *The Muslim Conquest and Settlement of North Africa and Spain*, pp. 101–102.

42. Roger Collins, *The Arab Conquest of Spain* (London, 1989), p. 87

43. Tâha, *The Muslim Conquest and Settlement of North Africa and Spain*, p. 190.

44. See E. Creasy, *The Fifteen Decisive Battles of the World* (London, 1874).

45. Philip K. Hitti, *History of the Arabs from the Earliest Times to the Present* (London, 1964), p. 501.

46. Ibid., pp. 500–501; Bernard S. Bachrach, *Early Carolingian Warfare: Prelude to Empire* (Philadelphia, 2001), pp. 26–32, 94–95, 170–177, 182–184, 187–190.

47. Tâha, *The Muslim Conquest and Settlement of North Africa and Spain*, p. 106.

48. Hitti, *History of the Arabs from the Earliest Times to the Present*, p. 168.

49. Ibid., p. 167.

50. Ibid., pp. 602–605.

Chapter 8

1. R. H. C. Davis, "The Warhorses of the Normans," *Anglo-Norman Studies: Proceedings of the Battle Conference* 10 (1987), p. 68.

2. Ibid., p. 69.

3. Ibid., pp. 71–72.

4. Ibid., pp. 71–80; Andrew Ayton, "Arms, Armour, and Horses," in Keen, *Medieval Warfare*, pp. 186–208.

5. Ayton, "Arms, Armour, and Horses," in Keen, *Medieval Warfare*, pp. 191–192.

6. Ibid., p. 191.

7. Davis, "The Warhorses of the Normans," pp. 79–80.

8. Kelly DeVries, *Medieval Military Technology* (Peterborough, Ontario, 1992), pp. 45–48.

9. Ibid., p. 13.

10. Ian Peirce, "Arms, Armour, and Warfare in the Eleventh Century," *Anglo-Norman Studies: Proceedings of the Battle Conference* 10 (1987), p. 244.

11. Ibid., pp. 244–245.

12. Leonid Tarassuk and Claude Blair, *The Complete Encyclopedia of Arms and Weapons* (New York, 1979), pp. 307–309.

13. Ibid., p. 309; R. H. C. Davis, *The Medieval Warhorse* (London, 1989), pp. 19–22.

14. DeVries, *Medieval Military Technology*, p. 15; Tarassuk and Blair, *The Complete Encyclopedia of Arms and Weapons*, p. 309.

15. On this see the clear summary of the debate in DeVries, *Medieval Military Technology*, pp. 95–100.

16. Bernard S. Bachrach, "Charles Martel, Mounted Shock Combat, the Stirrup, and Feudalism," *Studies in Medieval and Renaissance History* 7 (1970): 47–75.

17. Tarassuk and Blair, *The Complete Encyclopedia of Arms and Weapons*, p. 471.

18. Ewart Oakeshott, *A Knight and His Weapons* (Chester Springs, Penn., 1997), pp. 58–60.

19. Peirce, "Arms, Armour, and Warfare in the Eleventh Century," p. 250.

20. Ibid., p. 267; DeVries, *Medieval Military Technology*, p. 24.

21. Tarassuk and Blair, *The Complete Encyclopedia of Arms and Weapons*, pp. 471–472.

22. Oakeshott, *A Knight and His Weapons*, pp. 80–81.

23. DeVries, *Medieval Military Technology*, pp. 19–20.

24. Oakeshot, *A Knight and His Weapons*, pp. 48–49.

25. Ibid., pp. 27–29.

26. Ibid., pp. 25–27.

27. DeVries, *Medieval Military Technology*, p. 44.

28. Ibid., p. 44.

29. Tarassuk and Blair, *The Complete Encyclopedia of Arms and Weapons*, p. 145.

30. See Ian Peirce, "The Knight, His Arms and Armour, c. 1150–1250," *Anglo-Norman Studies* 15 (1992): plates 8, 9.

31. Tarassuk and Clair, *The Complete Encyclopedia of Arms and Weapons*, p. 259.

32. Peirce, "The Knight, His Arms and Armour, c. 1150–1250," p. 252.

33. Tarassuk and Clair, *The Complete Encyclopedia of Arms and Weapons*, p. 253.

34. Peirce, "The Knight, His Arms and Armour, c. 1150–1250," p. 256.

35. Tarassuk and Blair, *The Complete Encyclopedia of Arms and Weapons*, pp. 23–24.

Chapter 9

1. Peter Sawyer, "The Age of the Vikings, and Before," in Peter Sawyer, *The Oxford Illustrated History of the Vikings* (Oxford, 1997), p. 2.

2. John Haywood, *The Penguin Historical Atlas of the Vikings* (London, 1995), p. 8.

3. Jordanes IV.

4. Sawyer, "The Age of the Vikings, and Before," pp. 2–3.

5. Haywood, *Penguin Historical Atlas of the Vikings*, p. 10.

6. Sawyer, "The Age of the Vikings, and Before," pp. 8–11.

7. Ibid., pp. 12–13.

8. Quoted in Simon Keynes, "The Vikings in England, c. 790–1016," in Sawyer, *Oxford Illustrated History of the Vikings*, pp. 73–81.

9. Régis Boyer, "Les Vikings des guerriers ou des commerçants," in Régis Boyer, *Les Vikings et leur civilisations. Problèmes actuels* (Paris, 1976), pp. 211–240.

10. H. B. Clarke, "The Vikings," in Maurice Keen, ed., *Medieval Warfare: A History* (Oxford, 1999), pp. 40–41.

11. Preben Meulengracht Sørensen, "Religions Old and New," in Sawyer, *Oxford Illustrated History of the Vikings*, pp. 202–224.

12. Clarke, "The Vikings," in Keen, *Medieval Warfare*, p. 42.

13. Paddy Griffith, *The Viking Art of War* (London, 1995), pp. 142–143.

14. Ibid., pp. 162–181.

15. Pál Engel, *The Realm of St. Stephen: A History of Medieval Hungary, 895–1526*, trans. Andrew Ayton.(London, 2001), pp. 1–7; Pàl Liptàk, *Avars and the Ancient Hungarians* (Budapest, 1983), pp. 155–162.

16. Barta et al., *A History of Hungary*, p. 17.

17. Lipták, *Avars and the Ancient Hungarians*, p. 161.

18. Barta et al., *A History of Hungary*, p. 25.

19. Ibid., p. 22.

20. Ibid., p. 24.

21. Engel, *The Realm of St. Stephen*, pp. 10–12.

22. *Chronicon Ebenspengense*, quoted in Contamine, *War in the Middle Ages*, p. 34.

23. *Chronica* by Otto of Freising, quoted in Contamine, *War in the Middle Ages*, p. 33.

24. Gina Fasoli, *Le incursioni ungare in Europa nel secolo x* (Firenze, 1945), pp. 54–55.

25. Liutprand of Cremora I.13.

26. *Vita S. Deicoli*, quoted in Fasoli, *Le incursioni ungare in Europa nel secolo x*, p. 56.

27. Fasoli, *Le incursioni ungare in Europa nel secolo x*, p. 56.

28. Ibid., p. 57.

29. Ibid., p. 59.

30. Engel, *The Realm of St. Stephen*, pp. 13–14.

31. Fasoli, *Le incursioni ungare in Europa nel secolo x*, p. 71.

32. Engel, *The Realm of St. Stephen*, p. 16.

33. Fasoli, *Le incursioni ungare in Europa nel secolo x*, p. 62.

34. Contamine, *War in the Middle Ages*, pp. 33–34.

35. Fasoli, *Le incursioni ungare in Europa nel secolo x*, p. 66.

36. Ibid., pp. 66–67.

37. Ibid., p. 155.

38. Ibid., pp. 156–157.

39. Ibid., pp. 157–159.

40. Ibid., pp. 160–161.

41. Karl Leyser, "The Battle of the Lech, 955: A Study in Tenth-Century Warfare," *Historia* 50 (1965): 15–16.

42. Ibid., p. 17.

43. For the battle, see ibid., pp. 1–25; Fasoli, *Le incursioni bulgare*, pp. 202–212; Hans Delbrück, *History of the Art of War, vol. 3: The Middle Ages*, trans. W. J. Renfroe Jr. (Westport, Conn., 1982), pp. 115–129.

44. Leyser, "The Battle of the Lech," p. 14.

45. Ibid., p. 17.

46. Ibid., p. 18.

47. Ibid., pp. 18–19.

48. Fasoli, *Le incursioni ungare in Europa nel secolo x*, pp. 208–209.

Chapter 10

1. Anglo-Saxon Chronicle E 1066.

2. This account of the crossing is based mainly on Christine and George Crainge, "The Pevensey Expedition: Brilliantly Executed Plan or Near Disaster?" *Mariner Mirror* 79 (1993): 261–273. But see also the articles by C. M. Gilmor, "Naval Logistics of the Cross-Channel Operation, 1066," *Anglo-Norman Studies* 7 (1984): 105–131, and J. Gillingham, "William the Bastard at War," in C. Harper Bill, ed., *Studies in Medieval History Presented to R. Allen Brown* (Woodbridge, 1989), pp. 141–158. All three articles are reprinted in Stephen Morillo, ed., *The Battle of Hastings: Sources and Interpretations* (Rochester, N.Y., 1996).

3. Crainge, "The Pevensey Expedition," pp. 137–138.

4. Ibid., pp. 139–140.

5. On this see J. Gillingham, "William the Bastard at War," in Bill, ed., *Studies in Medieval History*, pp. 141–158.

6. Nicholas Hooper, "The Housecarls in England in the Eleventh Century," *Anglo Norman Studies* 7 (1984), p. 175.

7. Richard Abels, "Bookland and Fyrd Service in Late Saxon England," *Anglo-Norman Studies* 7 (1984).

8. Hooper, "The Housecarls in England in the Eleventh Century," 175.

9. *Rectitudines Singularum Personarum,* quoted in Abels, p. 60.

10. Abels in Morillo, *The Battle of Hastings,* p. 74.

11. On how a lance could be used see Contamine, *War in the Middle Ages*, p. 184.

12. Ian Peirce, "Arms, Armour, and Warfare in the Eleventh Century," *Anglo-Saxon Studies* 10 (1987), pp. 237–257.

13. Marjorie Chibnall, "Military Service in Normandy before 1066," *Anglo-Norman Studies* 5 (1982), pp. 65–77.

14. R. Allen Brown, "The Battle of Hastings" *Anglo-Norman Studies: Proceedings of the Battle Conference* 3 (1980), pp. 1–21.

15. My reconstruction of the campaign and battle is based mainly on William of Poitiers, the Anglo-Saxon Chronicle, and the Bayeux Tapestry, which together with the other primary sources are listed in the very useful S. Morillo, ed., *The Battle of Hastings: Sources and Interpretations* (Woodbridge, Suffolk 1996), pp. 3–53. My main secondary sources have been Morillo's introductory comments in ibid., pp. xxii–xxxii, R. Allen Brown, "The Battle of Hastings," *Anglo-Norman Studies: Proceedings of the Battle Conference* 3 (1980), pp. 1–2; Stephen Morillo, "Hastings: An Unusual Battle," *Haskins Society Journal* 2 (1990) pp. 95–104; Bernard S. Bachrach, "The Feigned Retreat at Hastings," *Medieval Studies* 33 (1971), pp. 344–347. All of these articles are contained in Morillo, ed., *The Battle of Hastings*. On normal warfare, besides Morillo's bookn very useful is also Matthew Strickland, ed., *Anglo-Norman Warfare* (Woodbridge, Suffolk, 1992).

16. Morillo, *The Battle of Hastings*, p. 234.

17. Florence of Worcster, *Chronicon ex Chronicis.*

18. So says William of Poitiers, *Gesta Willelmi.*

Chapter 11

1. Contamine, *War in the Middle Ages*, pp. 44–46.

2. Ibid., p. 109.

3. John France, *Western Warfare in the Age of the Crusadesn 1000–1300* (Ithaca, N.Y., 1999), p. 107.

4. Ibid., p. 79.

5. Contamine, *War in the Middle Ages*, pp. 46–47.

6. Philip Warner, *Sieges of the Middle Ages* (London, 1968), p. 11.

7. Contamine, *War in the Middle Ages*, p. 113.

8. France, *Western Warfare in the Age of the Crusadesn 1000–1300*, pp. 89–90.

9. Contamine, *War in the Middle Ages*, p. 114.

10. Warner, *Sieges of the Middle Ages*, p. 12.

11. Jim Bradbury, *The Medieval Siege* (Woodbridge, 1992), pp. 259–270.

12. Paul E. Chevedden in Donald J. Kagay and L. J. Andrew Villalon, eds., *The Circle of War in the Middle Ages: Essays on Medieval Military and Naval History* (Woodbridge, Suffolk, 1999), p. 36.

13. Ibid., p. 36.

14. Ibid., pp. 37–38, 43.

15. Bradbury, *The Medieval Siege*, pp. 252–254.

16. Warner, *Sieges of the Middle Ages*, pp. 29–30.

17. Ibid., p. 30; Bradbury, *The Medieval Siege*, pp. 150–251.

18. H. W. Koch, *Medieval Warfare* (London, 1978), pp. 45–55.

Chapter 12

1. M. Fischer and W. Pedrotti, *Le cittia Italiane and medioevo* (Colognola ai Colli, 1977), pp. 14–15.

2. Franco Cardini, *Quell'antica festa crudele. Guerra e cultura della guerra dall'età feudale alla grande revoluzione* (Firenze, 1982), p. 13.

3. Most of the definition based on an interview with Georges Duby, "Un modèle de perfection virile," *Les collections de l'Histoire. L'aventure des chevaliers* (March 2001): 8–11.

4. Ibid., p. 8.

5. Jean Flori, "Encore l'usage de la lance . . . La technique du combat chevaleresque vers l'an 1100," *Cahiers de civilisation médiévale* 31 (1988): 213–240.

6. This is the view put forward by Georges Duby in many of his writings.

7. Jean Flori, *La cavalleria medievale* (Bologna, 2002), pp. 8–10.

8. Ibid., p. 27.

9. Georges Duby, *La société au XIe et XII siècles dans la région mâconnaise* (Paris, 1953).

10. Georges Duby, *William Marshal the Flower of Chivalry*, trans. Richard Howard (New York, 1985).

11. R. Fossier, *Enfance de l'Europe Xe-XIIe siècles*, vol. 2 (Paris, 1982), p. 971.

12. Dominique Barthélemy, "Le pillage, la vengeance et la guerre," *Les Collections de l'Histoire. L'aventure des chevaliers*: 38–43.

13. Jean François Verbruggen, *The Art of Warfare in Western Europe During the Middle Ages from the Eighth Century to 1340* (New York, 1977), pp. 59–60.

14. Ibid., p. 30.

15. Contamine in Corvisier, *Histoire militaire de la France* I, pp. 89, 93.

16. On the different interpretations of their origins see the summary in ibid., pp. 90–91.

17. Ibid., p. 89.

18. Ibid., p. 100.

19. Ibid., pp. 91–92.

20. On this see also France, *Western Warfare in the Age of the Crusades, 1000–1300*, pp. 53–63.

21. Patrick Boucheron, "Au service du seigneur," *Les Collections de l'Histoire. L'aventure des chevaliers*: 16.

22. Verbruggen, *The Art of Warfare in Western Europe*, pp. 26–27.

23. Flori, *La cavalleria medievale*, p. 30.

24. Philippe Contamine, *La noblesse au royaume de France de Philip le Bel à Louis XII* (Paris, 1997), p. 280.

25. Duby, "Un modèle de perfection virile," *Les collections de l'Histoire. L'aventure des chevaliers*, p. 9.

26. Flori, *La cavalleria medievale*, p. 84.

27. *Gesta Francorum* c. 9 quoted in Verbruggen, *The Art of Warfare in Western Europe*, p. 53.

28. *Chanson d'Antioche* vv. 927–931 and 461–462, quoted in ibid., p. 53.

29. Fulcher of Chartres, *Historia Hierosolymitana* 3:468 in ibid., p. 54.

30. Flori, *La cavalleria medievale*, p. 127.

31. On what follows Michel Pastoureau, "Aux origines des armoiries," *Les Collections de l'Histoire. L'aventure des chevaliers*: 44–45.

32. Koch, *Medieval Warfare*, p. 117.

33. Ibid., pp. 120–121.

34. For an interesting survey of the topic, see Alessandra Perriccioli Saggese, *I romanzi cavallereschi miniati a Napoli* (Napoli, 1979).

35. The following comments mainly based on François Suard, " Les héros de la chanson de geste," in *Les Collections de l'Histoire. L'aventure des chevaliers*: 70–71.

36. Ibid., pp. 39–52.

37. Fulcher of Chartres, *Historia Hierosolymitana*, 3:335 and 375, quoted in ibid., p. 43.

38. Both examples in R. de Clari, *La conquête de Constantinople*, c. 66 quoted in ibid., p. 44.

39. Verbruugen, *The Art of Warfare in Western Europe*, p. 81.

40. Ibid., pp. 82–83.
41. The story is in Ibn al-Athir quoted in ibid., pp. 86–87.
42. Ibid., p. 85.
43. Ibid., pp. 170, 178.
44. Ibid, p. 95.
45. William of Malmesbury on Duke William.
46. Verbruggen, *The Art of Warfare in Western Europe*, p. 75; Contamine, *War in the Middle Ages*, pp. 229–230.
47. Contamine, *War in the Middle Ages*, p. 229.
48. Ibid., p. 230.
49. Ibid., p. 230.
50. Verbruggen, *The Art of Warfare in Western Europe*, pp. 96–97.
51. Contamine, *War in the Middle Ages*, pp. 230–231.

Chapter 13

1. Verbruggen, *The Art of Warfare in Western Europe*, p. 196.
2. Ibid., p. 145.
3. Riccardo Semplici, ed., *La battaglia di Campaldino a Poppi, 11 giugno 1289* (Firenze, 1998), p. 41.
4. Verbruggen, *The Art of Warfare in Western Europe*, pp. 141–142.
5. Ibid., p. 142.
6. Ibid., p. 196.
7. Ibid., p. 194.
8. Ibid.
9. Ibid., p. 148–149.
10. Contamine, *War in the Middle Ages*, pp. 35–36.
11. Otto of Freising II.13.
12. Ibid. IV.36.
13. Contamine, *War in the Middle Ages*, p. 36.
14. Otto of Freising II.12.
15. Lambert von Hersfeld, *Annales*, quoted in Contamine, *War in the Middle Ages*, p. 36.
16. Ibid., p. 37.
17. On this and what follows see Daniel Waley, *The Italian City-Republics*, 3rd ed. (London, 1988), pp. 53–54.
18. Ibid., p. 53.
19. Ibid., pp. 53–54.
20. Ibid., pp. 97–101.
21. Ibid., pp. 101–102.
22. For this and what follows see Giorgio d'Ilario et al., *Legnano e la battaglia* (Legnano, 1976).
23. The account based mainly on details in Verbruggen, *The Art of Warfare in Western Europe*, pp. 166–173; K. De Vries, *Infantry Warfare in the Early Fourteenth Century* (Woodbridge, Suffolk, 2000), pp. 9–22; and Lot, *L'art militaire et les armées au Moyen Age*, vol. 1, pp. 250–264.
24. The figure is taken from the text of the act of surrender by the castellan on 13 July 1302 in Lot, *L'art militaire et les armées au Moyen Age*, vol. 1, pp. 262–263.
25. De Vries, *Infantry Warfare*, pp. 12–14.
26. Lot, *L'art militaire et les armées au Moyen Age*, vol. 1, p. 255.

27. Ibid., vol. 1, pp. 203–204.

28. Giovanni Villani, "Istorie Fiorentine," in L. Muratori, ed., *Scriptores rerum italicarum* (Rome, 1728), vol. 13, i, c. 338.

29. Lot, in *L'art militaire et les armées au Moyen Age*, vol. I, p. 261, says 500 meters.

30. This on the basis of map in Verbruggen, *The Art of Warfare in Western Europe*, p. 167.

31. De Vries, *Infantry Warfare*, p. 15.

32. From *Branches des royaux lignages*, in Delbrück, *History of the Art of War*, vol. 3, pp. 437–438.

33. Lot, *L'art militaire et les armées au Moyen Age*, vol. I, p. 260.

34. Ibid., vol. 1, p. 260.

35. De Vries, *Infantry Warfare*, p. 10.

36. Verbruggen, *The Art of Warfare in Western Europe*, p. 173.

37. Georges Duby, *The Legend of Bouvines: War, Religion, and Culture in the Middle Ages*, trans. Catherine Tihanyi (Cambridge, 1990), p. 110.

38. Ibid., pp. 112–113.

39. Ibid., p. 20.

40. Ibid., p. 19, on the basis of of Verbruggen's calculations.

41. Ibid., p. 25.

42. Ibid., p. 26.

43. Verbruggen, *The Art of Warfare in Western Europe*, p. 223.

44. William the Breton's text is available in an English translation in Duby, *The Legend of Bouvines*, pp. 36–54.

45. Verbruggen, *The Art of Warfare in Western Europe*, pp. 223–229.

46. From the *Ursperg Chronicle* as quoted in Duby, *The Legend of Bouvines*, p. 27.

47. Verbruggen, *The Art of Warfare in Western Europe*, p. 228.

48. Ibid., pp. 228–229.

49. This interpretation differs from Verbruggen, *The Art of Warfare in Western Europe*, whose map (fig. 4, p. 221) shows the French facing east and Otto's troops west.

Chapter 14

1. Verbruggen, *The Art of Warfare in Western Europe*, pp. 207–208.

2. August C. Krey, ed., *The First Crusade: The Account of Eye-Witnesses and Participants* (Gloucester, Mass., 1958), pp. 163–193.

3. Robert C. Stacey, "The Age of Chivalry," in Michael Howard et al., eds., *The Laws of War: Constraints on Warfare in the Western World* (New Haven, Conn., 1994), pp. 31–32.

4. Ibid., pp. 27–39.

5. Ibid., p. 38.

6. Ibid., pp. 38–39.

7. Ibid., pp. 34–36.

8. Ibid., pp. 28, 32–34.

9. Jean Flori, *Les croisades. Origines, réalisations, institutions, déviations* (Paris, 2001), p. 10.

10. Ibid., p. 14.

11. Ibid., p. 24.

12. So the Jewish chronicler Salomon bar Simson in Elizabeth Hallam, ed., *Chronicles of the Crusades: Eye-Witness Accounts of the Wars between Christianity and Islam* (London, 1989), p. 69; also Flori, *Les croisades*, pp. 28–29.

13. Anna Comnena, *Alexiad*, as quoted in Hallam, *Chronicles*, p. 58.

14. Flori, *Les croisades*, pp. 26–59.

15. This partially on the basis of Hitti, *History of the Arabs*, pp. 636–637, with a slight change in the dates.

16. Ibid., pp. 636–637.

17. Flori, *Les croisades*, pp. 71–72.

18. Ibid., p. 72.

19. On all this see ibid., pp. 71–74.

20. Albert of Aachen, *Historia Hierosolymitana* in Hallam, *Chronicles* p. 74.

21. Amin Maalouf, *Le crociate viste dagli Arabi* (Torino, 1989), pp. 34–35.

22. Ibn al-Athîr, in Francesco Gabrieli, ed., *Arab Historians of the Crusades Selected and Translated from Arabic Sources* (London, 1969), p. 9.

23. Krey, *The First Crusade*, p. 173.

24. Al-Athîr in Gabrieli, *Arab Historians*, p. 7.

25. Al-Athîr in ibid., p. 8.

26. Verbruggen, *The Art of Warfare in Western Europe*, p. 205.

27. Al-Athîr in Gabrieli, *Arab Historians*, p. 8.

28. Guibert of Nogent, *Historia Hierosolymitana* in Hallam, *Chronicles*, p. 85.

29. Maalouf, *Le crociate viste dagli Arabi*, pp. 53–56.

30. Contamine, *War in the Middle Ages*, p. 61.

31. France, *Western Warfare in the Age of the Crusades, 1000–1300*, p. 212.

32. See ibid.; and R. C. Smail, *Crusading Warfare, 1097–1193* (Cambridge, 1995).

33. Charles R. Bowlus, in Michel Balard, ed., *Autour de la Première Croisade. Actes du Colloque de la Society for the Study of the Crusades and the Latin East*. Clermont-Ferrand, 22–25 Juin 1995 (Paris, 1996), pp. 160–161.

34. Ibid., pp. 163–165.

35. Quoted in ibid., p. 165.

36. France, *Western Warfare in the Age of the Crusades 1000–1300*, p. 208.

37. Ibid., p. 210.

38. Contamine, *War in the Middle Ages*, pp. 62, 64.

39. On the orders see as an introduction Flori, *Les croisades*, pp. 81–83; Alan Forey, *The Fall of the Templars in the Crown of Aragon* (Aldershot, 2001), pp. 184–216.

40. Flori, *Les croisades*, p. 82.

41. Forey, *The Fall of the Templars*, p. 195.

Chapter 15

1. Herodotus VI.102, 107.

2. Froissart, *Chronicles*, ed. and trans. Geoffrey Brereton (1979) I, p. 79.

3. Boccaccio, *Decameron*, introduction of Day One.

4. Christopher Allmand, *The Hundred Years War: England and France at War, c. 1300–c. 1450* (New York, 1991), pp. 20–36.

5. Ibid. p. 14.

6. Ibid., p. 17.

7. Trois Continents, *La guerre de cent ans*, pp. 51–52.

8. On the Jacquerie, see Nicholas Wright, *Knights and Peasants: The Hundred Years War in the French Countryside* (Woodbridge, Suffolk, 1998).

9. Ibid., pp. 54–58.

10. Ibid., pp. 56–58.

11. Ibid., pp. 59–61.

12. Allmand, *The Hundred Years War*, pp. 22–23.

13. Ibid., pp. 26–27.

14. John Bergsagel, "War and Music in the Middle Ages," in Brian Patrick McGuire, *War and Peace in the Middle Ages* (Copenhagen, 1987), pp. 291–292.

15. Quoted in Michael Prestwich, *Armies and Warfare in the Middle Ages* (New Haven, Conn., 1996), p. 201.

16. Froissart, *Chronicles* I, p. 75.

17. Prestwich, *Armies and Warfare in the Middle Ages*, p. 190.

18. As an introduction to the concept of battle see ibid., pp. 305–333; and especially Matthew Bennett, "The Development of Battle Tactics in the Hundred Years War," in Anne Curry and Micheal Hughes, eds., *Arms, Armies, and Fortifications in the Hundred Years War* (Bury St. Edmunds, Suffolk, 1994), pp. 1–20.

19. Froissart, *Chronicles* I, p. 69.

20. Ibid. I, p. 72.

21. Ibid. I, p. 71.

22. Ibid. I, p. 77.

23. Alfred H. Burne, *The Crécy War: A Military History of the Hundred Years War from 1337 to the Peace of Brétigny* (London, 1955), pp. 169–170.

24. See the summary of the debate in Prestwich, *Armies and Warfare in the Middle Ages*, pp. 319–321.

25. Lot, *L'art militaire et les armées au Moyen Age*, vol. 1, pp. 344–348.

26. Contamine, *Histoire militaire de la France* I, p. 138.

27. Froissart, *Chronicles* I, p. 83.

28. Ibid. I p. 84.

29. Contamine, *Histoire militaire de la France* I, p. 134.

30. Froissart, *Chronicles* I, pp. 85–86.

31. Ibid. I, p. 86.

32. Ibid. I, p. 91.

33. Roger Wynkeley's letter of 2 September, 1346 in Richard W. Barber, *Edward, Prince of Wales and Aquitaine: A Biography of the Black Prince* (London: Barber, 1978), p. 20.

34. Michael Northburgh's letter of 4 September 1346 in ibid., p. 24. Froissart (*Chronicles* I, p. 91) lists 1291.

35. Froissart, *Chronicles* I, p. 95.

36. Ibid. I, pp. 89–90.

37. Burne, *The Crécy War*, pp. 183–184.

38. On this and various other aspects of the battle see John Keegan, *The Face of Battle: A Study of Waterloo and the Somme* (London, 1978), pp. 78–116.

39. Andrew Ayton, "English Armies in the Fourteen Century," in Curry and Hughes, *Arms, Armies, and Fortifications*, p. 22.

40. Ibid., p. 26.

41. Ibid., pp. 26–31.

42. Ibid., p. 23.

43. Ibid., pp. 23–25.

44. Gray's *Scalacronica* quoted in ibid., p. 33.

45. Ibid., pp. 35–37.

46. Ibid., p. 45.

47. Contamine, *Histoire militaire*, p. 133.

48. Ibid., p. 138.

49. Ibid., p. 136.

50. Ibid., pp. 138–139.

51. Ibid., p. 137.

52. Philippe Contamine, *La guerre de Cent Ans: France et Angleterre* (Paris, 1976), pp. 235–236.

53. Contamine, *Histoire militaire*, pp. 138–139.

54. Ibid., p. 140.

55. Ibid., pp. 140–141.

56. Contamine, *La guerre de Cent Ans*, p. 240, citing Froissart's rendering of the king's words.

57. Contamine, *Histoire militaire*, pp. 146–147.

58. Ibid.

59. Ibid., pp. 145–150.

60. Quoted in ibid., p. 150.

61. Ibid., p. 159–152.

62. Ibid., p. 183.

63. Ibid., pp. 187–195.

64. Ibid., p. 189.

65. Ibid., p. 201.

66. Ibid., pp. 201–202.

67. Ibid., p. 105.

Chapter 16

1. Sarah Lambert, "Crusading or Spinning," in Susan B. Edgington and Sarah Lambert, eds., *Gendering the Crusades* (New York, 2002), p. 3.

2. Matthew Bennett, "Virile Latins, Effeminate Greeks, and Strong Women: Gender Definitions on Crusade?" in Edgington and Lambert, *Gendering the Crusades*, p. 16.

3. M. McLaughlin, "The Woman Warrior: Gender, Warfare, and Society in Medieval Europe," *Women's Studies* 17 (1990): 193–195.

4. Ibid., p. 106.

5. Contamine, *War in the Middle Ages*, pp. 241–242.

6. McLaughlin, "The Woman Warrior: Gender, Warfare, and Society in Medieval Europe," p. 203.

7. Bennett, "Virile Latins, Effeminate Greeks, and Strong Women," p. 25.

8. Keren Caspi-Reisfeld, "Women Warriors During the Crusades, 1095–1254," in Edgington and Lambert, eds. *Gendering the Crusades*, pp. 96–97.

9. Contamine, *War in the Middle Ages*, p. 142.

10. *The Journal of the Siege of Orléans,* quoted in Régine Pernoud, *Joan of Arc by Herself and Her Witnesses*, trans. Edward Hyams (London, 1964), p. 73.

11. Contamine, *War in the Middle Ages*, p. 142.

12. Caspi-Reisfeld, "Women Warriors During the Crusades, 1095–1254," pp. 99–101.

13. Ibid., p. 101.

14. Contamine, *War in the Middle Ages*, pp. 239–242.

15. Joan's words from her trial in Pernoud, *Joan of Arc by Herself,* p. 16.

16. Hauviette, wife of Gerard de Sionne, in ibid., pp. 17–18.

17. Colin in ibid., p. 18.

18. Ibid., pp. 21–22.

19. Ibid., p. 23.

20. Ibid., pp. 23–24.

21. Wilfred T. Jewkes and Jerome B. Landfield, *Joan of Arc: Fact, Legend, and Literature* (New York, 1964), p. 7.

22. *Chronique de la Pucelle* (Genève, 1976), pp. 271–272.

23. Ibid., p. 272.

24. Pernoud, *Joan of Arc by Herself,* pp. 58–59.

25. The Duke of Alençon at the retrial, Jewkes and Landfield, *Joan of Arc: Fact, Legend, and Literature,* p. 61.

26. Contamine, *Histoire militaire,* pp. 185–187.

27. Bradbury, *The Medieval Siege,* p. 172.

28. Contamine, Histoire Militaire, p. 165.

29. Ibid., p. 185.

30. Bradbury, *The Medieval Siege,* p. 173.

31. Pernoud, *Joan of Arc by Herself,* pp. 75–76.

32. Contamine, *Histoire Militaire,* pp. 185–187.

33. From the *Journal of the Siege of Orléans* in Pernoud, *Joan of Arc by Herself,* p. 76.

34. Ibid., pp. 76–78.

35. Contamine, *Histoire militaire,* p. 187.

36. From the testimony of the Bastard of Orléans at Joan's retrial in Jewkes and Landfield, *Joan of Arc: Fact, Legend, and Literature,* p. 57.

37. Pernoud, *Joan of Arc by Herself,* pp. 84, 85.

38. Ibid., pp. 84, 87.

39. Ibid., p. 86.

40. Jean d'Aulon at the retrial in Jewkes and Landfield, *Joan of Arc: Fact, Legend, and Literature,* p. 64.

41. The Duke of Alençon at the retrial in ibid., p. 60.

42. The Duke of Alençon at the retrial in ibid., p. 62; Kelly DeVries, "A Woman as Leader of Men: Joan of Arc's Military Career," in Bonnie Wheeler and Charles T. Wood, eds., *Fresh Verdicts on Joan of Arc* (New York, 1996), pp. 3–18.

43. Pernoud, *Joan of Arc by Herself,* pp. 94, 111.

Chapter 17

1. Novella CLXXXI in Franco Sacchetti, *Trecentonovelle.*

2. Delbrück, *History of the Art of War,* vol. 3, p. 314.

3. Reinhard Baumann, *I Lanzichenecchi. La loro storia e cultura dal tardo Medioevo all guerra dei Trent'anni.* Torino, 1996), p. 4.

4. Ibid, p. 5; Delbrück, *History of the Art of War,* vol. 3, p. 314.

5. For Gattamelata and the other mercenaries discussed see the short biographies in Tommaso Argiolas, *Armi ed eserciti del Rinascimento Italiano* (Roma, 1991) but especially the detailed rendering in E. Ricotti, *Storia delle compagnie di ventura in Italia,* 2nd ed. (Torino, 1893).

6. Contamine, *War in the Middle Ages,* p. 188.

7. Lot, *L'art militaire et les armées au Moyen Age,* vol. I, p. 414.

8. William Caferro, *Mercenary Companies and the Decline of Siena* (Baltimore, 1998), p. 4.

9. Michael Mallett, *Mercenaries and Their Masters: Warfare in Renaissance Italy* (Totowa, N.J., 1974), pp. 25–26.

10. Lot, *L'art militaire et les armées au Moyen Age,* vol. 1, p. 415.

11. Ibid., p. 415.

12. *The Life of Cola di Rienzo*, trans. John Wright (Toronto, 1975), p. iv.11.

13. Caferro, *Mercenary Companies and the Decline of Siena*, p. 11.

14. Michael Mallett, "The Condottiere," in Eugenio Garin, ed. *Renaissance Characters*, trans. Lydia G. Cochrane (Chicago, 1991), pp. 25–26.

15. Mallett, "The Condottiere," pp. 28–20.

16. Mario Del Treppo, "Gli aspetti organizzativi, economici e sociali di una compagnia di ventura italiana," *Rivista Storica Italiana* 85 (1973): 262–264.

17. Alan Ryder, *The Kingdom of Naples Under Alfonso the Magnanimous: The Making of a Modern State* (Oxford, 1976), p. 264.

18. Del Treppo, "Gli aspetti organizzativi, economici e sociali di una compagnia di ventura italiana," pp. 255–256.

19. Ryder, *The Kingdom of Naples Under Alfonso the Magnanimous*, p. 262.

20. Antonio Santosuosso, "Anatomy of Defeat in Renaissance Italy: The Battle of Fornovo in 1495," *International History Review* 16 (1994): 221–250.

21. Mallett, *Mercenaries and Their Masters*, p. 116.

22. Ryder, *The Kingdom of Naples Under Alfonso the Magnanimous*, pp. 269–270.

23. *The Life of Cola di Rienzo*, p. iv.11.

24. Del Treppo, "Gli aspetti organizzativi, economici e sociali di una compagnia di ventura italiana," pp. 264–270.

25. Ryder, *The Kingdom of Naples Under Alfonso the Magnanimous*, pp. 270–274.

26. Del Treppo, "Gli aspetti organizzativi, economici e sociali di una compagnia di ventura italiana," pp. 264–270. On this also Mallett, *Mercenaries and Their Masters*, p. 107.

27. Ibid., pp. 238.

28. Del Treppo, "Gli aspetti organizzativi, economici e sociali di una compagnia di ventura italiana," pp. 273–274.

29. Ryder, *The Kingdom of Naples Under Alfonso the Magnanimous*, pp. 266–267.

30. F. L. Taylor, *The Art of War in Italy 1494–1529* (Westport, Conn., 1973 [rpt. 1921 ed.], p. 11.

Chapter 18

1. G. Grosjean, *Die Schlacht bei Murten* (Zurich, 1975) p. 54.

2. Malcom G. A. Vale, *War and Chivalry: Warfare and Aristocratic Culture in England, France, and Burgundy at the End of the Middle Ages* (London, 1981), pp. 100–174.

3. Contamine, *War in the Middle Ages*, p. 139.

4. Ibid., p. 139.

5. Bert S. Hall, *Weapons and Warfare in Renaissance Europe* (Baltimore, 1997), pp. 65–66, 105.

6. Ibid., p. 115.

7. Ibid., p. 115–116.

8. Ibid., pp. 116–123.

9. Angelo Angelucci, *Gli schioppettieri milanesi nel XV secolo* (Milano, 1865), pp. 9–10.

10. Ibid., pp. 6–7.

11. Hitti, *History of the Arabs*, pp. 699–702.

Selected Bibliography

Primary Sources

Agathias. *Historiarum libri quinque.*

Ammianus Marcellinus. *Rerurm gestarum lirbi qui supersunt.*

Brundage, J., ed. 1976. *The Crusades: A Documentary History.* Milwaukee.

Cassiodorus, 1992. *Variae.* Trans. S. J. B. Barnish. Liverpool.

1976. *Chronique de la Pucelle.* Genève.

Erchemberto. 1995. *Storia dei Longobardi sec. IX (Ystoriola)*, trans. Arturo Carucci. Salerno.

Fiamma, Galvano. *Manipulus Florum.* Cronca milanese del Trecento.

Fredegar. 1960. *The Fourth Book of the Chronicle of Fredegar.* Ed. and trans. J. M. Wallace-Hadrill. London.

Froissart. 1979 [1968]. *Chronicles.* Ed. and trans. Geoffrey Brereton.

Gabrieli, Francesco, ed. 1969 [1957 Italian ed.]. *Arab Historians of the Crusades Selected and Translated from Arabic Sources.* London.

Gregory of Tours. *Libri Historiarum X* (History of the Franks).

Hallam, Elisabeth, ed. 1989. *Chronicles of the Crusades: Eye-Witness Accounts of the Wars Between Christianity and Islam.* London.

1992. *The History of al-Tabara.* Trans. Yohanan Friedmann.

Isidore of Seville. *Historia Gothorum.*

Jean de Venette. 1953. Richard A. Newhall, ed. *The Chronicle of Jean de Venette.* Trans. Jean Birdsall. New York.

Jordanes. 1991. *De Getarum sive Gothorum Origine et Rebus Gestis (Storia dei Goti).* Ed. Elio Bartolini. Milano.

Krey, August C., ed. 1958. *The First Crusade: The Account of Eye-Witnesses and Participants.* Gloucester, Mass.

1993. *Liber Pontificalis.* Ed. Raymond Davis. Liverpool.

1979. *The Life and Campaigns of the Black Prince.* Ed. and trans. Richard Barber. Bury St. Edmunds, Suffolk.

1975. *The Life of Cola di Rienzo.* Trans. John Wright. Toronto.

Maurice. *Strategikon.*

Menander. 1985. *The History of Menander the Guardsman.* Ed. R. C. Blockley. Ottawa.

Otto of Freising and Continuator. 1953. *The Deeds of Frederick Barbarossa.* Toronto.

Paul the Deacon. 1992. *Historia Longobardorum.* Ed. Lidia Capo. Vicenza.

Procopius. *History of the Wars.*

Sidonius Apollinaris.

Zosimus. *Historia nova.*

Secondary Sources

Abun-Nasr, Jamil M. 1971. *A History of the Maghrib*. Cambridge.

Allmand, Christopher. 1991 [1988]. *The Hundred Years War: England and France at War, c. 1300–c. 1450*. New York.

Amory, Patrick. 1997. *People and Identity in Ostrogothic Italy, 480–554*. Cambridge.

Angelucci, Angelo. 1865. *Gli schioppettieri milanesi nel XV secolo*. Milano.

Argiolas, Tommaso. 1991. *Armi ed eserciti del Rinascimento Italiano*. Roma.

Aurell, Martin. 1996. *La noblesse au Occident (Ve-XVe siècles)*. Paris.

Ayton, Andrew. 1994. *Knights and Warhorses: Military Service and the English Aristocracy Under Edward III*. Woodbridge.

Azzara, Claudio. 1999. *Le invasioni barbariche*. Bologna

Babcock, Michael A. *The Stories of Attila the Hun's Death: Narrative, Myth, and Meaning*. Lewiston, N.Y.

Babinger, E. 1978. *Mehmed the Conqueror*. Princeton.

Bachrach, Bernard S. 2002. "Charlemagne and the Carolingian General Staff." *Journal of Military History* 66: 313–357.

Bachrach, Bernard S. 2001. *Early Carolingian Warfare: Prelude to Empire*. Philadelphia.

Bachrach, Bernard S. 1994. *The Anatomy of a Little War: A diplomatic and Military History of the Gundovald Affair (568–586)*. Boulder, Colo.

Bachrach, Bernard S. 1993. *Armies and Politics in the Early Medieval West*. Variorum. Great Yarmouth, Norfolk.

Bachrach, Bernard S. 1972. *Merovingian Military Organization, 481–751*. Minneapolis.

Bachrach, Bernard S. 1971. "The Feigned Retreat at Hastings." *Medieval Studies* 33: 344–347.

Balard, Michel, ed. 1996. *Autour de la Première Croisade. Actes du Colloque de la Society for the Study of the Crusades and the Latin East* (Clermont-Ferrand, 22–25 Juin 1995). Paris.

Balbi, Marco. 1991. *L'esercito longobardo, 568–774*. Milano.

Balestracci, Duccio. 2001. *La festa in armi. Giostre, tornei e giochi nel Medioevo*. Bari.

Barber, Richard. 1994. *The New Knighthood: A History of the Order of the Temple*. Cambridge.

Barber, Richard W. 1978. *Edward, Prince of Wales and Aquitaine: A Biography of the Black Prince*. London.

Bartha, Antal. 1975. *Hungarian Society in the 9th and 10th Centuries*. Budapest.

Baumann, Reinhard. 1996 [1994 German ed.]. *I Lanzichenecchi. La loro storia e cultura dal tardo Medioevo all guerra dei Trent'anni*. Torino.

Beeler, John. 1983. "The State of the Art: Recent Scholarship in Late Medieval and Early Modern Military History." *Military Affairs* 47: 193–195.

Beeler, John. 1980 [1971]. *Warfare in Feudal Europe, 730–1200*. Ithaca, N.Y.

Bekker-Nielsen, Hans, et al., eds. 1981. *Proceedings of the Eighth Viking Congress. Århus 24–31 August 1977*. Odense.

Bennett, Matthew. 1994. "The Development of Battle Tactics in the Hundred Years War," in Anne Curry and Micheal Hughes, eds., *Arms, Armies, and Fortifications in the Hundred Years War*. Bury St. Edmunds, Suffolk, pp. 1–20.

Bliese, John R. E. 1998. "Saint Cuthbert and War." *Journal of Medieval History* 24: 214–241.

Bognetti, Gian Piero. 1966–1968. *L'età longobarda*. Milano, 4 vols.

Bowlus, C. B. 1995. *Franks, Moravians, and Magyars: The Struggle for the Middle Danube*. Philadelphia.

Boyer, Régis, ed. 1976. *Les Vikings et leur civilisation. Problèmes actuels*. Paris.

Bracciotti, Annalisa. 1994–1995. "Il ruolo di Peredeo nell'assassinio di Alboino." *Romanobarbarica* 13: 99–123.

Bradbury, Jim. 1992. *The Medieval Siege.* Woodbridge.

Bradbury, Jim. 1985. *The Medieval Archer.* Woodbridge.

Brown, R. Allen. 1980. "The Battle of Hastings." *Anglo-Norman Studies: Proceedings of the Battle Conference* 3: 1–21.

Burne, Alfred H. 1955. *The Crécy War: A Military History of the Hundred Years War from 1337 to the Peace of Brétigny.* London.

Caetani, Leone. 1911. *Studi di Storia Orientale.* Milano.

Caetani, Leone. 1905–1926. *Annali dell'Islam.* Milano.

Caferro, William. 1998. *Mercenary Companies and the Decline of Siena.* Baltimore.

Cameron, Averil, ed. 1992–1995. *The Byzantine and Early Islamic Near East.* Princeton, N.J.

Cameron, Averil. 1985. *Procopius and the Sixth Century.* Berkeley and Los Angeles.

Canard, Marius. 1965. "L'expansion arabe: Le problème militaire." *L'Occidente e l'Islam nell'Alto Medioevo.* Spoleto: 37–63, 309–335.

Capitani, Ovidio et al. 1984. *L'Italia dell'alto Medioevo.* Milano.

Cardini, Franco. 1994. *Dio lo vuole! Intervista sulla crociata.* Rimini.

Cardini, Franco. 1982. "Crusade and 'Presence of Jerusalem' in Medieval Florence," in B. Z. Kedar, H. E. Mayer, and R. C. Smail, eds., *Outremer: Studies in the History of the Crusading Kingdom of Jerusalem.* Jerusalem: Yad Izhak Ben-Zvi Institute, 332–346.

Cardini, Franco. 1982. *Quell'antica festa crudele. Guerra e cultura della guerra dall'età feudale alla Grande revoluzione.* Firenze.

Carpenter, Jean, and François Lebrun. 2001. *Histoire de la Mediterranée.* Éditions du Seuil.

Chalmeta, Pedro. 1994. *Invasión e Islamización.* Madrid.

Chejne, Anwar G. 1974. *Muslim Spain: Its History and Culture.* Minneapolis.

Chibnall, Marjorie. 1982. "Military Service in Normandy Before 1066." *Anglo-Norman Studies* 5: 65–77.

Christie, Neal. 1998. *The Lombards.* Bodmin, Cornwall.

Christie, Neal. "Invasion or Invitation? The Longobard Occupation of Northern Italy, AD 568–569." *Romanobarbarica* 11: 79–108.

Christophilopoulou, Aikaterina. 1993. *Byzantine History.* Trans. Timothy Cullen, 2 vols. Amsterdam.

Clante—Centro di Studi Chiantigiani. 1992. *Il Chianti e la battaglia di Montaperti.* Poggibonsi.

Clark, John. 1995. *The Medieval Horse and Its Equipment.* London.

Collins, Roger. 1998. *Charlemagne.* Toronto.

Collins, Roger. 1989. *The Arab Conquest of Spain, 710–797.* London.

Colombo, Alessandro. 1935. *Milano sotto l'egida del Carroccio.* Milano.

Contamine, Philippe. 1997. *La noblesse au royaume de France de Philip le Bel à Louis XII,* Paris.

Contamine, Philippe. 1992. "La fondation du Regnum Francorum," in André Corvisier, *Histoire militaire de la France, vol. 1: Des origines à 1715.* Paris.

Contamine, Philippe. 1992. "L'espace carolingien: dilatation, dislocation, invasion," in André Corvisier, *Histoire militaire de la France, vol. 1: Des origines à 1715.* Ed. Philippe Contamine. Paris.

Contamine, Pierre. 1984 [1980 French ed.]. *War in the Middle Ages.* Trans. Michael Jones. Oxford.

Contamine, Pierre. 1976. *La guerre de Cent Ans: France et Angleterre.* Paris.

Corfis, A., and M. Wolfe, eds. 1995. *The Medieval City Under Siege.* Woodbridge.

Corvisier, André. 1992. *Histoire militaire de la France, vol. 1: Des origines à 1715*. Ed. Philippe Contamine. Paris.

Coupland, Simon. 1990. "Carolingian Arms and Armor in the Ninth Century." *Viator* 21: 29–50.

Courtois, C. 1955. *Les Vandales et l'Afrique*. Paris.

Crainge, Christine, and George Crainge. 1993. "The Pevensey Expedition: Brilliantly Executed Plan or Near Disaster?" *Mariner Mirror* 79: 261–273.

Creasy, E. 1874. *The Fifteen Decisive Battles of the World*. London.

Crone, Patricia. 1980. *Slaves on Horses: The Evolution of the Islamic Polity*. Cambridge.

Crouch, D. 1990. *William Marshal: Court, Career, and Chivalry in the Angevin Empire, 1147–1219*. London.

Curry, Anne. 1998. "Medieval Warfare: England and Her Continental Neighbours, Eleventh to the Fourteenth Centuries." *Journal of Medieval History* 24: 81–102.

Curry, Anne, and Michael Hughes, eds. 1994. *Arms, Armies, and Fortifications in the Hundred Years War*. Bury St. Edmunds, Suffolk.

Davis, R. H. C. 1989. *The Medieval Warhorse: Origin, Development, and Redevelopment*. London.

Davis, R. H. C. 1987. "The Warhorses of the Normans." *Anglo-Norman Studies: Proceedings of the Battle Conference* 10: 67–82.

Delbrück, Hans. 1982. *History of the Art of War, vol. 3: The Middle Ages*. Trans. W. J. Renfroe, Jr. Westport, Conn.

Del Treppo, Mario. 1973. "Gli aspetti organizzativi, economici e sociali di una compagnia di ventura italiana." *Rivista Storica Italiana* 85: 253–275.

De Santiago Simón, Emilio. 1998. "The Itineraries of the Muslim Conquest of al-Andalus in the Light of a New Source: Ibn al-Shabbat," in Manuela Marín, ed., *The Formation of al-Andalus*. Aldershot, pp. 1–12.

De Valdeveavellano, Luis G. 1973. *Historia de España*. Madrid.

DeVries, Kelly. 2000 [1996]. *Infantry Warfare in the Early Fourteenth Century*. Woodbridge, Suffolk.

DeVries, Kelly. 1992. *Medieval Military Technology*. Peterborough, Ontario.

D'Ilario, Giorgio, et al. 1976. *Legnano e la battaglia*. Legnano.

Donner, Fred McGraw. 1981. *The Early Islamic Conquests*. Princeton.

Drinkwater, John, and Hugh Elton, eds. 1992. *Fifth-Century Gaul: A Crisis of Identity*. Cambridge.

Duby, Georges. 1990. *The Legend of Bouvines: War, Religion, and Culture in the Middle Ages*. Trans. Catherine Tihanyi. Cambridge.

Duby, Georges. 1985. *William Marshal the Flower of Chivalry*. Trans. Richard Howard. New York.

Duby, Georges. 1980. *The Three Orders: Feudal Society Imagined*. Chicago.

Duby, Georges. 1953. *La société au XIe et XII siècles dans la région mâconnaise*. Paris.

Du Jourdin, Michel Mollat. 1992. *La guerre de Cent Ans vue par ceux qui l'ont vécue*. Évreux.

Edgington, Susan B., and Sarah Lambert, eds. 2002. *Gendering the Crusades*. New York.

Elgood, Robert, ed. 1979. *Islamic Arms and Armour*. London.

Engel, Pál. 2001. *The Realm of St. Stephen: A History of Medieval Hungary, 895–1526*. Trans. Andrew Ayton. London.

Erbstösser. Martin. 1978 [1978 German ed.]. *The Crusades*. Trans. C. S. V. Salt. Newton Abbot.

Fasoli, Gina. 1945. *Le incursioni ungare in Europa nel secolo x*. Firenze.

Fauber, Lawrence. 1990. *Narses Hammer of the Goths: The Life and Times of Narses the Eunuch.* New York.

Fischer, M., and W. Pedrotti. 1977. *Le cittia Italiane and medioevo.* Colognola ai Colli, pp. 14–15.

Flori, Jean. 2002 [1998 French ed.]. *La cavalleria medievale.* Bologna.

Flori, Jean. 2001. *Les croisades. Origines, réalisations, institutions, déviations.* Paris.

Flori, Jean. 1998. "Guerre et chevalerie au moyen âge." *Cahiers de civilisation médiévale* 41: 353–363.

Flori, Jean. 1988. "Encore l'usage de la lance . . . La technique du combat chevaleresque vers l'an 1100." *Cahiers de civilisation médiévale* 31: 213–240.

Folz, Robert. 1974 [1964 French ed.]. *The Coronation of Charlemagne, 5 December 1970.* Trans. J. E. Anderson. London.

Forey, Alan. 2002. "The Military Orders and the Conversion of the Muslims in the Twelfth and Thirteenth Centuries." *Journal of Medieval History* 28: 1–22.

Forey, Alan. 2001. *The Fall of the Templars in the Crown of Aragon.* Aldershot.

Forey, Alan. 1993. "Military Orders and Secular Warfare in the Twelfth and Thirteenth Century." *Viator* 24: 79–100.

Forey, Alan. 1992. *The Military Orders from the Twelfth to the Early Fourteenth Centuries.* London.

Fossier, R. 1982. *Enfance de l'Europe Xe-XIIe siècles,* vol. 2. Paris.

France, John. 1999. *Western Warfare in the Age of the Crusades, 1000–1300.* Ithaca, N.Y.

France, John. 1994. *Victory in the East: A Military History of the First Crusade.* Cambridge.

Galley, Micheline, and David R. Marshall, eds. 1973. *Actes du Premier Congrès d' Études des Cultures Méditerranéennes d'Influence Arabo-Berbère.* Alger.

Ganshof, F.-L. 1952. *Feudalism.* London.

Gasparri, Stefano. 1984. "L'Italia meridionale contesa tra bizantini, longobardi, franchi saraceni," in Ovidio Capitani et al., *L'Italia dell'alto Medioevo.* Milano, pp. 169–197.

Geary, Patrick J., ed. 1997 (2nd ed.). *Readings in Medieval History.* Peterborough, Ontario.

Gerberding, Richard A. 1987. *The Rise of the Carolingians and the Liber Historiae Francorum.* Oxford.

Gil, Moshe. 1992 [1983 Hebrew ed.]. *A History of Palestine, 634–1099.* Trans. Ethel Broido. Cambridge.

Gillingham, J. 1989. "William the Bastard at War," in C. Harper Bill, ed., *Studies in Medieval History Presented to R. Allen Brown.* Woodbridge, pp. 141–158.

Gilmor, C. M. 1984. "Naval Logistics of the Cross-Channel Operation, 1066" *Anglo-Norman Studies* 7 (1984): 105–131.

Goffart, Walter. 1980. *Barbarians and Romans, A.D. 415–584. The Techniques of Accomodation.* Princeton.

Griffith, Paddy. 1995. *The Viking Art of War.* London.

Haldon, John. 1999. *Warfare, State, and Society in the Byzantine World, 565–1204.* London.

Hall, Bert S. 1997. *Weapons and Warfare in Renaissance Europe.* Baltimore.

Halsall, G. S. 1998. *Warfare in the Barbarian West, c. 450–c. 900.* London.

Halsall, G. S. 1995. *Settlement and Social Organization: The Merovingian Region of Metz.* Cambridge.

Hamidullah, Muhammad. 1973. *The Battledields of the Prophet Muhammad.* Hyderabad.

Hamidullah, Muhammad. 1959. *Le Prophète de l'Islam.* 2 vols. Paris.

Hamilton, Bernard. 1980. *The Latin Church in the Crusader States: The Secular Church.* London.

Haywood, John. 1995. *The Penguin Historical Atlas of the Vikings.* London.

Heather, Peter. 1996. *The Goths.* Oxford.

Heather, Peter. 1991. *Goths and Romans, 332–489.* Oxford.

Hewitt, H. J. 1971. *The Organization of War Under Edward III, 1338–1362.* London.

Hillenbrans, Carole. 1999. *The Crusades: Islamic Perspectives.* Chicago.

Hinds, M. 1996. *Studies in Early Islamic History.* Princeton, N.J.

Hitti, Philip K. 1984 (8th ed.). *History of the Arabs from the Earliest Times to the Present.* London.

Holmes, George, ed. 1997. *The Oxford Illustrated History of Italy.* Oxford.

Holt, P. M. 1986. *The Age of the Crusades: The Near East from the 11th Century to 1517.* Longmans.

Hooper, N., and M. Bennett. 1996. *Cambridge Illustrated Atlas of Warfare.* Cambridge.

Hummer, H. J. 1998. "Franks and Alamanni: A Discontinuous Ethnogenesis," in Ian Wood, ed., *Franks and Alamanni in the Merovingian Period: An Ethnographic Perspective.* San Marino, pp. 9–32.

Hyland, Ann. 1994. *The Medieval Warhorse from Byzantium to the Crusades.* Stroud.

Jackson, Peter. 2000. "The Mongol Empire, 1986–1999." *Journal of Medieval History* 26: 189–210.

Jandora, John W. 1985. "The Battle of the Yarmûk: A Reconstruction." *Journal of Asian Studies* 19.

Jewkes, Wilfred T., and Jerome B. Landfield. 1964. *Joan of Arc: Fact, Legend, and Literature.* New York.

Juynboll, G. H. A., ed. 1982. *Studies on the First Century of Islamic Society.* Carbondale, Ill.

Kaegi, Walter Emil Jr. 1992. *Byzantium and the Early Islamic Conquests.* Cambridge.

Kaegi, Walter Emil Jr. 1982. *Army, Society, and Religion in Byzantium.* Variorum Reprints.

Kagay, Donald J. and L. J. Andrew Villalon, eds. 1999. *The Circle of War in the Middle Ages: Essays on Medieval Military and Naval History.* Woodbridge, Suffolk.

Kauper, Richard W. 1988. *War, Justice, and Public Order: England and France in the Later Middle Ages.* Oxford.

Keen, Maurice, ed. 1999. *Medieval Warfare: A History.* Oxford.

Keen, Maurice. 1965. *The Laws of War in the Late Middle Ages.* London.

Kennedy, Hugh. 2001. *The Armies of the Caliphs. Military and Society in the Early Islamic State.* London.

Kennedy, Hugh. 1996. *Muslim Spain and Portugal.* London.

Kennedy, Hugh. 1994. *Crusader Castles.* Cambridge.

Kiszely, István. 1981. "On the True Face of the Longobards in Italy." *La cultura in Italia fra tardo antico e alto Medioevo. Atti del Convegno tenuto a Roma 1979.* Roma, vol. 2, pp. 887–892.

Koch, H. W. 1978. *Medieval Warfare.* London.

Koren, J., and Y. Nevo. 1991. "Methodological Approaches to Islamic Studies." *Der Islam* 68: 87–101.

Landau-Tasseron, Ella. 1995. "Features of the Pre-Conquest Muslim Armies in the Time of Muhammad," in Averil Cameron, ed., *The Byzantine and Early Islamic Near East.* Princeton, N.J., pp. 299–316.

Leyser, Karl. 1965. "The Battle of the Lech, 955: A Study in Tenth-Century Warfare." *Historia* 50: 1–25.

Liebeschuetz, J. H. W. G. 1990. *Barbarians and Bishops: Army, Church, and State in the Age of Arcadius and Chrysostom.* Oxford.

Liebeschuetz, J. H. W. G. 1992. "Alaric Goths: Nations or Army?" in John Drinkwater and Hugh Elton, eds., *Fifth-Century Gaul: A Crisis of Identity.* Cambridge University Press, pp. 75–83.

Lipták, Pàl. 1983. *Avars and the Ancient Hungarians*. Budapest.

Logan, F. 1983. *The Vikings in History*. London.

I Longobardi e la Longobardia. *Saggi*. Milano Palazzo Reale dal 12 Ottobre 1978. S. Donato Milanese.

Lot, Ferdinand. 1946. *L'art militaire et les armées au Moyen Age en Europe et dans le Proche Orient*. Paris, 2 vols.

Lyons, M. C., and D. E. P. Jackson. 1982. *Saladin: The Politics of the Holy War*. Cambridge.

Maalouf, Amin. 1989 [1983 French ed.]. *Le crociate viste dagli Arabi*. Torino.

Mackay, Angus, and David Ditchburn. 1997. *Atlas of Medieval Warfare*. London.

Maenchen-Helfen, J. Otto. 1973. *The World of the Huns: Studies in Their History and Culture*. Ed. Max Knight. Berkeley.

Makki, Mahmous. 1992. "The Political History of al-Andalus," in Dalma Khadra Jayyisi, ed., *The Legacy of Muslim Spain*. New York, pp. 3–87.

Mallett, Michael. 1994. "The Art of War," in Thomas A. Brady et al., eds., *Handbook of European History, 1400–1600: Late Middle Ages, Renaissance, and Reformation*, vol. 1. Grand Rapids, Mich.

Mallet, Michael. 1991. "The Condottiere," in Eugenio Garin, ed., *Renaissance Characters*. Trans. Lydia G. Cochrane. Chicago.

Mallett, Michael. 1974. *Mercenaries and Their Masters: Warfare in Renaissance Italy*. Totowa, N.J.

Man, John. 1999. *Atlas of the Year 1000*. Cambridge.

Mariani, Maria Stella Caló, and Raffaella Cassano, eds. 1995. *Federico II: Immagine e potere*. Padova.

Marín, Manuela, ed. 1998. *The Formation of al-Andalus*. Aldershot.

Marshall, Christopher. 1992. *Warfare in the Latin East, 1192–1291*. Cambridge.

Mathisen, Ralph Whitney. 1993. *Roman Aristocrats in Barbarian Gaul: Strategies for Survival in an Age of Transition*. Austin, Tex.

Mayer, H. E. 1988 (2nd ed). *The Crusades*. Trans. J. Gillingham. Oxford.

McGeer, E. 1995. *Sowing the Dragon's Teeth: Byzantine Warfare in the Tenth Century*. Washington.

McGuire, Brian Patrick, ed. 1987. *War and Peace in the Middle Ages*. Copenhagen.

McLaughlin, M. 1990. "The Woman Warrior: Gender, Warfare, and Society in Medieval Europe." *Women's Studies* 17: 193–209.

Molina, Luis. 1999. "Los itinerarios de la conquista: el relato de 'Arib,'" *Al-Qantara* 20: 27–46.

Morillo, Stephen, ed. 1996. *The Battle of Hastings: Sources and Interpretations*. Rochester.

Morillo, Stephen. 1994. *Warfare Under the Anglo-Norman Kings, 1066–1135*. Woodbridge.

Morillo, Stephen. 1990. "Hastings: An Unusual Battle." *Haskins Society Journal* 2: 95–104.

Munz, Peter. 1969. *Frederick Barbarossa*. London.

Muir, William. 1923 [1861]. *The Life of Mohammad*. Edinburgh.

Nixon, C. E. V. 1992. "Relations between Visigoths and Romans in Fifth-Century Gaul," in John Drinkwater and Hugh Elton, eds., *Fifth-Century Gaul: A Crisis of Identity*. Cambridge University Press, pp. 64–75.

Norgård Jorgensen, A., and B. L.Clausen, eds. 1997. *Military Aspects of Scandinavian Society in a European Perspective, A.D. 1–1300*. Copenhagen.

Norris, H. T. 1982. *The Berbers in Arabic Literature*. London.

Noth, Albrecht. 1994 (2nd ed.). *The Early Arabic Historical Tradition: A Source-Critical Study*. Princeton, N.J.

Oakeshott, Ewart. 1997 [1964]. *A Knight and His Weapons*. Chester Springs, Penn.

Oman, Charles. 1924. *A History of the Art of War in the Middle Ages*, 2 vols. London.

Pacaut, Marcel. 1970 [1967 French ed.]. *Frederick Barbarossa*. Trans. A. J. Pomerans. New York.

Page, R. I. 1995. *Vikings: Records, Memorials, and Myths*. Toronto.

Pamlényi, Ervin, ed. 1975. *A History of Hungary*. London.

Parry, W. J., and M. E.Yapp, eds. 1975. *War, Technology, and Society in the Middle East*. London.

Peirce, Ian. 1992. "The Knight, His Arms and Armour, c. 1150–1250." *Anglo-Norman Studies* 15: 251–274.

Peirce, Ian. 1987. "Arms, Armour, and Warfare in the Eleventh Century." *Anglo-Norman Studies: Proceedings of the Battle Conference* 10: 237–257.

Pernoud, Régine. 1964 [1962 French ed.]. *Joan of Arc by Herself and Her Witnesses*. Trans. Edward Hyams. London.

Perriccioli Saggese, Alessandra. 1979. *I romanzi cavallereschi miniati a Napoli*. Napoli.

Peters, F. E. 1994. *Muhammad and the Origins of Islam*. Albany, N.Y.

Pieri, Piero. 1952. *Il Rinascimento e la crisi militare italiana*. Torino.

Pizzani, Ubaldo. 1981. "The Influence of *De Institutione Musica* of Boethius up to Herbert d'Aurillac: A Tentative Contribution," in Michael Masi, ed., *Boethius and the Liberal Arts: A Collection of Essays*, pp. 97–153.

Porter, Pamela. 2000. *Medieval Warfare in Manuscripts*. Toronto.

Prawer, J. 1969–1970. *Histoire du royaume latin de Jérusalem*. 2 vols. Paris.

Prestwich, Michael. 1996. *Armies and Warfare in the Middle Ages: The English Experience*. New Haven, Conn.

Prestwich, Michael. 1980. *The Three Edwards: War and the State in England, 1272–1377*. London.

Pryor, J. H. 1988. *Geography, Technology, and War in the Maritime History of the Mediterranean*. Cambridge.

Raaflaub, Kurt, and Natan Rosenstein, eds. 1999. *War and Society in the Ancient and Medieval Worlds: Asia, the Mediterranean, Europe, and Mesoamerica*. Washington.

Reynolds, S. M. G. 1994. *Fiefs and Vassals*. Oxford.

Ricotti, E. 1893 (2nd ed.) *Storia delle compagnie di ventura in Italia*, 2 vols. Torino.

Riley-Smith, Jonathan, ed. 1995. *The Oxford Illustrated History of the Crusades*. Oxford.

Riley-Smith, Jonathan, ed. 1991. *The Atlas of the Crusades*. London.

Riley-Smith, Jonathan. 1986. *The First Crusade and the Idea of Crusading*. University of Pennsylvania Press.

Riley-Smith, Jonathan. 1973. *The Feudal Nobility and the Kingdom of Jerusalem, 1174–1277*. London.

Rogers, R. 1992. *Latin Siege Warfare in the Twelfth Century*. Oxford.

Rose, Susan. 2002. *Medieval Naval Warfare, 1000–1500*. London.

Rotili, Marc. "La civiltà dei Longobardi negli insediamenti protoitaliani." *La cultura in Italia fra tardo antico e alto Medioevo. Atti del Convegno tenuto a Roma 1979*. Roma, vol. 2, pp. 933–946.

Russell, F. H. 1975. *The Just War in the Middle Ages*. Cambridge.

Ryder, Alan. 1976. *The Kingdom of Naples Under Alfonso the Magnanimous: The Making of a Modern State*. Oxford.

Saggese, Alessandra Perriccioli. 1979. *I romanzi cavallereschi miniati a Napoli*. Napoli.

Santosuosso, Antonio. 2001. *Storming the Heavens: Soldiers, Citizens, and the Symbols of War*. Boulder, Colo.

Santosuosso, Antonio. 1994. "Anatomy of Defeat in Renaissance Italy: The Battle of Fornovo in 1495." *International History Review* 16 (1994): 221–250.

Savage, Elizabeth. 1997. *A Gateway to Hell, A Gateway to Paradise: The North African Response to the Arab Conquest*. Princeton, N.J.

Sawyer, Peter, ed. 1997. *The Oxford Illustrated History of the Vikings*. Oxford.

Sawyer, P. 1971 [1962]. *The Age of the Vikings*. London.

Scragg D. G., ed. 1991. *The Battle of Maldon, AD 991*. Oxford.

Sellier, Jean, and André Sellier. 2000. *Atlas des peuples d'Europe Occidentale*. Paris.

Semplici, Riccardo, ed. 1998. *La battaglia di Campaldino a Poppi, 11 giugno 1289*. Firenze.

Sennis, Antonio. 2000. "Invasioni barbariche e mondo mediterraneo. Alcune note." *Rivista di Cultura Classica e Medievale* 1: 121–127.

Sestan, Ernesto. 1968. "La composizione etnica della società in rapporto allo svolgimento della civiltà in Italia nel secolo vii," in Ernesto Sestan, *Italia medievale*. Napoli, pp. 22–49.

Sestan, Ernesto. 1984. "I longobardi." *Ovidio Capitani et ali., L'Italia dell'alto Medioevo*. Milano, pp. 71–117.

Setton, K. M., ed. 1969–1989. *A History of the Crusades*, 6 vols. Madison, Wis.

Siddorn, J. Kim. 2000. *Viking Weapons and Warfare*. Stroud, Gloucestershire.

Siegmund, Frank. 1998. "Social Structure and Relations," in Ian Wood, ed., *Franks and Alamanni in the Merovingian Period: An Ethnographic Perspective*. San Marino, pp. 177–212.

Smail, R. C. 1995 (2nd ed.) *Crusading Warfare, 1097–1193*. Cambridge.

Stacey, Robert C. 1994. "The Age of Chivalry," in Michael Howard et al., eds, *The Laws of War: Constraints on Warfare in the Western World*. New Haven, Conn.

Strickland, Matthew. 1996. *War and Chivalry: The Conduct and Perception of War in England and Normandy, 1066–1217*. Cambridge.

Strickland, Matthew, ed. 1992. *Anglo-Norman Warfare*. Woodbridge, Suffolk.

Stubbs, William. 1969 [1908]. *Germany in the Early Middle Ages, 476–1250*. New York.

Tabacco, Giovanni. 1974. "La storia politica e sociale. Dal tramonto dell'Impero alle prime fondazioni di Stati regionali," in Ruggiero Romano and Corrado Vivanti, eds., *Storia d'Italia, vol. 2: Dalla caduta dell'Impero romano al secolo xviii*. Torino, pp. 5–274.

Tâha, 'Abdulwâhid Dhanûn. 1989. *The Muslim Conquest and Settlement of North Africa and Spain*. London.

Tarassuk, Leonid, and Claude Blair. 1979. *The Complete Encyclopedia of Arms and Weapons*. New York.

Taylor, F. L. 1973 [rpt. 1921 ed.]. *The Art of War in Italy, 1494–1529*. Westport, Conn.

Thompson, E. A. 1982. *Romans and Barbarians: The Decline of the Western Empire*. Madison, Wis.

Thompson, E. A. 1948. *A History of Attila and the Huns*. Oxford.

Treadgold, Warren. 1995. *Byzantium and Its Army, 284–1081*. Stanford, Cal.

Trois Continents. 1999. *La guerre de cent ans*.

Vale, Malcom G. A. 1981. *War and Chivalry: Warfare and Aristocratic Culture in England, France, and Burgundy at the End of the Middle Ages*. London.

Verbruggen, Jean François. 2002. *The Battle of the Golden Spurs*. Rochester, N.Y.

Verbruggen, Jean François. 1985. "L'armée et la stratégie de Charlemagne," in Helmut Beumann et al., eds., *Karl der Grosse. Lebenswerk und Machleben*, vol. 1. Düsseldorf, pp. 420–436.

Verbruggen, Jean François. 1997 [1954 Dutch ed.]. *The Art of Warfare in Western Europe During the Middle Ages from the Eighth Century to 1340*. Trans. S. Willard and S. C. M. Southern. Woodbridge.

Yûsuf, S. M. 1945. "The Battle of al-Qâdisiyya." *Islamic Culture* 19: 1–28.

Waley, D. P. 1988 (3rd ed.). *The Italian City-Republics*. London.

Waley, D. P. 1975. "Condotte and Condottieri in the Thirteenth Century." *Proceedings of the British Academy* 61: 337–371.

Waley, D. P. 1968. "The Army of the Florentine Republic from the Twelfth to the Fourteenth Century," in N. Rubinstein, ed., *Florentine Studies: Politics and Society in Renaissance Florence*. London, pp. 70–168.

Wallace-Hadrill, J. M. 1966. *The Barbarian West, 400–1000*. London.

Warner, Philip. 1968. *Sieges of the Middle Ages*. London.

Wenskus, Reinhard. 1961. *Stammesbildung und Verfassung: Das Werden der frühmittelalterichen Gentes*. Cologne.

Wheeler, Bonnie, and Charles T. Wood, eds. 1996. *Fresh Verdicts on Joan of Arc*. New York.

Wright, Nicholas. 1994. "Ransoms of Non-Combatants." *Journal of Medieval History* 17: 323–332.

Wolfram, Herwig. 1988. *History of the Goths*. Trans. Thomas J. Dunlap. Berkeley.

Wolfram, Herwig. 1970. "The Shaping of Early Medieval Kingdoms." *Viator* 1: 1–20

Wood, Ian, ed. 1998. *Franks and Alamanni in the Merovingian Period: An Ethnographic Perspective*. San Marino.

Wood, Ian. 1994. *The Merovingian Kingdoms, 450–751*. London.

Wright, Peter Poyntz. 1996. *Hastings*. Moreton-in-Marsh, Gloucestershire.

Zarrinkûb, 'Abd Al Husain. 1975. "The Arab Conquest of Iran and Its Aftermath," in R. N. Frye, ed., *The Cambridge History of Iran*, vol. 4. Cambridge, pp. 1–56.

Chronology of Medieval Warfare

Italy

France

987–1328 Capetian Dynasty in France
1214 Battle of Bouvines
1302 Flemings defeat French at Courtrai
1337–1453 One Hundred Years War between France and England
1346 Battle of Crécy
1347 English capture of Calais
1348–1350 First wave of Black Death
1356 Battle of Poitiers
1360 Treaty of Brétigny
1415 Battle of Agincourt
1429 Joan of Arc at the siege of Orléans
1450 English defeat at Castillon

Britain

919 Viking settlement in Britain
991–1016 Viking attacks on Britain
1066 Norman invasion of England
1066 Battle of Stamford Bridge
1066 Battle of Hastings
1314 Edward II defeats Scots at Bannockburn
1337–1453 One Hundred Years War between France and England
1346 Battle of Crécy
1347 English capture of Calais
1348–1350 Black Death
1356 Battle of Poitiers
1360 Treaty of Brétigny
1415 Battle of Agincourt
1429 Joan of Arc at the siege of Orléans
1450 English defeat at Castillon

Spain and Portugal

409–585 Suebian kingdom in Spain
507–711 Visigoth kingdom in Spain
711 Muslim conquest of Spain and Portugal begins
778 Charlemagne's forces defeated at Roncesvalles
1214 Spanish *reconquista* begins

German Lands and Central Europe

768–814 Charlemagne
772–804 Saxon campaigns
788 Conquest of Bavaria
789 Campaign against the Avars
795 Destruction of Avar kingdom
862–955 Magyar invasions
862 First raids in German lands
881 Charles III the Fat crowned Emperor in the West
899 Raid in Italy

900   Raid in Bavaria
933   Defeat of the Magyars at Riade
937–954   Continuous raids in Italy, Germany, and France
955   Defeat of the Magyars at Lechfeld
1315   Swiss defeat Duke of Austria at Mortgarten

Viking Invasions

790–840   Raids along the British coast
820   Raid in Gaul
835   Raids in Normandy
866   Conquest of Northumbria and East Anglia (870)
c. 870   Conquest of Iceland
874   Conquest of Mercia
882   Oleg the Wise founds the Kingdom of Rus at Kiev
896   Viking settlement at the mouth of the Seine
911   Viking Rollo receives Norman lands as fief
991–1016   Viking attacks on Britain

Byzantine Empire

533   Byzantines begin reconquest of North Africa
536–553   Byzantines war against the Ostrogoths in Italy
1071   Byzantine defeat by the Seljuk Turks at Manzikert (eastern Turkey)
1204   Crusaders capture Constantinople
1453   Fall of Constantinople to the Ottoman Turks

Muslim Territories

c. 570   Birth of Muhammad
573–634   Abu Bakr caliph
632   Muhammad takes refuge at Medina (Year One of the Hegira)
634   Begins conquest of Syria and Iraq
636   Defeat of the Byzantines at the Yarmûk
637   Defeat of the Persians at Qadisiyya
642   Conquest of Egypt
643   Begins the conquest of North Africa
649   Conquest of Cyprus
711   Conquest of northwestern India
711   Begins the conquest of Spain and Portugal
827   Conquest of Sicily begins
1071   Ottoman Turks defeat Byzantines at Manzikert
1096–1270   Crusades
1099   Capture of Antioch and Jerusalem
1187   Saladin reconquers Jerusalem
1219   Mongol invasions in Central Asia
1237–1240   Mongols conquer southern Russia
1291   Fall of Antioch and Acre
1453   Fall of Constantinople to the Ottoman Turks

Index